A SHORT HISTORY
OF WESTERN
PERFORMANCE SPACE

DAVID WILES

CAMBRIDGE
UNIVERSITY PRESS

CAMBRIDGE UNIVERSITY PRESS
Cambridge, New York, Melbourne, Madrid, Cape Town, Singapore, São Paulo

Cambridge University Press
The Edinburgh Building, Cambridge CB2 8RU, UK

Published in the United States of America by Cambridge University Press, New York

www.cambridge.org
Information on this title: www.cambridge.org/9780521813242

First published 2003

A catalogue record for this publication is available from the British Library

Library of Congress Cataloguing in Publication data
Wiles, David.
A Short History of Western Performance Space / David Wiles.
p.   cm.
Includes bibliographical references and index.
ISBN 0 521 81324 7 – ISBN 0 521 01274 0 (pbk)
1. Theatre – Europe History.   2. Theatres Europe History.   I. Title.
PN2570.W56   2003
792′.094 – dc21   2003043815

ISBN 978-0-521-81324-2 hardback
ISBN 978-0-521-01274-4 paperback

Transferred to digital printing 2007

A SHORT HISTORY OF WESTERN
PERFORMANCE SPACE

This innovative book provides a historical account of performance space within the theatrical traditions of western Europe. David Wiles takes a broad-based view of theatrical activity as something that occurs in churches, streets, pubs and galleries as much as in buildings explicitly designed to be 'theatres'. He traces a diverse set of continuities from Greece and Rome to the present, including many areas that do not figure in standard accounts of theatre history. Drawing on the cultural geography of Henri Lefebvre, the book identifies theatrical performances as spatial practices characteristic of particular social structures. It is not a history of contexts for dramatic literature, but the history of an activity rooted in bodies and environments. Wiles uses this historical material to address a pressing concern of the present: is theatre better performed in modern architect-designed, apparently neutral empty spaces, or characterful 'found' spaces?

DAVID WILES is Professor of Theatre at Royal Holloway, University of London. His previous publications have been mainly in the field of Elizabethan and Greek theatre, including *Shakespeare's Clown: actor and text in the Elizabethan playhouse* (Cambridge, 1987) and *Greek Theatre Performance* (Cambridge, 2000). This is his seventh book.

Contents

Illustrations

PLATES

FIGURES

Acknowledgements

I am grateful to all who have read individual chapters and given me their comments and encouragement: David Bradby, Jacky Bratton, Ali Hodge, Georgia Kallara, Patrick Landskaer-Wilson, Dick McCaw, Fiona Macintosh, Kate Matthews, Maurice Wiles, and Nurit Yaari. Richard Beacham, Hugh Denard, Mary-Kay Gamel, Edith Hall, Gayna Wiles and many others have provided me with bibliographical advice. Students in the Department of Drama and Theatre at Royal Holloway who have taken my course in Theatre Spaces have assisted me with their researches and experimentation. The Department has supported my sabbatical leave, which was supplemented by a grant from the Arts and Humanities Research Board. The Faculty of Arts at Royal Holloway has assisted with the cost of reproduction rights. Victoria Cooper at Cambridge University Press has been a consistent source of support. I am grateful to my wife Gayna Wiles for many things, but particularly for undertaking the drawings. Without them, this book would have been a much poorer thing.

CHAPTER I

Introduction

'I always nod off in a theatre'
(Peter Brook)[1]

When I enter an empty theatre, I feel a surge of anticipation, sensing the potential for intense human contact. But like Brook, when I watch a play in that theatre I have a habit of nodding off. Watching actors in a workshop situation, I sense what the show *could* be, but in the transposition from workshop to theatre something all too often vanishes. When nervous incoming drama students arrive for their induction in my institution, they are asked to find a space somewhere on the campus, to make it their 'home', and let a play grow out of it.[2] The exercise produces work that is committed and creative. An intense bonding with place occurs. Ten days later, the students are asked to take their 'play', transpose it, and make it work in the studio theatre. The work dies. Invariably. The moral of the exercise is absorbed slowly and painfully, while work goes on being transposed and allowed to die. The questions resulting from the exercise are often framed in terms of finding the right play for the space, or the right space for the play, but the only satisfactory solution is to refuse altogether the dichotomy of 'play' and 'space', of 'content' and 'form'. The play-as-text can be performed *in* a space, but the play-as-event belongs to the space, and makes the space perform as much as it makes actors perform. To eliminate the dichotomy of play and space is no easy task, however. In professional theatre the show is a commodity subject to constant transposition: it moves from the designer's model box into the rehearsal room, into the theatre just before the tech; then perhaps it will move from the studio theatre to the main house, which may be empty or full, and then transfer to a London venue, or be taken to a festival – yet the show is deemed throughout to be an ontological constant. This history of western performance space grew out of my frustration with commodity theatre. The world was not always thus.

A history of western performance space . . . of all these difficult terms, perhaps the most intractable is *history*. In a survey of theatre history that served
a generation of American students, Oskar Brockett justifies his procedures
on the basis of convention: 'It is usual to acknowledge a distinction between
the theatre as a form of art and *the incidental use of theatrical elements in other
activities*.' No answer is offered to the insistent twentieth-century question:
what is the difference between theatre-as-art and mere theatricality? beyond
the remark that this is *usual*. Brockett continues . . . 'This distinction is especially important here, for it would be impossible to construct a coherent
history of all the theatrical devices found in humanity's diverse undertak-
ings through the ages. Therefore, this book is primarily about the theatre as
an institution – its origin and subsequent development.'³ The key word is
Therefore. Brockett's history is not a function of what exists out there, but a
function of its own rhetorical needs. Theatre-as-institution is a concept that
serves the needs of the professional theatre historian, and Brockett adds his
name to the distinguished list of those who have constructed such histories.
The *institution* is thereby revalidated, with 'theatre' again cleanly separated
from the theatrical. An 'origin' followed by a 'development' bolsters the
status of the *institution*, and affirms that the word/concept *theatre* has a
timeless meaning. The circularity is a convenient one. You write the thing's
history to prove it has an essence; because it has an essence, you write its
history . . . Which is all hunky-dory if you happen to like the 'institution' –
but many do not:

> I can no longer sit passively in the dark watching a hole in the wall, pretending
> that the auditorium is a neutral vessel of representation. It is a spatial machine
> that distances us from the spectacle and that allies subsidy, theatre orthodoxy
> and political conservatism, under the disguise of nobility of purpose, in a way
> that literally 'keeps us in our place'. I can no longer dutifully turn up to see the
> latest 'brilliant' product of such-and-such in this arts centre, where I saw the latest
> 'brilliant' product of others only yesterday, a field ploughed to exhaustion.

The author of this 1998 manifesto – Mike Pearson – is now a Professor of
Performance Studies. Scarcely had 'theatre studies' (or 'drama') crystallized
as an academic discipline in the 1960s and 70s around the Brockett view of
things than 'performance studies' arose to split the subject apart, subjecting
theatre studies to a withering anthropological gaze. Pearson's manifesto
has new creative objectives in mind, relating to 'performance' outside the
institution of theatre:

> I want to get rid of the theatre 'object', the play, the 'well-made-show', the *raison
> d'être* of the critic . . .

I want to problematize and renegotiate all three basic performance relationships: performer to performer, performer to spectator (and vice versa), and spectator to spectator . . .

I want to find different arenas for performance – places of work, play and worship – where the laws and bye-laws, the decorum and learned contracts of theatre can be suspended.

I want to make performances that fold together place, performance and public.[4]

Pearson's reference to 'performance relationships' is inspired by Richard Schechner, the guru of Performance Studies in New York. Schechner regards it as axiomatic that three primary transactions comprise the theatrical event: (1) between performers, (2) between audience members, (3) between performers and audience. The position of detached subject vanishes from this conception of theatre because no-one can stand outside these transactions. At stake here, fundamentally, is the subject–object relationship. Pearson rejects the common assumption of Theatre Studies that the detached subject, the critic, will examine the object out there called the play, framed both in space (the hole in the wall, the arts centre) and in time (the well-made show with beginning, middle and curtain call). Pierre Bourdieu has defined in the broadest terms the problem of the 'knowing subject', who unnoticed inflicts on practice a 'fundamental and pernicious alteration . . . in taking up a point of view on the action, withdrawing from it in order to observe it from above and from a distance, he constitutes practical activity as an *object of observation and analysis*, a *representation*.'[5] To watch a performance practice as an external critic or observer is thus to change it, to turn it from an *event* into a *representation*. In physics, relativity theory confirms that objective viewing, once dubbed 'scientific', is a scientific impossibility.

In 1987, Schechner gave secondary status to the interaction 'between the total production and the space(s) where it takes place', but conceded that what seemed secondary might in time become primary.[6] In his book *Environmental Theater* (1973), he never analysed the qualities of the Performance Garage where he created his environments. Pearson, however, aspires to 'fold together place, performance and public', and is no longer willing to subordinate the environmental to the interpersonal. While Schechner in the utopian 1960s performed in the enclosing privacy of a garage where he and his group felt they could write their own new rules for social interaction, Pearson in 1998 senses that the only way to escape the dead hand of the theatrical past is to work in found spaces that impose given rules. To separate self from space had become harder by 1998. In my final chapter I shall argue that twentieth-century theatre has been characterized by the rise and fall of the 'empty space'. 'I can take any empty space and call it a bare stage,' said Brook in the classic statement of this theory; and again: 'no fresh and new experience is possible if there isn't a pure, virgin space ready to receive it'.[7] Brook's empty space is like the blank canvas of a modernist painter. By the end of the twentieth century it became clear that, just as virgins always have characters, so every canvas has a specific texture, colour and form, and an invisible label marked 'Art'. Pearson's dismissal of the latest brilliant product of an arts centre is not just the eternal disenchantment of the creative artist, but reflects a philosophical understanding that space is never empty, and can never be a 'neutral vessel of representation'.

I have much sympathy with Pearson's point of view – a passion for performance mixed with frustration once trapped in spatial machines that grind out predetermined theatrical meanings. This book is written from the conviction (1) that there are new ways forward; (2) that the best way to understand the present is to look backwards; and (3) that theatre worth experiencing (to say 'watching' would already imply a certain detachment, but 'experiencing' may still be too passive a term) necessarily folds together 'place, performance and public'.

The context for a history of performance space is a history of *space*. Classical and medieval space was finite and bounded, but the renaissance and the enlightenment introduced the new conception that space was infinitely extensible. Plate 1 depicts the classical cosmos, with the earth at the centre, seven planets attached to translucent spheres revolving clockwise around it, then the stars revolving anti-clockwise, and in the ninth sphere the Prime Mover of the universe, here interpreted as Queen Elizabeth. Looking at the universe from his tiny planet, so recently displaced from its seat of honour at the centre of the cosmos, Descartes (1596–1650) cultivated the detached scientific gaze: reality viewed from a non-place somewhere on the margins. While surveying his universe from the sidelines, Descartes drew conclusions about himself. Since his intellectual milieu had ousted human beings from the sacred centre, Descartes would repair the damage by locating his *ego* – a resident homunculus of some non-material kind – in the centre of his brain in the centre of his head (fig. 1). Miraculously, he restored the satisfying centripetal order of the classical cosmos. Visual sensation, Descartes considered, passed through the optic nerves to be mapped onto this gland in the middle of the brain, where the mysterious ego could study the image. What Descartes installed in the centre of the skull was effectively a miniature theatre where the self could contemplate reality and decide how to deal with it, before sending appropriate messages down the hydraulic system to the body.[8] This miniature theatre was a secure home for the self or *ego* to reside in, safe from the Inquisition that nobbled Galileo, but

Plate 1   The classical cosmos. Frontispiece to J. Case, *Sphaera Civitatis* (1588).

the price was a certain detachment, reality viewed for ever at one remove. When Pearson declares that inside a modern theatre the spatial machine distances him from the spectacle, what he seeks to escape is the Cartesian condition.

Descartes is a seminal figure in the history of western theatre. Mediated by the drawings of LeBrun, his theory of the Passions would inspire a

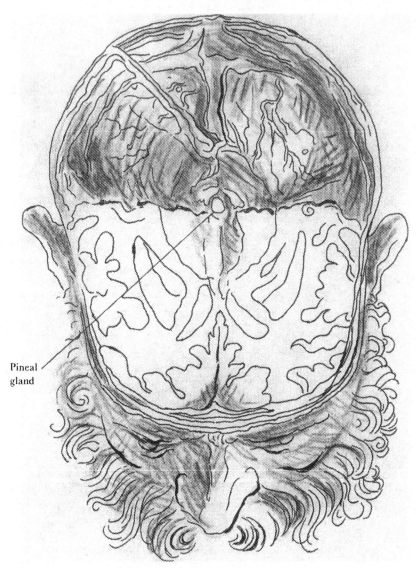

Pineal
gland

Figure 1   Descartes's diagram of the brain.

system of acting.[9] The face, being physically closest to the little theatre in the brain, was the piece of the body best equipped to present the different passions:

ACTOR'S EGO	→	ACTOR'S FACE	→	FOOTLIGHTS	→	SPECTATOR'S OPTIC NERVE	→	SPECTATOR'S EGO IN INTERIOR THEATRE

The corollary of Cartesian space was, eventually, the retreat of the actor into a frame. If the authentic homuncular *ego* is already peering out at the action through the cornea, then it makes sense to gaze in at the stage performance through another focalizing lens created by a proscenium arch. If the action shown on this stage has the distant quality of a dream, well and good because life itself has the quality of a dream, the only certainty being the cogitating *ego* of the dreamer, secure in its darkened seat in the stalls within the skull. Cartesian space is an ocular space. The invisible *ego* not only views the action but also quells the actors with the controlling power of its gaze. It does not submit to any embodied immersion in space – space as apprehended through kinetics, smell, sonic vibrations or an osmosis running through packed shoulders. The Brockett school of theatre historiography based itself on the naturalness of the divide between active actor and passive spectator – a phenomenon which we might term the Cartesian theatrical dichotomy. Since that dichotomy is historically contingent, a new kind of history needs to be written.

Many historians of space have found inspiration in Michel Foucault's invitation: 'A critique could be carried out of this devaluation of space that has prevailed for generations . . . Space was treated as the dead, the fixed, the undialectical, the immobile. Time, on the contrary, was richness, fecundity, life, dialectic.'[10] Most works of theatre history present theatre spaces as immobile lifeless containers within which unfold the rich and fecund careers of authors and actors. Foucault's emphasis on space related to his analysis of the present:

The great obsession of the nineteenth century was, as we know, history: with its themes of development and of suspension, of crisis and cycle, themes of the ever accumulating past . . . The present epoch will perhaps be above all the epoch of space. We are in the epoch of simultaneity: we are in the epoch of juxtaposition, the epoch of the near and far, of the side-by-side, of the dispersed. We are at a moment, I believe, when our experience of the world is less that of a long life developing through time than that of a network that connects points and intersects with its own skein.[11]

Back in 1967, this was a prophetic vision of the network society held together by instant global communications, a world in which memory is obliterated and death hidden from view. The new importance given to space by postmodernism generated a new intellectual challenge:

A whole history remains to be written of *spaces* – which would at the same time be the history of *powers* (both these terms in the plural) – from the great strategies of geo-politics to the little tactics of the habitat, institutional architecture from the classroom to the design of hospitals, passing via political and economic installations.[12]

Though theatre escaped Foucault's attention, his words apply with equal force. The relationship between theatre(s) and power(s) is complex and ongoing.

In his 1967 lecture 'Of other spaces', Foucault outlined a tripartite history of space. He saw medieval space as the space of emplacement, of localization. Some places were inherently more important or sacred than others, and in the grand cosmological scheme, there were natural and unnatural places for different beings to inhabit. In the second historical phase, the new cosmology of Galileo led to the Cartesian perception that all matter was *res extensa*, an extension into an infinite space where everything was in flux. The space of 1967, finally, is seen by Foucault as the spatiality of a site defined only by its relationships – though in practice many residues of the two earlier spaces remain. Foucault develops the concept of the 'heterotopia' as a counter-site that speaks about other sites, and he cites the theatre as one example among many. To illustrate his thesis, let us imagine the monumental Opéra or Comédie that faces the Mairie in the central square of the French city. Once this was a *utopia* where coherent fables and discourses could be framed, but in 1967, inhabited by radical directors, it has become a *heterotopia* suitable only for undermining language and dismantling myths.[13] The history of theatrical performance can be constructed in relation to Foucault's tripartite scheme. In the space of *emplacement*, performances took place in locations that had an inherent significance such as a shrine, a high street, so-and-so's ancestral home. In the space of *extension*, theatres could be built in any convenient place where people were able to gather. Their gaze was directed towards a stage, and via the perspectival décor towards a Euclidian infinity. In the modern space of the *site*, Foucault's invitation in 1967 was to link the theatre with heterotopias like the brothel or the oriental garden which represent, contest and invert other spaces in society. A generation later, Foucault's idealization of alternative (hetero-) spaces seems a little dated. To opt out of globalization and inhabit an 'alternative' culture seems more problematic than it did in the sixties.

For Foucault, a decisive historical rupture occurred with the birth of the 'classical order' at the start of the seventeenth century, the age of Descartes. Words ceased to be mystical signs, and language became transparent. In order to illustrate the new Cartesian space of extension, and demonstrate how realist art magically obliterates the viewer, Foucault described Velasquez's painting known as *Las Meninas* (1656). In this painting we discern the gaze of the royal couple in a tiny mirror at the centre, whilst the artist who paints their portrait is seen on the canvas, along with other figures in the studio. Velasquez's painting, Foucault maintains, gives the lie to a classical notion that art in some objective way reflects reality out there, because the reflected subject is tantalizingly hidden from view. Viewers of the canvas, he claims, unable to see themselves in the mirror, experience the 'essential void' implicit in classical representation.[14] There is one difficulty with this analysis. Foucault would have seen the painting exhibited in the Prado, with a mirror placed on the opposite wall in order to give the modern viewer a thoroughly postmodern experience of multiplied gazes. The painting was actually commissioned for the private viewing of the King, allowing the King alone in his study to see himself in relation to a life-size image of his female heir.[15] The painting created a space of illusion, but there was no void in the royal mirror. Foucault stripped the painting of its spatial context, and thus failed to grasp how the meaning he saw was a function of its modern staging. Foucault provides us with an object lesson rather different from the one he intended. What we see as a classical and enduring 'work of art' is made so by its context in a museum. Modern theatre buildings likewise transform scripts into classics, with meanings cut loose from spatial context.

Henri Lefebvre's *The Production of Space*, published in French in 1976, and in English translation in 1991, is a product of the same intellectual climate as Foucault's work, but is more materialist in its standpoint. It is a magisterial enterprise that draws together Marxist, phenomenological and feminist strands in modern French thought. Lefebvre was inspired by the utopian Marx of the 1844 Philosophical Manuscripts, a young Marx driven by a vision of the natural human being, rather than the late Marx who subordinated all aspects of life to the economic. Lefebvre's history of space, like that of Foucault, is rooted in a critique of Cartesian metaphysics:

By conceiving of the subject without an object (the pure thinking 'I' or *res cogitans*), and of an object without a subject (the body-as-machine or *res extensa*), philosophy created an irrevocable rift in what it was trying to define. After Descartes, the

Western Logos sought vainly to stick the pieces together and make some sort of montage. But the unification of subject and object in such notions as 'man' or 'consciousness' succeeded only in adding another philosophical fiction to an already long list . . . Western philosophy has *betrayed* the body . . . The living body, being at once 'subject' and 'object', cannot tolerate such conceptual division . . . Today the body is establishing itself firmly, as base and foundation, beyond philosophy, beyond discourse . . . We are speaking, therefore, of the abolition of western metaphysics, of a tradition of thought running from Descartes to the present day . . .[16]

Where Foucault is frequently content to refer back to discourses – about sexuality or madness, for example – Lefebvre insists on the materiality of the body. His insistence that knowledge is rooted in the body rather than Logos or discourse has obvious implications for the study of theatrical performance.

The core thesis of Lefebvre's book is the axiom: '*(Social) space is a (social) product.*'[17] Space is *social*, for each society produces its own space, a space simultaneously mental and physical. Space is always *produced*, in the sense that it is always a set of relationships, never a given, never inert or transparent, never in a state of nature untouched by culture. There is no such thing as an empty space:

Vis-à-vis lived experience, space is neither a mere 'frame', after the fashion of the frame of a painting, nor a form or container of a virtually neutral kind, designed simply to receive whatever is poured into it. Space is social morphology: it is to lived experience what form itself is to the living organism . . .[18]

Lefebvre defines three ways of relating to space: we can perceive the *spatial practices* of a society; we can conceptualize space in the form of certain coded *representations of space*; and we can live space within *representational spaces* that embody complex symbolisms.[19] The final category includes theatre and other forms of art, and offers the possibility that established practices and conceptualizations may be contested.

Lefebvre criticizes idealist notions of space. He also offers a critique of traditional Marxism, with its abstract conception of ideology, and the explanatory power it gives to pure economics. He challenges structuralist and semiotic approaches to space which propose that a disembodied ego can read or decode space without being part of it, and argues, for example, that the early work of Barthes fails on the one hand to account for the body, on the other to account for power. Space, Lefebvre maintains, is not 'read' but experienced by means of the body which walks, smells, tastes and in short lives a space. Power, meanwhile, lies outside codes and is rooted in violence.[20] The Paris school of theatre semiotics, inspired by Anne Ubersfeld, has developed an influential account of performance space based on the premiss that the passive spectator 'reads' the stage action.[21] The semiotic approach can be seen now as an academic response to a form of theatre in which the director, aided by the scenographer, replaced the author as the principal creative artist. The semiotic approach, like the mode of theatre on which it was posited, fails to challenge the Cartesian theatrical dichotomy: the split between stage and auditorium, between the performance as object and the spectator as disembodied subject. Lefebvre's phenomenological critique of semiotics invites us to start elsewhere.[22]

Lefebvre outlines a history of space, moving from early 'absolute space' to the 'abstract space' of modern capitalism. Absolute space addresses itself to the body and cannot be conceptualized. It is an activated space, a sacred space, in form always a microcosm of the universe. The Greek agora at the centre of the community was part of 'absolute space' because of its religious and political functions. When the Romans erected buildings around the forum, they set up a façade, destroying the absolute space of the Greek agora. Roman architecture, according to Lefebvre, characteristically creates a rift between the construction and the decorative form which conceals the construction, and so creates a different space, one that no longer '*comprehends* the entire existence of the . . . city-state'.[23] The period from the twelfth to the nineteenth century is seen as a period of steady accumulation, with an explosion of sovereign power in the sixteenth century, and the Cartesian conceptualization of space in the seventeenth. The abstract space of the twentieth century, heralded by the romantics, is at once fragmented and homogeneous. On the one hand culture has become global and uniform; on the other, the fragmented bodies of women in Picasso's paintings exemplify a new mode of perception, the body as a collection of parts and shapes, cut to pieces by the male gaze of the artist.[24] Abstract space is related to the abstraction of labour, and the conversion of all things to their unitary commercial value.

Lefebvre's opposition of absolute and abstract spaces has a number of corollaries. He charts the rise of a geometric and visual order, connected to the ascendancy of the written word over the spoken:

Any non-optical impression – a tactile one, for example, or a muscular (rhythmic) one – is no longer anything more than a symbolic form of, or transitional step towards the visual . . . The eye, however, tends to relegate objects to the distance, to render them passive. That which is merely seen is reduced to an image – and to an icy coldness.[25]

It is principally through the eyes that the detached Cartesian subject accesses the world. Lefebvre traces the primacy of seeing back to the manipulation of light in Gothic cathedrals, whilst recognizing that the remorseless rise of the visual has not gone unchallenged, for example by innovations in eighteenth-century music. Lefebvre's thinking chimes here with Foucault, who demonstrated how nineteenth-century doctors or jailers exerted power through the gaze.[26] Lefebvre forces us to recognize the extent to which modern theatre has become predominantly ocular. Spectacular sets, reinforced by stage lighting, air-conditioning, protective arm-rests and an architectural emphasis on sightlines, makes the experience of theatre-going a pre-eminently visual experience. We might take as a symptom of the modern condition the 750 lanterns suspended above both the Lyttelton and Olivier auditoria in London's Royal National Theatre. The cost of making any desired lighting state possible has proved to be an impoverished acoustic.[27] Vitruvius' account of the Roman theatre illustrates how times have changed: in a theatrical culture centred on oratory and music, it was the acoustic properties of the theatre that demanded almost all the architect's attention. Good acoustics mean that the actors can hear the audience, not only laughter and applause but tiny rustlings and shufflings that demonstrate the quality of attention, so that communication becomes a two-way process.[28] Good modern sightlines imply one-way traffic: passive spectators can see the actors, but the actors are blinded by the lights.

In respect of architecture, Lefebvre contrasts the 'monument' with the mere 'building':

Monumental space offered each member of a society an image of that membership, an image of his or her social visage. It thus constituted a social mirror . . . The monument thus effected a 'consensus', and this in the strongest sense of the term, rendering it practical and concrete. The element of repression in it and the element of exaltation could scarcely be disentangled.[29]

Thus the user of a cathedral, breathing the incense and hearing the singing, partakes bodily in a world of sin and redemption, which is to say an ideology. Greek theatre is cited as another consensual space which 'presupposes tragedy and comedy, and by extension the presence of the city's people and their allegiance to their heroes and gods'. In monumental space, architectural volumes generate rhythms, processional movements and musical resonances that allow bodies to find each other at the level of the 'non-visible'. When monuments lose their force through the oppression or dispersal of a people, Lefebvre argues, they yield to a chaos of mere buildings that are not integrated with 'moments' of social practice. With the loss of the old unity, buildings often receive façades as signs of monumentality,[30] and he could have cited the classical façades of Georgian and Victorian theatres to support his point. Lefebvre associates the 'monument' with the domain of Absolute space, where time was once related to space through the occasion of the calendrical festival. The modern disjunction of space and time is for Lefebvre another Cartesian dichotomy. Modern theatre is forced to inhabit the alienating time and space of 'leisure', where nevertheless some dialectical forces of change may originate.[31]

In his concern with monumentality, Lefebvre articulates a widespread concern of the 1970s. The director Antoine Vitez in 1978, for example, declared himself torn between the constraints of an 'edifice' which imposed a particular kind of production, and the opportunities to create more freely in a space that is a mere covering or shelter.[32] By this time the practical choice facing theatre practitioners was stark. Should one work in inherited theatre spaces that were built for and perpetuate outmoded spatial practices? Should one work in the concealment of a 'shelter' that appears to be neutral and have no relationship to the work of art which it covers and contains? Or should one look for a new monumental form that is a social mirror of late twentieth-century society? Lefebvre seeks a dialectical resolution of the tension between monument and covering in the form of a transgressive 'counter-space' – a vaguely defined term that evokes Foucault's 'heterotopias' and the new generation of fringe theatres.[33]

In the field of performance theory, the most powerful call for the primacy of space has come from the Polish director Tadeusz Kantor. Stanislavski, Meyerhold, Grotowski and Adolphe Appia, the pioneer of modern stage design, represent the dominant twentieth-century line with their championship of the actor. Brecht argued for the story, and was content to work in conventional theatre buildings. Craig was ultimately more interested in shaping the stage than in actor–audience relationships. Artaud hinted at a new direction with his notion of 'spatial poetry', but it is above all Kantor who rooted his understanding of theatre in an understanding of space. His creative roots lay in painting, not the interpretation of texts, and this led him to conceive theatre as a medium where objects and places counted for as much as the human body. He describes space as the 'ur-matter' of theatre, alive and independent of the artist:

> Space is not a passive r e c e p t a c l e
> in which objects and forms are posited. . . .
> SPACE itself is an OBJECT [of creation].
> And the main one!
> SPACE is charged with E N E R G Y.
> Space shrinks and e x p a n d s.
> And these motions mould forms and objects.

> It is space that G I V E S B I R T H to forms!
> It is space that conditions the network of relations and tensions
>   between objects.
> TENSION is the principal actor of space.[34]

He has no truck with the theory that the play should inhabit an 'empty' space, and his conception of space being energized relates to the insights of subatomic physics.

Like Foucault and Lefebvre, Kantor identified the early twentieth century as a critical moment when the old order of seeing was overthrown. The turning point for his own work came in the Second World War, when he used real materials to create the 'found reality' of a bombed-out house:

> In that memorable year of 1944,
> I pronounced another important word:
> real p l a c e.
> Theatrical place,
> but not the official place
> reserved for the presentation of a drama . . .

Since performances took place covertly, in defiance of a Nazi prohibition, the courageous spectators had no sense that they were witnessing an illusion. Physically, they were located inside a piece of environmental art, an installation. In his subsequent career Kantor would reject conventional theatres in pursuit of 'real place'. The theatre, he wrote, 'a site of centuries-old practices, indifferent and anaesthetized, is the least suitable place for the m a t e r i a l i z a t i o n of drama'.[35] He set one of his plays or happenings in a theatre cloakroom, preferring this "poor" space to 'a "s a c r e d" site in the temple of art'.[36] His fundamental tenet was that drama should be reality and not illusion. Ocularity was to be rejected. 'A theatre piece should not be *"looked at!"* '[37]

Henri Lefebvre, together with Foucault and Kantor, provide the outlines of a history of space, around the pivots of Cartesian or perspectival viewing and early twentieth-century modernism. Within these parameters, the question which follows is how to write a history of *the theatre*? Having rejected traditional theatre buildings, Kantor refused to site himself within 'the general history of the theatre'.[38] My own reflections on historiography were stimulated by contributing to *The Oxford Illustrated History of Theatre*. The editor, John Russell Brown, offered his team a strong sense of purpose. The work would be a 'celebration of theatre's greatest achievements' and would 'enhance our present playgoing, reading, and exploration'. Directors, actors and designers would benefit from the book, since this history was to

be 'an active agent in the future life of an inherited repertory of plays'.[39] On
the dust-jacket, a photo of Anthony Sher as Lear's fool in a Royal Shakespeare Company production provided the reader with a point of reference,
fusing the modern and the classic, the popular and high tragedy. The jacket
located the RSC both as a lens through which to view the past, and as an
institution revalidated by the pages of our history.

The task was, I think, well executed. But supposing we changed the
lens . . . Supposing we orient our history not in relation to the RSC but
to a manifesto statement by Welfare State: 'In current terminology we fuse
fine art, theatre and life style but we aim to make such categories and role
definition in itself obsolete.'[40] The received term 'theatre' is seen as a block
to the kind of work this company undertakes. Michael Kirby comments in
similar terms on the theatre of happenings inspired by John Cage:

Just as no *formal* distinctions between poetry and prose can be made in some cases,
and passages of 'prose' are published in anthologies of 'poetry,' and as traditional
categories of 'painting' and 'sculpture' grow less and less applicable to much modern
work, so theatre exists not as an entity but as a continuum blending into other
arts. Each name and term refers only to a significant point on this continuum.[41]

Rosalind Krauss has examined the category of 'sculpture' in her essay 'Sculpture in the expanded field', her focus being a postmodern earthwork that
defies traditional categories.[42] In the pre-modern period, she argues, a
'sculpture' was a commemorative monument that belonged to a particular place. In the age of modernism, the 'sculpture' became a free-standing
work of art, and its base was fetishized (most obviously by Brancusi) to
compensate for the fixity of place that a sculpture no longer possessed.
In the postmodern period, whilst artists make earthworks that are neither architecture nor objects nor landscape, historians continue to use the
term 'sculpture' in order to construct a paternity for contemporary work
and make the new seem familiar. Theatre/performance is likewise sited
in an expanded field. The word 'theatre' like the word 'sculpture' runs
the risk of homogenizing pre-modern site-specific events, modern artistic
events supposedly housed in 'empty' theatrical spaces, and contemporary
performance art. The histories of Brockett, Brown and others essentialize
theatre in accordance with the generic assumptions of early modernism.
The present book offers a series of parallel narratives in an attempt to create
a dialogue with traditional historiography. While refusing theatre a single
transhistorical essence, I nevertheless wish to identify a set of continuities
relevant to a cluster of performance activities that I recognize as theatrical.
My perspective is necessarily that of the present.

Theatre history is a genre that emerged some three centuries ago. Luigi Riccoboni, for example, was an Italian actor–playwright working in Paris in 1738 when he published his *Historical and critical reflections on the different theatres of Europe*. As an itinerant performer, he was aware of cultural differences, and in an age of European rivalries he framed his history around national traditions. Five major assumptions shaped his account of the past:

Perpetual progress. 'The aim of this work is to create an awareness that modern theatre, though it has reached a level of propriety far higher than it in its beginnings, is still far from the point of perfection that many worthy people seek.'

Continuity. 'Comedy . . . has never suffered interruption since it ceased to appear on the stages of the Romans. After forgetting its first greatness, it lowered itself to run from town to town, and showed itself in public places.'

Essentialism. 'The essential goal of theatre is to create illusion, and this can only be achieved through verisimilitude.'

Text/space split. 'Having spoken of the physical Theatre, I come to the Plays that were performed there.'

An agenda for the present. 'My plan is to treat the reform of the theatre in a separate work; but I thought I should begin with the history of all the European theatres.'[43]

Riccoboni's history ends with a sample of his dramatic writing and a plea for a new system of actor training. He is an engaged writer, using history to support his favoured brand of practice. The classical terms 'comedy' and 'tragedy', attached freely to medieval theatre, link his own performance practice back in a shadowy but unbroken line to origins in Greece and Rome, and serve as his touchstones of theatre-as-art. Riccoboni found it hard to achieve a rigorous definition of 'theatre', however. In order to refute a claim that the French stole a march on the Italians by launching medieval theatre through the monologues of troubadours, he chooses to deny that monologues are strictly part of theatre.[44] Though Riccoboni insists in a scientific manner that history requires proof rather than conjecture,[45] his polemical purpose is refreshingly clear, and a reminder that his twentieth-century successors have also written with present-day agendas. They could not do otherwise.

Despair of knowing the past is a feature of the present. A challenging postmodern approach to historiography is spelled out by Hans Kellner:

I do not believe there are 'stories' out there in the archives or monuments of the past, waiting to be resurrected and told. Neither human activity nor the existing records of such activity take the form of narrative, which is the product of complex cultural forms and deep-seated linguistic conventions deriving from choices that have traditionally been called rhetorical; there is no 'straight' way to invent a history, regardless of the honesty and professionalism of the historian.[46]

The historian of today, in other words, cannot represent the truth about the past, the past as it *really* was, any more than a naturalistic play can represent 'true' human behaviour, and a 'real' social milieu. The historical work, like the play, is a construct. Whether one shares Kellner's epistemological position, or regards it as a recipe for cynicism and despair, the fact is that in most university departments of drama in Britain the once mandatory 'survey of theatre history' has dropped from the syllabus. The task has lost its intellectual credibility. The available textbooks offer a normative view of theatre that has little appeal for those more interested in creating devised, movement-based, community-based or intercultural work. Where theatre history is included in the syllabus, it is offered as a series of disembodied fragments. Students often sense the loss, longing for the securities that a chronological overview used to provide.

To illustrate Kellner's case by an example – I have no personal doubt that the Globe was built in 1599, that on a winter's day some chilly and desperate actors dragged timbers across the frozen Thames . . . The past did indeed happen. But as soon as I cast this information in narrative form, I begin to tell an ideologically laden story about the world's greatest playwright, the romance of the acting profession, or the economic underpinning of art. For Kellner, it is the act of contemplation that is valuable. Since in his view 'history is not "about" the past as such, but rather about our ways of creating meanings from the scattered and profoundly meaningless debris we find around us',[47] it follows that writing history is a creative act, based in an attempt to analyse the present. Kellner has no hesitation in supporting the traditional academic qualities of honesty and professionalism. Primary sources remain the building blocks for any historical enterprise.

It is a condition of historical writing that the past is shaped within a given rhetorical or narrative structure. I have borrowed my holding structure in this book from Richard Southern's *Seven Ages of the Theatre*, a pioneering work when first published in 1962. Southern taught in the first university drama department in the United Kingdom, and his concern was to write a history of theatre forms that would be neither a history of dramatic writing nor a history of staging techniques. As a stage designer, he was driven by a practitioner's agenda, to replace the proscenium stage in the theatres of his day with an open thrust stage on the Elizabethan model, following in the footsteps of Tyrone Guthrie. Southern defines seven evolutionary phases through which theatre passed, understanding each new phase as an

accretion around the essential figure of the player. After the simple cos-
tumed player came elaborate outdoor festivals. Then professionals replaced
amateurs and started to work indoors. Playhouses were built, then roofed
and given scenery. The nineteenth-century theatre of illusion was followed
in the twentieth century by the rejection of illusion. Southern's history of
performance space is structured by a Darwinian organization of time, and
this has certain corollaries. His is a teleological history, constructed from the
vantage point of professional English theatre practice in the 1950s. From
its broad sweep across world theatre, the focus narrows steadily towards
England. His title, *Seven Ages . . .*, has a Shakespearean ring, hinting at
the way Elizabethan theatre will dominate the fourth age in his narrative, the age of maturity, pointing towards his own espousal of the 'open
stage'. Southern's single line drawn through time assumes that theatre has
a single origin, a single identity. 'The essence of theatre,' he states, 'lies in
the impression made on the audience by the way you perform. Theatre
is essentially a reactive art.'[48] The player is the core, but the essence is to
be sought in the audience's reaction. The radicalism of Southern's book in
1962 lay in its perception that theatre turned upon actor–audience relationships defined by space, but his phrase 'reactive art' assumes that theatre is *a
priori* an 'art' distinguishable from 'ordinary communication'. Four decades
later, the distinction between art and not-art seems vulnerable. Research
into popular culture, symbolic practices in ritual, children's play, and the
semiotics of everyday behaviour make the distinction untenable. We are
now more aware of how 'art' is a historical construct, a product of the way
a publisher's blurb, a museum wall, a concert hall or the boards of a stage
place objects and activities inside an aesthetic frame.

In *Space in Performance: making meaning in the theatre*, a book firmly
located in the territory of 'theatre studies' rather than 'performance studies', Gay McAuley concentrates on text-based productions of classic plays
because this form has such 'historical importance in western culture', but
she is at pains to deny that any value judgements are involved. She cites
a 1994 conference at the Centre for Performance Studies at Sydney, where
it was the firm consensus of theatre practitioners that creativity could no
longer be located in text-based work, and she suggests that this perspective
may be shared by practitioners in other anglophone countries, while in
continental Europe more generous public funding of theatre accounts for
a more positive attitude to text-based practice. At the end of her book,
after describing actor–audience relationships in popular nineteenth-
century theatres, she comments that 'people of the current generation
must go to a rock concert or a football final to experience the kind of

performance energy that Kierkegaard found at the Königstädter Theater in Berlin.'[49] Like McAuley in Sydney, I am in contact with several different theatrical cultures. There is an official culture centred around productions of classic plays, commanding a high level of social prestige. The texts performed are an international common currency, and a useful means by which an Australian academic (for example) can speak to an American and European readership. There is an alternative culture (no longer a youth culture as in the sixties) that made its voice heard at the Sydney conference. The work of Kantor, Mike Pearson and Welfare State belongs to this second artistic culture, minimally resourced and operating outside prestigious urban centres. There is also a commercially based popular culture, fostering many modes of performance other than theatre, including stand-up comedy, dance shows, circus and pantomime. To these three main performance cultures, one can add the non-western ritual theatre witnessed by western travellers, theatre-in-education, carnival practices, performance art and much more. In this environment, Southern's notions of essence and common source have become redundant. I have attempted to be more catholic than McAuley in dealing with a plurality of theatrical cultures – at the cost of giving short shrift to countless influential and distinguished playwrights and directors.

As a historian trying to make sense of a pluralist world, I perceive a set of continuities relating to spatial practices that involve 'performers' and 'spectators'. Qua historian, I am tied to narrative. My role is not to paint the past or set it to music, but to tell stories. My strategy will be to tell seven parallel stories about seven discrete performance practices. If Lyotard is right that the grand narrative has become intolerable, the genre of the short story, the micro-narrative, may still be admissible. Each of my seven histories describes a practice that belongs to a specific space, with the physical relationship of performer, spectator and environment determining the communication that takes place. Since space, as Lefebvre insists, is always socially produced, aesthetic practices are at every point bound up with socio-political and philosophical assumptions. These seven chapters are not exhaustive, and more micro-histories could have been constructed. Seven, however, seemed sufficient to create the sense of a spectrum.

I have rooted each chapter except the last in classical antiquity. Here I lay myself open to charges of traditionalism, and a political case could be made, for example, for starting a chapter on processional space in ancient Egypt. I have started in Greece for three important reasons. First, I wanted to set up a dialogue with traditional historiography, and indicate that many performance practices other than tragedy and comedy can be traced to

Greece. Second, Greece has been a continuing reference point for western practitioners, who have shaped their work in response to a particular understanding of the classical world. And third, I did not wish to entangle myself in notions of primitive antecedents, and a fruitless search for the origins of theatre,[50] since developments in anthropology have made it clear that the 'primitive' is now an unacceptable notion. My histories are not histories of progress but merely of change. Because Southern saw Olivier as an 'artist', he invested bygone shamans of New Guinea with the same aesthetic aura. Like modernist artists who purchased African masks in order to hang them as sculptures on their studio walls, he garnered a set of masked rites from around the world and placed them in the first two evolutionary phases of 'theatre'. An intercultural approach that seemed radical in its day now has an unacceptable political loading. The concern of this book is limited to western Europe, broadening in the twentieth century to embrace eastern Europe and the USA. My purpose is to subject western culture to an anthropological gaze. My purpose is not to naturalize European practices, in order to make them normative, but to defamiliarize them, and position them as the rituals of a particular cultural system.

Though I begin with Greece, Rome is the major nodal point, the place where one seat of religio-political authority gave way to another, and where more recently the Treaty of Rome was signed in order to erode the concept of the nation state – the concept which has shaped so much historiography from Riccoboni to the *Oxford Illustrated History*. Although I have often focused on England and France, I have attempted to describe typical European practices. The distinctive history of western European society is characterized by the interaction of classical paganism, Christianity and scientific rationalism, and particular ways of organizing space are bound up with those three major codes of practice and belief. My search has rather been for continuities than for changes, for the *longue durée* and not brief flowerings, for typical rather than avant-garde practices.

My focus will be upon activities where, as Michael Kirby puts it, a matrix of space, time and character is superimposed on the actual place and time of performance, and on the identity of the performers.[51] I shall concentrate on practices that involve the enactment of narratives, and on practices that involve live performers. Philip Auslander, inspired by the Derridean critique of 'presence', has pointed out that there are certain ontological problems involved in sustaining the category of liveness. Screenings, for example, are an increasingly important component of performance art, and the modern pursuit of liveness can be seen as a function of mediatized viewing.[52] Although I find more audience spontaneity and sense of community in my local cinema than I do in my local theatre, I have left cinema-going and television-watching to one side as distinct spatial practices, the subject of an unwritten chapter.

The first of my seven spaces is 'sacred space' – a space which its users hold to be more imbued with absolute reality than the everyday, secular space lying round about it. This notion of the sacred is linked to Foucault's space of 'emplacement' and to Lefebvre's 'absolute space'. I begin with the 'sacred' since this is more obviously an ancient than a modern category, but it is not my intention to smuggle in a theory of origins and imply that the first actors were those who climbed onto the altar of Dionysus at harvest time. My argument is a different one. Classical paganism assumed that certain places were sacred because they were gateways to the underworld or belonged in some other way to the gods. Christianity was less comfortable with the idea that the divine retained a material presence, but nevertheless developed different ways of sacralizing space. Though the Cartesian universe is strictly homogeneous, and admits no boundaries separating divine from human spheres, the impulse to sacralize space remains a latent force in the modern world.

I deal next with performance in outdoor public spaces, starting with processional theatre that passes up and down the street or aisle, and moving in the next chapter to performances in the piazza or marketplace. The spatial order is an order of power. A linear movement through the streets defines the shape and order of the town and of its processing inhabitants. The central *place* of the town (to use the evocative French term for a central square) may be a site for displays of centralized authority, but it is also commonly a space for buying and selling, and thus a place where performers have offered up their bodies on trestle stages as wares to be consumed. The metaphor of consumption leads to my fourth space, the banquet where performances help diners to feast their eyes and ears. In my fifth narrative, I pass to a specific philosophical conception of the sacred, the idea that a geometric circle reflects the order of God's universe. Throughout antiquity, the cosmic order correlated with an ideal of political order. When the Copernican view of the material universe prevailed, and the incomprehensible cosmos was shut off by means of a roof over the heads of the audience, the circle remained as a device which allowed society to contemplate its own internal structure. Plato is not only the key theorist of the cosmic circle, but also, through his simile of the cave, introduces my sixth spatial paradigm, whereby the spectator, conceived now as an individual, looks from outside into a magical cube where the ideal order of the universe is manifested. Renaissance rulers found Plato's idealism gratifying, and the Cartesian order consolidated the idea that an invisible wall should separate the viewer from what is viewed, using the magic of theatrical illusion to satisfy a hunger for the numinous, in an age when religion had become too divisive a topic for actors to treat. In my final chapter I look at the central thesis of modernism, lying behind the great revolutions of France and Russia, that the human being is a *tabula rasa*, and that fresh beginnings are possible. It followed from this thesis that the artistic forms of classical antiquity could be discarded, along with all conventions that mirrored society. In the theatre, the new technology of stage lighting provided the basis for an environment that seemed neutral and infinitely malleable. Theatre architecture turned out to be one of modernism's greatest failures, flexible, versatile theatres stripped of social messages proving a conceptual impossibility. The *machine à jouer* proved as chimeric as Corbusier's *machines à vivre*.[53] When postmodernism declared that we can never create *ex nihilo*, we can only rework fragments of the past, many theatre people heard the voice of common sense prevailing.

CHAPTER 2

Sacred space

There is an irresistible human impulse to demarcate certain spaces as sacred, separate from the profane spaces of everyday life. For Lefebvre, the sacred is always bound up with relationships of power. He writes of the moment when 'through the actions of masters or conquerors' a portion of agro-pastoral space received a new role, and appeared 'as transcendent, as sacred (i.e. inhabited by divine forces), as magical and cosmic'.[1] This sacred space, comprising fragments of nature such as springs or mountain-tops, is termed by Lefebvre 'absolute space', for nothing seems prior to it. It is a 'nucleus of coherence', both activated by and activating social energies. In Lefebvre's model, the town quickly becomes the master of the countryside, and builds temples to assert its dominance; it defines itself as a mirror of the universe, and becomes the privileged focus for the countryside around it. The meanings of absolute space are addressed 'not to the intellect but to the body',[2] and the traditional language-based concept of 'ideology' is obsolete:

What would remain of a religious ideology – the Judaeo-Christian one, say – if it were not based on places and their names: church, confessional, altar, sanctuary, tabernacle? What would remain of the Church if there were no churches? . . . Ideology *per se* might well be said to consist primarily in a discourse upon social space.[3]

Lefebvre's materialist analysis, seeing religion as a function of power, contrasts with phenomenological approaches that seek to describe religious experience. In his classic study of 'homo religiosus', *The Sacred and the Profane*, Mircea Eliade devotes his opening chapter to 'sacred space', defining the sacred and the profane as 'two modes of being in the world'. Modern occidentals mostly participate in the second, finding great difficulty in understanding how a stone or a tree can be regarded as sacred. 'It should be said at once that the completely profane world, the wholly desacralized cosmos, is a recent discovery in the history of the human spirit.'[4] For Eliade, writing in the heyday of existentialism, 'the sacred is pre-eminently the real'.[5] *Homo religiosus* desires constantly to inhabit sacred spaces because those spaces seem more objectively real, whereas the modern occidental regards sacred space as an illusion. The great urge of *homo religiosus* was to live as close as possible to the centre of the world, and he therefore defined each house, temple and city as a centre through rites of foundation and through techniques of orientation. A position at the centre allowed *homo religiosus* to communicate with the other world, and to possess a fixed point amidst a surround of chaos. Jerusalem for the Jews and Delphi for classical Greeks were rocks that marked the navel of the world.[6]

The Chinese–American geographer, Yi-Fu Tuan, prefers to see the religious impulse in human nature as an aspect of the aesthetic impulse, which finds embodiment in 'symbolic spaces' that are necessary to the ordering of life, and satisfy a desire for moral beauty.[7] Tuan combines a modern American perception that 'culture is performance' with a traditionalist Chinese perception that human beings crave an ordered universe more than individual freedom. He identifies the political state as an 'aesthetic–moral construction on a grand scale', sustained by rituals and ceremonies which locate the individual or group within some larger setting, which explains why perceptions of god and emperor are often closely linked.[8] Sacred space is a function of the desire to experience order and beauty, a condition of which is the erection of symbolic boundaries. Order and beauty are more likely to be found in a demarcated wilderness than in the sprawling homogeneous mass of a modern American city.[9] Against Tuan we may set the European postmodern position exemplified by Jean-Luc Nancy, who argues that God is definitively dead, and there can be no recourse to the wilderness:

From all the rites and all the liturgies, not the least canticle is left over: even the *believer* who prays can only *quote* his prayer. Not the least genuflection remains. Music, theater, or the dance have taken it all over . . . All that remains of the experience of the temple or the desert is destitution before the empty temples . . . Space is everywhere open, there is no place wherein to receive either the mystery or the splendor of a god.

The question: who or what is God? is bound up with the question: where is God? Divine places, Nancy argues, are irrevocably lost, and with them a sense of community based on communion.[10]

Western culture knows three basic forms of divine place. First is a fragment of wilderness, most commonly a stone, a spring or an ancient tree. When Peter Quince's actors elect to rehearse at the 'Duke's oak', or Falstaff dressed as a diabolic hunter–stag visits Herne's oak at midnight, two traditions merge: a popular folkloric tradition linked vestigially to pagan nature worship of the kind Tacitus describes among the Anglo-Saxons, and a literary tradition drawing on the sacred groves of Graeco-Roman antiquity.[11] The venerable age of these Shakespearean oak trees makes them appear to be a portion of 'absolute space' not contaminated by human society or history. In London today, the smell of authentic English oak amidst an environment of concrete office blocks helps to sacralize Shakespeare's Globe, and create a modern shrine, differentiated from concrete structures like the Barbican and National Theatre complexes. It is probable that, when set amongst the timbered houses of Elizabethan Southwark, those beams were plastered over and the walls painted to simulate marble but the aesthetic and spiritual needs of the late twentieth century imposed different symbolic requirements.[12]

The second form of divine place is the tomb. In pre-modern Europe the spirits of the dead continued to exert force where their bodies lay. Lefebvre writes that 'absolute space is above all the space of death, the space of death's absolute power over the living'.[13] Ancient cults were often centred on the tombs of heroes, and shrines were associated with the dead. In Delphi the bones and teeth of the Python killed by Apollo were housed in a kettle in the sunken seat of prophecy. The Athenian Acropolis was the tomb of Erechtheus, the first king of Athens, born like a serpent from the earth. Eleusis was the place where Persephone vanished into a cavern. The Spartans carried the bones of Orestes to Sparta, and the Athenians carried the bones of Theseus to Athens to sacralize and strengthen their respective cities.[14] Just the same dynamic underlay the Christian practice of making pilgrimage to the Church of the Sepulchre in Jerusalem, or placing the relics of martyrs within their cathedrals. Today, however, Stratford-upon-Avon is sacralized more by Shakespeare's birthplace than by his remains in the churchyard.

The third major form is defined by the way its internal symbolism relates to an eastward orientation. When the Jews in the desert set up an elaborate mobile tabernacle, they ensured that the door was to the east. To the west was the veiled ark of the covenant, with candles to the south and the table with loaves and vessels to the north.[15] In Greek temples the sacrificial priest faced the rising sun. Medieval churches faced east in accordance with the classical tradition, supported by the rationale that this was the direction of Jerusalem. In all three religions, numerological symbolism helped tie human architecture to the architecture of the cosmos.[16] Orientation in regard to sunrise, mid-day and sunset ensured that space within any ritual observation was bonded to time. If worshippers could not place themselves at the physical centre of the universe, they could at least integrate themselves in the cosmic order and thus come closer to the divine, closer to the real.

European writings on theatre provide no equivalent to the *Natya Sastra*, which defines at length the ceremonies required to erect an Indian playhouse, and integrate it with the political and cosmic order. The pillars have to be erected in the right state of the moon. Offerings are made in the four cardinal directions, with foodstuffs of colours that correspond with directions. The four principal pillars correspond with four castes, so the space also mirrors the social order. Images of the gods are laid out around the space, in whichever direction corresponds with their natures – though most watch from the direction of the audience. Food and mantras are offered to the gods, and the space is purified with fire and water. A ritual combat results in the spilling of human blood. The participants must neither be deformed, nor ascetics incapable of appreciating the sensuous pleasures of theatre. If all this is done, says Bharata, the king, the region and the city will achieve splendid results, whilst failure will affect the success of the performance and the karma of the participants.[17]

In pre-modern western performance we observe the same desire to invest space with sanctity by letting it sum up and embody principles of social and universal order. With the coming of humanism and individualism, sacred space ceased to provide the same 'nucleus of coherence'. When the earth was no longer sited at the centre of the cosmos, there could be no sense that the world had a spiritual centre, and east became a function of rotational mechanics. If there is no pre-Copernican equivalent to the *Natya Sastra*, that is perhaps because the western philosophical tradition has always insisted on a dichotomy between human beings and their physical environment. Created in the form of a god, the western human being has been separated from the natural world. In polytheistic religions, particular gods can be associated with particular spaces and directions, but monotheism makes space homogeneous, for God is at once everywhere and nowhere. Just as office planners and residents of suburbia may turn to *feng shui* to counter the alienation of human beings from their environment, so many theatre practitioners look to the eastern tradition for a new sense of connexion with place. Ariane Mnouchkine is one of many western directors who has followed the ideal of interculturalism, and anecdotal evidence tells of how actors attending workshops at her theatre felt it incumbent on them to remove their shoes, kneel, touch the studio floor with their fingers, kiss their fingers, bow and then rise.[18] This piece of theatrical folklore illustrates the sense of embarrassment felt by the western actor when confronted by the idea that the stage itself is sacred, and not just a row of boards.

A sense of the sacred is maintained by ritual. Walter Burkert sees sacred space as a function of ritual: 'The sacred spot arises spontaneously as the sacred acts leave behind their traces: here sites of fire, there stains of blood and oil on the stone – rudiments of altars of differing types and functions.'[19] Yet spaces also make performances sacred, in an endless and reciprocal relationship of reinforcement, and the one should not be seen as prior to the other. The distinction between theatre and ritual has been a main plank in western aesthetics from Aristotle onwards, ritual supposedly being concerned with the sacred whilst theatre deals in the imitation of reality. In the wake of movements such as theatre of cruelty, agit-prop, and performance art, the Aristotelian distinction between reality and imitative art seems once again to have become unsustainable.

Aristotle associates the dithyramb, the choral hymn to Dionysus, with the origins of tragedy.[20] Pindar, a contemporary of Aeschylus, wrote a dithyramb for the Athenians:

> Come to the chorus, Olympians,
> and send over it glorious grace, you gods
> who are coming to the city's crowded incense-rich navel
> in holy Athens
> and to the glorious, richly adorned agora.
> Receive wreaths of plaited violets and the songs plucked
>   in springtime . . .[21]

This is the text of a dance performed in the Athenian Agora. Pindar's dance defines the urban altar as the *omphalos* or navel of Athens. The altar is sacralized by the burning of incense, by the circular dance around it, and by the throwing down of spring flowers. This dithyramb was probably performed as part of the Anthesteria, the 'flower-festival' when children wore floral garlands to symbolize their emergence from infancy, so the act of throwing down flowers was probably associated with the life-cycle as well as the seasonal cycle. The dance establishes cosmic coherence of the kind sought by the *Natya Sastra*. The altar was transmuted into absolute space, and became a fixed point of orientation in regard to the universe. The image of the navel linked the political geography of Athens to the Olympian pantheon, and mother earth to the bodies of the dancers. Pindar's text survives because an ancient critic thought it a good exemplar of the 'austere' poetic style,[22] and we have to work hard to reembody such poetry in the performance space that gave words their meaning. Our text survives because it was not only a piece of Dionysiac ritual but also an original poetic composition. Since the Greek gods liked to be honoured with new creations, it makes no sense to regard ritual and creative originality as polar opposites.

The worship of Greek gods commonly involved reenacting their deeds as a means of showing respect. Though ill-documented, the Greek mystery play was an important dramatic form. In the sanctuary of Apollo at Delphi, a circular area straddling the processional route up to the temple was the scene for a reenactment every eight years of Apollo's killing of the Python, offspring of the earth-goddess. The boy of noble birth who represented Apollo had to descend into the valley and journey far away for rites of purification, returning with foliage that served to make victory wreathes in the ensuing Pythian games.[23] Through reenacting Apollo's crime against the earth-serpent, the Greeks expiated evil, and states at war with each other were able to send musicians, athletes and charioteers to compete without rancour. Memories of the Python linked the sanctuary of Apollo to the immemorial cult of Earth, and reinforced the idea that Delphi was both a tomb and the sacred centre of the earth. At the Pythian games, musical contests were shaped by the combat of god and Python, and the circuit of the chariot race was imbued with cosmic symbolism. Place, time and performance were integrated in a way that modern categories of 'concert' and 'sport' make incomprehensible.

Athenian legend associated the origins of drama with the mountain village of Ikarion. Here Sousarion is supposed to have invented the first comic chorus, and Thespis to have turned from chorus-leader to 'actor' before bringing drama to the city, competing for the prize of a *tragos* or goat. Here also Dionysus first succeeded in introducing wine to the land of Athens.[24] A tradition of performing tragedies is attested in Ikarion in the fifth century, the period of the classical playwrights.[25] The playing space is today abandoned and overgrown, as if a monument of no significance to posterity. It has been ignored by tourism and the humanist tradition in scholarship because it embodies an alien sacral understanding of theatre. The statue of the god in his temple looks out towards the place where tragedy is danced (fig. 2). Although the direct alignment of the temple points to the position of the priest standing before the east-facing altar in order to sacrifice, the doorways inside the temple are off-centre, directing the gaze of the statue towards the playing space. A few thrones of honour mark the front of the audience. The rest of the audience must have gathered on the slope behind the thrones. The playing space is entirely irregular, its shape defined by the topography, and it is little more than a place where a

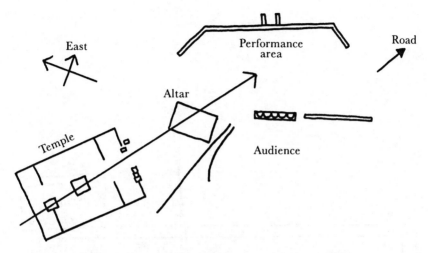

East

Performance
area

Road

Altar

Temple

Audience

Figure 2   Theatre of Ikarion (based on a plan by C. D. Buck).

procession arrived at its destination. The tradition that Thespis performed
on a cart is entirely consistent with the terrain. An inscription tells us that the
temple belonged to Pythian Apollo, and a base in the centre of the temple
is generally assumed to have held a navel-stone. The rites at Ikarion must
have replicated those of Delphi, where Dionysus supplanted Apollo during
the four winter months which embraced the season of tragic and comic
performance. The navel-stone not only placed the Ikarion community at
the centre of its own universe, but also gave the state of Athens a centre
that partook of Delphi's sanctity. Comedy and tragedy were Athenian forms
successfully exported to the rest of the Greek world, and it was important
to the Athenians, bound up with their sense of ownership, to feel that those
forms were rooted in a portion of Athenian soil.

In the city of Athens, the relationship of playing space to the temple of
Dionysus is or became rather different (fig. 3). The first structure on the site
was a stone temple, and we can assume that a sacrificial altar once lay to the
east of it. Both statue and priest would have faced the rising sun, and sunrise
was the moment when the performance ceremonies began. The audience
would have sat on the slope of the Acropolis to watch the sacrifice, and
dances in front of the altar. At some point in the period of Sophocles and
Euripides the hillside was hollowed and set on a more convenient axis for
seating. A colonnaded hall was built dividing the sanctuary from the theatrical area. With the building of a circular, stone auditorium in the fourth

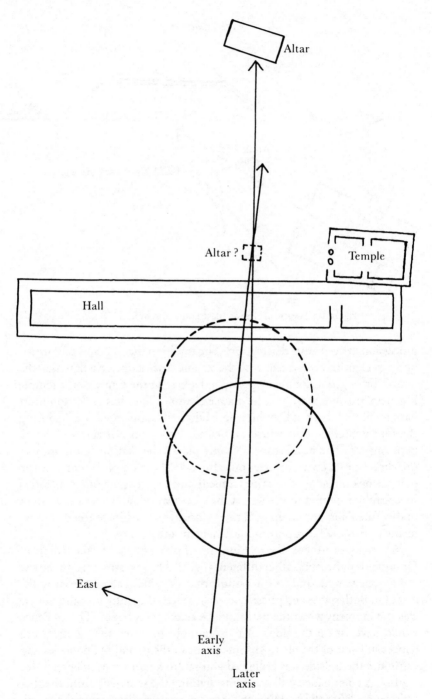

Figure 3   The Theatre of Dionysus in Athens. Reconstruction of the first two phases.

century, a different notion of the sacred came into play, the sacredness of geometry governed by its own internal laws, and the link between theatre and temple became weaker still.

At the start of the day of performance, we know that libations of wine were poured in the orchestra, and the blood of a young pig was spilled in a circle to sacralize the space. But whether tragedy and comedy were intrinsic to the cult of Dionysus has been hotly debated.[26] Some see 'ritual' as a term which defines the substance of Greek tragedy and comedy, others see it merely as an enclosing frame. The principal problem is that tragedies and comedies enacted many stories, only a few of which dealt with Dionysus. The major theatre festival began with a day of dithyrambs, supposedly dances in honour of Dionysus, but here again other myths supplanted those of Dionysus thanks to a competitive drive for originality.[27] The split between Dionysus and the stories enacted in his honour must have been linked to the architectural split between shrine and playing space. The great binary divide between 'theatre' and 'ritual', which western culture insists upon so vigorously, is rooted in this bifurcation of the sanctuary.

Athenian tragedy nevertheless worked to reinforce the cultic infrastructure of Athens, and of Greece at large in accordance with Athenocentric perceptions. Play after play ends by showing how its story explains a particular ritual performed in a particular space. A clear-cut example is the conclusion to Euripides' *Erechtheus*, a play set in Athens. Erechtheus' daughter has been offered as a human sacrifice to ward off Theban attack, and two other daughters have killed themselves at the same spot in accordance with an oath. The goddess Athene declares:

Bury her there where piteously she breathed her last, and these her sisters too in the self-same grave, true nobles, they who did not break their oaths to a beloved sister. Their souls did not descend to Hades. I have lodged their spirits in the ether, and I shall make their name famous throughout Greece, 'the Hyacinthids', so mortals can invoke them as gods.[28]

Athene goes on to describe the sacrifices and dances that must be performed at this place, the Hyacinth rock, annually and before battle. If enemies sacrifice in this secret place, she says, Athens will be defeated. Euripides in this play used the Theatre of Dionysus to reinforce the sacredness of another actual Athenian space. In a piece of political one-upmanship, he commandeered the name of the Spartan hero Hyacinthus whose daughters were sacrificial victims, and he may have introduced the notion that a particular known rock was actually an ancient tomb. He reinforced the faith of the Athenians, currently being attacked by Sparta, that their land was under divine protection provided they honoured the gods. His play demonstrated that the whole of Athens was in fact a sacred space, comprising a network of sacred nodal points.[29] By separating the acting space from the temple, the Athenians opened it onto the city. This was not an act of secularizing or deritualizing, but of turning the power of Dionysus to new ends. The uniqueness of Dionysiac cult lay in its ability to reenact, travesty, and reconstruct rites performed in other contexts in order to define a new collective identity for the assembled celebrants. The nature of Dionysus as the eternal foreigner and creature of the margins legitimated practices which had a powerful meaning for the participants, and little for those in another era who encountered the plays as texts.

No act of reading can completely obliterate the ritual or sacred aspect of classical Greek drama. The case is different with the Roman playwright Terence, whom the renaissance appropriated as the great exemplar of humanism. Terence's most quoted line comes from a play that bears the Greek title *The Self-Punisher*: 'I am human: nothing human do I think alien to me.' The fact is that Romans did find Greek modes of 'self-punishment' thoroughly alien, and this would have been entirely clear in the performance context of the Megalesian games. The festival celebrated the *Megale Meter*, Cybele the 'Great Mother'. The goddess was actually a black stone, imported to Rome some forty years earlier from Asia Minor as a spiritual support to assist the Romans in their war against Hannibal, and within the temple was incorporated as the head of an anthropomorphic statue. When the stone was brought to Rome, it was accompanied by castrated priests, in memory of the mythical Attis who cut off his genitals when driven mad by the jealous goddess. During the festival, the sanctuary was opened to visitors, and the eunuchs danced through the streets with their feminine garments and long hair – though citizens were forbidden from participating. In the period of the Empire, the rites of Attis were formalized like a Christian passion play. Attis' image was attached to a pine tree, representing the scene of his castration. Priests and devotees danced wildly and slashed their breasts or genitals. The pine and image were then buried in a solemn funeral, to be resurrected joyously next day.[30] The context of Terence's *Self-Tormentor* was thus a wild Greek cult, to which the Romans were exposed for the period of a week. A forbidden sanctuary was opened up for events which included Terence's play. The goddess in her temple on the Palatine Hill was the honoured spectator, just like the wooden statue of Dionysus in Athens. The steps of her temple provided an auditorium, and the stage was erected on a triangle of ground in front (fig. 4).[31] This was an irregular space like Ikarion, not a rational and harmonious space. The

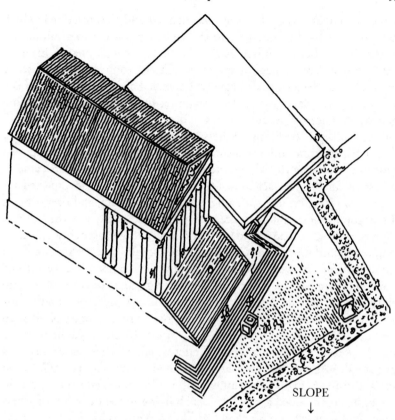

SLOPE
↓

Figure 4   Temple of Cybele (after P. Pensabene).

humanist Terence of the renaissance was a Terence visualized in relation to symmetrical and harmonious auditoria, with the seat of honour given to a human ruler not a black-faced statue.

The link to cult is even clearer in the case of Terence's *Eunuch*, performed before the goddess in 161 BC. When he chose to adapt a Greek comedy about a man who impersonates a eunuch so as to rape a virgin, Terence inverted the myth that shaped the festival, transforming male self-castration to male gratification. The young men in Terence's comedy defy all the social rules that governed the behaviour of Roman youth. Whilst the audience appeared in Roman dress, the actors wore Greek costume to mark their otherness. Terence's plays were Greek rites which played out, in a normally forbidden environment, sexually incontinent, anti-patriarchal and non-militaristic behaviour antithetical to all official Roman values. The dangerous Greekness of the event was defined and circumscribed, which may explain why direct address to the audience was cut to a minimum. Terence had to beware of the charge that he had 'contaminated' his originals. Over a century later, a speech by Cicero lambasts the magistrate responsible for the Megalesian games. There had been a breakdown of law and order, with slaves pressing in, trapping the senators and terrorizing their wives. Cicero does not stress the danger to life and limb involved, but the sacrilege. Traditionally, he says, if a dancer stopped dancing, or a piper fell silent, an offence against the gods would have to be expiated through performing the whole ceremony again. Some spectators came to the games for the spectacle, but others out of piety. Cicero expected his listeners to recognize that the games were a religious act, and he attributes distant sounds of rumbling to the outraged goddess. The way the cult was summoned from abroad is held up as evidence of its great sanctity.[32] Roman conquerors purloined from Greece not only statues and priests but also a cult called comedy, with its rules of masking and competition. Performed as an uncontaminated Greek rite on sanctified ground, Terence's plays were felt to give pleasure to the goddess, and thus bestow protection on the city.

All Roman 'theatres' in the time of Terence were temporary or adapted structures. When Pompey built the first stone theatre in Rome in 55 BC (fig. 5), he described it as 'a temple under which we have placed steps for spectators'.[33] At the top was a huge shrine of Venus Victrix, built on an apse and rising as high as the summit of the Capitoline Hill. The statue in the shrine commanded a vast complex, looking in the direction of a new Senate House at the opposite end (see fig. 27). Pompey's conception of the theatre–temple was plainly inspired by Greek theatre–temple complexes like Pergamon, and Latin imitations like Praeneste. It is likely that the original stage wall was a temporary wooden structure, allowing the temple to be viewed from the gardens and Senate, with the auditorium appearing from the Senate to be a huge flight of temple steps.[34] A later emperor paid his respects to Venus, then walked down the central steps in silence to take up a throne of honour in the orchestra.[35] It is easy to imagine how Pompey would have used the temple to associate his own victories with the goddess of Victory.

The humanist tradition tends to dismiss Pompey's goddess as a cipher, an excuse to legitimize the building of a permanent theatre. Standard modern reconstructions eliminate the flight of steps, thereby turning the temple into an appendage rather than a focus of the architectural scheme.[36] Vitruvius' geometric account of the Roman theatre, which we shall examine in chapter 6, encouraged the Christian renaissance to consider that theatre

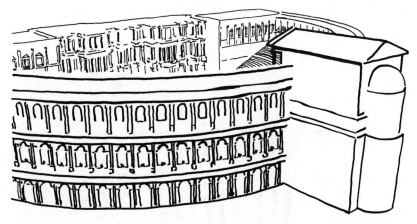

Figure 5   The relationship of temple and auditorium in the Theatre of Pompey (after a
realization by the Theatron project, University of Warwick).

and religion belonged to different realms of human existence. As Yi Fu
Tuan indicates, we must beware also of a modern tendency to place politics
and religion in different compartments. Imperial Rome and Hellenistic
Greece, unlike Republican Rome and classical Greece, recognized monarchs as akin to gods. Philip of Macedon entered his palace theatre at dawn in
336 BC alongside statues of the twelve Olympian gods, presenting himself as
the thirteenth god, but an assassin gave the lie to this self-aggrandizement,
and stabbed him on the floor of the orchestra.[37] Mark Antony was embraced
by the Greek world as Dionysus, Cleopatra as Aphrodite, and Octavia as
Pallas Athene. When Antony came to Athens, he built himself a Dionysiac
bower out of branches, hung with tambourines and fawnskins, up above
the theatre in the commanding position which equated with that of Venus'
temple in Rome.[38] Pompey associated himself with Venus because Venus
was patron of Troy, the city from which the first Romans were supposed to
have descended. We can be righteously cynical about the claims of Philip,
Antony and Pompey, or we can with Tuan see them as attempts to give stability and aesthetic form to the world order. These men used the sacredness
of a sanctuary to enhance their own political power, but in so doing they
also reasserted the religious dimension of theatre.

Pompey's rival Julius Caesar responded with a grand scheme to build
a temple on the slopes of the Capitoline Hill, a theatre that would be
commanded by the most prestigious temple in Rome. On the land which
Caesar had cleared, his adoptive son Augustus preferred, more modestly,
to build a free-standing structure in front of the rebuilt Temple of Apollo,

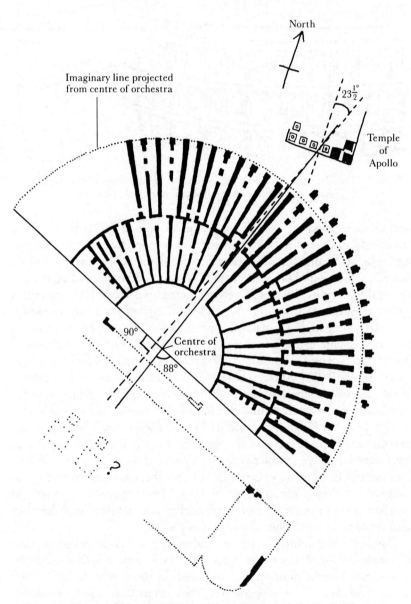

North

Imaginary line projected
from centre of orchestra

$23\frac{1}{2}°$

Temple
of
Apollo

90°

Centre of
orchestra

88°

Figure 6   Theatre of Marcellus (based on the archaeological plan by P. Fidenzoni).

a long-established site for theatrical performance. On the face of it, the building appears to be a secular space: Pompey's auditorium minus the Temple of Venus. But when we examine the geometry carefully, we find that temple and theatre are linked (fig. 6). Bruno Poulle recently argued that the axis of the theatre meets the axis of the temple at an angle of $23\frac{1}{2}°$, which is an angle of great astrological significance, the angle of the ecliptic. Augustus made much of his links with Apollo, and propounded an official myth that he was conceived in the temple on the winter solstice. The axis of the theatre thus links it to the scene of Augustus' mythic conception, and to the position of the sunrise on the solstice. Poulle also notes that his two axes converge on an ancient Greek image of Athene embedded in the centre of the pediment. However, the geometry of the theatre is more complex than Poulle recognized. The line which he identifies is set at 90° to the stage wall, and runs close to a centre point defined by the outermost perimeter of the theatre, but he fails to observe that it does not actually run through the centre point of the orchestra, towards which all the radial lines are pointed. Poulle did not consult Paolo Fidenzoni's official account of the excavations published in 1970.[39] Fidenzoni, without explanation, defined a skewed axis line from the centre of the orchestra to the centre of the temple, and this appears to be an access route allowing the emperor or statue of Apollo to be carried from the temple to a place in the orchestra. There is nothing difficult about drawing concentric circles on paper and on the ground, so the explanation cannot lie in simple incompetence on the part of the builders or archaeologist. Greek astronomers recognized that the planets did not run in perfect circles around the earth, and developed 'eccentric' or 'epicyclic' models to explain how their orbits were defined by centres at a slight remove from the earth.[40] The multiple centre points of the Theatre of Marcellus can only be explained on the basis that the theatre was conceived as a model of the cosmos. The relationship to the temple remains fundamental, but Poulle's explanation needs refinement in the light of more research.

Roman theatre was always a religious practice, a point entirely clear to early Christians, but largely incomprehensible to the renaissance and modern worlds, which have tended to associate religion with spirit rather than place. Renaissance theatre builders took little heed of Vitruvius' remark, in his treatise dedicated to Augustus, that temples of Apollo (who was patron of mimes and pantomime) and Liber (the Roman Dionysus) should be placed near a theatre, implicitly in order to allow the relevant statues to be carried in to watch the performance.[41] Without the architectural extravagance of Pompey, or Caesar's brazen appropriation of the Capitol, Augustus founded his rule on religious authority. While Pompey tried to build an alternative to the old centre of Rome, and sanctify untouched land, Augustus saw that a sense of the sacred had to be rooted in spatial memories, and he built on a site sanctified by previous performances given before Apollo. The political statement made by his building was related to a statement about the universe, and the mysterious physical order established by the gods. The subtle asymmetry of the building was a reminder that not everything is subject to the order of human beings. Whether or not the audience were conscious of the asymmetry, they would have sensed a quality of aliveness and movement in the building, which experientially would have felt like the product of something more than rational human planning. The axis would conveniently have allowed the early morning sun to fall for a moment on the emperor and the golden statue of Marcellus beside him in the orchestra, bestowing a further role to the cosmos. Two structures on either side of the portico behind the stage wall must be temples, replacing others destroyed in the clearance operations.[42]

When the Roman empire became Christian, theatres were not closed immediately because the Christian emperors needed to supply the populace with their traditional entertainments, but there was a slow process of attrition.[43] Saint Augustine was willing to accommodate Terence as literature, but regarded theatre performance as a creation of the devil.[44] The opening of St John's Gospel asserts the primacy of language: 'In the beginning was the word . . .' John's conception of sacred space is set out in his account of how Jesus met a woman of Samaria at a holy well. The woman recognizes Jesus as a Jewish prophet and infers that she should worship God not on the mountain sacred to her ancestors but in Jerusalem. Jesus replies: 'Woman, believe me, the hour cometh, when ye shall neither in this mountain, nor yet at Jerusalem, worship the Father . . . God is a spirit, and they that worship him must worship him in spirit and in truth.'[45] Likewise St Peter made a serious mistake when he proposed building shrines on the mountain-top after seeing apparitions of Christ, Moses and Elijah.[46] Sacredness cannot inhere in physical spaces, but only inside the human soul.

Early Christians worshipped in interior spaces – partly for reasons of security. When they needed more space, they moved from dining-rooms which recalled the institution of the mass to basilicas.[47] The basilica was a covered rectangular meeting-hall, overseen by a figure of authority in a bay at one end, and its lack of religious association was precisely what made it acceptable. When the Roman emperor Constantine was converted to Christianity, he may be said to have converted Christian spatiality back to

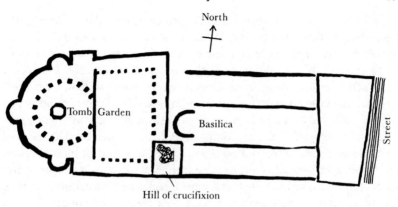

Figure 7   Church of the Sepulchre, Jerusalem.

paganism in many regards.[48] He introduced the notion of the 'Holy Land', and the idea that geographical locations could be inherently sacred. He built a basilica in Jerusalem on top of an old temple of Venus (fig. 7), and conveniently found on the spot remains of the true cross. Whether his choice of site was arbitrary or based on tradition remains controversial. Later, roughly in alignment with the building, Constantine uncovered a tomb which he claimed as the tomb of Christ, and a procession through the basilica led the pilgrim towards the tomb. Constantine also placed a cross on top of a small natural outcrop that once served as base for a statue of Venus, and within a few years this was taken for the scene of the crucifixion. Within a generation or so, a domed mausoleum was built over the tomb, inaugurating the second architectural mode that Rome bequeathed to medieval and renaissance Christendom. The rotunda signified that the tomb was the centre of the world. It was another few centuries before the grave of Adam was located in the same spot, confirming that the site was a physical centre of absolute coherence, a fixed point around which the Christian world could locate itself. Under Constantine, Christian faith acquired an optical dimension.[49] Pilgrims who visited the holy places nevertheless continued to privilege the Word. A Roman woman who spent Easter visiting the Mount of Olives, Gethsemane, the pillar of the flagellation, Golgotha, and the cave in which Christ was buried, heard readings of the relevant biblical texts and joined the weeping, but saw no full physical reenactment. It was enough for the bishop to walk out from the tomb to represent the resurrection.[50] The limitations of the Christian 'word', however, were already apparent, for the Greek had to be translated simultaneously into Latin and Aramaic.[51]

Christianity espoused the Platonist principle that the body was the prison-house of the spirit or soul. While some Christians reviled the human body, others came to see it as a microcosm which replicated the order of God's creation, but in either event theatre was unacceptable. Like other pagan activities such as athletics, chariot-racing, gladiator fights and bath-houses, it held the body up for human admiration.[52] Worse, it transformed the body, allowing men to become women through donning masks, sub-verting the order of God's creation. The Christian premiss that the soul was enclosed inside an inferior body was related to a taste for interior space. The Greek gods were thought to inhabit the sky, or mountain-tops or live beneath the earth or in the sea, and most Greek acts of worship took place around an altar in the open air. Since Greek theatre was concerned with relations between the human and the divine, it was important to see actors stamping on the beaten earth, gazing into the sky, and standing before a wild and open landscape or seascape. Roman Stoic beliefs to some extent antic-ipated Christianity, regarding the gods as a more generalized presence, and implying that human beings should aim to control nature, not respond to its animate properties. The Romans enclosed their theatrical stages within high walls, and used an awning to shut out the sun, so insulating the fes-tive or tragic world of the play from the natural world and from everyday life. Christianity completed this flight from nature, and the dissident views of Adelbert in eighth-century Germany illustrate the hegemonic power of interior space. A man of humble origins, Adelbert founded a sect which appealed to the lower orders. He erected crosses in meadows and beside springs, and called on people to come to chapels in the open fields, not pray in the cathedrals of bishops. No-one should go to confession in church, he claimed, for he already knew their secrets.[53] For Adelbert, church buildings represented hierarchical authority, but also the power of authority to peer at the soul inside the body. The enclosing church was a metaphor for the body that enclosed the soul.

Greek theatre used the vertical axis to articulate relations of human and divine, and for this reason flew gods in on a crane, but its major concern was conflict on the horizontal human plane. In early tragedy, two opponents characteristically enter from opposite sides of the orchestra, and in Hellenistic comedy rival families live behind the two doors on the left and right sides of a long horizontal stage.[54] The Roman theatre of the imperial age placed more emphasis on verticality, structuring the stage façade with three orders of columns to reflect the hierarchical principles of society. Christianity was even less interested in representing conflict on the horizontal plane of human society, and focused its attention on Christ's movement down to Hell, back up to earth and finally to heaven.[55] When Procopius described Justinian's cathedral in Constantinople, he commented on its dome which seemed suspended like the vault of heaven. The person coming inside to pray found his mind 'risen towards God and walking in the air, feeling that He cannot be far away'.[56] Sunlight filtering through windows at the base of the dome added to his sense of nearness to the divine. The dome was an alternative sky, and the church an alternative universe.

As we have seen, there was a necessary ambivalence in Christian attitudes to sacred space. The martyr Stephen condemned the Jewish temple of Solomon, saying 'the most High dwelleth not in temples made with hands; as saith the prophet, Heaven is my throne and earth is my footstool'.[57] Stephen's God was thus the eternal spectator in the sky, in contrast to Greek gods who manifested themselves in their idols. Dionysus in Athens, like Cybele and Venus in Rome, was not a diffuse presence apprehended via filtered sunlight, but was able to watch plays through the eyes of a particular statue placed in a central viewing position. The Greek and Roman spectator shared the subject-position of the divine statue, a position from which everything could be seen and known. In the Christian world this mode of spectating vanished. Whilst Antony–Dionysus in pagan Athens could see the play and audience laid out beneath him, Justinian took up his place at the centre of the cathedral in Constantinople, where he could be seen better by God and by human beings. There was no single vantage point from which the architectural ensemble could be apprehended, and it was necessary to process through the space in order to appreciate it.[58] In medieval Christendom, the watcher was always being watched by an invisible God. Perfect sightlines were never a priority. The important thing was to arrange a complete performance space in a way that reflected God's order.

When Charlemagne was Holy Roman Emperor, an important compromise was reached between Roman and Christian performance traditions. Amalarius of Metz, a reformer attached to the imperial court, interpreted the mass as a three-part drama tracing Christ's ministry, death and resurrection. The church became a kind of theatre in which different and shifting roles were allocated to the priest, the bishop, the choir, the deacons, the congregation. The altar as visual focus of the ceremony was reconfigured at different points in the ceremony to signify different imaginary spaces. When the priest prayed, the altar became first Jerusalem and then the Mount of Olives, but when bread and wine were placed upon it, it became the table used for the last supper. When the bread was transformed into

Christ's body, the altar was transformed into the hill on which Christ was crucified, and finally became the tomb. The practice of placing relics of saints or fragments of the cross under the altar helped this identification of altar with tomb. Behind the altar and facing the congregation was the bishop's throne, identifying the bishop with the role of God the father, looking down upon the earthly drama at the altar. In Amalarius' theatrical conception of the mass, a fluid and symbolic use of space allowed constant play between interior and exterior worlds. The altar was at once the external space where Christ was sacrificed and the internal space of the human heart. The linen on the altar symbolized both Christ's shroud worn in the tomb and purity of mind.[59] This theatrical perspective was developed further by Honorius of Autun who proclaimed in around AD 1100:

We know that those who played tragedies in theatres represented combat to the people through gestures. Thus does our tragedian represent the combat of Christ to the Christian people in the theatre of the Church with gestures of his own, and so he impresses them with the victory of Christ's redemption.[60]

While the mass was being reconstituted in theatrical terms at the heart of the Holy Roman Empire, the formal theatrical tradition was by no means moribund. The one playwright whose work survives from this period, linking the 'holy' Christian tradition to the secular Roman tradition, is an aristocratic nun called Hroswitha. Hroswitha lived in the convent of Gandersheim, but had close links with the imperial court. She used the formerly pagan medium of theatre to reflect upon the fundamental question of sacred Christian space.

In the opening scene of *The Conversion of Thais the Prostitute*, an ascetic hermit summarizes a line of teaching which can be traced from Pythagoras and Plato's *Timaeus* to St Augustine and Boethius, and governed the 'sacred geometry' of medieval churches.[61] The hermit explains that the human being is a microcosm, and needs to obey God's law just like the stars of the cosmos. The harmony of body and soul is analogous to the mathematical harmonies that shape the music of the celestial spheres. Hroswitha's parable–play which follows illustrates these teachings by means of an ironic inversion. The prostitute of the title, a character-type borrowed from Terence, repents her sins. The hermit condemns her to a foul and enclosed cell without toilet facilities where her body becomes putrid, and she can moan but not sing. She regrets that 'there is no place where I may fittingly and religiously call on the name of the Divine Majesty'.[62] The hermit is obdurate, until in the end a vision forces him to recognize that the body beautiful will be resurrected along with the soul, since a pristine couch awaits Thais in heaven. The cell which forms the visual focus of the play is shown to be a kind of anti-church, the antithesis of the splendid convent church of Gandersheim. What a church should be, Hroswitha implies, is a reflection of cosmic harmony, with an acoustic that creates perfect music. The way of the nuns at Gandersheim was not the way of the early fathers in the desert. To honour God, it was now necessary to honour the body, and to create beautiful buildings as a microcosm of God's universe. The domed form of the church at Gandersheim defined it as a microcosm of the perfect circular cosmos.

The Martyrdom of the Holy Virgins Faith, Hope and Charity is set in pagan Rome, and depicts the torture of three beautiful sisters called Faith, Hope and Charity. The virgins are buried by their mother, assisted by a chorus of matrons. The power and coherence of the play is clear once we recognize that its place of performance must have been the convent church of Gandersheim. In the centre beneath the dome was the symbolic site of Christ's tomb, but also the actual tomb of Otto the Illustrious, grandfather of the present Holy 'Roman' Emperor. The association of the convent church with Rome was reinforced by the relics of two canonized popes, carried from Rome to consecrate the building. In the vicinity were the tombs of Oda, the foundress of the convent, and her three virgin daughters who were the first three abbesses. The Roman mother and three daughters of Hroswitha's play stand for the mother and daughters buried in the church; the three dead abbesses signify the Pauline virtues of faith, hope and charity. The play drew its meaning from the human remains in the crypt or under the altars, and in turn reinforced the sacredness of the space. The matriarch, named Wisdom and standing allegorically for Oda, becomes a figure for God the Father in Hroswitha's feminized view of Christianity. The female playwright's adoption of the Roman medium of theatre is related to a new valorizing of the body beautiful as a microcosm of God's creation.[63]

The medium of spoken theatre allowed Hroswitha to create scenes of ugliness and torment to polemical effect, but did not work to generate a contemplative spiritual experience. Her plays portray the human city, for which Rome was the archetype, and not the city of God, for which Jerusalem was the model. Hroswitha's poem on the *Apocalypse* is a piece more obviously written for aristocratic nuns to perform in their own persons, creating a very different quality of experience, and identifying the church with the heavenly Jerusalem. The biblical *Apocalypse* was a central text for romanesque and gothic architects.[64] Hroswitha's verses appear to have been written to accompany a sacred pageant where it was not the spoken but music and images that allowed the divine to be apprehended.[65]

In the course of the middle ages, theological emphasis shifted from Christ the symbolic lamb (his attribute in Hroswitha's *Apocalypse*) to Christ the sufferer who gave his human body. The architectural correlative in western architecture changed from the dome to the groundplan of the elongated Latin cross, a symbol of suffering and an iconic replica of the human body. The basilica, the dome and the cross are the three fundamental forms that have characterized sacred space in the Christian era. The dome would reappear in the Italian renaissance, to mark a return of the idea that the human body was not a site of suffering but the image of God.[66]

The Russian historian Aron Gurevich has analysed the medieval sense of space with particular acuteness, arguing that before the use of industrial tools nature seemed an extension of the human ego:

So, medieval man's relationship with nature was not that of subject to object. Rather, it was a discovery of himself in the external world, combined with a perception of the cosmos as subject. In the universe, man saw the same forces at work as he was aware of in himself. No clear boundaries separated man from the world: finding in the world an extension of himself, he discovers in himself an analogue of the universe. The one mirrors the other.[67]

The church building thus related both to the microcosm of the individual and to the macrocosm of God's universe. There could be no question of the spectator as subject seeing the performance as object of their gaze, because a sense of self could not be separated from that which one saw in the external world. One could not see the building as the inert container of a drama because the church building was itself an extension and replication of one's own embodied self.

Romanesque churches gave new emphasis to the east–west axis. The east, the direction of the sunrise, was associated with heaven and eternal life. By analogy with the orientation of Constantine's tomb of the resurrection in Jerusalem, the west end in romanesque churches was associated with death and judgement.[68] Whilst romanesque churches remained in some measure basilicas, processional spaces that *contained* tombs, paintings and dramatic enactments, translucent gothic architecture aimed to obliterate all sense of containment. Lefebvre describes the 'visual logic' of the new architecture as a 'decrypting' of the past,[69] moving the focus away from those magical relics in the crypt that concerned Hroswitha. In theatrical terms, the gothic church gave increasing emphasis to the principle of end-staging.[70] The all-important eye was drawn eastwards and upwards, away from the here-and-now. The priest no longer faced the congregation but looked away to the east. The essence of holiness now lay less in the bodies of saints than in the consecrated bread which symbolized, like the building, the body of Christ. The bread had always to be held up and displayed to the congregation after it had been transformed into Christ's body, a moment announced by a bell for those struggling to see. A wooden screen was installed between the choir and the nave to support a huge crucifix, creating distance, partial vision and an enhanced sense of mystery for those standing in the nave eager to see the miracle of transubstantiation.[71] The screen made the length of the church seem greater, while the statue on the crucifix caused the eyes to lift heavenwards, demonstrating that the miraculous bread had become a divine body. The figures of Mary and John beside the cross showed that the screen represented the need for mediation, contact with the deity being attainable only via the priest at the altar. Systematic concealment made the sacred objects seem even more sacred. The crucifix was covered by a cloth during Lent, and the high altar was masked by a curtain, enhancing the sense of privileged vision offered by the Easter ceremonies.

Hroswitha was not the only woman to champion dramatic performance as a component of Christian piety. Herrad, a German abbess at the end of the twelfth century, lamented that youths had corrupted the old tradition of performing biblical stories at Christmas and Easter. Though these plays had been introduced to strengthen faith and convince doubters, she accepted reluctantly that readings would now have to be substituted for unproductive performances, but clung to the basic theoretical defence of enactment: Christ commanded his disciples to copy him in washing feet on Maundy Thursday, and in partaking of the last supper.[72] A pendulum swung throughout the middle ages: on the one hand, performance instilled faith; on the other, the excitement generated by performance encouraged anarchy. The wealthy convent of Barking in Essex typifies these tensions. In 1279 the play of the Slaughter of the Innocents was banned because the choirboy performers took this as a day of liberty under the rule of a parodic boy bishop, and the archbishop decreed that the nuns should henceforth perform the ceremony on their own without any audience.[73] A century later the pendulum swung back when the abbess Katharine of Sutton decided to combat the chilly devotion and torpor of the congregation by enhancing the Easter *Quem Queritis* ritual, postponing its performance to the end of matins. In this musical enactment, the three Marys discover Christ's empty tomb, and an angel asks them *Quem Queritis?* 'Whom do you seek?'[74]

The abbey church, now ruined, was built in the twelfth century in the form of a cross (fig. 8). The high altar can be equated with Christ's head; the nave to which the public were admitted may be considered the space of the lower body. The public in the nave were separated from the high altar by a

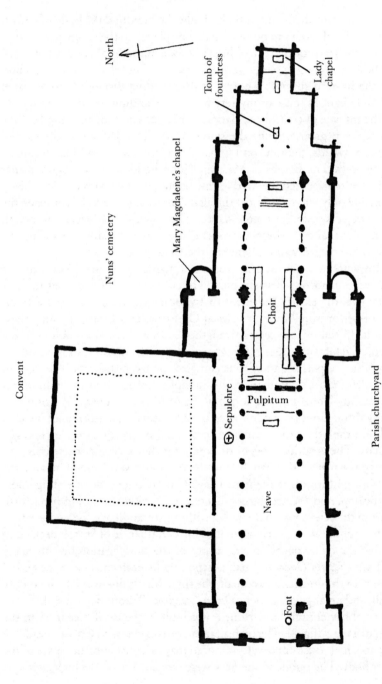

North

Tomb of
foundress

Lady
chapel

Mary Magdalene's chapel

Nuns' cemetery

Convent

Choir

⊕ Sepulchre

Pulpitum

Nave

Parish churchyard

O Font

Figure 8   Reconstruction of Easter play at Barking Abbey (based on A. W. Clapham's plan of the foundations).

wooden rood screen, and a high stone wall called the *pulpitum*, not to mention the altar rail and step, so the mysterious candle-light reflected on the gold leaf of the altar could only be glimpsed through a doorway. The church at Barking also had a gendered symbolism. The most remote and impenetrable area lay to the east, in added chapels beyond the high altar allocated to the virgin foundress Ethelburga and to the Virgin Mary. The cloister lay to the north, in accordance with a convention that north was the female side, and the side on which women traditionally sat,[75] while the south gave onto the parish churchyard. The sunny south thus correlated with the public world, the dark north with the enclosed world of the convent community. In English *Quem Queritis* plays, Christ's tomb was always placed on the north side of the choir, and the directional symbolism at Barking was enhanced by the fact that the nuns' cemetery lay on the other side of the wall.

Since matins ended at dawn, and the three Marys reached the tomb at dawn, the performance at Barking bound dramatic time to real time, increasing the audience's sense that it lived inside not outside the world of the drama. The first rays of the sun would have shone through the east window in the direction of the sepulchre soon afterwards. The politics of gender must have encouraged the institution of this play, which shows that women were first to see and touch the risen Christ. Only a male was permitted to handle the eucharist, and the ceremony thus fell into two parts. First the priest went into the sepulchre and brought out the consecrated bread in a crystal container from within the breast of Christ's statue. He displayed the bread while introducing the anthem 'Christ is risen!', and then led a procession carrying the bread through the church to the high altar, symbolically enacting Christ's journey from the privileged space of Jerusalem to the public space of Galilee. The three Marys then began a more realist or emotionally expressive mode of enacting the resurrection story. The abbess placed pure white robes on three chosen nuns, and purified them by absolving them of their sins.[76] The three nuns sang in a 'weeping and humble voice' in the choir before coming into public view. In the gloom, candle-light picked out their white robes. Carrying ointments, they approached the temporary structure that represented the sepulchre and encountered two angels. A *persona* (literally, a 'mask') appeared from behind the altar to present the risen Christ, coming first to Mary Magdalene and then to the three women together. The altar in question must have stood in front of the *pulpitum*, allowing the parishioners a rare sense of unimpeded vision.[77] Mary Magdalene announced the resurrection to priests who represented Christ's disciples, and it was now her turn to initiate the anthem 'Christ is risen!' Thanks to Katharine of Sutton's reform, a nun was seen to acquire parity with a priest in the celebration of Easter. She could not handle the eucharist, but her forebears had touched the feet of Christ. The nuns' role, like that of Magdalene, was to bring the Easter story to the public.

Modern accounts of the *Quem Queritis* ceremony often wrench the 'play' from its place in the greater drama played out over Easter week, with the leading tragic role of Christ taken variously by the priest, the abbess, the portion of bread, the statue with its hollow breast, and the mysterious *persona*.[78] On Palm Sunday the consecrated bread was taken out to a pavilion in the churchyard, and then carried into the church to symbolize the entry into Jerusalem whilst the nuns and crowd carried palms and branches and the choirboys sang in welcome. On Wednesday the curtain before the high altar was removed to anticipate the tearing of the temple veil at the moment of Christ's death. On Thursday the abbess in the refectory broke bread and gave each nun wine to drink in a reenactment of the last supper. All the nuns washed and kissed the feet of the poor, then each other's feet, and finally in the chapter house the abbess and prioress washed the feet of the other nuns – just as Christ washed the feet of his disciples. On Friday, a day of silence, the image on the crucifix was unwrapped and placed on the ground so the nuns could kiss its five wounds. The statue was then set on the high altar and taken down to simulate the removal of Christ's body from the cross, the wounds were washed, and the statue was carried to the tomb. Saturday was given over to events of a more symbolic nature, with the lighting of the huge Easter candle and the blessing of new water to signify renewal. On Sunday before dawn, the nuns enacted the 'harrowing of Hell': nuns and some priests crowded into the chapel of Mary Magdalene to represent Old Testament figures in purgatory, until a priest as Christ hammered on the door to release them. Easter day finally ended at vespers with a procession to the font, bringing to the furthest public end of the church news of the resurrection. The extinguishing of the great candle signified the formal end of Holy Week, but the drama continued when the nuns at rogationtide processed out to nearby churches, symbolically spreading the news to all parts.

These Easter ceremonies both derived their meaning from the space of the church, and fed the church with meaning. Gothic architecture was designed to exploit the medium of light.[79] Twenty-four candles were extinguished one by one before dawn on Thursday and Friday to signify death, and a blaze of candlelight on Saturday at sunset signified new life. The cruciform plan of the church was bound up with an awareness of Christ's suffering body. The stripping and scrubbing of the altars on Maundy Thursday was followed by the washing of feet, feet which next day would make contact with the stone floor when the nuns crept on their knees to kiss the statue. Every corner of the Abbey had its meaning. The foundress was honoured by psalms sung at her tomb. The new fire was kindled outside the chapel of St Paul because Paul spread the gospel abroad. The scholars venerated the cross outside the chapel of St Laurence because this martyr copied Christ's crucifixion. The chapel of Mary Magdalene was used to signify purgatory because Magdalene was rescued from sin. The abbess venerated every cross in the convent on Good Friday morning and the priest censed every room after Easter matins to ensure that the sanctity of the church extended to the living space of the nuns. A complete value system was articulated in space, and the articulation of space was bound up with the articulation of time; outside this space and time the nun had no identity.

Iain Mackintosh rightly attacks the functionalist fallacy in modern theatre architecture which assumes that sightlines and legroom are the key to a good theatrical experience.[80] For both nuns and parishioners, sensory deprivation, including fasting, loss of sleep and kneeling on a cold stone floor, were combined with restricted vision to create a powerful theatrical experience. The ordinary parishioner received communion once a year at high mass on Easter day, so all this sensory involvement came to a climax with the eating of Christ's body after the *Quem Queritis* drama had been witnessed. The taste of the bread, the smell of the incense, the touching of the crucifix, the resonance of the singing and glimpses of action in ever-changing light all supported a sense that Barking Abbey had become a second Jerusalem. For parishioners in the nave, a normal feature of the eucharist was its near invisibility. They could hear the words, and sense emotions in the singing, but could only glimpse the host from afar. Katharine of Sutton took a small but potentially dangerous step in making Christian truth visible to the common people.

The laity in the nave normally had their view obstructed by wood and stone barriers that connoted privilege. They could hear the words, but the words were in the exclusive language of Latin. In the exclusiveness of medieval sacred space lay the seeds of its destruction. The Protestant reformation substituted the sacredness of the word for the sacredness of space, and the word was spread through the vernacular Bible. The idea that the divine could be apprehended by the eyes was discarded. In reformation London, the centre of spiritual life shifted from the interior of St Paul's Cathedral – where the images had been smashed, the altars and their relics removed and the frescoes blotted out – to the churchyard. Here weekly sermons were preached from an octagonal booth surmounted by a cross. The preacher, an hour-glass at his right hand, relied on the power of the word to hold a huge audience entranced. The privileged sat in galleries attached to the walls of the cathedral, while the rest stood. As visual aid, the preacher pointed to a white-robed penitent who would perhaps be condemned or perhaps forgiven. This penitent was not a mimetic image but a living example of the sin described by the preacher. The power of the location derived from the presence of the dead who lay beneath the audience, and could be smelled on a hot day, helping focus attention on the fate of the penitent after death. The church had been desacralized, but the churchyard retained the aura of the sacred.[81]

John Donne, poet and Dean of St Paul's, set out a standard Protestant assumption when he preached: 'The organ that God hath given the natural man is the eye; he sees God in the creature. The organ that God hath given the Christian is the ear; he hears God in his Word.'[82] Visual sensations would now belong to the secular world, the world of creation, whilst God revealed himself through the words of the Bible. The printing of the Bible helped to separate the Word from the human body, and the printing press has been described as 'father of the reformation', creating a new disembodied understanding of 'the word'.[83] In Cartesian terms, the visual dimension related to matter or space, *res extensa*; the word related to the soul, or *res cogitans*. Visual sensations would now be excluded from the Protestant church, and associated with the secular domain. Whitewashed walls turned the church into an empty space where the worshipper could concentrate without being distracted from the task of hearing the Word. Michael O'Connell relates the white church interior and the abolition of dramatic role-playing to an anxiety about what New Historicism has termed 'renaissance self-fashioning'. The psychology of an earlier age, he states, would 'accept the role that a liturgical celebration thrusts upon it. But a self not so constituted will need reassurance that the role is not a role. Bare walls can reflect back to a worshipper a self unmediated by distracting or competing human images.'[84] In other words, the modern sense of self is bound up with what Peter Brook calls 'empty space' – a theme to which I shall return in my final chapter. The Easter drama in Barking Abbey assumed that no boundaries enclosed the self. As Gurevitch puts it, the world was an extension of the self and the self was an analogue of the medieval world. The nun who played Mary Magdalene *was* Mary Magdalene because she was a sinner and had just confessed. Locked in Magdalene's chapel, she was locked in the world of sin, excluded from the high altar on which the eucharistic body of Christ would rest. Looking at the icon of Magdalene in the chapel, she looked at herself. Parishioners kneeling rheumatically in the nave, however resentful they might be at paying tithes, knew that the prayers and ceremonies of the nuns touched their souls. One cannot easily isolate one's inner mental space when one's knees are in contact with cold flagstones.

The changes that took place in Protestant Europe were replicated in the Catholic world following the Council of Trent. In Spain, for example, pulpits were installed so a sermon could be preached at mass, the walls were whitewashed, and heavy gold frames were placed around religious paintings to separate art from reality. Reformers like Ignatius Loyola and Teresa of Avila emphasized the distinction between the external form of prayer and true mental prayer. Dramatic enactments of all kinds were banished from the church. Though religious drama still flourished on the streets at Corpus Christi, the sacred space of the church was demarcated, and was no longer to be contaminated by drama and entertainment. The notion of 'absolute space' had gone; a space was not inherently sacred, but was made so by devout usage. The sacred space and the theatrical space became antithetical concepts.

Michel Foucault saw the middle ages as 'a hierarchic ensemble of places: sacred places and profane places; protected places and open, exposed places, urban places and rural places . . . It was this complete hierarchy . . . that constituted what could very roughly be called medieval space: the space of emplacement.'[85] The medieval sacred site defined by its fixed location within a finite universe gave way to a multitude of heterotopic sites defined purely by their relative status. Foucault argues that Galileo's cosmology now made it impossible for three domains to reproduce each other: the microcosm of the body, the sacred building, and the macrocosm of the universe. This fragmentation of categories left no room for any given space to be defined as a source of coherence, and thus as intrinsically sacred. Freemasons continued through the Enlightenment to yearn for the temple of Jerusalem where the plan of the divine architect was revealed, but no cultural and philosophical consensus allowed such a building to be built.

The Baroque period kept the social space of theatre conceptually distinct from the religious space of a church. Motifs drawn from classical architecture and iconography signified that the theatre interior belonged to a pagan tradition, and could not be a site of spirituality; by the start of the nineteenth century, classical porticoes delivered the same message to the street. Georges Banu writes that by filling the space of the ancient orchestra with people the baroque theatre 'made the public its centre, as if to confront it in the absence of God with the emptiness of its own values, and thereby invite it, indoors in closed court, to create its own reflection in a hall of mirrors where one image is multiplied to infinity'.[86] While theatre spectators of the baroque period used actors as a means of looking at each other, those of the romantic age searched increasingly for a mystery beyond themselves, which they glimpsed in the depths of a pictorial stage image enhanced by gas lighting. The power of proscenium theatre to create a quasi-religious image of the ideal is a theme to which I shall return in chapter 7.

Romanticism merges with modernity in the Festspielhaus at Bayreuth, where Wagner required his spectators to forget other inhabitants of the darkened auditorium, and lose themselves in evocations of Germanic myth. The burghers of Bayreuth wanted Wagner to build a monumental theatre, but he preferred 'the outline of the idea', in the form of a simple wooden shell.[87] It was the inner workings of the theatre – the lighting and sets, that had to be perfect in accordance with his assumption that spirituality belonged to the inner world of the human being. The auditorium was reconfigured in an open Hellenic style to allow perfect sightlines, but the determining feature was the proscenium arch 'whereby the scene is removed as it were to the unapproachable world of dreams, while the spectral music sounding from the "mystic gulf", like vapours arising from the holy womb of Gaia beneath the tripod of the Pythia, inspires [the spectator] with the clairvoyance in which the scenic picture melts into the truest effigy of life itself'.[88] The invisibility of the orchestra helped to ensure that the sacred lay in the mental space of the spectators, and not in the physical environment their bodies occupied. Though Wagner compares his shrine to that of Pythian Apollo in Delphi, his earth-goddess is merely a metaphor. Wagner rejected the idea of building in one of the great German-speaking cities or in a royal court, and surrounded his theatre with parkland, because he wanted his audience to make a pilgrimage to a place where there were no social distractions.[89] Wagner succeeded in securing a different and more reverent mode of spectator behaviour. With the passage of time, the annual festival controlled by his descendants has made the boundary line between art and ritual indistinguishable.

Modernist ideals of art at the end of the nineteenth and start of the twentieth centuries were bound up with notions of the sacred. There was a new admiration for ancient and 'primitive' cultures, where the roots of art in religion seemed obvious. The avant-garde ideal of 'art for art's sake' has been described as a form of 'resacralization', allowing modern art to supplant the original functions of religion.[90] Adolphe Appia declared in 1922 that a theatre should be the 'cathedral of the future'.[91] The most important sacred object for Appia was the body, and he used the mystical medium of light to enhance its sculptural properties. At Hellerau, working with the eurhythmic dancers of Emile Jacques-Dalcroze, he helped create a 'milky

Elysian atmosphere' where light would appear from an invisible source, and the boundary line between stage and auditorium would be erased to create a sense of coming together as once in cathedrals.[92] Edward Gordon Craig ecstasized about the 'mystical' qualities of the Arena Goldoni, with its Platonist circle of seating, where he planned to set up a theatre school on the eve of the First World War. He was working at the time on *St Matthew's Passion*, but moved away from the idea of using a church for the performance, feeling that Bach had also distanced himself from the institution of the church.[93] Antonin Artaud, in order to recover a metaphysical form of theatre, proposed to abandon traditional theatre buildings for sheds owing something to 'churches, holy places, or certain Tibetan temples'. He wanted the audience to be placed in the middle of these sheds so the action could happen in a vast area above and around. Though he rejected the 'dictatorship of words', and wanted to substitute the ideal of 'spatial poetry', the precise material details of architecture did not concern him.[94] What these three seminal modernists have in common is a desire for the sacred, but an unwillingness to harness themselves to any specific code of belief complete with a liturgy that involved shaping space in a specific way.

A generation later, we find the same impulse in Jerzy Grotowski:

I do not think that the crisis in the theatre can be separated from certain other crisis processes in contemporary culture. One of the essential elements – namely the disappearance of the sacred and of its ritual function in the theatre – is a result of the obvious and probably inevitable decline of religion. What we are talking about is the possibility of creating a secular *sacrum* in the theatre.[95]

In order to achieve the paradoxical goal of secular sacredness, Grotowski considered three things to be necessary. First was the use of collective myths which 'are not an invention of the mind but are, so to speak, inherited through one's blood, religion, culture and climate'. Christian myths loomed large in Grotowski's work, but national myths were perhaps equally important. In an age that lacked a common faith, he argued, it was possible only to confront these myths, and find truth through profaning them.[96] Second was the elimination of the stage–auditorium dichotomy, because theatre is ' "what takes place between spectator and actor" '.[97] Third, the actor had to become a species of monk or martyr, discarding the masks of daily life:

The actor must not *illustrate* but *accomplish* an 'act of the soul' by means of his own organism. Thus he is faced with two extreme alternatives: he can either sell, dishonour, his own 'incarnate' self, making himself an object of artistic prostitution; or he can give himself, sanctify his real 'incarnate' self.[98]

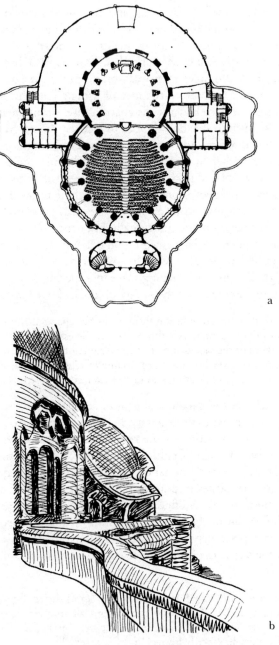

Figure 9   The first Goetheanum.

Sanctity for Grotowski thus resided in the body of the actor, and not in the laboratory space which the actor occupies. The space was simply an inert container small enough for the spectator to feel the breathing and smell the perspiration of the holy actor.[99] When Richard Schechner writes of Grotowski's work that 'We are face to face with a medieval cosmology, intensity, belief and (perhaps) practice', his note of caution is well advised.[100] Because Grotowski would not extend the domain of the sacred beyond the human body, he could make no link between the external architecture of his Laboratory Theatre and his fictional setting, for example the Krakow–Athens–Auschwitz setting of *Akropolis* (1962). The notion of a secular sacred space was beyond his grasp, as long as he worked within the medium of theatre.

The most ambitious and coherent attempt I know to create a sacred theatre in the twentieth century was Rudolf Steiner's Goetheanum (fig. 9), destroyed by fire at the end of 1922 when its fittings were barely complete. Steiner was an unorthodox Christian who saw Christ as a form of the Sun-god. He found the divine in nature and in the cosmos, and insisted on the close bond of the human microcosm to the macrocosm. He felt that his spiritual teachings were better expressed through drama than lectures. Having worked on the symbolist dramas of Maeterlinck and a reconstruction of the Greek Eleusinian Mysteries,[101] he wrote a sequence of 'mystery plays'. At the same time he developed a system of eurhythmy, similar to the eurhythmics that fascinated Appia, concentrating on the link between movement and the sounds of speech.[102] When he performed his mystery plays in makeshift theatres in Munich, he found that they lacked the necessary environment. He and his followers therefore built the Goetheanum at Dornach in Switzerland, whilst the guns of the First World War sounded across the border, as a space to realize these dramas – though in the event, the major production undertaken in the building was Goethe's *Faust*.[103] According to Steiner's philosophy:

One stands within spiritual science as if in a nut-kernel and carries in oneself the laws according to which the nutshell, the building, has to be designed . . . Everything presented in words, that is performed eurhythmically or in the Mystery plays, or whatever else it may be, must ring through the auditorium or give visible shape in such a way that the very walls give their assent, the paintings in the dome add their approval, as a matter of course; that the eyes take it in as something in which they directly participate. Every column should speak in the same way that the mouth speaks when it gives voice to anthroposophically oriented spiritual science! And precisely because it is at the same time science, art and religion, an anthroposophically oriented spiritual science must develop its own conception of architecture, quite distinct from all other architectural styles.[104]

The idea that words must take visible shape is a distinctive feature of Steiner's eurhythmic theatre practice. It follows from his holistic pagan–Christian view of the cosmos that shell and kernel must interlock, that the Mystery play cannot be separated from the place of its performance.

Steiner saw Greek temples as an expression of mankind's bond to the earth, shutting out the world above, whilst gothic cathedrals expressed a movement away from the earth. He was less interested in liturgy than in the rich decoration of medieval cathedrals that represented a community endeavour. In the baroque age the spiritual impulse was lost, but the opportunity now existed to move forward. Steiner's theatre–temple took the form of two intersecting domed circles. The smaller circle to the east was associated with spirit, the larger with the senses, and human beings needed a balance of both. The principle of the dome created centredness and repose, but the doubling created a nave which articulated a journey. The journey towards the solar temple which structures the first three mystery plays is expressed by the form of the space. For the east end Steiner designated a statue representing three figures from the plays: a Christlike everyman pulled two ways by spiritualism and the senses. A series of different elements from the western tradition combined to make the Goetheanum a sacred space.

(1) orientation. Steiner was one of the first to perceive the directional significance of Celtic stone circles.[105]

(2) centredness. The (double) foundation stone was placed where the circles intersect, and from here a lecturer would speak.

(3) decoration. Capitals were carved to express the spirit of movement, echoing the eurhythmic dancers. Painted ceilings and coloured glass expressed the flowing spirit of their creators.

(4) numerology. Seven different types of wood, for example, were used to make the seven columns on each side.

(5) curvature. In contrast to many modernist architects who linked their spiritualism to minimalism and favoured rectilinearity, Steiner (like Gaudi) sought movement. The walls swelled outwards to express the expansion of the spirit.

(6) microcosm. The anthropomorphic form of the building is clear from the groundplan.

We may think of all this as an inherited vocabulary of symbols. Steiner, however, insisted that the building could not be interpreted as a cluster of mere signs because the spirit of those who had given their money, labour and artistry was part of the material structure. He called the theatre a larynx for the speech of the gods, and protested that one cannot explain intellectually the symbolism of one's larynx.[106]

The irreplaceable first Goetheanum was developed from within, as an expression of the spirit. The second was conceived from without, presenting its moulded concrete shapes to the world, and asserting its links with the hillside on which it stood.[107] The interior arrangements were of a more conventional and multi-functional kind, including a rectilinear proscenium stage with standard technical equipment. Steiner's mystery plays, as still performed in this theatre, seem to the uninitiated to be intensely wordy and lacking in dramatic tension. For those attuned to the thinking, they are reputed to have a profoundly cathartic effect. The importance of the project in a wider European theatrical context lies in its decisive rejection of the modernist principle that a theatre should be an inert container for a play. Steiner's creation of a sacred space for sacred plays stemmed from a revisionist Christianity which proclaimed that humans are bonded to their environment. He also held, like Spengler, that architecture was an expression of its age,[108] which helps explain why at the end of his life he did not try to repeat his earlier creation.

Orthodox modern Christianity does not encourage the same sensitivity to space. When T. S. Eliot wrote *Murder in the Cathedral* for the Chapter House of Canterbury Cathedral in 1935, the power of the event relied on the fact that the protagonist, Becket, had been murdered only yards away. The gothic stalls on which archbishops sat, the resonance, and the claustrophobic absence of exits from the stage contributed to the ambience. Eliot's final chorus asserted the power of sacred space:

> For the blood of Thy martyrs and saints
> Shall enrich the earth, shall create the holy places.
> For wherever a saint has dwelt, wherever a martyr has given his
>   blood for the blood of Christ,
> There is holy ground, and the sanctity shall not depart from it
> Though armies trample over it, though sightseers come with
>   guidebooks looking over it . . .
> From such ground springs that which forever renews the earth
> Though it is forever denied . . .[109]

The irony is that the play promptly transferred to the London stage, dislocating the text from its space. Eliot went on to root his next cycle of poems, *Four Quartets*, in spaces of personal and spiritual significance, exploring the interplay of past and present, but the remainder of his dramatic output took the form of living-room dramas with coded Christian messages written for the mainstream London stage. The conventions of Ibsenesque living-room drama forced upon him a unity of time and uniformity of language that made them increasingly less interesting, either as theatre or poetry.[110] Eliot wrote dismissively in 1951 that 'people who deliberately go to a religious play at a religious festival *expect* to be patiently bored'.[111] It is unclear how far Eliot's gravitation to the West End stemmed from snobbery and the desire to reach a chic audience, and how far it stemmed from a democratic desire to bring poetry to a popular audience. Perhaps Eliot was right to see the problem in the audience. The wife of his director who saw many performances of *Murder in the Cathedral* recalled that one of the most 'shared' took place in a basement of Lloyd's Bank during the Blitz.[112] No doubt this sharing was due to the proximity of death, the sense of entrapment and the awareness of what political oppression entailed – an experience that could not be replicated either in the Chapter House or the West End. Whatever Eliot's motivations, his failure on the level of principle to align drama with place as inseparable aspects of 'performance' is characteristic of his age.

For orthodox Christianity, space is and has long been an unresolved issue. Britain's most famous modernist religious building, Coventry Cathedral, is a rectilinear volume of empty space that functions admirably as an art gallery displaying Sutherland's remarkable tapestry and Piper's windows. The altar remains in its orthodox position, and the modernist architecture bears no relation to any modernist reconception of the liturgy. When Benjamin Britten presented his *War Requiem* to inaugurate the building in 1962, there was no question of action augmenting the oratorio, and Britten was dismayed by the acoustics.[113] He used Wilfred Owen's poetry to awaken memories of war, but the building embodied no answering memories. The ruins of the adjacent medieval cathedral destroyed by bombing, on the other hand, have proved an admirable setting for the reenactment of Coventry's medieval mystery plays, because that space is dense with associations. The problem of the modernist 'empty space', with its dissociation of place and performance, is one to which I shall return in my final chapter. In that context I shall show how Brook's ideal of 'holy theatre' led him to adopt the Bouffes du Nord as a space of memories. The theatre designer Iain Mackintosh comments that Brook's 'success suggests that an old theatre may be a sacred place and that the ghosts of past productions are a reality and, if friendly, a benign presence. Slap on too much new paint and too much gilding and those ghosts will leave.'[114] William Faricy Condee, in another study of modern theatrical space, echoes the principle that a 'found space' is valued because of the 'ghosts' which are found there.[115] It is clear that both churches and theatres rely on the intuitive feeling that a space has a presence. Those intuitions are bound up with material traces of the past that trigger collective memories. For this to happen, a shared symbolism is necessary.

There is an experiential truth in Jean-Luc Nancy's assertion that there are no more divine places, but his argument is methodologically flawed, for it presupposes a primitive golden age when people lived rather than quoted a liturgy, and he has no means of saying when that age ended. Tuan's argument that spirituality is often bound up with a sense of statehood captures an important aspect of modern experience. National shrines such as Epidaurus, Bayreuth and Stratford-upon-Avon demonstrate how art satisfies the desire to believe in a transcendental force. A reverence for Englishness combines with a reverence for art to give Shakespeare his iconic status. The Shakespeare Memorial Theatre achieved cultural eminence in the mid twentieth century with the increasing availability of transport, but the aura of Stratford has come under threat in the twenty-first century with the building of 'Shakespeare's Globe', 200 yards from the foundations of the original Globe. Historically accurate features, like Norfolk reed on the roof or lime-and-goat's-hair plaster used for the facing, assure the spectator that this is a sacred space. Green oak, with its evocative smell and tactile appeal, functions as a symbol of the timeless, the natural, the authentic. Saddled with a modernist theatre building, Stratford now has weakening claims to be the premier site of Shakespearean pilgrimage.

When the Globe was being built, John Drakakis alleged that the project involved merely:

the fabrication of a narrative of tradition replete with a quasi-religious iconography, and a shrine at which to worship . . . The building will become the site of a seance designed to resurrect in certain conditions the spirits of Burbage, Heminge, Condell, Will Kemp, Robert Armin, Shakespeare, of course, and now Sam Wanamaker.[116]

Drakakis would have felt his worst fears confirmed on 22 April 1995, the eve of Shakespeare's birthday (the day also of England's patron saint): the future artistic director of the theatre, Mark Rylance, led a procession that started at Shakespeare's statue in Westminster Abbey, passed via Middle Temple Hall where *Twelfth Night* was performed in 1602, to the half-finished Globe to lay roses, before finishing at Southwark Cathedral.[117] Rylance rounded off his day with a public discussion of some eighteenth-century drawings which reconstructed the geometry of the Globe in accordance with Masonic beliefs in a divine architect.[118] The bond between church and theatre could scarcely be clearer. Rylance's self-ironizing yet serious procession was part of a long project of sacralizing the space. Drakakis points out that we 'cannot know what it must have *felt like* to be a spectator' because the brothels, open sewers and so forth are missing, and he argues that the new building is therefore 'erected upon nostalgia and sentiment'. Though his reasoning is unassailable, his perspective is limited. It is a feature of successful performance spaces that a sense of the past is inscribed in the present. The 'nostalgic' desire for a lost golden age – the wandering of the Israelites through Sinai, the Trojan Wars when gods spoke to heroes, the day of Christ's resurrection – has always been a feature of religious feeling. The idea that a theatre should be a sterile laboratory where the live human organism can be inspected in time present is a curious manifestation of modernity.

Eliade's analysis remains valid in the twenty-first century:

> The profane experience . . . maintains the homogeneity and hence relativity of space. No *true* orientation is now possible, for the fixed point no longer enjoys a unique ontological status; it appears and disappears in accordance with the needs of the day. Properly speaking, there is no longer any world, there are only fragments of a shattered universe, an amorphous mass consisting of an infinite number of more or less neutral places in which man moves, governed and driven by the obligations of an existence incorporated into an industrial society.[119]

The new Globe offers a challenge to the notion that urban space is homogeneous and infinitely malleable. It offers the spectator a reassuring sense that he or she inhabits a structured 'world' or 'cosmos', and not the fragmentary condition of postmodernity. It provides a physical centre around which values can be constructed. It may indeed be the case that Shakespeare's Globe is a calculated artifice, yet the faith that Shakespeare was the genius of the second millennium has its effect on the audience. And the behaviour of the audience is a main part of the performance. The problem with Drakakis' cultural materialism is that, for all its moral and intellectual rigour, it cannot account for what makes an intense theatrical experience.

Sacred space is not something we can shrug off as a preoccupation of the past, something which concerns the origins more than the present of theatre. The issue of the 'sacred' raises profound questions about performance today. In an age when theatre has lost its centrality as a social institution, the issue of the 'sacred' raises questions about why people pursue art in general and the theatre in particular. I shall take as my final case study Welfare State International, an English company that has tried since 1968 to bring mythic and ritual structures to spiritually impoverished modern communities.[120] In the late 1980s the company decided that street theatre too often turned into mere spectacle, and they shifted the focus of their work from local residencies to a base in Ulverston in Cumbria. The decision to create a permanent home, wrote John Fox the founder of the company, 'reflected a need to move away from "Theatre", where practitioners live in a bubble

Plate 2   Lanternhouse, or 'Tower of Dreams'. Graphic by John Fox.

with a timespan of six months at most (three behind and three in front) and a need to make something more permanent and substantial and maybe more necessary'.[121] In an age when Margaret Thatcher caused radicals to lose their faith that political intervention would ever change the world, the new role of Welfare State became a more spiritual one, and included the devising of private rites of passage. This new vocation raised the problem of 'ceremonial space':

Now few of the population practise Christianity so the forms of the available ceremonies for weddings and namings aren't really appropriate. Church architecture with its cross form, with all its hierarchy, with a man dressed in black in the pulpit at the front, everything about it is forcing a certain thought pattern. So we need a new architecture.

The outcome was a converted school called Lanternhouse (plate 2), completed in 1998, and named after the annual processional lantern ceremony which the company introduced to the town. The blue latticed framework of a spire tops the tower, echoing the adjacent church and hills, but within the spire is a large microwave dish symbolizing modern communications. This emblem sums up the uneasy encounter in Ulverston of past and future, of local and global identities. Fox has described the town as midway between 'Trident mega-death and Wordsworth deodorant' – between the nuclear submarine base at Barrow and the prettiness of tourist Lakeland. Lanternhouse is poised in the centre of a contradictory environment. At the rear of the original building the company erected a Cumbrian cruck barn made of green oak with no nails, a symbol of nature and authenticity. This was subsumed within a new structure when funds arrived from the national lottery, but remains as a space within a space, a kind of ecological shrine. When planning the new building, Fox had no very clear ideas about function:

If you build a space which is very beautiful, which helps people focus their energy in a relaxed way, what performance do you put in that space? Do you put any performance in? Who does the performance? Why do you have performance? When do you have the performance? Do you have it every full moon? Do you have it every winter when it's dark and people get miserable? In summer do you have it as a massive place where people can come and exchange stories? They're intriguing questions which we're going to try and solve.[122]

Lacking either Rudolf Steiner's complex framework of symbols, or a traditional role in the local community, Fox falls back on a vaguely Jungian repertory of archetypal images. The company tend to assume that a ceremonial space can be established anywhere where it is possible to achieve the right degree of focus, and have yet to determine the long-term function of the permanent sacred centre they have created. The building has yet to acquire its own memories and traditions. Meanwhile, the problems which Fox addresses remain more interesting than his answers. The company's move to Ulverston reflects a widely felt desire at the end of the twentieth century to recover a portion of 'absolute space' in a world where 'abstract space' is the norm, and to find a new role for a socially engaged theatre in a post-political age.

CHAPTER 3

Processional space

In 1997 a report on parades in Northern Ireland stated:

We were struck by the intensity of the views and feelings of nearly all those with
whom we discussed the parade issue. We have had to enquire into matters which
operate at levels deeper than rationality . . . Put simply, the parades issue goes to
the heart of the deeply fractured society that, sadly, Northern Ireland represents.

The review panel applauded a recent sociological analysis which related the
marching season to the feeling of young unemployed men that they were
neither Irish nor British. This analysis argued that

symbolic practices in which the young play such a significant part today – the
bonfires, the painting of kerbs, the creation of flags, arches and bunting, the
marching bands and the parades themselves – are the specific means by which an
exclusive Protestant identity is represented and renewed in the loyalist mind. Here
primarily an embodied ideology is at work. It is the sound of the Lambeg drum
rather than the resonance of political ideology which brings tears to the eyes of a
loyalist.'[1]

A ban imposed on Orange marches is perceived by many 'loyalists' as an
attack on their personal and collective identities. Their symbols of identity
are not locked in a simple time-warp. The orange sashes of the older generation no longer have resonance for the young, who adopt different uniforms
according to the different estates which they inhabit. Clothing and banners
are less important than space. Their identity is bound up with the sense of
belonging to a particular place. Painting the colours of the Union Jack on
a kerbstone transforms a bleak road in a depressed estate into an emblem
of purpose. The Orangemen who speak of how their 'liberties' depend on
the right to march to Drumcree church via the Garvaghy Road, and not
by an alternative route offered by the authorities, are not simply seeking
an excuse for confrontation with Catholic residents. They are seeking a
role to perform in a global community that seems to have left them aside.

The significance of Irish processions is not easily grasped by a modern English mentality; the same gap in understanding makes it hard for many in the twenty-first century to understand the attachment to processions which characterized the pre-modern world, where identity was construed in less egocentric terms. 'Processions' and 'theatre' now belong to different conceptual categories.

Processional theatre has four different aspects or functions: pilgrimage, parade, map and narrative. First of all, a procession is usually a *pilgrimage* to somewhere, to some sacred destination. Victor and Edith Turner argue that pilgrimage is an expression of 'communitas' because, though the moral unit remains the individual, all pilgrims engage in a common activity. The trials of the journey, the Turners write, permit the pilgrim a cleansing of the doors of perception, a new innocence of the eye as the world upon arrival is seen afresh.[2] In pilgrimage theatre, the spectator who matters most is the pilgrim. A *parade*, by contrast, is an arrangement of human beings for the benefit of a separate audience, and the physical goal of the parade is only of secondary importance. A parade displays, actually or symbolically, an ordering of power. The third function of processional theatre is to articulate space, to lay out on the ground a symbolic *map*. The route of the procession is bequeathed by tradition and understood as a 'sacred way'. It defines a space either by marking a boundary, or by marking an axis, and processing along the sacred way lays a claim to ownership of the space. Fourthly, the procession is a *narrative*. As it passes the static spectator, an arrangement in space becomes an arrangement in time. The sequence of places passed by the procession may also carry the bones of a story, clarified when the procession halts at key locations.

In Northern Ireland time and repetition have turned the goal of Drumcree church or the gates of Derry into sacred destinations. However, these are 'parades' and not 'pilgrimages' in the first instance, hence their political sensitivity. The routes are claims to ownership. The march around the walls of Derry asserts Protestant control of the centre, through reenacting the story of how apprentice boys in 1688 closed the gates against a Catholic army. The march up to the gates on 12 August reenacts the arrival of the Protestant army that relieved the besieged city, and orange insignia recall that this army served William of Orange. The siege becomes a metaphor for the feeling of loyalists that they have no friends either in Britain or in the Republic or indeed in the USA. Beyond the demarcation of space, the level of mimetic enactment is relatively slight. The shutting of the gates of Derry in December, and burning of an effigy of the Jacobite governor, are more obviously 'theatrical' events with a narrative element.

In many pre-modern processions, much more detailed forms of simulation were undertaken.

A famous example is the annual 'marriage of the sea' in Venice, when the doge carried a ring to the mouth of the lagoon, and threw it into the open sea in a symbolic marriage.[3] This water-borne procession illustrates the four functions of processional drama that I have identified. The procession was a Christian *pilgrimage*, for it occurred on Ascension Day, and the doge's journey to the open sea echoed Christ's departure from earth; after the ceremony, participants prayed at the monastery of St Nicholas, patron saint of sailors, next to the mouth of the lagoon. The gigantic barge *paraded* the power of Venice before a huge gathering of visitors, commemorating Doge Orseolo's expedition on Ascension Day in the year 1000, when he claimed possession of the Adriatic with the blessing of the pope. The patriarch of Venice sailed from the Castello, not from St Mark's, and his separate route defined the separate and subordinate nature of church power in the Venetian republic. The journey which began with mass in St Mark's basilica drew a *map* of the city and its power-structure, linking the ceremonial centre of Venice to the periphery, where the secure waters of the lagoon met the dangerous Adriatic. The ceremony enacted a *narrative* with several layers: the great expedition of Doge Orseolo, the paradigmatic human wedding, and behind these the story of the fisherman who took St Mark (whose image now flew on the mast-head) to the mouth of the lagoon to drive back a ship full of demons.

To speak of theatricality is to evoke an actor–audience relationship, and in processions that relationship necessarily cuts in two directions. The Venetian doge viewed the crowds on the water-front as much as they him; the sailors who followed his galley in smaller craft were both spectators and part of the spectacle. This ceases to be a methodological problem once we dispense with passive models of the theatre spectator. It is the presentation of narrative which justifies bracketing processions with the category of theatre. A Greek *theatron* was a watching-place that could be erected to view a procession as readily as a tragedy. The only stone-built *theatron* surviving from the age of the classical playwrights is at Thorikos (fig. 10), a mining town on the coast of Attica. The sides are curved but the central line of seats follows a straight line with the consequence that there is no single point of focus. The rationale for this arrangement is that it allowed up to 3,000 people to view the climax of a procession which climbed from the harbour and arrived to confront the god Dionysus in his temple. A column of people could be seen presenting their animals to the idol in the temple stage-left, and then sacrificing those animals on the altar stage-right. The

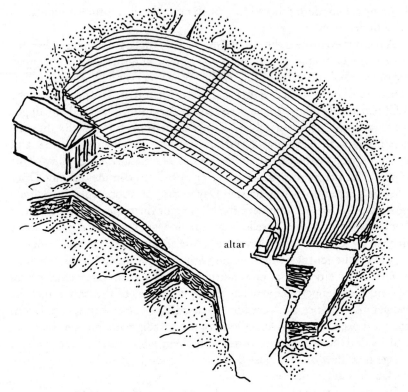

altar

Figure 10   Theatre of Thorikos (after Richard Leacroft).

performance of dances and plays was incidental to the main business of a
Greek festival: marshalling a procession that culminated in a sacrifice, to
be followed by a distribution of the sacrificial meat.[4]

In Athens, the Dionysiac procession likewise arrived in the theatre from
the audience's left, along a processional route lined with monumental
tripods that commemorated theatrical victories, and in the circular theatre the linear dancing of the ten tribes turned into the circular dancing
of dithyrambs.[5] Greek tragedy and comedy set up a tension between the
static individual, who would often gravitate physically to the point of equilibrium at the centre of the circle, and the collective, processional chorus.[6]
The relationship between art and ritual in tragedy was a complex one. In
Euripides' *Electra*, Electra enters the acting space in a one-person procession, and stops in the centre of the orchestra to perform a ceremony of
mourning over the imaginary grave of her father, when the chorus arrive

and ask her to participate in the Heraia, the annual collective march of Argive women to the outlying Temple of Hera. Electra declines, picturing herself as one who is trapped in both time and space. The Heraia was a ceremony that tied the centre of the community of Argos to the shrine of its patron on the periphery, defining the physical integrity of the state. Like all protagonists of tragedy Electra has become separate from the community, defined in the play by the chorus who are her peer group.[7] Greek theatre space can be understood as a site where the procession halts and is broken, where communal action and forward progress are interrupted.

Ancient theatres often made the performance space a thoroughfare. We have, for example, a rubric for the town of Oenoanda which explains how representatives of different villages and cities led bulls through the theatre en route for sacrifice in the course of a dramatic festival.[8] In the Theatre of Pompey in Rome (see figure 27) one processional axis ran down the temple steps, through the centre of the auditorium and the stage façade to Pompey's new Council Chamber, while a broad avenue ran laterally across the stage. The two side doors on Pompey's massive stage façade make little sense as entry points for an actor in tragedy or comedy, because they are set too far to the side to create adequate sightlines.[9] Though we need more accurate archaeological information, the length of the façade seems to create little focus for a single actor but makes admirable sense as the backdrop for a procession.[10] When Agamemnon's long procession of spoils from the east was drawn across the stage in one of the plays which inaugurated Pompey's theatre, this processional drama blurred the boundary between Pompey's real triumph and the fictive triumph of the play.[11] We saw in the last chapter how the Augustan Theatre of Marcellus was likewise planned in relation to a sacred processional axis or axes passing between the temple, the central door in the stage wall and some kind of arch to the rear of the complex; the stage meanwhile stood on a lateral axis which allowed a triumph to pass directly over it en route for the Forum. After the destruction of Israel in AD 71, we learn that the triumphal procession 'passed through the theatres to give the masses an easier view'.[12]

The distinction between procession as *pilgrimage* and procession as *parade* can be related to a distinction between two types of city within European culture. Athens began as an agglomeration around a sacred and defensive space, the Acropolis, while the adjacent port of Peiraeus was built up in the classical period according to a second model, the grid. In the first model, human beings adapt themselves to the disposition of nature and the gods; in the second, human order is imposed upon nature. In Athens the major processional route wound an irregular course to reach the Acropolis – in Rome it circled up to the Capitol. In planned cities of the Hellenistic world and Roman empire, however, a different logic was followed. The main ceremonial space was located where the two principal avenues intersected. The medieval world broadly adopted the irregular model, the renaissance reverted to geometry. The first model allows few vantage points for viewing a grand display, and the roads are in any case too narrow; participants, however, have a strong sense of their own place in the procession because irregular turns in the route offer them changing perspectives on their fellows, and bottlenecks force each part of the procession to be aware of the next. The natural mode here is the *pilgrimage*, a journey past a series of sacred locations to a destination vested with antiquity. The second model allows splendid vantage points for spectators on stands or at windows, who may be lucky enough to see the whole array. Straight avenues allow marchers to move in disciplined formation, with ample space for floats. Participants have a sense of their own subdivision, but not of the whole *parade*. The journeying is more important than the destination. The *mapping* function is more important in the first model, the *narrative* function in the second.

Two processions from the Greek world will illustrate the difference. The modern visitor to Delphi can still experience the climax of the Sacred Way, as it winds up the hill towards the giant altar of Apollo. The route is lined with an irregular array of statues, inscriptions, victory monuments, treasuries and natural features associated with the primeval Sibyl or the Python. The history of Greece was laid out here for those who processed. The novelist Heliodorus in the 2nd/3rd century AD describes a typical procession at Delphi, when one community amidst many others made its way up to the altar at the time of the Pythian games. The Aenians from Thessaly are making their four-yearly pilgrimage to Delphi, the symbolic navel of the earth. Delphi has a special resonance for them, because their symbolic ancestor or founding father was Pyrrhus son of Achilles, killed beside Apollo's altar at Delphi. The supposed tomb can still be seen, close to the giant altar, and next to it the Thessalian shrine where the Aenians feasted on sacrificial meat. Heliodorus pictures two groups of Aenian girls: a group of singers singing a song to Pyrrhus that tells his story, and a group of dancers balancing heavily scented baskets on their heads. Behind them ride two groups of young men on horses, and one (the hero of the novel) is identified by the crowd as a reincarnation of Pyrrhus. The procession comes to a climax when it circles the tomb and sacrifice. The girls scream in order to dramatize the killing of the animals and call to mind the martyrdom of Pyrrhus at this spot. The sense of sacred space is linked to the sacred time of the festival. The heroine of the novel, a priestess of Artemis dressed to resemble the goddess, joins the procession at dawn, stepping into the first rays of the sun. Reenactment of the myth at a special place and time gives the obscure Aenian state a sense of belonging within the heterogeneous Greek world. The novelist also evokes for us the participatory behaviour of the crowd. The people of Delphi admire the beauty of the young Aenian, and lower-class women bombard him with flowers; the visitors, on the other hand, ogle the Delphian priestess at the rear of the procession. Both groups enjoy their double vision of performer and role. The heroine is not confused with Apollo's sister, nor the Aenian youth with the hero of ancient myth, but the affinity is recognized.[13] The sense of interpersonal competition that characterized the athletic contest in the stadium belonged equally to the procession.

This procession along Delphi's Sacred Way can be contrasted with the grand procession of Dionysus which rolled through the broad, rectilinear avenues of Alexandria in 275/4 BC as part of the Ptolemaia, a festival celebrating the regime of the Greek Ptolemys.[14] As in Delphi, the formal destination was a sacrifice and banquet, but this was not an ancient feast-day of Dionysus: the purpose was rather to celebrate a new Greek dynasty, and bestow semi-divine status on its members. The procession began in the stadium, offering an optimal viewing position to a body of spectators. Satyrs as marshals cleared the way through the streets, and it was probably from the streets that the colonized Egyptian population would have witnessed this display of imperial power. We only hear of one sacred location visited, and that was a new one: a shrine to the wife of Ptolemy I, mother of the present ruler Ptolemy II. The procession was dominated by pageant wagons, vehicles far too huge to have penetrated the streets of Athens or Delphi. The narrative function which in Delphi fell to singers here fell to *tableaux vivants*.

The satyr–marshals were followed by women with incense, by actors who were going to perform later in the theatre, and by prizes for the athletes who would compete in the stadium. The first pageant wagon held a gigantic statue of Dionysus, pouring a 'libation' of wine in the rite that opened almost every Greek ceremony, and was followed by wild bacchanalian women. The second wagon held a mechanical statue of a seated woman who stood up to pour a libation of milk. This was not just a technological miracle but also a clue to what would follow, an image that had to be decoded by the audience. The woman was identified as Nysa, the name of Dionysus' Greek nurse (hence the milk), but also of the mountain in modern Pakistan which Alexander the Great identified as the site where

Dionysus was reared. The Ptolemys had inherited Alexander's eastern empire, and claimed descent both from him and from the god Dionysus, so Dionysus' return from the east was to be the theme of the procession. The use of dazzling and animated statues helped break down the division between human and divine spheres of existence. This proximity of mortals and gods – which in Delphi allowed the priestess of Artemis to become her embodiment – was a feature of Greek religion that Hellenistic rulers embraced with enthusiasm.

The next two carts, the biggest in the procession, carried a wine-press and a leaking wine skin. This image worked on many levels: wine as the emblem of Dionysus, his gift to the Greeks; wine to celebrate a Greek industry imported to Egypt; conspicuous waste to celebrate the wealth of the regime; a prelude to the elite banquet on the Acropolis; largesse distributed to the crowd in the stadium and probably also in the streets; smell to mingle with that of incense and assault the senses; a trail of wine along the street that would transform everyday space into a sacred way. After all the accoutrements of the banquet, three more tableaux resumed the narrative: a miniature, bejewelled bedchamber where Dionysus was born, the cave on Mt Nysa where Dionysus was reared by nymphs, and a statue of Dionysus returning from India riding an elephant. These three were followed by a stream of exotica from the east: trophies, livestock including elephants, and images of conquered peoples. The myth of Dionysus' return served to legitimate Greek conquests and acts of plunder.

The next wagon depicted Dionysus being cured of the sex-mania inflicted on him by his jealous stepmother, and the erectile figure of Priapus indicated the nature of his madness. Again, the image could be read on many levels: a stage in the life-story of Dionysus; an emblem of fertility suggesting the wealth and longevity of the regime; an image of catharsis suggesting public order brought by the Ptolemys; a scene to glorify the island of Kos, where Ptolemy II was born. The last wagon brought the story firmly into historical time, and provided the key to the whole. A statue of Ptolemy I, honorand of the festive season, stood beside Alexander, his notional ancestor, famed conqueror of the east. Statues of Virtue and Priapus symbolized Ptolemy's attributes. A statue representing Corinth symbolized a bond with mainland Greece. The wagon was followed by women in the guise of rescued prisoners, symbolizing Greek cities liberated by Alexander from Persian rule. The whole procession led up to this placing of Ptolemy I in the city of Alexandria as a second Alexander the Great. The technique of using wagons and tableaux was taken up in the medieval and renaissance periods as a means of creating similar religio-political narratives that legitimated a structure of power.

Ptolemy's Dionysiac procession has much in common with the Roman 'triumph' awarded to a victorious general.[15] In a triumph the general appeared in person, though his face might be painted to resemble a statue. He appeared in the costume of Jupiter, setting up the same ambiguity between human and divine spheres that we have seen in the Greek world, and his destination was Jupiter's temple on the Capitol. The story of his campaign was told through a series of images: spoils, prisoners, models of captured places. A model of the Alexandrian lighthouse, for example, marked the fall of Alexandria. The general's chosen triumphal route through the irregular streets of Rome told a story, for it would pass by particular places associated with friends and ancestors before joining the Sacred Way and entering the Forum, the ceremonial heart of the community. Here prisoners were slaughtered in a rite of sacrifice before the general climbed the hill to greet the statue of the god whom he temporarily embodied. In Ptolemy's procession men dressed as satyrs, often riding mules, provided an element of comedy but not political satire. In the Roman republic, an egalitarian ideology required that the general, whilst being honoured, should also be mocked by common soldiers or satyrs at the rear of the procession. There was a strong element of pilgrimage since the general had returned from foreign parts and was making a ceremonial entry into the city. His entry was symbolized by passage from the Campus Martius, which represented the world of war, through a triumphal arch. The Roman triumph had a profound influence on medieval and renaissance processions, when the new ruler would enter the gates of his city and make his way to the principal church, via archways and other locations laden with symbolism.

The Christian world did not choose in the same way to emulate the Roman funeral, another processional drama of great cultural significance.[16] During the republican period, a realistic wax effigy represented the dead nobleman in order to blur the boundaries of life and death, past and present. Under the empire it became customary that an actor skilled in mimicry should play the dead man. Throughout the period actors wore masks in the procession to impersonate the dead man's ancestors, and in imperial times putative ancestors might extend back as far as Aeneas and Romulus. The procession thus told a historical story. The official aim was to inspire the young to serve the state in emulation of earlier generations, whilst an unspoken object was to affirm the right of a few families to dominate the political system. In imperial times we hear also of satyrs accompanying the procession, and the mime who played the Emperor Tiberius offered a burlesque performance, bantering with the crowd to demonstrate the late emperor's solidarity with the people. This vision of physical immortality and shrugging off of death was incompatible with a Christian code of belief.

When Tertullian at the end of the second century objected to Greco-Roman processions, his Christian anger was directed at the parading of idols.[17] As a form, stripped of its pagan gods, processional drama proved entirely congenial to Christianity. The two great story-cycles of Christian myth resolve themselves easily into the form of a journey: first the journey to and from Christ's birthplace in a stable in Bethlehem, and second, the journey to the scene of Christ's death outside the walls of Jerusalem. The 'stations of the cross' line the sides of Catholic churches today as a memory of the ancient processional route in Jerusalem known as the *via dolorosa*, the route which Christ travelled to his crucifixion. Churches became processional spaces which created their own closed system of symbolic topography. In Constantine's Jerusalem the basilica funnelled processions westward towards the sites of the crucifixion and the resurrection (figure 7), while in Bethlehem the Church of the Nativity directed a procession eastwards towards the grotto deemed to be the birthplace. It was the eastward conception that became normative.

Having examined Easter Sunday in the last chapter, I shall cite an Easter Monday play to illustrate the processional form of medieval church drama. On Easter Sunday, Christ revealed himself to Mary Magdalene, and his next appearance according to St Luke was to two disciples on the road to Emmaus. The play which told this story was integrated into the structure of Vespers. The celebrants moved away from the altar towards the font at the west end singing Psalm 112, a poem full of inversionary themes: child worshippers, the sunset, God looking downwards from above, the poor sitting next to princes, barren women becoming mothers. The return eastwards was accompanied by Psalm 113, again full of relevant verbal images: the Israelites heading for the promised land, the Red Sea moving aside, mountains moving away like sheep and turning to water. The scene from St Luke was slipped into this return procession. Two disciples entered through the right-hand doors at the west end, whilst a bare-footed priest with a crucifix entered through the left door to represent Christ; Christ thus took the north side, the side of death. The figures addressed each other as they walked down the aisle, before reaching a stage set up in the nave to signify the 'Castle of Emmaus'. Here the trio stopped, and Christ broke bread and revealed his identity before disappearing. In Rouen cathedral in the twelfth century, the source of our fullest account, Mary Magdalene now appeared in the pulpit, showing the disciples grave-clothes which proved that Christ had risen, whereupon the procession resumed its course to the east end.[18] The correlation of real time (evening on Easter Monday) with the time in Luke's account helped a procession in the here and now of Rouen cathedral to coalesce with a biblical journey, allowing past and present to become one. In the Christian view of the world, time and space were not cyclic but directed at a specific goal: east, i.e. heaven and Armageddon. The procession embodied the sentiment, alien to a modern mind-set and to modern architectural practice, that life had inherent direction.

If we move on to the papal city of Avignon in the late fourteenth century, we can see how processional drama kept finding new vitality.[19] At a time of increasing devotion to the Virgin Mary, the schismatic pope established a new annual festival celebrating the admission of the Virgin at three years old to the temple in Jerusalem, where she would spend her childhood as a kind of nun. The drama devised for this festival helped identify the pope's new home in Avignon with the archetypal city of Jerusalem. It asserted the power of the church through demonstrating that Mary grew up in a temple and not a domestic environment. Girls, musicians and men dressed as angels joined the procession as it left the chapter house. Comedy at the rear was provided by the Devil, dragged howling and roaring in his chains by the Archangel Michael. In the plaza outside the west door of the church, nobles and commoners joined the procession, carrying candles to place before the altar, while strong youths used horizontal spears to create a mobile crush-barrier. Once inside the church the three-year-old protagonist climbed onto a stage in the middle of the nave. One by one, performers representing the nine orders of angels climbed onto the stage, sang their praises to the child Mary and climbed down on the eastern side. Mary's parents took their turn, so did a young man dressed as a woman called 'Church', while another playing a crone to symbolize Judaism was turned back. Finally the howling Devil was led up onto the stage, and the child kicked him, whereupon he too fled westwards. Praises completed, the child was escorted to the altar and presented to the bishop. The spectators all became participants in the drama through travelling the same journey as the Virgin, a journey from which sinners were excluded. Weather permitting, the drama concluded with a procession through the streets of the city, angels on horseback escorting the child Mary, ensuring that the whole of Avignon became a second Jerusalem.

In the twelfth century, Romanesque architecture was characterized by a dominant western façade, suggesting that Christ the Saviour opened his arms to the world outside the church. The western door, surmounted by a carved image of Christ sitting in judgement, became a doorway to revelation and salvation.[20] Written into the new architecture was a journey from the common world of the street, through a west door associated with death and judgement, to the east which represented eternal life. Gothic architecture gave increasing emphasis to the mystery and remoteness of the east end. The idea that the space of the church represented a spiritual journey became less important with the domed and centrally focused churches of the Italian renaissance. These were designed for static human beings to contemplate the harmony of the visible cosmos in the here-and-now of creation. The linear church procession no longer seemed to express life's transcendent truths.

Medieval cities were defined by their defensive walls. Outside lay anarchy and poverty, inside lay a world of regulation, hierarchy and relative affluence. Royal entries inspired by Roman triumphs were among the most important dramas of the medieval and renaissance world, defining the relative powers of state and city authorities. When the Wars of the Roses ended, Henry VII of the house of Lancaster approached the gates of York to be greeted by two huge roses, a red Lancastrian rose and white Yorkist rose, and a single crown was lowered to cover both in a sign of reconciliation. Henry's entry into this once hostile city illustrates the importance of the processional mode.[21] The route began when the king crossed the Wharfe and met the city sheriffs ten miles away at the limit of their jurisdiction. Five miles away they were joined by the mayor, the aldermen in red and the council in violet. Then came other townsmen of lesser status with no right to wear gowns, and afterwards the church – monastic institutions followed by representatives of the different parishes. In this display of feudal order there was no question that the dominant figure was the king. However, once the great colour-coded procession reached the city gates, the king could no longer be framed by his escort, and had to step into a new role. He rode into a city that had been transformed, the frontages entirely covered over by tapestries and fabrics. York became Jerusalem, and the victorious king stepped into a role constructed for him, not Jupiter but Christ.

Henry was greeted in sequence by three kings with gifts and by the Virgin Mary in order to consolidate this identity. King Ebranke, the legendary founder of York, handed Henry a crown, Solomon handed him a sceptre symbol of wisdom, and David a victor's sword. The choice of Solomon, builder of the temple, and David, conqueror of Jerusalem, reinforced the idea that York was now Jerusalem. The greetings took place at symbolic locations. Ebranke stood at the city gates, and passed over the keys of the city he founded. Solomon stood on the bridge over the Ouse, whose waters symbolized wisdom. David, positioned beside the seat of civic authority, spoke from a miniature castle, a microcosm of the walled city. The Virgin greeted Henry from the pageant wagon used for the play of the Assumption at Corpus Christi, and this wagon had a winch that allowed her to ascend to heaven to rejoin her son, Henry's only overlord. Between these four 'stations', each transition was marked by a sprinkling of substances from above – rose-water, sweetmeats, and finally a snow-storm of wafers – which enhanced the sense that Henry was engaged in a spiritual and transformative journey. Henry and his entourage finally entered the west door of York Minster, and terminated their procession at the altar. A role had been defined for Henry that required he be merciful like Christ towards a city which, for all its offences, was a version of the Holy City.

In this procession, Henry was both principal spectator, passing a number of theatre sets erected along the route for his benefit, and protagonist, playing a role for those who lined the streets. When he returned to the city the following summer, with 10,000 men behind him to show how he had consolidated his rule, the balance shifted. Members of the different craft guilds lined up on either side of the street to pay their respects within the city, and the mayor humbly carried his mace before the king. The king ordered the guilds to present their Corpus Christi pageants before him, and he sat at a window to watch. He was now the empowered spectator, the citizens merely performers.[22] 1 August was a date normally allocated to electoral and contractual business, and Henry asserted his power by wrenching the Corpus Christi ritual from its temporal context.

York is famous for the cycle of plays performed on wagons on Corpus Christi day. The feast was introduced in 1311 to honour the body of Christ (the *corpus Christi*), the centrepiece of the mass. The consecrated bread was carried through the streets on this day to demonstrate that church authority extended across the whole community. The festival functioned throughout Europe as a cusp when a sacred half of the year dominated by Christmas and Easter – i.e. the narrative of how Christ was born, died and rose again – gave way to a more secular half of the year dominated by civic and parish feasts,[23] and in Corpus Christi pageants sacred and civic themes met. Christ's *body* was an appropriate symbol for representing the corporate nature of an ideal community, its members conjoined and harmonious but far from equal. In many parts of Europe the consecrated bread, carried through the streets under a canopy, was escorted by static images of scenes relating to the New Testament narrative. In York, these tableaux gave way to a procession of short enacted dramas.[24] Whilst the church hierarchy organized one procession focused on the Host, the guilds of York organized a quite separate procession on the previous or following day, ending in the marketplace. A competitive relationship between the civic corporation and the church, which had economic jurisdiction over large swathes of the city, helps to explain why processional drama was developed in the streets of York to such a point of sophistication. The attribution of specific pageants to specific guilds allowed each guild to proclaim its status within the body of York society. When the Butchers performed the death of Christ, the tainted nature of their profession was reflected in the representation of murder, and the blood used in the pageant would have come from their slaughter-houses. The Butchers were a guild of relatively low status, but the necessary place of butchery in the scheme of urban life was asserted, and participation reflected the privilege it was to be freemen of the city.

Processional theatre was a practical mode that allowed a huge cast to perform before a huge audience in a city of confined spaces. In York the wagons started to process at first light, when the first group gave their first rendition of 'the creation', and it must have been well after dusk when the last performance of 'the last judgement' was given in the marketplace. Each wagon stopped in turn before ten or twelve tiny auditoria rented out to citizens who charged for entry, while many of the affluent watched from windows. Despite much research, we still do not know whether performances were given side-on, offering intimate experiences to those who had paid for seats, perhaps 10 per cent of the population, or whether the wagons were open platforms allowing the performers to play to all in the street behind them, whilst the elite watched from one side, paying to be seen as well as to see. Whether the streets of York constituted a democratic or an elitist auditorium thus remains a great unknown. York is unusual in the extent to which the pageant wagons housed fully scripted dramas, and the logistical complications of halting the procession to play these dramas must have been enormous. Across Europe different communities worked out different systems and timetables according to their particular size, topography and social structure.

To use a term coined by Bakhtin, the processional Corpus Christi play exemplifies the medieval 'chronotope' of the journey.[25] Medieval processional drama bears a close relationship to epics like the *Canterbury Tales* or Arthurian romances in the sphere of literature. The time–space conception of the journey was an aesthetic structuring device that helped to make sense of medieval living. Whilst late nineteenth-century bourgeois theatre was preoccupied with psychological interiority, and thus favoured the representation of human beings enclosed in inner rooms, the medieval world preferred linear representations. Life on earth was part of a longer journey to another world. Aron Gurevich observes that: 'Travel in the Middle ages mainly took the form of pilgrimage to the Holy Places. Striving to perfect oneself morally involved topographical displacement . . . The locus occupied by a man had to conform to his moral status.'[26] Personality, Gurevich continues, was defined centrifugally, through projecting the self onto the outside world. Individual qualities were always linked to a social role.[27] The mobile modern world likes to think of the individual and his or her environment as separable entities, but in the medieval world the soul was tied to the body till death, and the body was tied to the space it habitually occupied – where it grew its food, made its clothes and would eventually be buried. York provided its citizen 'body' with a complete means of subsistence, and few would migrate outwards or change their status. The bond of the body with the space it occupied meant that movements through space acquired strong symbolic force. Gurevich remarks that Christianity, inspired by St Augustine, broke with the pagan cyclic world view shaped by the rhythms of agriculture. Time became linear and irreversible. Historical time was detached from the notion of eternity, and given structure by Christ's incarnation.[28] In Christendom the forward march of the human race from Creation to the Last Judgement could best be represented through the mode of the procession. Political and religious dimensions were intertwined in the medieval period, as they had always been in Greece and Rome, but in the renaissance the individual human ruler became ever more dominant. Perhaps our best piece of visual evidence for an early modern procession is the painting in London's Theatre Museum known as *The Triumph of Isabella*, famous for a pageant wagon depicting the nativity (plate 3).[29] The painting is part of a sequence recording a parade through Brussels on 31 May 1615. The houses along the processional route have been covered in fresh green branches, transforming the everyday commercial milieu of the street into a May-time world of festival. The painting in the Theatre Museum omits the procession of the guilds with their patron saints at the start, and the militia who followed them, as well as the statue of Our Lady of the Sablon at the rear, escorted by church and city authorities. It depicts the third section which interweaves medieval pageant wagons surviving from the reformation with neo-Roman triumph-wagons. Scenes related to the Virgin Mary are juxtaposed with triumphal scenes depicting the virtues of the Archduchess Isabella. In pride of place at the rear of this section, on a huge wheeled ship made years before for the funeral of the emperor, sit the Virgin and child, above Isabella and her consort. (The prow of the boat is moving into the frame top right in the photograph.) The image demonstrates that a kind of divinity lies in the royal blood of Isabella,

Plate 3   Detail from Denis Van Alsloot *The Triumph of Isabella* (1615). Oil painting.

daughter of Philip II of Spain and granddaughter of the Emperor Charles V. A wagon bearing a tree of Jesse with Mary on top of the genealogical tree reinforces the value of lineage (wagon in the centre of the photograph). While James I of England at this time was asserting the 'divine right of kings', touching the sick to cure them of scrofula, Isabella preferred to use the religio-triumphal procession to certify the sacredness of her Hapsburg body. We have seen the same dynamic at work in regard to Ptolemy II, a transference rather than an obliteration of the religious impulse. There is no reason to doubt that, after the traumas of the reformation, most of the Catholic burghers who lined the streets of Brussels and filled the windows derived security and spiritual comfort from equating monarch and Virgin. If a statue could be endowed with sanctity in the premodern world, so could an archduchess. Gradually, in the baroque world, monarchs ousted traditional religious images as the major focus of public emotion and of public processions.

Isabella's procession had no use for a script. The audience's pleasure was partly acoustical, for Apollo and the nine muses provide an orchestra. It was partly sensory, for the dark clothes of the bourgeoisie contrast with the red and gold opulence of the procession. But most important was the pleasure of decoding the signs and reading a narrative. The key was the giant parrot cage at the head of this procession which marked the formal occasion of the triumph: Isabella's victory in a competition, firing her crossbow at a parrot emblem on top of the spire of Our Lady's church. This miracle or triumph legitimates a double identification of Isabella with Our Lady, and with the Roman goddess Diana the archer. The narrative of Mary's ancestry, the annunciation, and the birth of a child who demonstrates his wisdom in the temple builds up to the fusion of the two main protagonists on Charles V's vessel. The virtues of Isabella (personifications which occupy the wagon top left in the photograph) merge with the virtues of Mary. Each figure and each banner contributes another detail to the interlocking pattern of meaning. Without the aid of dialogue, a story unfolds, inviting analysis, admiration and reverence. Devils interacting with the crowd like ancient satyrs destabilize the experience of viewing, and call into question neatly ordered systems of control in a world where humans have only a partial vision of truth.

Our sources inevitably privilege the elite, who caused records of great occasions such as Isabella's triumph to be perpetuated. Law suits provide our best access to the behaviour and attitudes of the unprivileged. Events in the Somerset city of Wells in 1607 offer us a vivid picture of a popular processional culture, rooted in pagan folklore, clinging to the infrastructure of church and aristocracy, but threatened now by a new set of values.[30] John Hole, the city's constable and largest employer, was one of many English puritans who objected to traditional modes of celebration, and he was angry enough to drag many fellow citizens to the Star Chamber, and consequently into our historical records. Wells was a much smaller community than York, with a population of perhaps, two thousand. Technically a 'city' by virtue of the cathedral which looms over the streets, its scale was and remains

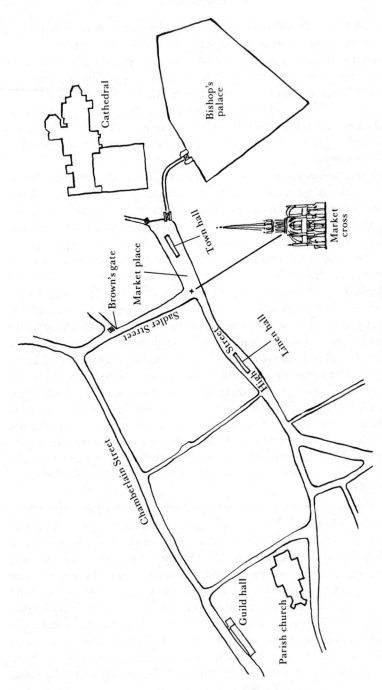

Cathedral

Bishop's palace

Brown's gate

Market place

Town hall

Market cross

Sadler Street

High Street

Linen hall

Chamberlain Street

Guild hall

Parish church

Figure 11   City of Wells in the Elizabethan period.

that of a medium-sized town. Wells gained a charter in 1589, bringing independence from the oppressive jurisdiction of the bishop. The main processional route ran along the High Street from west to east, from the market cross to the parish church (fig. 11). It was here and not in the cathedral that the mayor and corporation had their official seats. The High Cross was a raised and covered structure which guarded the entry to the market, and provided a viewing platform that allowed dignitaries to look down the High Street, and up Sadler Street to Brown's gate. Topographically, Wells can be regarded as a microcosm of London, where processions flowed westward along Cheapside to St Paul's.[31] Equivalent to the Tower of London, the locus of feudal power in Wells was the bishop's fortified palace, immediately west of the marketplace.

The first phase of what we might call the 'marching season' occupied the month of May. At first light on 1 May, a drummer led twenty people to fetch in the may. They brought in boughs from the woods to build bowers for the May Lord and his Lady at either end of the processional route, one close to the cross, the other by the entry to the churchyard, and they set up a red and white maypole in the High Street near the cross. On the four Sundays which followed, the drummer, the morris troupe and hired musicians organized dancing in the streets before and after the hours of compulsory church service. Couples of male and female danced hand in hand up the street, and some continued beyond the city to nearby houses or villages. Under their 'Captain' and 'Lieutenant', a group of thirty or forty youths processed up and down the streets firing off guns in a threatening if not dangerous manner. These rites of May articulated the community according to its different age and gender categories. Young couples marked their youth by collecting spring buds; unmarried men performed their masculinity through marching and playing with guns. Children under eight paraded as virgins on Ascension day, 14 May. When the greenery of nature invaded the city, the natural order returned and class structures were abolished. The elected May Lord was a 'gentleman', and his Lady a mere barber's wife. Thorny may blossom hung on the doorways to keep evil spirits from entering the houses, and these spirits were left outside to inspire a sense of anarchy on the street.

The maypole was the first cause of serious trouble. When a haberdasher's wife, Ann Yarde, performed her Sunday morning promenade along the High Street to the parish church, she balked at passing the maypole, which she dubbed a spotted calf like the idol worshipped by the Israelites in the desert. Next Sunday the festive militia processed up and down with a painting of a calf coloured like the maypole and framed like an icon.

They took pot-shots at it with their guns, sounded their trumpets at the constable as he stood under the High Cross, and a man dressed in 'satyr' skins bleated like a calf in front of Mrs Yarde's door in the marketplace. In Catholic times, no-one objected strongly to the juxtaposition of Christian cross and pagan maypole in the High Street, but now a wealthy citizen claimed a right to her private conscience and to freedom of the streets. The young men responded with a charivari, a traditional processional form designed to bring anomalous individuals into line with the community.[32]

June was dominated by an 'Ale' in the parish church, a feast held to raise money for bells and repairs to the steeple. The cost of church maintenance was now supposed to come from rates in Protestant England, but the dean of the cathedral who had responsibility for the parish church gave his permission for old-style fund-raising, and much pent-up energy was released. Over five days, residents of the five major streets and their environs processed via the High Cross to the banquet in the churchyard, carrying their food with them. They contributed money for ale and refreshments on arrival, and processed home by the same route. In this parish event, the community therefore defined itself topographically. In medieval society, identity was tied to space, with different occupations clustered in different parts of town. The mayor and many burgesses with the dean and his canons attached themselves to the rear of the procession when it reached the cross, led on by two dummies, a Giant and Giantess, representing pagan forces that conferred protection.

The first two days were relatively low key, but on the third day, the inhabitants of Chamberlain Street, associated with the affluent Mercers, produced two spectacular displays. First came George and the Dragon. The young men of the May militia provided an 'Irish' entourage for the saint, and the royal family of Egypt must have worn imported fabrics sold by the mercers. In the evening in the marketplace, the dispersal point of the procession, St George rescued the King of Egypt's daughter by killing the dragon. In the second display, a child representing the goddess Diana in her chariot was accompanied by six choristers dressed as nymphs, singing ecclesiastical music. The participation of the choir marked the physical integration of borough and cathedral, but the May Lord had to twist the arm of a reluctant choirmaster to gain this contribution. The pageant told the story of Actaeon, and we may infer that it too concluded with an evening enactment, probably a male dancer wearing like Falstaff in *Merry Wives of Windsor* the horns of a deer. It is not hard to conceive why the mingling of pagan themes with Christian music offended puritan sensibilities.

The fourth day belonged to the area south of the river, where the dominant tradesmen were dealers in animal flesh – tanners, chandlers and butchers, and their street would have been distinctly malodorous. This group celebrated their place in society by adopting a carnivalesque mode. 'Old Grandam Bunch', carried in a barrow while she made filthy black puddings from intestinal matter, offered an ironic image of butchery, incidentally demonizing widows cut off from family networks. The procession included a charivari burlesquing puritans opposed to the Ale. One man impersonated the pewterer Hugh Mead, presenting him as a tinker, which provoked the real Mead to come down from the High Cross, confiscate the hammer and saucer, and try to pull the rider from his horse. A real-life butcher waved a pair of scales to show that he played a grocer, threw grains into the crowd, and proclaimed they were better than the raisins of Humphrey Palmer the grocer. A farmer dressed himself as a spinster in a red petticoat, spinning worsted wool at high speed with spindle and distaff in the manner of John Hole's employees. He bantered with his companions about the destiny of the wool, and sang a song beginning 'Hole, hole . . .'. Another couple rode face to face with a desk between them, representing a usurer and notary, and bantered about the difficulty of lending money to decayed tradesmen. This particular charivari brings out the economic realities underlying the conflict. Hole was an incomer, who had migrated to Wells and become a citizen by virtue of his capital, creating employment for some five hundred impoverished peasants and townspeople by getting them to make cloth for worsted hose. The new economic regime, whereby one capitalist doled out piecework to many, required that people should conceive themselves as individuals; processional drama required that people should conceive themselves as parts of an integrated community, parts of the *corpus Christi*. While Hole's modern solution to poverty was job creation, the traditional solution lay in collective festive action. On the third Sunday in May, for example, men from Wells took their May-games to nearby Croscombe, for an Ale held to support an impoverished weaver.

The Ale was concluded a few days later on market day when many strangers were in town.[33] Images of Mead and Hole were painted on a vertical board, with Ann Yarde standing between them. A bowling alley was set up on a plank, so the balls could pass through nine holes beneath the painting of Mrs Yarde. A ballad was sung proclaiming this 'holing game' best of all the summer shows. The ballad was later circulated, and the May Lady entertained the dean's wife with it. Improvised banter punned on the boards being a 'yard' long, and the prize was a crown since the Yardes lived at the sign of the Crown. One punning insult has a particular resonance:

'Holing is against the King's proclamation and not sufferable in the streets, and therefore if you would needs Hole it go Hole it in the Mead.' In the new capitalist regime, the space of leisure and celebration would become the demarcated and marginal space of the meadow (mead) or park; the once public space of the streets would in future belong to business and to private individuals, not to collective expression. For puritans, the dominant social unit was the family not the town or parish, and it was alleged by the revellers that these closed family units were riddled with adultery. The churchwardens continued the fight by taking Hole to the diocesan court in the cathedral a year later, accusing him of adultery with Ann Yarde while her husband was in London and her household at a festival. Here, they implied, lay Hole's true motive in opting out of collective celebrations.

Six years later, Hole had conceded defeat, abandoned the attempt to impose a modern socio-economic order on the town, and moved away. The queen with the bishop and many courtiers came to visit Wells and performed a formal entry through Brown's gate, greeted by the mayor and aldermen.[34] The streets were decorated, and beggars removed. The city presented itself to the queen as a regulated medieval community defined by occupational categories, and six craft groupings offered their traditional pageants, in hierarchical order. Scaffolding was set up to create adequate seating for the courtiers. The 'hammermen' from the east of town who worked in metal and wood represented themselves through pageants of Noah (a woodworker) and Vulcan (a metalworker). The shearmen and tuckers from the west side had only a banner, perhaps a sign of how far Hole and his pieceworkers had taken over the making of cloth, while the company of Weavers had disintegrated entirely. The dealers in animal flesh sustained their clowning persona: men in animal skins hauled a float packed with men dressed as old maids adorned with bits of cow – versions of Grandam Bunch. The shoemakers followed, performing on their wagon an ambitious drama about Crispin and Crispianus, patron saints of their company, with a shoemaker's daughter playing the romantic lead. The play of the tailors was concerned with the death of John the Baptist, an appropriate figure for this company because he declined to wear any form of tailored clothing. The Mercers drew up the rear with their two plays of St George, and of Actaeon.

In many respects these shows were an anachronism. The closed and regulated economy of the medieval town was collapsing. Religion and theatre had come to seem a contradiction in terms. Plays on biblical themes like Noah and John the Baptist were no longer an accepted mode for representing Christian teaching, certainly not in the public street alongside

Roman goddesses and a cartload of witches. St George would vanish, to reappear in the romantic era as the hero of a Christmas mumming play, taken from house to house or pub to pub with every illusion of being an ancient rite.[35] In Catholic Europe, similar changes took place under the influence of the counter-reformation. St George remained an acceptable figure, but his dragon was dismissed as apocryphal.[36] Plays on pageant wagons continued to flourish in Spain on Corpus Christi day, but they were regulated and performed by professionals, starting and finishing their journey in church to make quite clear the divide between sacred and secular spheres.[37] The shoemakers of Wells were most in touch with modern times, performing a story of romantic love and rags to riches, inspired by Thomas Deloney's popular bourgeois novel.[38] Their play owed more to fashions in the professional theatre than to traditions of street performance.

Though guild performances on wagons would soon be a thing of the past, the consensus established in 1613 between the queen, the bishop and the burgesses of Wells points to the immediate future. King James' *Book of Sports* in 1617 would legitimize Ales on Sunday and other street festivities. After the hiatus of the Commonwealth, many civic traditions would be resurrected, placing increased emphasis on the monarchical power of the mayor. It was many years before John Hole's preference for private living finally won the day – not till the eighteenth century when polite society withdrew from English popular culture, retreating to enclosed spaces such as pleasure gardens and assembly rooms. Special places – heterotopias in Foucault's terminology – were demarcated for entertainment and celebration. In Richard Sennett's view, the major motor of change was architectural:

The monumental squares of the early 18th Century, in restructuring the massing of the population in the city, restructured the function of the crowd as well, for it changed the freedom with which people might congregate. The assemblage of a crowd became a specialized activity; it occurred in three places – the cafe, the pedestrian park, and the theater.[39]

Back in 1607 there were no heterotopias. The parish church was a space for banqueting as well as worshipping; the market was a space both for selling and for performing shows; the High Street was not only a space where people lived and sold their goods but also a space of ceremony. The residential squares of the eighteenth-century city created a public space that was empty, devoted purely to private leisure, and this emptiness was a sign of political order; the straight, wide streets of the neo-classical city likewise signified the triumph of human rationality. Wells High Street at the end of the middle ages was a space of disorder, swelling in the middle to accommodate a 'shambles' of market stalls and a linen hall raised on posts in the centre, and twisting in a slight S-shape echoing the natural course of the rivulet that flowed down it. No two vantage points offered the same view, and nowhere offered a complete view. Every building had its individual associations. The form of the street was not the product of planning, but stemmed from ancient spatial practices. The architectural form encouraged the collective expression of fantasies that could be anarchic, fantastical and satirical.

Paris is the most striking example of the way the new baroque architecture, with its immense vistas, turned the city street into a space that bespoke royal power, offering no scope for popular self-expression, neither intimate enough to make ordinary tradesmen feel comfortable, nor irregular enough to suggest that everyone had their niche in the social order, but ideal for soldiers marching in disciplined formation.[40] The baroque streets of Paris were laid out in accordance with the principles of perspectival art which required that one commanding eye – that of the ruler – should have a view of the totality. The city became a kind of stage set for the royal spectator. In the manner of Foucault's Panopticon, the eye of power looked in all directions down radiating streets, implementing absolute control.[41] After the revolution, the festivals of the republic found no way of accommodating themselves to streets which embodied the absolute power of a single monarch, and carried memories of recent bloodshed. The taste of the Revolution was for festivals in open spaces. Whilst in ancient Rome triumphal processions proceeded from the Campus Martius to the Forum, in revolutionary Paris this direction was reversed. The open and quasi-rural Champs de Mars where the first revolutionaries gathered to assault the Bastille became the sacred space, the goal of processions. The great monuments of the ancien régime were concealed by greenery as in medieval May-games to obliterate symbols of the past.[42] Richard Sennett argues that these revolutionary marches into open, empty environments, far from stimulating violent crowd behaviour, actually numbed the crowd. 'The space of liberty', he writes, 'pacified the revolutionary body.'[43]

The spatial practices of northern Europe have not, since the enlightenment, encouraged processional drama to flourish. Different theoreticians have accounted for the growth of modern individualism in different ways. For Richard Sennett, the failed efforts of Parisian revolutionaries to regenerate pagan ritual epitomize the failure of human planners to harness a public sense of transcendental powers. He associates the thinking of urban planners with Harvey's discovery of the circulation of the blood, suggesting that streets were designed in the enlightenment to allow individuals to circulate endlessly. The Parisian revolutionaries who evacuated their festivals to the Champs de Mars believed that 'Pain could be erased by erasing place. This same erasure has served different ends in a later time, the purposes of individual flight from others rather than moving closer towards them.'[44] When planners aim to promote comfort and convenience, Sennett argues, what they achieve is physical desensitization. For Walter Benjamin, the isolated individual thrown up by commodity capitalism is epitomized by Baudelaire's *flâneur*, a man who wanders through the Parisian arcades, safe from traffic, observing the crowd but never part of it. While Victor Hugo idealized and spiritualized the revolutionary masses, Baudelaire's *flâneur* is condemned to be a lonely spectator.[45] Michel de Certeau draws a memorable picture of the postmodern *flâneur*, walking through a city that is stripped of dirt, memory and particularity. Footsteps, he suggests, have the unique qualities of a spoken utterance. To walk is to escape an imposed spatial system.[46] When de Certeau idealizes the act of walking through the city as a means of claiming freedom and identity, he takes it for granted that the act of walking is a singular and not a collective statement.

Though far from moribund in the twentieth century, processional drama now has had a residual quality, a sense that it exists to perpetuate the past. The Christian tradition has been sustained by Easter dramas most notably in Greece and Spain; in England, the need to keep traffic circulating rules out any possibility of reviving Mystery plays in their full processional form.[47] Street demonstrations have provided another important occasion for processional performance. Perhaps the most influential experiments have been those of Peter Schumann, whose Bread and Puppet Theatre played a part in American protest marches during the Vietnam War, when his huge puppets, masks and dummies stood out above the crowd, his arrangement of images being 'spatial analogues to actions', telling a story through juxtaposition. Slow ceremonial movement was a feature of the style, creating a sense of the sacred that could never be attained by ordinary actors with bare faces. Schumann's aim was always 'to prevent the degradation of ceremony/ritual into art, i.e. mere form, aesthetic pattern', and his work was infused by the principle that 'theatre is a form of religion'. Processions are a demonstration of order, and the sense of a transcendent moral order infused Schumann's work. After the Vietnam period, Schumann no longer chose to use American streets as his theatre, but preferred fixed locations. He travelled to Nicaragua in order to devise politicized Easter passion plays for communities of a kind that he could not find in the USA.[48]

Another major modern category is 'carnival', a thriving form in many parts of the Mediterranean world, but confined to pockets in northern

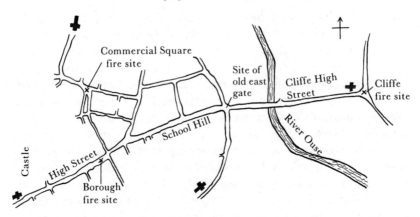

Figure 12   Lewes, showing main processional route.

Europe, where it escapes being prettified and insipid. London's major carnival is an import from the Caribbean, and a means by which a particular ethnic community celebrates its collective identity. In Chinatown at Chinese New Year, residents likewise assert their collective identity by feeding dragons that dance through the streets. Ethnicity now defines community more strongly than other markers of age, occupation and residence. It is outside major cities that processional drama is mainly to be found. I shall conclude with an English example that seems buoyant at the time of writing, the annual bonfire festival held in Lewes, Sussex, on 5 November.[49] 'Bonfire' in Lewes is never demeaned and trivialized by the term 'carnival'.

The town retains its medieval street plan (fig. 12). A long, irregular main street runs roughly west–east, heading downhill towards the river Ouse. The focal area at the top of School Hill is now defined by a war memorial, the market and town hall having become less visible presences. Across the river, the main street becomes Cliffe High Street, defining another community that both is and is not part of Lewes. The town is hemmed in by hills on either side, which fosters a sense of spatial integrity. Historically, the festival in Lewes falls into three phases: the revolutionary period, framed by the two great Parisian risings of 1789 and 1848, the age of Victorian imperialism, and the modern world. In the first period a relatively unstructured working-class crowd of the kind idealized by Victor Hugo lit fires in the street and rolled flaming barrels down the hill, until Whig shopkeepers called in a large militia in 1847.[50] In the second period, four highly structured societies each laid claim to a separate area of the town. Each had a fire-site in its own territory, close to a public house. After a series of processions, each society burned three principal effigies: Guy Fawkes (the Catholic who tried to blow up the Houses of Parliament in 1605), the pope, and a contemporary figure who seemed to epitomize the Romish or anti-British spirit. Plate 4 shows the mock Bishop of Borough Bonfire Society preaching a sermon alongside the effigy. This phase came to an end in 1905, when large fireworks and street bonfires were banned. Today there are five societies, which march through the town while traffic is diverted to the bypass and eventually burn their effigies in the safety of a meadow. Up to 60,000 spectators crowd into the streets and onto the fire-sites, causing much anxiety about public safety. The principal effigy is a surprise, revealed only in the final procession to the fire. In 2001 there was a certain inevitability, eight weeks after the destruction of the World Trade Center in New York, when the Cliffe effigy turned out to be a 9-metre(30-foot) Osama Bin Laden seated on a lavatory pan.

A historical narrative is embedded in each procession as it passes. Giant effigies of Guy Fawkes and the Pope of 1605 provide the dominant point of reference. Banners portray William of Orange landing on 5 November 1688 to restore Protestant rule. Seventeen flaming crosses, lit outside the town hall, commemorate Protestant martyrs burned at the stake in that spot. The rioters of 1847, prevented from rolling their barrels down the hill, are commemorated by a race with flaming half-barrels down Cliffe High Street, by more barrels trailing behind each procession, and by barrels ceremoniously dropped into the river. The smuggler costume (black masks and striped Guernsey jumpers) commemorates the uniform worn by those seeking to evade recognition and arrest in the mid nineteenth century. Each society has a set of historical costume-types worn because that is the society's tradition, adding to an overall sense of historical continuity. A continuum links the sixteenth-century counter-reformation to Osama Bin Laden or whatever other demonized figure is represented by the principal effigy. The procession as a whole recounts an on-going contest between Britain and the foreign other.

The space of Lewes is transformed by the banishment of the motor car. The discomfort of the participants who march for many hours, often in the rain, battered by the sound of firecrackers and in constant danger of suffering burns, enhances their sense of embodiment in place and space. Their normal sense of self is disrupted by the hypnotic experience of marching for so long. The flames and smoke divert attention from ground-level commercial frontages to the ancient outline form of the streets, and significant places become vested with memories. Pyrotechnic wreathes, for example, are illuminated at the War Memorial to bring back memories of the 1918 Armistice. The march to the fire-site does not have the quality

Plate 4   Street bonfire outside Lewes town hall in c.1901. Ink and wash drawing.

of a pilgrimage since these are strictly places of exile; the sites of greatest symbolic potency are the nodal points where street bonfires used to be lit until 1905 (see figure 12). Here 'bonfire prayers' are solemnly chanted by the mock Archbishop ('Remember, remember . . .'). Men and increasing numbers of women around midnight pile up discarded brands and jump through the flames as medieval men once jumped through midsummer bonfires. In the nineteenth century the main topographic concern was to mark out separate territories, with the four processions uniting on the High Street to define their common membership of the town. The concern today is to claim collective ownership of the streets over against the rival claims of domestic life, cars, visitors, commerce and above all the regulatory authorities. Tension between the police and the societies is constant. In 1999 a fire engine thundered dangerously through the crowds in what seemed more a display of power than a serious concern for public safety. A policeman at a high window attempted to control the crowd by means of a public address system, but was ignored almost as a matter of principle. In 2001 there was less tension because severe floods in 2000 had drawn people and authorities together.

The Lewes processions grew steadily larger in the last decade of the twentieth century, and so did the audiences. The festival survives being annihilated by public regulation because it is a tradition, and feeling for it in the town is intense enough to affect Council elections. A long-established white population with broadly working-class values feels that Bonfire is part of its identity, and an escape from imposed systems of regulation. The values of politicians, profit-and-loss economics, and mainstream Christian morality are not those of Bonfire. Media coverage is avoided. The values which Bonfire represents are oppositional, conservative, nostalgic and more or less xenophobic. Particularly within the dominant Cliffe Bonfire Society, the residual anti-Catholic rhetoric of Orangemen and a youthful interest in modern paganism give a religious tinge to the event. The processional drama of Lewes asserts communality. It communicates through things that people make with their hands – emblems, costumes, fireworks, music – and not through language that may be conceived as the property of intellectuals, or through technology. Bonfire does not claim to be a form of *art*, so when I claim that the processions constitute a form of 'drama' I engage in some act of appropriation.

CHAPTER 4

Public space

'Drama originated in a public square and constituted a popular entertainment.' Thus the romantic Russian poet, Alexander Pushkin, began his thumbnail history of theatre in order to campaign for a popular nationalist form of tragedy. He rejected the bogus realism of 'a building divided into two parts, one of which is filled with spectators who have agreed, etc . . .' in favour of a trestle stage in the public square, or some equivalent, that relies on no such pretences or false divisions. The history that Pushkin constructs is simple but compelling. Drama abandoned the public square for the halls of the elite, where alas it 'lowered its voice', 'doffed the mask of exaggeration', and 'shed its universally comprehensible language.'[1]

Pushkin's vision communicated itself to two compatriots, whose influence has been extensive. First, Mikhail Bakhtin:

The marketplace of the Middle Ages and the Renaissance was a world in itself, a world which was one; all 'performances' in this area, from loud cursing to the organised show, had something in common and were imbued with the same atmosphere of freedom, frankness, and familiarity . . . The marketplace was the center of all that is unofficial; it enjoyed a certain extraterritoriality in a world of official order and official ideology, it always remained 'with the people.'[2]

For Bakhtin, then, the marketplace was a site of freedom and the home of popular culture. For Vsevolod Meyerhold, the ideal was not so much the open market as the fairground booth, where the art of the strolling player, *cabotinage*, is for ever on display. The marketplace is central to his account of theatre history:

Having sensed its own inadequacy, the mystery began gradually to absorb the elements of popular entertainment as personified by the mummers, and was forced to go from the ambo, through the parvis into the churchyard, and thence out on to the marketplace . . . Perhaps it has always been so: if there is no cabotin, there is no theatre either . . .[3]

Pushkin's two disciples thought along similar lines. Both espoused an aesthetic of the grotesque, which they associated with the marketplace or fairground. This aesthetic emphasized the body rather than psychology, masks rather than faces. There are important differences, however. Meyerhold celebrates the triumph of the visual over the verbal, while Bakhtin emphasizes the language of the marketplace. Meyerhold anticipates both a modernist theatre which sought to communicate through images, and the ideal of a body-based physical theatre which has shaped so much radical work in the late twentieth century. Bakhtin, though despairing of monologic naturalism in the theatre, had no sympathy for modernist experimentation. His influence on theatre has percolated more slowly than Meyerhold's, and has centred on the notion of 'carnival'.

Marketplace and fairground represent somewhat different ideals, increasingly so with the passage of time. Medieval fairs were often located in and around marketplaces, and were in the first instance places for buying and selling, free from heavy tolls and the restrictive practices of the guilds. Fairs were markets open to vendors from outside the community, and normally attracted many visitors, functioning perhaps two or three times in a year. With the rise of capitalism, which is to say the dominance of shops over markets, the function of fairs began to change. Driven from prestigious urban centres, fairgrounds became important heterotopias, operating on the social margins. The concept of the marketplace is more closely bound up with locality, for each community possesses its market. The concept of the fair became associated with itinerancy, and the absence of a fixed community. Meyerhold's ideal was the romantic strolling actor, a player who belongs to nowhere.

Bakhtin conjured up a marketplace where peasants buy and sell at the centre of his imagined community, and appears to be a place where one might escape the order of Stalin's command economy; he passes over the fact that medieval markets were instruments of regulation. The doubtful nature of Bakhtin's historiography emerges when we turn from Bakhtin's account of a Roman carnival visited by Rabelais in 1549 to Rabelais' own description.[4] Bakhtin passes off the mock battle as a specimen of popular culture, but when we read the original account the festival turns out to be organized by the Cardinal Du Bellay in front of his palace to celebrate the birth of a French prince. A mock castle is built in the square and one of Diana's nymphs is rescued. The performers are aristocrats, the nymphs are played by gentlewomen, and the audience includes not only the populace but Dukes, Cardinals and persons of fashion from far and wide. The enthusiastic popular audience is caught up in a ceremony that celebrates

Plate 5   Pieter Brueghel the Younger: *A Village Festival*. Oil painting.

an aristocratic and French ideology. Bakhtin's carnival became a potent twentieth-century myth, but the marketplace of his imagining is of scant historical authority.

Meyerhold's claim that the 'fairground booth is eternal' is equally troublesome to the historian.[5] If we look at booth theatres of the early modern period, pictured by Dutch artists like the Brueghels, we see a stage that is open to all. A fundamental change took place in the seventeenth century, when the fairground booth became an indoor theatre. Images of eighteenth- and nineteenth-century fairgrounds depict façades before which actors appear, delivering a prologue or dumb-show that will lure a paying public through the doors of the makeshift building.[6] The change was in the first instance economic. In sixteenth- and early seventeenth-century Dutch paintings, the actors we see are amateurs who belong to guilds or Chambers of Rhetoric;[7] later the performers are professionals, and it is in their economic interest to close off and privatize the performance space. Already, in Jonson's *Bartholomew Fair* (1614), Littlewit's puppet show is located in an interior space, a microcosm of Jacobean professional theatre. *Bartholomew Fair* play was written in part to celebrate King James's paving of Smithfield Market, an act of control and containment.[8] At a more philosophical level, we may discern in the enclosure of the booth a new conception of space. In the pre-Copernican world, the performance was visible to all, and was for its duration the fixed point at the centre of its own small universe. When the elite demanded perspectival viewing, the fairground gradually adapted.

Pieter Brueghel the Younger pictures a typical booth stage in his painting of a village fair near Antwerp (plate 5).[9] Sitting at table, a priest and an adulterous wife are sited at the centre of the image, acting out a scene from the extant play *Playerwater*.[10] The trestle stage has been placed beside an archery butt and in front of a tavern to create some sense of enclosure. On a symbolic level, the play on the stage represents body as distinct from spirit, sin opposed to virtue. Above the adulterous couple, separated by empty space, is the church door, and directly beneath is a fire suggestive of hell. The artist has also positioned the stage on two diagonal axes: between archers and butt to signify that love results in punishment; between the tavern and the evicted family to signify the perils of wasteful behaviour. The appended lines of the tavern are organic, for play and tavern are equally concerned with the satisfaction of bodily desire. Meanwhile other spectators watch a procession make its way diagonally across the picture plane, bearing two images, St Antony the hermit, and St Hubert the bishop. The dichotomy of wilderness and church, nature and culture, relates to two possible goals of this procession: either the church with its grand church house behind it, or the well of pure water at the end of the street. The painting is a meditation on salvation, and the female figure on stage points to her choice: the tavern which represents the flesh. There is no position of objective knowledge for the viewer of this complex painting; the eye wanders at will over the canvas, constructing meanings as it chooses, not yet disciplined by scientific perspective. The medieval spectator of *Playerwater* was likewise in no position to make objective judgements. One spectator hands a stool to an actor, breaking the binary actor–audience divide; some peer from underneath the trestles. The spectators are participants by virtue of participating in a festival, surrendering temporarily to the flesh just like the protagonists, and accepting their status as fallen human beings. The performance only exists if the spectators help to make it. The actors of *Playerwater* are fellow celebrants, not hired professionals. Within the farce itself, the cuckolded husband in the coal hod is besmirched by the act of spying. To watch is to be a participant, not a moral judge.

In the Cartesian world of ocular, infinitely extensive space, fairground theatre changed. Spectators passed through a façade to an interior space, where they ran no risk of being viewed by the Almighty, or his earthly delegates. Seeing but not seen, they waited for the curtains to open, and reveal the depths of mystery behind a second hidden interior. What delighted Meyerhold was to play with façades, and then strip them away to reveal the post-religious void behind. In the light of Kantor's new aesthetic of real place, or found space, Meyerhold's fascination with fairground illusion can be seen for what it is, a historically rooted ideal. The fairground booth, like all other manifestations of theatre, is historically produced, not eternal.

It is a commonplace of theatre history that Greek drama began in the Agora, the marketplace of Athens. A dictionary compiled from unknown sources explains the Greek word for 'bleachers' with reference to the wooden seats in the agora 'from which they used to watch the Dionysian contests before the theater in the sanctuary of Dionysus was built', and relates the word 'orchestra' to a dancing place in the agora. Another source explains the building of the Theatre of Dionysus by the collapse of wooden seating during a performance at the start of the fifth century.[11] It is now known that the 'archaic' agora was sited on the north-east slope of the Acropolis, site of the modern Plaka, and it was probably here and not in the flat classical agora that comedy and tragedy began.[12] A new space for dancing and drama was hollowed out on the south slope of the Acropolis, another for political assemblies on a nearby hill called the Pnyx; the level classical agora was a space for processions, courts and rites around altars, but not for large-scale drama. This fragmentation of civic space had long-term consequences for western culture.

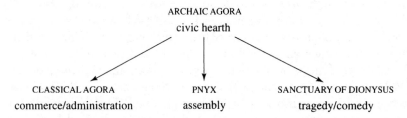

ARCHAIC AGORA
civic hearth

CLASSICAL AGORA   PNYX   SANCTUARY OF DIONYSUS
commerce/administration   assembly   tragedy/comedy

Tragedy and comedy abandoned the symbolic centre, where the domestic 'hearth' of the city would always remain. Commerce and the political executive moved to the new Agora, the assembly moved to the Pnyx, and drama moved to a 'theatre'. In the sophisticated and planned cities of the Hellenistic world the Athenian separation of theatre and agora became standard practice, but there seemed no long-term logic in separating the functions of theatre and political arena.[13] Advances in acoustical design meant that a dancing place and a speaking place could conveniently be one and the same, so theatres doubled as places of assembly. Drama was framed by Greek culture as an ethico-political activity, located outside the space of purchase, consumption and daily social intercourse.

Plato was an opponent both of democracy and of theatre, and he dismissed democracy as 'theatrocracy'.[14] When he imagines his ideal city, he considers what he will say to wandering tragedians. I will not, he declares 'allow you to set up stage in the agora and bring on your actors whose fine voices will carry further than ours. Don't think we'll let you declaim to women and children and the general public . . .'[15] In Plato's traditionalist city there was to be no theatre, no assembly-place where all the free males of the city could sit down together, only a multi-functional agora. He supported participatory dancing but not passive spectatorship. He aimed in his Cretan utopia to create a centred community with one topographical hub, designed for centred human bodies that did not as in a theatre auditorium separate doing from thinking and feeling. He could not, however, reverse the tide of history. The major dramatic forms of the democratic Greek world from tragedy to mime and pantomime were associated with theatres, where men could sit and contemplate. There is no evidence in Greek cities of Plato's day and after for any theatre of the marketplace.[16]

Rome was different. No permanent auditoria were built in Rome until the end of the Republican period when, in a grand imperial gesture, Pompey built a stone theatre as a monument to his personal greatness. The ruling class in the Republic held that such places would have encouraged the populace to sit, look at themselves gathered in a circle, debate, and so insidiously turn themselves into democrats. When the lower orders voted, they stood in the Comitium, and quickly dispersed. We saw in chapter 2 how Terence's *Eunuch* was performed before the image of the Great Mother, in a cramped and asymmetrical space, with the audience on temple steps. The theatres of the Roman Republic were temporary and multi-functional. We learn from the prologue to Terence's *Mother-in-Law* that this play was performed in a space also used for gladiator-fighting.[17] Gladiator-fighting in this period was a blood-spilling ritual which accompanied the celebration of a nobleman's funeral, and the normal place where gladiator fights took place was the Roman forum – later called the Forum Romanum to distinguish it from other forums built by emperors.

Unlike the Greek agora, the Roman forum was a space for public performance. The Roman architect Vitruvius explained to the Emperor Augustus why forums should not be built like agoras: 'for the reason that it is a custom handed down from our ancestors that gladiator shows should be given in the forum'. The differences, he argues, should be as follows: Columns around the periphery should be more widely spaced than in Greece (thus providing a better view from the surrounding arcades). On the upper level there should not be walkways as in Greece but balcony seating that can be let out for the games to bring in public revenue. While Greek design emphasizes spaciousness, Vitruvius wants the scale of the forum to be planned in relation to the population, so there is no overcrowding or sense of emptiness. The Greek agora is normally square, but the forum should be rectangular 'suited to the conditions of shows'.[18] It has been suggested that the distinctive oval shape of imperial amphitheatres derives from structures set up within the rectangular Forum Romanum, the original home of gladiator-fighting.[19] The logic of the rectangle is that one end should serve each of the two combatants. Vitruvius goes on to emphasize that the scale of the public buildings adjoining the forum should be proportionate to the ground area. Where the Greek emphasis lay in creating openness, the Romans created a sense of volume. It is the enclosed nature of the Forum that made it a powerful space for performance.

In the Forum of republican Rome, performances gained their meaning from the rich associations of place.[20] As we saw in the last chapter, the Forum was in part a processional space, where the Triumph halted and prisoners were ceremonially slaughtered. Funeral processions also finished here, the corpse was placed in public view, and speeches were made over the body. Actors wearing masks of the dead man's ancestors sat on a stage in order to reincarnate the past. The most famous account of a funeral is that of Julius Caesar.[21] The event began traditionally with the death of gladiators. The funeral was then staged as a participatory Greek tragedy, to mark the way Caesar like heroes of old was passing from the status of mortal to the status of a god. Antony moved from the role of messenger to the role of chorus leader, breaking into a hymn. The audience divided into two and sang wailing songs in the Greek manner, accompanied by a piper as in tragedy. The corpse was initially concealed, with only a waxwork on display, so Antony could draw back the curtains as if opening the doors of the *skene*, and reveal the horror at a climactic moment, uncovering the body and holding up the bloodstained robes on a spear. An actor then delivered a speech in the person of Caesar, weaving lines of tragedy into his text. The planned scenario broke down at this point, the audience took possession of the body and cremated it at the east end of the forum.

The topography is crucial to our understanding of events. The *rostra*, the official stage used for speeches and displays, had formerly been sited on the north side, in the middle of the Forum, allowing the audience to gather round and contemplate each other in relation to the life-story and ancestry of the dead nobleman. Recently, however, Caesar had moved the stage to the west end, transforming the Forum into an end-staged theatre. The speaker gained added presence and authority from the Temple of Concord behind him, while the audience could lose themselves in the emotions of the narrative. The new staging allowed Antony to speak with the Capitoline Hill as his backdrop, and indicate with his right arm the link between Jupiter in his temple above and the body of the man-turned-god beneath. The body of the dead hero was physically separated from the rapturous audience, making it easier for them to see it not as a human body but as divine. Caesar's decision to move the stage was a major step in transforming a republican space into a hierarchical imperial space. A massive temple was subsequently built to mark the spot where Caesar was cremated. This symbol of imperial power would create a linear axis to which all other shrines were subordinated. On the occasion of the funeral, however, the people rejected the structures of power mapped out in space, and reappropriated the Forum of the Roman People.

The Forum Romanum was regarded as a sacred space. Its association with gladiator-fighting and other death-rites is bound up with the fact that it lay on an ancient burial site, and housed the tomb of Romulus. Supposedly there was once access to the underworld from here. Mysterious shrines like the 'Curtian lake' had no agreed meaning but were carefully preserved. It

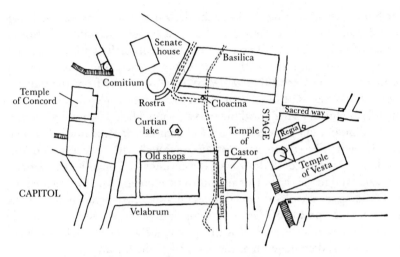

Figure 13   The Roman Forum in the time of Plautus (after J. Isager).

was at the same time the centre of Roman political life. The plebeians had little constitutional hold over the nobility who controlled the Senate, but in real terms they exercised considerable power, using the Forum as a place of display where they could heckle, jostle and riot in order to pressurize the ruling class. While the nobility tended to live up on the cooler and healthier Palatine Hill, the plebs lived close to the Forum in the republican period, a place where they could still sell their wares and drink in the taverns. The republican Forum was regarded as a place that belonged to the plebs, and it was here – in the adjacent Comitium or later in the Forum itself – that the plebs gathered to vote. In 122 BC Plutarch tells us that the nobility built wooden seating inside the Forum in order to charge for the seats. The populist leader Caius Graccus forcibly removed them during the night before the performance so the poor could view unimpeded.[22] It is not clear whether the novelty lay in building ground-level seats that sealed off the arcades, or whether the novelty lay in charging. At all events, the people's right of access was a sensitive issue.

If the Forum served for visual displays and speech-making, there can be little doubt that it also served for theatre performances. Plautus' *Curculio* contains a detailed description of the Forum, which has aroused great interest in archaeologists, but surprisingly little interest amongst theatre historians (fig. 13). The *choregos* responsible for hiring out costumes steps onto the stage in a metatheatrical interlude, and fills in time by discussing the virtues and vices of those who inhabit different parts of the Forum. The passage only makes sense as a comic routine if we assume that the comedian, rather like the Porter in *Macbeth*, is gesturing at different sections of his audience. The topography is precise, though some the jokes behind the words are lost, and we can reconstruct exactly where the gaze of the actor fell. I translate for clarity and not for the wit and rhythm of the language:

I trusted them [the costumes] to Phaedromus [hero of the play] himself. Anyway, I'll keep a look out. But until Phaedromus emerges, I shall point out where you'll have no trouble meeting all sorts, so an assignation will be easy, whether you like them pure or sullied, honest or crooks. If you want to meet a perjurer, go to the *Comitium*. If you want a bragging sort of liar, the shrine of *Cloacina*. For rich married roués – try under the *Basilica*, and there also whores of a certain age, and men offering a deal. Collectors of banqueting fees – try the *fish market*. In the *lower forum*, fine men and rich are promenading. In the middle, by the *canal*, people who simply want to display themselves. The conceited, the prattlers, the slanderers are above the *Lake*, boldly insulting others for no reason, when plenty of true things could be said about them. Beneath the *Old Shops*, there are those who lend and borrow at interest. Behind *Castor's Temple*, there are those whom you should not trust too quickly. In the *Tuscan Alley*, there are men for sale: they will turn for you, or oblige when others turn. In the *Velabrum* – bakers, butchers, readers of entrails, and the rich married wasters at Madame Leucadia's. But stop, the hinge is creaking. I must hold my tongue. [*Exit as* THE PARASITE, VIRGIN, PIMP *and* BANKER *enter from the brothel.*][23]

The inference must be that the stage was placed at the east end of the Forum, in the position of command later used for the praetor's tribunal and the platform built to commemorate Caesar's pyre. The actor first gestures with his right hand at the speaker's platform – the 'rostra' – on the edge of the Comitium, contrasting the lies of politicians with the truth of theatre. He then passes down the right-hand side, pointing to decadent men intent on a party, and works his way up the centre, where some sort of auditorium must have been erected. At ground level close to the stage (the lower Forum) are some nobility, who display their authority by walking in and out. In the middle above the canal are people in prime position to be seen by their fellow citizens. At the back are hecklers who barrack the actors from time to time, and others who disrupt concentration by talking since they cannot hear well.[24] The actor then turns to his left, seeking out people hidden in the arcades or behind the temple façade, and homosexual prostitutes hidden in the side street. He gestures further away towards the plebeian quarter of the Velabrum, and ends by returning to frustrated husbands. On the right, they find whores by places of business, and somewhere on the left is a brothel.

The context of the speech sets up the commercial basis of the performance, for the speaker claims to have rented out his goods to unreliable actors. The Forum is presented as a market where food and bodies are for sale. The prominent role of the banker in the play reflects the importance of commerce in the Forum. There was a tension within the Forum between monuments reflecting aristocratic power and the everyday commercial activities of the plebs, and Plautus' play was bound up with those tensions, contributing to the power struggle by providing a plebeian reading of the space. To be sure, a noble *aedile* funded the performance, but if the play did not please the crowds, the *aedile* would be humiliated.

Staged at the east end of the Forum, the play was not overwhelmed by a grand monumental backdrop. The position made it possible to subvert aristocratic values. At the beginning of the play, when the hero comes on with the paraphernalia of a banquet, the entry is set up as a burlesque procession. This entry, if made stage right, would have used the Sacred Way, the processional route used for triumphs and funerals. If we assume that Plautus gave the central doorway to the temple in accordance with the normal convention of Greek New Comedy, then that doorway would have corresponded with the Regia behind it, where the Pontifex Maximus celebrated many important ceremonies. The brothel stage left would then have corresponded with the temple of the Vestal Virgins, emblems of female purity. The play did not transport the audience to a fictional world, as in the 'mimetic' drama of Greece, but subverted the here-and-now of the Forum. The meaning of the text turned upon the real space of performance.

Plautus' *Curculio* accords rather well with Bakhtin's mythical carnivalesque theatre of the marketplace, which 'does not know footlights'.[25] The figures on stage are grotesques. Their masks are emphasized – the owl-eyes of the heroine, the green face of the pimp. A song sung to the creaking doorway points up the materiality of the stage set. The transformation of the Forum into a festive performance space asserted the claims of the people over against officialdom. This was an interactive theatre, with no hermetic boundary separating actors from spectators. The actor works his audience, turning the laugh from one area to another, looking into the recesses so all in the Forum are part of the show. And it thrives on the language of insult. Interaction is most apparent in the play when the parasite returns from his mission and forces his way through spectators seated on stage,[26] incorporating them into the performance and foisting on them a Greek identity. Plautus' Choregos is something of an anarchist, for he refuses to defer to the officers of Greek democracy, including inspectors of the Agora; he is anti-intellectual, for he pretends that the spectators in his path are drunk and windy philosophers; and he is aggressively het-erosexual when he describes the game of give and take played by undis-ciplined slaves in the street. The actor challenges the audience when he threatens to push people off the stage, or trample them underfoot, but be-neath the playful confrontation lies solidarity: the reassurance that ordinary Roman people are not bureaucratic, cerebral and sexually decadent like the Greeks.

In a later discussion of carnival, Bakhtin shifts his emphasis away from the idea that the marketplace is the preserve of the people. He describes carnival as a pageant without the footlights that for him symbolize the divide of spectators from actors. The result is a space of interaction. 'People who in life are separated by impenetrable hierarchical barriers enter into free familiar contact on the carnival square.'[27] The Roman marketplace was not so much the people's autonomous territory, as a privileged space where the classes could interact. Facing the stage on which *Curculio* was performed stood the Temple of Concord, the architectural symbol of equilibrium between the classes. The socio-political conditions which produced that particular balance of power, and the theatrical mode which reflected and embodied it, was short-lived. When the activities of making, buying and selling were driven from the Forum, and the place was dominated by aristocratic or imperial monuments that compelled human beings to locate themselves in relation to planned architectural axes, Plautus' anarchic mode of making theatre became impossible. The disordered architectural form of the Forum Romanum made it quite unlike any other public space in Rome, and it would never entirely lose the potent sense of place that stemmed from its history and topography, and stirred powerful emotions through the memories that it embodied.[28]

The forums of imperial Rome and planned Roman cities were spaces rather than places, constructed in accordance with human reason. No longer sites of an overt class struggle, they continued to provide the stage set for countless micro-performances when prosperous citizens on a daily basis processed through the centre of the city with an entourage of clients, feeling that their existence had no meaning unless conducted under the gaze of fellow citizens. Arcades lent themselves to promenading. The temple of Capitoline Jupiter reflected the power of the state, and represented the head in relation to the rectangular body of the forum. The Basilica reflected the rule of law, and the architectural balance of the whole engendered a feeling that the citizen inhabited an ordered society. Vitruvius failed to recognize that the future of gladiator-fighting under the empire lay in purpose-built amphitheatres, where better control of the populace could be achieved.

The contained expression of public feeling in Augustus' vision belonged to the Circus, amphitheatre and theatre, but not to the Forum at the centre of civic life. With the coming of Christianity, and the decline of urban living, the forum ceased to represent a moral ideal. What mattered under Christianity was not the visible body of the citizen but the soul of the individual, not the order created by emperors and rationalistic architects but the immanent divine plan. Christian builders were concerned with the interior volumes of churches, not the exterior volumes of civic spaces.[29] Churches and other individual buildings were planned, but the towns and cities that grew up around them were the product of individual decisions. No-one attended to the provision of public open spaces because a sense of selfhood no longer depended on the public gaze.[30]

We look in vain at medieval English towns like Lewes or Wells to find a focus of civic life equivalent to the Roman forum. Both are built around a High Street, broadened in the middle to accommodate stalls and later a hall raised on stilts suitable to accommodate Elizabethan strolling players. In Wells, the High Street links the marketplace (smaller than it is today) to the parish church (see figure 11). Important people (like Mrs Yarde) lived beside the marketplace, not the plebs of Wells. The marketplace was dominated by the High Cross, used by the Constable as a place of surveillance, and the market bell which stood on top of the fountain that supplied the town with drinking-water. A raised hall was added in the sixteenth century. The old marketplace of Wells was a space of confinement and control.[31] It lent itself to morris dancing, but was too cluttered for more elaborate forms of ceremonial. A tanner in 1607 planned to dress as a bishop and deliver a mock sermon from the emblem of civic authority, the market cross, but the idea proved too dangerous.[32] The other available performance spaces out of doors were the High Street, suited to expansive processions, and the sacred spaces around the church and cathedral. The parvis, the huge open space before the cathedral, was a place to view hundreds of painted sculptures, but was on too large a scale for human actors.[33] Renaissance London resembled Wells, on a larger scale. The forum of Londinium had vanished without trace, and the focus of civic display was the processional route along Cheapside. Muddy fairgrounds like Smithfield lay outside the walls, on the margins of civic life.

Continental towns often retained larger open spaces for markets, and these were generally kept separate from the parvis in front of the church. With no two markets being alike, every market was imbued with a sense of local identity. Inhabitants felt their own environment to be unique, and this generated a sense of belonging. The aesthetic appeal of these market spaces lay in their heterogeneous, unplanned nature.[34] The term 'carnival *square*' adopted by Bakhtin's translator is an unfortunate one because in England, where there is no tradition of the piazza as a civic space, the term 'square' implies geometric neo-classical planning. The best-documented example of theatre in the medieval marketplace or 'carnival square' is the Passion Play performed in Lucerne at Easter 1583 (fig. 14). The play was performed in the Wine-Market, a space which was also used for carnival games, plays about saints, farces and interludes on trestle stages. Elie Konigson, in his careful analysis of the records, points out that the Wine-Market was not strictly a public space but belonged to the wealthy merchants and guilds whose houses gave onto it.[35] The urban elite, who controlled all the commercial activity of the town, commissioned the play and took the leading roles, along with members of the clergy. The distinction between streets and marketplaces was rarely clear-cut in the middle ages, and the Wine-Market of Lucerne was more a broad thoroughfare than an urban node, a sloping trapezoidal component in a chain of open spaces. The urban elite turned it into a theatre by erecting an auditorium behind and around the fountain at the west end, creating a focused enclosure dominated by the impressive building which divided the thoroughfare at the east end. The effect was to create a space with the properties of an outdoor church. The crosses of the crucifixion were placed uphill at the east end, in front of Heaven. The fountain recalls the position of the font, and in this space of new life stood the crib. Hell-mouth was placed north-west, reflecting the proximity of tanners and cordwainers, makers of smells and smoke. Through creating a church in the open, the urban elite asserted their own prestige over against that of the church authorities, and the glory of their Catholic town over against Protestant neighbours. They had no spatial models or conceptions to fall back upon other than those of the church.

The seating arrangements likewise recall a church. The elite and the clergy sat on stands immediately behind the actors on the south and north sides, or viewed from their windows. Like monks in privileged choir stalls, they had a good view of the dramatic action, and particularly of the resurrection, which took place at the symbolic position of the high altar. The common people sat as it were in the nave, on a large stand behind the fountain. As Konigson points out, the action at the east end was a great distance away from the common people, and vertical sightlines prevented them seeing much of the action at the west end. In this environmental space, the actors would probably not have given a frontal performance for the benefit of the distant plebs. The commoners of Lucerne were excluded by this performance from a privileged world, and confined to the role of

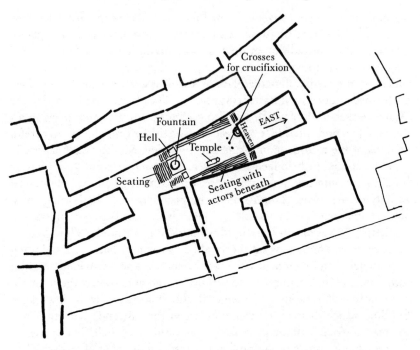

Figure 14   The centre of Lucerne, arranged for performance in 1583 (based on a
street-plan by E. Konigson).

onlookers. The hereditary elite transformed their working environment
into a sacred space, using the symbols of Christianity to boost their own
social status. The play in 1583 was an unusually elaborate affair, and the
Wine-Market was often configured in a less hierarchical manner, with the
audience concentrated on the two long sides, and with raised stages sometimes erected in the centre. Carnival time would have allowed the lower
orders more chance to assert their place in society. The historical realities
of Lucerne at Easter 1583 could scarcely differ more from Bakhtin's utopian
marketplace. The Lucerne play belongs to a particular historical moment.
The power of church had waned, whilst a hereditary urban aristocracy was
still prepared to expend its wealth on tokens of status like theatre, and
this group had yet to be overwhelmed by the individualist, capitalist and
humanist values of the bourgeoisie. Perhaps the groundplan displays the
first hints of perspectival thinking. All would change in the seventeenth
century, when theatre moved indoors, and the notion that drama should
be the collective expression of a community had vanished.

It was in Italy, where renaissance planners wanted to mould urban space rather than let it evolve organically, that the ideal of the Roman forum first became influential. The forum implied arcades, a sense of enclosure, and buildings of consistent design and height which would create the feeling that the sky was a roof. The scale should allow comfortable viewing of the dramatic action, and for Palladio this meant that the width of the piazza should not be more than 2.5 or less than 1.5 times the height of the buildings.[36] The rectangular Roman groundplan was preferred to the Greek square. When Philip II commissioned the building of new cities in the New World, he specified the rectangle 'as this proportion is best for festivals in which horses are used and any other celebrations which have to be held'.[37] The *piazza, plaza* (Spanish) or *place* (French) is a Latinate term which significantly has no German or English equivalent, signifying the 'place' that matters, the centre of the community, the space for collective performances.

I shall take the city of Venice as my case study for the renaissance city, and focus on a set of engravings by the Venetian artist Giacomo Franco, published in 1610/14, which records in an idealized manner the traditional festive life of the piazza.[38] In around the 1770s, these engravings were reinterpreted in a series of oil paintings by Gabriele Bella, a Venetian painter of equally obscure origins.[39] The Piazza San Marco, ceremonial centre of Venice, was widened, harmonized and bordered with new buildings in the sixteenth century to make it more like an imperial forum, reflecting the glory of the Venetian state. The ramshackle stalls of butchers and other vendors were demolished at this time.[40] The Piazza then became a fit place where the nobility of Venice, like the Roman nobility of old, could perform their evening promenade. As in republican Rome, there was a tension between the people and the elite over who controlled the symbolic centre, and Franco's patriotic images reflect a strategic equipoise between people and elite. One image, for example, shows the newly elected doge being carried perilously through a crowd of paupers in the Piazza, distributing largesse in a rite of humility that recalls Coriolanus. In Bella's image, the poor are pushed aside before the doge arrives, so authority goes unchallenged.

Franco's frontispiece depicts Venice as the centre of a globe (fig. 15), and the Piazza with its phallic Campanile is the centre of Venice. An English visitor at this time describes the great Piazza as the 'place', 'market-place' or 'forum' of Venice, but also as the 'street of St Mark', struggling to find the right English term. He describes the Piazza as *orbis forum* (the forum of the globe), not *urbis forum* (the forum of the city).[41] Though propagandist

Figure 15   Venice as microcosm (after G. Franco).

images like that of Franco played their part, Venice was in a real sense the centre of the world economy, the place where east met west. Braudel describes the way Venice ensnared other economies, and forced them to conduct trade through her port.[42] The centripetal force exerted by the Piazza San Marco encouraged foreign merchants to conduct their business in Venice. Though the architecture was impressive, it was the complex of performances supported by the architecture which made the Piazza a magnet. Another prefatory image in Franco's volume shows the view from the canal, looking through the two classical Pillars of Justice and the Piazzetta towards the main Piazza (fig. 16). The city presents itself to the arriving visitor as a perspectival stage set.

Franco introduces his festive sequence with the Corpus Christi procession, symbol of civic order (plate 6). The Piazza is articulated by a corridor of awnings and by three permanent flagstaffs aligned with the three domes. The result is a sculptural composition designed to delight the eyes of people

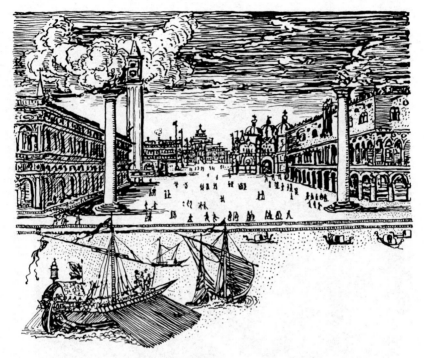

Figure 16   The Piazzetta seen from the canal (after G. Franco).

watching from windows, with bodies and architecture in perfect harmony.
The front of the procession emerges from the Basilica, where it has been
viewed by the doge and foreign ambassadors; the most imposing floats, alle-
gories of Venetian naval might, pass under the awnings on their way in. The
watching crowds are a model of silent order, impressed by the splendour
of floats, relics, precious metals and the communion host. The procession
of the host was particularly important at this time because the pope had
excommunicated Venice, and the parade displayed the city's defiance.[43]
In Bella's eighteenth-century version the parade survives but the intensity
of the crowd has gone. The procession is viewed as part of the texture of
Venetian life, stripped of its religious and political force. At Corpus Christi,
the Piazza of St Mark becomes the parvis, the forecourt to the Duke's
splendid chapel (fig. 17). In York the Corpus Christi procession could
never be viewed as a totality, and its slow movement through narrow streets
encouraged the development of speech to enhance the pageantry; in the
great piazza of Venice, however, spectacle predominated over speech. While
medieval towns usually separated off the secular space of the market from

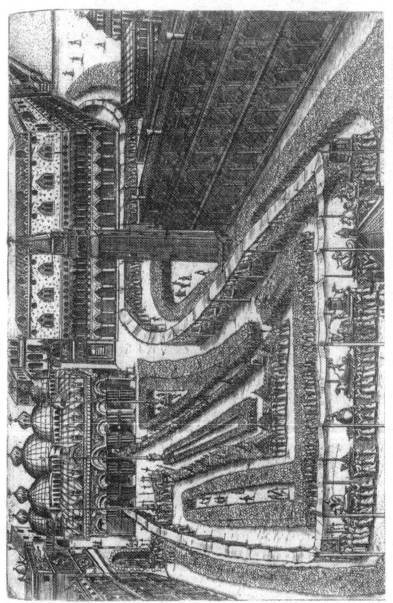

Plate 6   G. Franco: engraving of Corpus Christi procession in the Piazza San Marco. From *Habiti d'huomeni* . . . (1610).

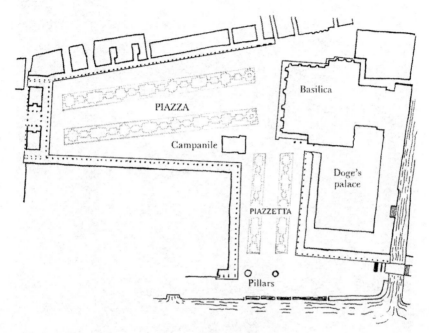

Figure 17 Piazza San Marco, with eighteenth-century processional markings
(after C. Moughtin).

the sacred space of the parvis before the cathedral, renaissance Venice
merged sacred and secular to create a single centre.

By way of contrast we turn from this emblem of order and state power
to the entertainments of the people, conducted in their own space: a small
'campiello' in front of a parish church (plate 7). Female spectators watch
from balconies while men display their male prowess. Multiple activities
are depicted as if happening simultaneously, in accordance with medieval
pictorial convention. Though Franco creates an image in perspective, this
is no renaissance piazza but a medieval public space, amid heterogeneous,
crowded buildings. In the foreground, the bridge creates a natural stage for
the game of swinging from the goose's neck, which allows women to taunt
men by swinging the goose away from them. On a trestle stage, men kill a
cat by butting it with shaven heads. In the centre of the *campiello*, a square
stage is set up for dancing. Two men with hands tied will perhaps try to
kiss the two dancers. Ground level on either side is used for bear-baiting
and for climbing a pole greased by the fat of two ducks. Behind, a bull is
run through the streets, preventing any possibility of passive spectating.

Plate 7   G. Franco: engraving of popular entertainments in a campiello. From
Habiti d'huomeni . . . (1610).

Franco's orderly composition belies the violence that takes place, as men pit themselves against animals to display their virility. The only women in the public space of the *campiello* are the two dancers who stand on the raised stage protected by armed men. Women in this image control the private space of the dwelling, men the public space of the *campiello*.

For Bella the parish church in this image evokes Santa Maria Formosa, focus of the ancient Candlemas festival of the Twelve Marys. This medieval festival in its organization and symbolism had formerly emphasized the role of women, and the centrality of the parish in Venetian life, but was radically scaled down in the wake of the Black Death. The spatial dominance of the renaissance Piazza San Marco was tied to a weakening of the cellular structure of medieval life, centred on the parish church, the *campiello* beside it where women fetched water, and the dwellings round the *campiello*.[44] Renaissance carnival activities in the Piazza San Marco and elsewhere were controlled not by the people but by groups of aristocratic young males called Compagnie dei Calze, from the badges they wore on their hose (*calze*). Their activities at carnival time included erecting stages for the performance of Latin plays.[45] Franco portrays two of these cliques playing football in mid-Lent, on the margins of the city.

Bella gives the dancers no stage in his version, indicating that eighteenth-century women ran less risk of being molested. He does, however, represent the stage set up for another local event in St Luke's Square, outside a pharmacy (plate 8). A flagstaff is a kind of umbilicus, turning the *campiello* into the centre of its own universe.[46] On the backless baroque stage is the dummy of an old woman representing Lent, and this will be sawn in half to symbolize the fact that it is the half-way point in Lent. Sweets found inside it will be distributed. Meanwhile, a masked man entertains the crowd by bobbing in a bucket, trying to seize a live eel with his teeth. The sexes and social classes mingle, though the gentry mainly watch from windows. Red and blue hangings draped from windows transform the identity of the *campiello* from a shopping centre to a theatre. There is a deep logic of place at work in this image. The play is a rite of healing, associated with the pharmacy, which in turn is associated with the fact that Luke, the patronal saint of the parish, was a doctor. Bella's idyll points to a renewed vitality in community life, though one wonders if ritual has not begun to transmute itself into romantic folklore.

Franco depicts the opening of the carnival season amidst the irregular buildings of the Piazza di San Stefano, where according to his caption people of all social classes gathered in the evening. The masks worn by participants allowed social barriers to dissolve, and were a spur to the creation

Plate 8   G. Bella: A play in the Campo di San Lucha. Oil painting.

of improvised performances. Franco depicts a man dressed as Pantalone, the lecherous old Venetian of the commedia dell'arte, serenading a courtesan. Beside the courtesan is a woman in male attire, her identity revealed by her platform soles, while another masker dressed as a fool prances in the background. To appear in the piazza at carnival time was to perform, and the wearing of masks encouraged many to adopt roles culled from the theatre. The distinction between celebration and theatre is obliterated in Franco's image. Carnival opened beside San Stefano's church on the saint's feast day (St Stephen's Day) known throughout Europe as the Feast of Fools, so place and time were bound up in the act of celebration. Soon, however, the centripetal force exerted by the Piazza San Marco won out, and San Stefano lost its importance. The medieval idea that each parish had its own identity and moment of pre-eminence was overwhelmed by the drive towards centralization. The bond between space and time that once reassured people they lived in an ordered cosmos was broken. A French tourist observed in 1680:

The Piazza of St Mark is the great theatre where the people display themselves at Carnival. There is not a mask in Venice which fails to go there an hour before sunset. However large the piazza may be, it can scarcely contain the host of masks, and those who want to see them.[47]

Accordingly, Bella represents the ceremonies of St Stephen's day in the Piazza San Marco, and depicts serried rows of spectators seated outside coffee houses watching the 'noble' masks pass before them. We have passed into the age of objective viewing. The arcades of the Piazza provide a convenient shadowy hiding place for passive spectators, who as visitors or citizens of a centralized state have lost their bond with locality.

From the climax of the carnival season, Franco selects the *Powers of Hercules*, performed on a stage set up in the centre of the Piazzetta, the part of the Piazza San Marco which runs down to the canal and abuts the Doge's palace (plate 9). The two Pillars of Justice beside the quay make the Piazzetta an enclosed and focused space for performance. The ceremonies involved a festive execution, that of twelfth-century enemies of Venice who were symbolized by a bull. In medieval times twelve pigs were also executed, but such grotesque features were abolished in the sixteenth century in the interests of decorum. The doge watches from his balcony, while the Senate and visitors watch from temporary seating set up around the sides of the Piazzetta. On the stage, a castle topped by fireworks symbolizes Friulian castles conquered by the Venetians in the twelfth century. Workers from the Arsenal perform an acrobatic display of agility and Herculean strength, while bulls are run on the margins to create an invigorating sense of danger: to watch is to participate, and objective viewing is impossible when the viewer is under physical threat. In the foreground, butchers conduct a burlesque military procession.[48] We see in this image the people asserting their place in society, celebrating their physical strength, their right to mock, and their residual right to a bloody and grotesque spectacle offensive to upper-class taste. At the same time, the people offer a form of tribute to their social superiors. As in ancient Rome, the Piazza provides a space where the classes can view each other, and power can be negotiated. The social stability of Venice owed much to rites of this kind. Later, Bella would copy Guardi's painting of this scene, where the centrepiece is a huge baroque

Plate 9   G. Franco: engraving of Giovedi Grasso ceremonies in the Piazzetta San Marco.
From *Habiti d'huomeni . . .* (1610).

Plate 10   G. Franco: engraving of mountebanks in the Piazza San Marco. From *Habiti d'huomeni . . .* (1610).

edifice. The event slowly turned from a spectacle of the people into a technological spectacle for the people.[49]

The last of Franco's images that we shall examine depicts an everyday scene: mountebank doctors in the Piazzetta standing on trestle stages to vend their wares to an audience dominated by foreigners (plate 10). In the foreground, the mountebank handles a snake, while his assistant takes from a chest a medicine that will cure all ills, including snakebite. The doctor follows a standard routine, claiming a link with St Paul who drove snakes from Malta.[50] Next to him, an actress plays the lute, whilst a masked Pantalone, with a masked *zanni* beside him, gazes at her lecherously, indicating that the medicine is also an aphrodisiac. This image provokes renewed questions about today's formal definitions of 'theatre'. An Elizabethan visitor was already having trouble with categories when he described how mountebanks 'draw people about them by music and pleasant discourse like Comedies, having a woman and a masked fool to act these parts with them'.[51] Mountebanks often staged plays in the commedia dell'arte style to follow their vending of medicines: crowds gathered to see the play, and the purchase of medicines funded the enterprise.[52] In Franco's engraving, the vending of medicines and the stock commedia scene merge in a single image. Humour and self-parody were a normal part of the performance, and we should not dismiss the audience as simpletons. It is impossible to tell how far they paid for a utopian dream, and how far they paid for good entertainment to continue. The famous eighteenth-century playwright Goldoni obtained his first commission from a mountebank, whom he praises as a doctor of great learning and skill.[53] The Paracelsan medicine offered by mountebanks was probably more effective – certainly less dangerous – than orthodox medicine based on the classical teachings of Galen.

The trestle stage lends itself to performance in the marketplace. It is quickly set up and removed. It allows the mountebank to dominate the crowd, from a position of power. It also throws the emphasis on the actor's body, since the spectators' heads are close to the actors' legs. Mountebank theatre was a theatre of the body, for it paraded the grotesque nature of ageing and disease, and offered in return for money the dream of a physical cure. Franco's female performer may be a prostitute, offering the male spectator her own form of cure.[54] This was a theatre of the grotesque body, for the audience were close enough to see every physical blemish on the performer. There was no scope on these noisy planks for courtly dancing or aetherial lighting effects creating an image of untouchable beauty. Commedia dell'arte performances on trestle stages offered the audience exactly the same reward as mountebank routines. The dream of liberation from

Plate 11   G. Bella: Fairground booths in the Piazzetta. Oil painting.

the failings of the body was expressed through the libidinous energy of a Pantalone, the defiance of gravity by an acrobatic Arlecchino, and the conquest of the courtesan by a callow *innamorato*. In Bella's version of this scene (plate 11), Franco's five players in the foreground still play in the Piazzetta, having become fully fledged commedia dell'arte characters. The boundary between life and performance has been clarified. The trestle stage is dwarfed by four huge wooden booths, erected close to the quay for easy removal. On balconies outside, men lure the public in to watch feats and prodigies of whatever kind. A Meyerholdian world of private fantasy has been created within the public space of the piazza.

The open spaces of Venice, from the small campiellos to the great Piazza, served both to focus performances and to inspire performances. The American phenomenologist Christian Norberg-Schulz proposes that spaces such as the Piazza San Marco should be analysed in terms of their 'genius loci', a concrete experiential quality that cannot be reduced to geometric abstraction. Strong spaces are those where the topographical site, the pattern of human settlement, and architectural specifics coalesce.[55] The concept is a useful one. The *genius loci* of the renaissance Piazza San Marco is strong for the same reasons as the Forum Romanum. It is the centre of the city, the point where natural topography requires journeys to begin and end. It is the seat of government, justice and state religion, but is also bound up with commerce. Its lack of symmetry is a reminder that the spatial logic of the site transcends the rationality of a classical planner. And it is the seat of collective memories. The Pillars of Justice, for example, are spoils from the east, emblems of patron saints past and present, and the scene of rites that represent the doge's obligations to his people.

The concept of *genius loci* risks essentializing place at the cost of obscuring historical change. In the renaissance period qualitative differences between the Piazza and Piazzetta were stronger than now. Before Napoleon secularized its west end, the Piazza was framed by two churches, and had overtly sacred associations, while the Piazzetta had stronger juridico-commercial associations, and the Campanile served to articulate these two polarities. Coryate's observation that high-status mountebanks on stages occupied the Piazza, while low-status charlatans on ground level haunted the Piazzetta,[56] points to a vanished texture that shaped life in the period. Today it is the monumental architecture of the Piazza San Marco that stands on show for the tourist, a shell within which cultural events can happen. The cultural geographer Don Mitchell makes a useful distinction between two incompatible urban ideals: 'public space' and 'landscape'. The first he associates with interaction, inclusiveness and conflict; the second allows one to bask 'in the leisure of a well-ordered scene', and provides visitors with the illusion of control.[57] The Piazza today tends increasingly towards 'landscape', a 'scene' which the tourist/spectator can possess.

The images of Franco and to a lesser extent Bella represent the Piazza San Marco as 'public space'. It was not a fixed template for human activity, but subject to constant metamorphosis through the seasons of the year. It was dominated by masks, rostra and mock castles at carnival, candle-light at Easter, booths and wooden arcades at the Ascensiontide fair, processional awnings at Corpus Christi, shacks, stalls, pillories and stages for mountebanks and executions at other times. The doge's balcony, the statues on the Basilica, the windows above the arcades, the flagstaffs and pillars come in and out of focus in the course of this cycle. The physical presence of the renaissance and baroque Piazza was fluid. In the modern world the space has taken a fixed form, reinforced in its geometry by floodlighting. For Lefebvre, the Venice of today succeeds in remaining a 'theatre-city – where actors and public are the same in the multiplicity of their roles and relation'. He identifies, however, a tension between the dominance of the state, expressed through monumental architecture, and citizens who resist the state through different rhythms they impose upon space. The rhythms constituted in public spaces by acts of promenading, trade and intrigue override the measured, unirhythmical time derived from the power of the modern state.[58] The renaissance state was not perceived as an abstraction like the modern state, but as a set of human beings whose power rested on the way they inhabited the Piazza. The dead or tormented bodies of criminals exposed in the Piazza were a constant sign of this power. Today the Piazza is a thriving site of cultural activity, and the workings of political power are effaced.

If there is a mismatch today between the architecture of the Piazza San Marco and the spatial practices of its occupants, as Lefebvre maintains, perhaps the same is not true of lesser piazzas. The 'Teatro Povero di Montichiello' is a cooperative company which, since the late 1960s, has performed every summer in a small village piazza in Tuscany.[59] The performers are villagers, who create their own scripts and to a large extent perform themselves. The term 'poor theatre', borrowed from Grotowski, evokes the fact that this is a theatre which does not need the trappings of set, elaborate effects and characterization. The plays performed in the piazza have characteristically juxtaposed a past dominated by landlords and other forms of oppression with a present in which the traditional rural economy struggles to survive. A seminal performance in 1969 dealt with the narrow avoidance of a massacre in 1944, when many villagers were lined up against the fortified wall to be shot. The performance of these annual dramas does much to keep alive a sense of community and commitment to the old way of life. The centripetal force of the piazza, with its topography derived from the logic of rural life, makes it the inevitable point where the community can converge to witness and discuss an 'autodramma' reflecting on its own condition. The performances draw on historical memories embedded in the piazza, without aestheticizing or celebrating mere architectural beauty, in order to dramatize the relationship between past and present. Italian hill villages tend to be spaces of memory, with plaques and street names commemorating the achievements of individuals now dead, they encourage collective living through close-packed housing and life on the balcony, and they create the sense of a natural performance space through the contrast between tiny alleys and open areas with viewing points from above. The English village green creates a more timeless sense of the past, and lacks the same focus. The piazza at Monticchiello provides the basis for a form of popular theatre bound to place. The first animateurs of the company contrasted their work with that of Jérôme Savary, who used a circus tent to tour popular, participatory theatre around Europe. This theatre of the piazza was not transferable like the 'Grand Magic Circus', and thus created a stronger sense of democratic participation. British community theatre companies are commonly obliged to work in school halls, clubs, parks or transient found spaces, and the idea of animating a community around its defining space seems not to be an option. The school halls characteristically used by Ann Jellicoe are a poor substitute for the Mediterranean piazza.[60]

The continuous political ferment of Paris provides a useful comparison with Venice, which retained its renaissance architectural form at the cost of political stagnation. Medieval Paris had plenty of covered halls and private courtyards, but because of its overcrowding was remarkably lacking in public open spaces, which helps to explain the very early adoption of the Hôtel de Bourgogne as an indoor playhouse. We have one exceptional record of Les Halles, the food market, being used for a performance on Shrove Tuesday 1512, when the Basoche, the festive guild of law clerks, abandoned their normal site of performance in the Great Hall of the Palais de Justice. It is unclear whether one of the covered halls was used or the tiny courtyard by the executioner's scaffold, where whores were whipped and debtors exhibited.[61] Street theatre began to flourish with the arrival of renaissance architecture. When Henri IV completed the Pont-Neuf and the triangular Place Dauphine on the island at the mid-point of the bridge, he provided Parisians with a leisure space for promenading and enjoying a panoramic view. The pavement on the bridge provided space for entertainers to divert

Figure 18   Tabarin performing in the Place Dauphine (after an engraving
by Abraham Bosse).

the promenaders.[62] An engraving by Abraham Bosse depicts Tabarin, the
most famous and successful of all street performers, playing in the Place
Dauphine, soon after its completion in 1620 (fig. 18). Stage right stands
Mondor, the refined mountebank, his medicine chest beside him; on stage
left his assistant Tabarin waggles his famous hat. The pair were probably
brothers. Behind them are musicians who help to draw in the crowd from
the bridge, and two lovers who will feature in a farce. Bosse portrays the mix
of gentry, women, peasants and children who come to the performance,
and indicates how the thirty-two uniform buildings of the Place provide
architectural support for the trestle stage. The stage faces the entry from
the bridge, and Bosse's viewpoint is that of the king's statue.

   Henri's efforts to make Paris desirable, a place where gentlemen might
happily reside, fostered an entrepreneurial mode of theatre-making. Tabarin
made huge profits from the sale of products such as medicines and scripts.
The coarseness of his routines fed off the elegance of Henri's architecture.
Mondor would play the civilized intellectual, and Tabarin would keep undermining him with the earthy logic and scatological humour of the peasant. If Mondor was the head, Tabarin was the grotesque body; if Mondor
is renaissance man, Tabarin is medieval man. Which is the most gentle-
manly (*honnête*) of animals? asks Tabarin. Man, replies Mondor, because
he possesses reason – followed by the pure white ermine, and birds of the
air. No, says Tabarin: dogs because they lick each other's arses clean, followed by pigs, who eat up turds on the roadside to spare the sight of passers
by.[63] Tabarin spoke for the embodied human beings who crowded onto
the bridge to escape the squalor of daily life. Medications for the grotesque
body attested by so direct and blunt a man must have been an irresistible

purchase. The Place Dauphine was an expression of rationality implanted in the chaotic city. The classically harmonious environment supported the dream of a classically harmonious body.

When renaissance ideals of the city gave way to baroque, street theatre lost its support from the environment. While renaissance planners drew attention to the centre of the piazza, conceived as a place of balance and repose, baroque planners were interested in perspectival vistas. The gaze was turned towards distant obelisks, churches and palaces symbolic of absolute royal power. While the statue of Henri IV stood outside the Place Dauphine, looking benevolently on the activities of citizens in the centre, baroque squares placed a huge royal statue in the middle, visible from the surrounding streets. The king was the only performer who counted in the perspectival theatre constituted by the new avenues and squares. The role of the citizen was to be a perpetual spectator.[64] Louis XIV not only initiated the sequence of vistas that led out from the Louvre along the Champs Elysées, but also demonstrated his despair of urban life by evacuating to Versailles. Though street theatre continued to flourish in the environs of the great fairs of St-Germain and St-Laurent, on the margins of the city, hints of the new spatial order were apparent as early as 1618, when the Abbey of St Germain allowed a group of actors to fence part of its fairground in order to charge for entry.[65] Enclosed booths were the next step. In the eighteenth century, these booth theatres within the fair became fashionable places for the aristocracy to visit in an evening. Performance in the open continued, but only as a second-class activity.

The revolutionaries found no way of reappropriating the medieval and baroque public spaces of the city for their festivals. As we saw in the last chapter, the ideal of liberty was associated with empty, open space, and specifically the Champs de Mars. Sennett comments on the festival stage-managed by David in 1792: 'Nothing stood in David's way: the great festival reached its consummation out in the open, in unobstructed space, in a pure volume. At that denouement, confusion and apathy reigned.'[66] The renaissance principles of enclosure and intimacy, needed in order to generate performance energy and a sense of community, were lacking, to disastrous effect. Sennett notes that the execution of Louis XVI took place in an 'empty volume'.[67] The axial centre of the Place de la Concorde was occupied by the broken statue of Louis XV, so there was no natural point of concentration, no convergence of sightlines on the spot chosen. Baroque architecture was designed to prevent acts of theatre and popular self-expression. We might compare the fate of Charles I, who enjoyed a renaissance death in 1649 on his 'memorable scene' framed by the Palladian pillars of Inigo Jones'

Banqueting House. Walls on three sides of a courtyard created focus for the drama of his execution.[68]

In the wake of the 1830 revolution, Victor Hugo in *The Hunchback of Notre-Dame* (1831) romanticized medieval Paris as a city whose disparate bells chimed in a true symphony. The novel's protagonist, Pierre Gringoire, is Hugo's alter ego, a dramatist and aesthete whose play fails through the vagaries of a socially divided audience, and the inherent falsity of theatrical convention. Just as Hugo's *Hernani* reduced the theatre to chaos in 1830, so Gringoire's production for the Basoche in the Palais de Justice fails to hold its audience on Twelfth Night 1482. A disappointed Gringoire goes out to join the people in the Place de Grève in front of the Town Hall, awaiting the Lord of Misrule's procession. In the firelight he sees a vision that will haunt him, a gypsy girl dancing and performing tricks with a Persian carpet for her stage. Then he loses himself in the narrow dangerous streets, and is hustled into another impoverished *place* where a tavern is backdrop for the sinister 'Court of Miracles'. Hugo was attracted by the gothic world because it offered an escape from the values of bourgeois culture. The Place de Grève is the site of Hugo's dream: the dream of an authentic and harmonious street performance, the quintessence of popular theatre. However, the street artist does not live in the Place de Grève in the shadow of the gibbet, but inhabits another *place*, a site of menacing, carnivalesque energies that point to revolution. Hugo's novel epitomizes a modern dilemma: on the one hand, performance in the *place* or piazza is a romantic ideal, an escape from the bourgeois condition; on the other, it points to political anarchy. It is clear from Hugo's novel what drove Napoleon III and Baron Haussmann twenty years later to drive long straight boulevards through the twisted streets of medieval Paris, allowing soldiers to reach the barricades and prevent revolution, and the bourgeoisie to pass safely from their suburban homes to the Opéra in the city centre.[69] The streets became safe for those who wished to promenade or visit a *café-concert*. The new spatial logic was one of mobility, free movement from one interior space to another. The streets of Paris became conduits. Squares became intersections of conduits, or alternatively places of retreat that restored a fragment of nature to urban residents. Nothing could be further removed from the Venetian model of the city, where each community, ghettoes included, was focused on its own gathering point, and all were clustered around one major gathering point that defined the identity of the city.

In the wake of the May 1968 uprising, when students and workers laid claim to the streets of Paris, Ariane Mnouchkine used the fairground as her metaphor and device for representing the congruent events of the 1789

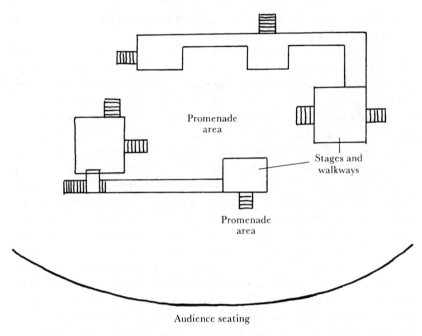

Figure 19   Design by Ariane Mnouchkine and Roberto Moscoso for *1789*
(from a plan in *Travail théâtral*).

revolution (fig. 19). Her cast became acrobats, puppeteers, jugglers and
storytellers in order to present a chronicle of triumph and repression. She
was inspired by fairground theatres in the *places* of market towns like Cam-
brai, and by the idea that the bourgeoisie in their windows had a different
view from the people milling below.[70] The actors used five trestle stages,
whilst part of the audience stood and moved about in their midst, and the
rest – the bourgeoisie, as it were – sat on raised seats along one side.
Mnouchkine's *1789* can be understood in retrospect as a characteristic
twentieth-century attempt to reconcile popular theatre with political engagement. Part of the audience was physically immersed and interactive,
while part looked down in judgement. The tension here can be traced back
to the divide between Greek and Roman ideals of theatre. By separating the
theatron from the *agora*, and linking it to the political assembly, Greece insti-
tutionalized the idea that theatre is justified by the ethical–political insights
it offers to a physically immobile public. When transforming the forum
into a festive environment, Plautus worked to the opposite Roman assumption: a performance is a *ludus*, a game in which the audience has to play its

active part. Ultimately, in Mnouchkine's work, the Greek conception wins out, because the performance takes place in a 'theatre'. Her Cartoucherie de Vincennes was a new industrial 'found' space, not a bourgeois playhouse, but it still set up an absolute barrier between the real world and its mimesis. In Petrograd in 1920, the storming of the Winter Palace was reenacted before an audience of 100,000, with a carnivalesque combat of whites and reds.[71] There was no similar opportunity in 1971, after the failure of the 1968 uprising, for Mnouchkine to use public space in the same way. Those who attended Mnouchkine's simulated carnival headed outwards towards the margins of Paris, since the urban centre had proved resistant to transformation.

I shall end with some observations on Covent Garden, London's unique attempt at a renaissance piazza. Periodizing terms are always controversial, and there is for example no clear-cut divide between 'medieval' and 'renaissance' Venice. The word 'renaissance' seems important in this context because it evokes an attempt to emulate the ideal of the Roman forum. Lewis Mumford, in his magisterial account, *The City in History*, passes straight from the medieval to the baroque, and declares flatly that 'there is no renascence city'.[72] For him, the renaissance was merely a geometric clarification of the medieval. His historiography reflects his taste in the 1950s for the centrifugal ideal of the garden suburb, and his despair of squalid or impersonal city centres. Wartime bombing did little to foster the urban ideal. The concern of planners today to reanimate urban centres obliges us to look again at our conceptions of the past. The defeat of grandiose plans by the Greater London Council to redevelop Covent Garden in 1973 was an important nail in the coffin of modernism.[73] This was the year of the oil crisis, when dreams of infinite 'progress' came to an end. In lieu of the brave new world of modernity, a traditionalist public space was created in the centre of London where pedestrians could interact comfortably, and traders in small shops make a profit. Street theatre has proved crucial to the success of the concept. Performers earn a modest living, their work supported by traders because they draw in the public. Here and throughout western Europe, street theatre has become part and parcel of a new urban ideal.

From the start, Inigo Jones' piazza seems to have been a space where the social classes interacted. The civil war put an instant end to dreams of aristocratic exclusivity. Wealthy tenants jostled with vegetable sellers, puppeteers and frequenters of coffee-houses. The prestige of the piazza as a residential site declined, but its commercial status was enhanced with the building of a Victorian covered market.[74] The great victory of 1973 was the decision to preserve and reanimate the market in its relationship to the surviving arcades. The importance of street theatre owes much to the architectural particularity of the site. On the west side of the piazza, echoing the temple of Jupiter Capitolinus which dominates imperial Roman forums, Jones placed the classical façade of St Paul's Church. Traditionalists objected, in the course of building, to a west-facing altar, so the axis was reversed, and the façade was left without a function, offering entry to nowhere.[75] The level of the Piazza was raised in the course of time, removing the monumental steps. This façade without a function has proved a natural stage set, offering both visual and acoustical support to the performer standing in front of the columns. The covered market creates a sense of enclosure, with spectators in the Punch and Judy public house on the balcony having a grandstand view. Performers book the space for half-hour slots and pay no rent, though they are required to carry insurance.

Economic logic points to solo performance, for two performers working together cannot earn double the money. Members of the audience are regularly brought into the act to create interaction of character, and break the actor–audience divide. The performers work variants on a limited repertory of circus-based skills. A tightrope stretched between the classical columns justifies their architectural presence. Unicycling and juggling allow the performer to echo their imposing verticality. The passageway running behind the columns encourages the technique of imitating unsuspecting passers-by – a device developed by continental street theatre artists in the 1990s. The placing of props to create symmetrical visual compositions has proved a necessary formal device if the performer is to take command of this classical space. The repertory is limited because originality almost always fails. The risk and frequency of failure is perhaps what gives street performance its excitement. If we leave aside the blood, the pleasures of viewing are not so dissimilar from the pleasures of watching gladiators fight in the Forum Romanum. The performer has to take on the crowd and win. He mocks individuals, just like the *choregos* in *Curculio*, in order to create a sense that the performance is a contest.

The church façade offers the most prestigious and profitable site (fig. 20). Performers with static acts, often impersonating statues, line the promenade down St James' Street from the underground station. Energetic acts can use the uncomfortably cobbled area north of the covered market now that the police, in accordance with a new ideal of public space, have been instructed to turn a blind eye. Inside the covered market are two more licensed spaces for performers. The gendering of space is very marked when one contrasts the male-dominated, confrontational acts in front of the vertical columns

Figure 20   Street performance in front of St Paul's Church, Covent Garden.

of the church with the operatic and instrumental performances given in the womblike basement area inside the market, where many of the performers are female. Out in the open air, the performers – almost exclusively male – celebrate the grotesque body, and typically remove an extravagant outer layer of clothing to reveal an ungainly torso. In the basement area, spectators do not have to be seized, but gather to watch from the safety of a higher level, or café seats where they cannot be asked for money. In this female space, the public are offered sound rather than image, beauty rather than ugliness, art rather than fun. The erotic body is a zoned phenomenon, and belongs to Soho, not Covent Garden.

These traditional dichotomies are symptomatic of a deep conservatism in street theatre. In the basement space, the performers play in front of Past Times, a chain store selling replicas of historical domestic objects, and this placing seems symbolic. Covent Garden creates a nostalgic and sanitized image of what urban life used to be.[76] The public want traditional acts to reinforce their sense of inhabiting a transhistorical environment. This is not a medieval market, where the necessary things of life are bought, and commercial relationships are personalized through haggling, but a kind of performed market in which all participants are complicit performers. Yet we should not dismiss Covent Garden as something entirely synthetic. The street performers of today are not so dissimilar from the mountebanks of renaissance Venice, who were also trapped in formulaic performances, as small cogs in a macro-economic mechanism, and useful symbols of civic freedom. The utopia that Covent Garden invites the tourist to dream of never existed. Like Turlupin, modern street performers contest a world of infinite illusion through their insistence on the body and its physical presence. They create a provisional community through creating participatory experiences. The sketch depicts Richie Rich, one of the most accomplished Covent Garden regulars, working the crowd in front of the church. Rich rides high on his phallic unicycle, swiping with his juggling sword at a passing pigeon, creating a sense of the unrepeatable moment. His aboriginal tattoos are indelible signs that the space is public but the body is his own. The tattooed face is not a removable Meyerholdian mask, but an assertion of the grotesque body that challenges a world of façades.

CHAPTER 5

Sympotic space

In April 2001 I took the opportunity of seeing (or experiencing) the celebrated Catalan company Comediants present their gastro-comic spectacle
Boccato di Cardinale in a circular banqueting tent erected within the grounds
of the Casino in Barcelona's Olympic Village. The visible kitchen became
an orchestra, with tunes played on saucepans. The waiters were assistant
performers. Each course of the banquet was preceded by a thematically
linked entertainment: a fish-masked man performed the Tour du Poisson
on his unicycle, Bacchus in the guise of a tout appeared on his barrel before
the opening of the red wine, and so forth. Groups of performers traversed
the space, while individual entertainers circulated around the tables with a
menu of routines. Small groups of diners–spectators were welded into larger
groups, first on a table-by-table basis, and later as an ensemble when the
tent became a cosmic emblem of the four seasons to accompany the final
Mignardises Quatre Estacions, each quartile becoming one of the seasons,
curtained off and then reunited to create a circle of bonded participants.
The 'cigars' were flutes, allowing the audience to perform in the finale. The
aim of Comediants' gastro-comic form was to break down divisions, not
only between theatre and catering, but also between diner and diner, diner
and player. Commensality, the sharing of food, both symbolizes and effects
unity. A manifesto in the programme explained that, over thirty years, the
company had often been commissioned to bring the festive spirit to banquets and celebrations. They regard their routines as dishes to be savoured
by the five senses. 'Like culinary recipes, every stage oeuvre may be more
or less balanced, with more or less taste, rhythm and texture, but always
obeys an undertaking: to transform the space, to impose a time different
to daily-life, and to tell stories mixing different languages.'[1] The polyglot
mix of Catalan, Spanish, French and fragments of English, combined with
music, created an acoustical variety show; while the turns created a piquant
balance between the grotesque, the erotic, the magical, the athletic and

the absurd, with each of the principal performers developing a distinctive persona.

Barbara Kirschenblatt-Gimblett in a recent issue of *Performance Research* surveys a broad range of performance art that involves cooking, and concludes with a question:

What would theater history look like were it written backwards from the Futurist banquets and Dali dinners and performance art? Canonical histories of theater take as their point of departure that which counts as theater in the modern period – namely, theater as an autonomous art form – and search for its 'origins' in fused art forms of the past. Thus, Oscar G. Brockett's *History of the Theater* is a history of drama and its performance: it does not view courtly banquets, tournaments, royal entries, and street pageants as performance genres in their own right but as occasions for plays and playlets. Such histories attend not to the fusion of *opera gastronomica*, the Renaissance musical banquet, conceived from the outset to play to all the senses, but to the seeds of what would become an independent art form. A history of the theater in relation to the senses – and specifically the interplay of table and stage, the staging of food as theatre, and the theatrical uses of food – remains to be written.[2]

She defines here the conundrum facing any would-be objective historian: one can only view the past from the viewpoint of the present, so the question becomes, *which* present? A long history could be constructed to culminate in the work of Comediants. They drew on a rich performance tradition that includes, for example, Joseph Furttenbach's cosmic dining theatre designed in the mid seventeenth century (fig. 21).[3] The sketch includes tiny astrological symbols which indicate how cosmic forces were intended to act on the embodied diner–spectator.

The idea that a performance should resemble a well-balanced meal is a commonplace in Indian aesthetics, but deeply alien to mainstream western thought. In Indian thinking, just as the eater relishes the *rasa* derived from the six tastes, so the spectator relishes the *rasa* that is a kind of extract or essence derived from a mixing of the eight basic emotional states.[4] In western thought, the mind–body dichotomy rules out any such moral approbation of tasting and digesting. Plato likened rhetoric to the production of dainties, which the body unlike the soul cannot distinguish from healthy medicaments, and set the tone for Christianity's devaluation of bodily experience. Augustine would later declare that God had taught him to take food like a medication.[5] The sharing of meat from sacrificial animals was central to most Greek and Roman religious festivals, but alien to Christianity. St Paul advised Greek Christians in Corinth to eat privately at home before coming together for the solemn but strictly symbolic Lord's Supper.[6] The

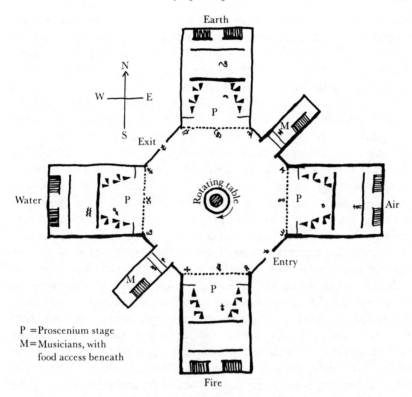

Figure 21   The Schawspilsaal at Ulm (after J. Furttenbach).

real eating of a Dionysiac festival could not be reconciled with a Christian religion that mistrusted sensory pleasure, and this religious context helps to explain the long suppression of the gustatory aesthetic in the western tradition.

In the twentieth century Brecht, with his background as a guitar-toting cabaret artist, was well placed to reopen debate. In a famous discussion of his 'epic' opera *Mahagonny*, Brecht portrayed opera as a 'culinary' form which originated as a source of pleasure. He both celebrates and mistrusts the 'culinary' aspect of opera, arguing that his own opera 'may not taste particularly agreeable' but is nevertheless 'culinary through and through', and thereby 'brings the culinary principle under discussion'. What Brecht particularly values in opera is the principle of variety in the separation of words, music and staging, and he argues that the Wagnerian ideal of fusing different art forms leads to mere intoxication. At the end of his essay, however, he records a movement in his own work away from the culinary towards the didactic.[7] To reconcile the ethical and the pleasurable proved in the end as difficult for the Marxist as it was for the Christian. The ethically driven western tradition has always found it difficult to value 'variety' as an aesthetic ideal. The reinscription of the body in performance art offers a more radical challenge to the western moral agenda. I recently watched a Spanish performance artist, La Ribot, turn her nude body into a set of scuptures in the South London Gallery.[8] Television monitors at the start showed her preparing parts of her body by pressing them with garlic and rubbing in herbs. Towards the end, she drank very simply a large glass of water, and one watched the water vanish into her slender body. By such means she called attention to the link between self and body that male-oriented ethical codes tend to deny. The title of her performance, 'Piezas distinguidas', plays on the 'distinguished' status of high art, and the process of 'distinction' that separates one pose from another, one part of the body from another. La Ribot takes us by another route to the aesthetic ideal of variety.

In the ancient world, Variety thrived alongside tragedy and comedy. Its home was not the theatre but the symposium, the drinking session that concluded a private banquet. It was in the symposium that two aspects of Dionysus converged: god of wine and god of dramatic performance. A study of the symposium allows us to comprehend a pagan aesthetic which exalted Variety and sensory pleasure, and has always lurked as a hidden presence in western thinking about performance. One of the problems in tracing the history of Variety is the fact that an oral, improvisational and musical form leaves few texts as memorials of its passing. The best ancient record that we have is Xenophon's more-or-less fictional account of a symposium hosted by a rich Athenian called Callias on a hot summer's night in 422 BC to celebrate the victory of his young boyfriend in a pugilistic contest.[9] The setting is a standard *andron* (men's dining-room) with, one must assume, the standard number of seven couches laid out around the edge of the square room (fig. 22).[10] Each couch was expected to accommodate two reclining drinkers. To recline for long periods supported by the left arm appears an act of decadence, but in fact requires the musculature acquired in carrying a shield; for the modern body it proves an acutely uncomfortable position. Xenophon's symposium unites Socrates, accompanied by members of his philosophical coterie, with a group of Athenian aristocrats. As a rich man, Callias can afford the services of a Sicilian impresario-cum-pimp, who owns three slave performers. In Plato's *Symposium*, the flute girl is sent packing, so the philosophers can concentrate on debate, and such entertainments are dismissed elsewhere in Plato as bourgeois (literally: 'of the *agora*').[11] Xenophon was a man of action who did not share Plato's asceticism. In his text,

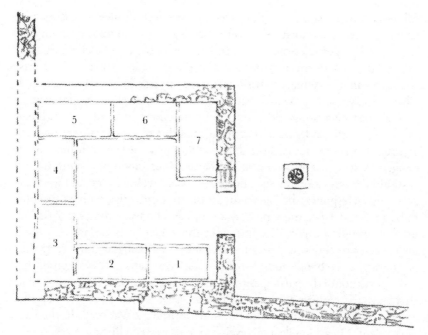

Figure 22   A typical *andron* excavated in a house in Athens (after John Travlos).

the entertainment is both a stimulus to conversation and a moral test of the participants.

The performer's space is the centre of the room, the ceremonial centre where the wine is mixed with water in the desired proportion. There is just space enough for solo performers to be secure that a drinker will not lean over and touch them. The three performers are young and beautiful: a boy who plays the *kithara* (a form of lyre), a girl who plays the *aulos* (double pipes) and a girl who specializes in acrobatics. The performance touches all the senses: the wine-cup is passed around the circle, perfume is rejected in favour of honest sweat, kisses are the prize in a competition, and music complements the visual beauty of the human body. The programme is as follows:

instrumental music
juggling hoops
acrobatics (somersault through circle of blades)
boy's athletic dance
boy sings
acrobat reads and writes while spun on a potter's wheel
mime-play of Dionysus and Ariadne.

All the acts are musical. The piper accompanies everything except the song, where the boy accompanies himself; she also accompanies the singing of guests, and plays frenetically when the parasite – the unofficial entertainer in the party – performs a burlesque of the boy's dance. Each of these acts stimulates an intellectual discussion, and the impresario becomes frustrated when the discussion grows so animated that the entertainers are forgotten.

The most interesting and anomalous entertainment is the unscheduled mime play at the end. Socrates contests the value of variety entertainment, arguing that acrobatics contort the body and make it less beautiful, while dangerous acts do not belong to the harmonious mood of a symposium. Instead of magic, he requests a beautiful dance evoking Graces, Hours or Nymphs. In response, the Syracusan devises his mime-play, which turns out to be an erotic dance showing how a drunken Dionysus comes to Ariadne on their wedding night. The beauty of the naked body cannot be prised apart from sexual desire. The guests seem to hear dialogue, but clearly this is a mimed interchange audible only in the imagination. It is a sign of the moral fortitude of the participants, braced by Socrates' ethical teaching, that they leave the performers untouched, and seek sublimated love or socially approved partners elsewhere. Xenophon's attitude to Variety is in the end ambivalent. On an intellectual level, he seems to share Plato's reservations, but as a writer he communicates his delight in the pleasures of the form. Socrates maintains that Callias' love for his boyfriend, the relationship which occasions the symposium, will turn Callias into a better citizen, and sexual desire is not regarded as inherently evil in this pre-Christian world. A good Athenian must negotiate the world of pleasure and the erogenous provocations of the symposium, not cut himself off.

In the centuries that followed, variety entertainment in the symposium drew increasingly on the world of formal theatre. When Philip of Macedon gathered together representatives of the Greek world in 336 BC to celebrate the wedding of his daughter and prepare the ground for an invasion of Persia, he invited Neoptolemus, the greatest actor of the age, to come to his palace in Vergina. In the evening Neoptolemus performed at a symposium extracts from various tragedies, selected for their relevance to the occasion; next morning at dawn he performed a tragedy in full.[12] The theatre outside the palace and the multiple sympotic spaces within have both been preserved. Two of the banqueting rooms are grander than the rest – about 8 metres (8.8 yards) square – and one of these must have been used. One of the floor mosaics survives, demarcating the performance space from the border where eleven large or fifteen standard couches would once have stood.[13] The centre spot, used for the wine-mixing and subsequently for the solo performer, is defined by the centre of a rose, with tentacles spreading out towards the guests. Many Hellenistic floors include theatrical motifs, especially masks, to define the theatrical nature of a sympotic space, but here in Macedonia the design is more abstract, with female nature-spirits in the corners. We infer from a similar event that Neoptolemus would have used costume, props and a supporting chorus.[14] On another occasion Philip took the middle couch at a symposium in order to impose his authority, but the archaeological remains suggest that at Vergina he must have organized the space in the traditional way, which placed the host by the doorway. The presence of a pair of royal banqueting rooms signifies balance, not autocratic monarchy. The architecture of Greek sympotic space was designed to be egalitarian, with the passing of a cup around the circle allowing each symposiast an equal share of attention.

The idea that the sympotic *andron* was a space of performance became deeply rooted. Centuries later, Plutarch debated which dramatic form was most appropriate to it, and his list of possibilities included performed dialogues by Plato, Sappho's poems, tragedy, Aristophanic comedy, the comedy of Menander, satire, pantomime, farce and instrumental music.[15] From Plutarch's sustained discussion of the symposium we can extrapolate a counter-aesthetic, an alternative to the Aristotelian mode of discussing dramatic performance. Drama in the symposium and drama in the public theatre respond to two different ideals:

SYMPOSIUM	THEATRE
variety	unity
digestion	purgation (catharsis)
private	public
enclosed	open air
evening	morning
performer-centred	author-centred
solo	choral
body naked	body masked
slave performers	free performers
participatory	judgemental
creates friendship (*philophrosyne*)	creates wisdom (*sophrosyne*)

Variety (*to poikilon*), argues Plutarch, is more pleasurable in a meal, and more healthy than uniformity, provided it does not lead to excess, and performed entertainments contribute to the pleasures of 'variety'.[16] The role of the host, the director of the symposium, is crucial: he can turn the *andron* into a public theatre, or he can 'give place only to those words, spectacles and games which achieve the sympotic purpose: namely, to build through pleasure an enhanced or new friendship among participants.'[17] The essential objective of the variety performance is thus the bonding of the audience. The enclosed environment isolates the guests from the democratic *polis*, and creates a world where the individual is subjected to the intense pleasures and dangers of wine, sexual encounter and performances. Michel Foucault saw the symposium as a place for practising the *technê* of the self. Greek morality, in his interpretation, was not a code but an ethics, a set of aesthetic–moral practices that generated mastery of the self.[18] To engage in the pleasures of the symposium was a complex and demanding undertaking in the Greek world.

Florence Dupont makes a useful distinction between the 'hot culture' of the symposium and the 'cold culture' of the book. In the symposium, she argues, the word could never be separated from the conditions of its enunciation, and each performance was unique. The symposium was a space of cultural memory, where works were continually remade in time present. Wine in the Greek world had a mystical function, linked to the presence of Dionysus, creating the conditions for such spontaneous remaking. Aristotle in his *Poetics*, she maintains, separated language from its performance, and saw plays as representations rather than events. Through effacing the conditions of a work's enunciation, he turned works into 'cold' monuments that would assist in the cultural unification of the Greek world.[19] Dupont reinforces the importance of the sympotic aesthetic for our understanding of performance.

Two other works from the ancient world are worth placing alongside Xenophon's portrait of the classical symposium, setting up rather different ideals for the future. We can go back several centuries to Homer's *Odyssey*, where the blind bard Demodocus sings at the end of two royal feasts whilst playing his lyre. The setting is a *megaron*, a large square or rectangular hall that forms the architectural core of the palace, with its roof supported by columns. The bard sits on a chair with his back to a column, in the midst of the company. His first tale, a violent quarrel at a feast, sets up an ethical ideal: the banquet should be a place for harmony and friendship. After food has been shared, the bard's aim is to create shared emotions, but on this occasion Odysseus' experiences prevent him participating in the communal good cheer, so he takes over the storyteller's role, and creates silence with his own more tragic tale.[20] Some important attributes of the classical symposium are missing in the Homeric world. We find no idealization of Dionysus and the mystic properties of wine. The guests are seated, not reclining in a simulation of decadence. Aristocratic women are present and eroticism has no place. Though the setting is indoors, the hall is huge and the audience is inclusive rather than exclusive – the name Demodocus meaning 'received by the people'. In the world of Homeric monarchy there is no distinction between domestic and public space, but the role of the public audience in this society is to listen, not participate as equals. The columns would have made it hard for spectators to focus on a mobile performer, but they can arrange themselves in such a way as to fix their eyes on a single chair. When Homer describes the attempts of Odysseus to conceal his emotions, he helps us understand what made the bard something more than a disembodied voice.

The most famous account of a Roman banquet is found in a satirical epic by Petronius.[21] A naïve Greek guest describes a dinner hosted by a freed slave of enormous wealth called Trimalchio. Trimalchio appears to be the butt of the comedy, and is often taken to represent Nero, but by the end of the account the narrator is shown to be the greater fool. As in the comedies of Plautus, Rome is superimposed on a parody of Greece, making it hard to read the social reality behind the fiction. Roman-style wives, for example, function as Greek-style prostitutes. This is essentially a Roman dinner, not a Greek symposium, and drinking is neither ritualized nor demarcated from eating in this Roman environment. The Greek symposium celebrated youth, but Trimalchio is obsessed with death; Greek symposia celebrated the body beautiful, but Petronius conjures up a grotesque world, where the eating and excreting human body is incompatible with Greek ideals of beauty. The presentation of food is the core of Trimalchio's dramatic entertainment: the slave who chops up and distributes a boiled calf, for example, does so in the person of Ajax, the Greek hero who attacked animals in a fit of madness. The narrator has constant difficulty in distinguishing planned entertainments from accidents, as when a beautiful male acrobat falls off his ladder and lands on Trimalchio's couch. Petronius' account reflects real imperial banquets animated by an aesthetic ideal, that artifice and reality should be indistinguishable. This collapsing of categories was associated with celebration and conviviality, while the magic and opulence of the occasion reflected the charismatic qualities of the host. When emperors ceased to be gods, and the Christian God was understood to be quite separate from the transient material universe he had created, such magic-making became unsustainable. In the renaissance, when rulers again aspired to absolute power, the ideal of the theatricalized banquet was resurrected.[22]

Whilst Greek drinkers placed themselves in the round in order to participate as performers offering songs, recitations and speeches, Roman diners

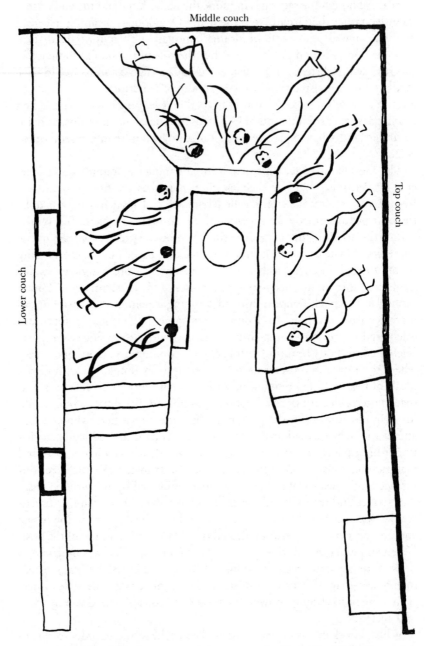

Figure 23 Plan of outdoor *triclinium* excavated at Pompeii, with diners.

positioned themselves to be recipients of a spectacle. The Roman tradition was to place three couches around a table, allowing nine diners to recline with their heads close together in intimate conversation (fig. 23). The visual focus of the Roman *triclinium* was not the centre, but the doorway, placed off-centre in Greece but centrally in Rome. This doorway allowed grand entrances to be made with spectacular dishes, and a succession of such entries dominates Trimalchio's feast, the space in front of the door serving as a performance area. Dining arrangements thus replicate theatrical arrangements, with the Greek *andron* enfolding the performance space, the Roman *triclinium* confronting it. In Trimalchio's feast, there are more guests present than three couches could accommodate, reflecting the increased scale of imperial dining-halls, which made conversation difficult and the importing of entertainments essential.[23] Trimalchio places himself beside the doorway in the position which belonged to the host of a Greek symposium, allowing him in this end-staged Roman context to assume the unexpected role of compère.

Plutarch identifies three basic seating plans in antiquity: the Greek, the Roman and the Persian.[24] It was the monarchical Persian model, which offered a central place to the king, that eventually won out. The principle that the raised seat of honour in the middle belonged to the monarch was embodied architecturally in the basilica, where the apse provided a frame to glorify the host.[25] Medieval dining halls followed this monarchical model. In a typical medieval hall, the dais at the top end created a dividing line between the 'household of magnificence' and the 'household of service'.[26] A bay window next to the dais threw light on those who sat at high table. On the dais and behind were the living quarters of the noble family, while the floor of the hall was a public space accessible through doors in the screens at the bottom end. The screens gave onto a passage that led to the kitchen, the servants' quarters and the exterior. Minstrels often occupied a gallery above the screens, facing their lord. Long tables down the sides of the hall left free space in the centre. The public space of the floor, not the privileged area of the stage, was the space used by performers.

Solo variety entertainers played an important part in medieval feasts. A self-reflexive tale attributed to a French minstrel called Trubert, probably dating from the thirteenth century, gives some idea of the art of the minstrel or *jongleur*. *Le vilain au buffet* tells how a Count holds court, and opens his house to all who wish to be his guests. An ugly villein called Raoul decides to attend, but the steward is resentful, and places him not at the communal table but on a *buffet* or chest. The Count offers scarlet livery to the best entertainer, and Trubert lists the ensuing repertory. *Riot* was probably a mime play, the *Herberie* a monologue spoken by a street vendor:

> one acts the drunk, the other the fool,
> some dance, another sings,
> the rest play *Riot*,
> the third some patter;
> those who live by minstrelsy play the viol before the Count.
> All listen to the storyteller:
> some recite the *Herberie*
> where there are many japes, and much laughter . . .

At the end of the meal, before the Count can wash his hands, Raoul goes to the space of performance before high table, the steward remonstrates, and Raoul gives him a 'buffet' on the face, and hands over his napkin like a knight's glove. He explains that he is merely returning the loan of a *buffet*, and this jest wins him the livery. The Count slowly begins to laugh, and the rest of the hall follows.[27] The principal performer in any medieval dining hall was the nobleman on the stage, not the minstrel on the floor, who had his back to most of the audience. The open fire in the middle of the hall lit the minstrel's back, but helped illuminate the face of the noble diner, and that face guides the responses of the hall. Trubert's tale is itself a calculated jest, full of direct speech that offers much scope for role-play and characterization. Trubert implies through the poem that he too should be rewarded by a magnanimous host. Raoul is a projection of himself, establishing a grotesque lower-class persona that is the antithesis of nobility and 'courtesy'. When the Christian Count eats, he gratifies his lower body, and Raoul is a manifestation of that lower body. Raoul performs his jest before the Count can wash his hands, and put the corrupt world of the body behind him. What is interesting about Trubert's minstrelsy is the complex relationship he sets up between the other world of his narrative and the present context of performance at court. The appeal of the solo variety artist lies in the way he puts his personality on the line, engaged in a battle for the audience's approval. When the solo act becomes a 'play' with multiple performers, that engagement with the audience is diluted.

Our best example of sympotic theatre in the middle ages comes again from France. Roger Berger, through a meticulous examination of the context, has demonstrated that *Le Jeu de la Feuillée* by Adam de la Halle must have been performed in the course of an overnight drinking ceremony in the town of Arras on Thursday 4 June/Friday 5 June 1276.[28] The occasion was the annual gathering of a guild or brotherhood, which began with heavy drinking to cement social bonds. In a bourgeois milieu, unlike a feudal one, relationships of equality could be celebrated. Whilst Trubert's minstrelsy reinforced a hierarchical bond, and emphasized the duties of a superior towards his servant, Adam de la Halle's play celebrated a horizontal bond, and maximized participation. The 'brotherhood' brought together two disparate groups, the bourgeoisie of Arras and the local minstrels, and its major concern was the burial rites of members. After the drinking ceremony, three 'mayors' would be elected to serve for the coming year: one for the bourgeoisie, one for minstrels resident in the town, and one for minstrels from outside. The gathering took place in the great hall of the brotherhood, close to the 'small marketplace'. This marketplace was a distinctly secular environment, its only religious monument being the curious pyramidal chapel of the brotherhood.

The setting of the play is Arras, the immediate environment of the performance. The cast is large, and many of the characters are known to have been real-life bourgeois members of the brotherhood. The largest part belongs to Adam himself. Berger plausibly argues that Adam, his father and their circle of bourgeois friends played themselves, whilst minstrels played the anonymous fantasy roles. The narrative structure is loose, and variety of mood is more important than storyline. There are few clear entries and exits. It used to be thought that the play was performed in the marketplace, but it is hard to see how effective sightlines or audibility could be achieved out of doors, and curfew regulations forbade such events at night.[29] We have rather to imagine how people left their places at table, flowed into the space between the tables, and flowed back to their seats, while the rhythm of the verse preserved momentum. The script moves between three distinct locations. First is an ill-defined open area where a monk exhibits bogus relics, and topographical allusions suggest the nearby marketplace: this was the *platea*, the body of the hall. Second is a table where three fairies come to consume a banquet, prepared for them by Adam. This would have been the high table on the dais, where later the three 'mayors' would sit and dine. The fairies on their dais make a formal entry and exit, and have little interaction with the company, while a Wheel of Fortune is displayed beside them as a spectacular set piece. The 'tavern' would have been set at the lower end of the hall, where wine and food were brought through the screens from the kitchen, and a gallery may have been available above the screens, allowing water or urine to be poured on those below. The same spatial schema can be found in two earlier plays written for the brotherhood by Jean Bodel.[30] The hall was a microcosm of the medieval world, the high end associated with the ethereal fairies, the low end with the world of the body.

The play begins with Adam's formal farewell to a wife who is beautiful no longer. Eating and drinking make all human beings grotesque, and the common possession of a grotesque body unites all members of the brotherhood. The fairies, who are not grotesque, derive from a pagan world where the body is not perforce harnessed to sin.[31] As in Petronius and Trubert, the fluid boundary between the here and now of the social occasion and a dramatic fantasy world creates dramatic tension, within a dining space that makes no physical division between stage and auditorium. We must imagine the play as it unfolded in time. The event began with a formal solo recitation by Adam, a set-piece farewell poem that was interrupted by friends at table, and evolved only gradually into a physically enacted performance. Adam's father Henri was in reality a wealthy businessman, but the play presented him as impoverished and greedy, so ironic acts of self-projection were involved. The final drunken tavern scene and evocation of the morning after echoed the real social context of nightlong drinking. Adam's group left at the end of the play to present a candle to Our Lady because this was the main rite of the guild. Fiction and reality were united by the ritual context of the performance. The world of the medieval symposium at Arras was nocturnal, pagan and bourgeois, in contrast to more familiar forms of medieval drama presented in daylight under the auspices of the church.

In the late middle ages and renaissance period, the idea of eating a meal in public began to disturb aristocratic sensibilities. The grotesque act of eating was hard to reconcile with the persona of one whom God had placed in office. The introduction of the fork in place of fingers symbolizes the new attitude: a desire to separate self from the physicality of the body, a reluctance to contaminate the aristocratic body with ugliness.[32] Dininghalls went on being used for theatrical performance, but the act of eating was gradually separated from the act of watching. Minstrels gave way to actors as viewing was separated from eating. English banquets on Twelfth Night illustrate the changes that took place at the end of the middle ages. Commemorating the night when three kings visited Christ, Twelfth Night was the most important occasion on the calendar for kings to feast, and for mock kings to parody royal feasting.

King Henry VII celebrated Twelfth Night 1494 in Westminster Hall, the parliament chamber, and used the feast to consolidate his relationship with the city of London.[33] Aristocratic theatre was universally understood as a mode of completing a banquet. However, to eat dinner with the mayor, a commoner, would have been politically demeaning, so the king asked his chamberlain to substitute for him at table at court, and joined the mayor after dinner. Galleries were erected around the side of the hall for the entertainment, allowing the public to view their monarch enthroned on stage beneath a cloth of state, with his queen, court and foreign ambassadors around him. Tapestries were hung on the walls, improving the acoustic and turning the hall into a visually rich, festive environment. First on the programme was a professional, scripted play given by the king's company of actors. This was interrupted before the moralizing finale: the director of the king's choristers rode in on horseback in the person of St George, accompanied by a model dragon spitting fire, and rescued a virgin from the dragon in order to present her to the queen. Rushes on the floor would have absorbed the clash of hooves. The arrival of the horse and the building of a castle in the hall inverted the normal sense of indoors and outdoors. The spontaneity of the entry created the sense not of a rehearsed performance but of an event, and the sixties term 'happening' evokes the kind of disruption that must have been secured.[34] The third presentation, highest in status, was the 'mumming' or 'disguising' (the term 'masque' not yet being used), when twelve male courtiers led in twelve female courtiers, all in elaborate disguise, and presented the king and queen with a dance, the men demonstrating their athleticism, the women their deportment. The evening ended with a symbolic 'running banquet'. The disguised male courtiers, with other gentlemen behind them, took on the role of servants, and delivered sixty dishes to the king and queen – not real sustenance, but meals simulated in confectionery – while the mayor on his separate dais was given only twenty-four dishes to define his relative status. The conception of the shared meal was sustained, but the grotesque reality of public eating was avoided. The integration of food and performance supported the feeling that this was a concelebration, not a passive act of viewing. It was also a public mapping of hierarchical relationships, with plebeian actors in the lowest position. Scripted theatre, which today's literary culture might regard as highest in status, here ranked lowest.[35]

Leslie Hotson has pieced together a detailed account of the way Queen Elizabeth celebrated Twelfth Night a century later in 1601, on the eve of Essex's rebellion, desperate to establish her position amidst a dissident court.[36] The meal and the play at Whitehall have now become two separate performances. Elizabeth dined with the Russian ambassador, obliged to eat in front of her courtiers because sharing bread was a symbolic matter for the Russian emperor, but removed from the eyes of the public. She sat on her own stage in the Chamber, with plate brought from the Tower serving as her backdrop, while courtiers performed the role of menials serving her food, and choristers provided entertainment. The play in the Great Hall

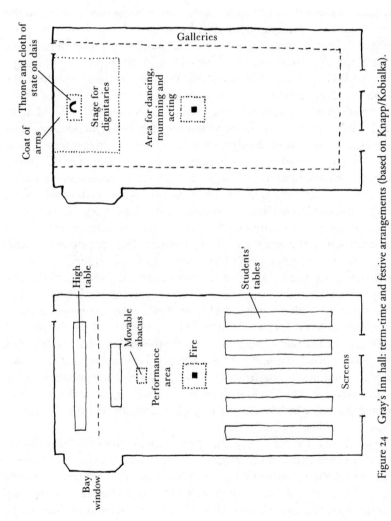

Figure 24 Gray's Inn hall: term-time and festive arrangements (based on Knapp/Kobialka).

in the evening was an affair for the public. Galleries were set up on all sides of the hall, and tapestries were hung. The queen sat on the dais, with cloth of state framing her and enhancing her importance. Duke Orsino, her young Italian guest of honour, stood beside her in the position where the young and romantic Essex had stood seven years earlier. First the courtiers danced, and then professional actors performed a play. A symbolic banquet rounded off the evening in the queen's private apartments: after the queen had tasted it, the whole elaborate display of confectionery was destroyed by the maids-in-waiting – a ritual which broke the dream and restored normality.

The play was the object of Hotson's quest, and few have been convinced by his claim that this was Shakespeare's *Twelfth Night*.[37] The Chamberlain's memorandum refers to a debate about securing the 'play that shall be best furnished with rich apparel, have great variety and change of music and dances, and of a subject that may be most pleasing to Her Majesty'. The Chamberlain must have obtained what he wanted because Orsino was to report a 'mingled comedy with pieces of music and dances'.[38] The word 'variety' once again epitomizes that which complements a banquet. Somehow the Chamberlain and players had to reconcile the aesthetic demands of a banquet with the very different qualities of a repertory developed in the playhouse. It is clear from Hotson's study that the principal theatrical performance on this occasion was the one given by the queen seated on her stage, an old woman playing an amorous virgin. The performance by common players on the floor of the hall was directed towards her, and was refracted through her gaze to the audience. With the audience seated on all sides, the focus was not on the play but on the relationship of play and queen.

Christmas festivities at Gray's Inn in 1594/5 provide another example of late-medieval theatre in a dining-hall (fig. 24).[39] The 'Prince' on this occasion was a student elected for the season by his fellows, and the whole event can be seen as a form of theatre-in-education, allowing young aristocrats to prepare for power. On the inaugural night, when there was plenty of room on the floor of the hall, the Prince watched an armed knight in the person of his champion ride on horseback around the central open fire – just as St George had done a century earlier. A budget was granted for the season's entertainment, and it may have been at this point that a stage was built over the dais, and galleries banked from floor to ceiling. The ensuing 'grand night' is famous as the occasion when Shakespeare's *Comedy of Errors* was performed, at the end of an evening that had grown chaotic through overcrowding. It is clear that the play was performed in the medieval fashion in front of the Prince, and not in front of the screens at the lower end of the hall. One study surmises that a wide, shallow stage was built between the fire and the permanent low dais, but this would require us to privilege the play too much, raising the actors higher than the Prince and his court.[40] It is much more likely that an extensive raised stage covering the upper end of the hall was used for the Prince, his courtiers and distinguished guests, while the actors performed on the floor in front of the stage, in the area used for dancing and mumming. Given the number of bodies crammed into the space, not to mention candle-power, it seems questionable whether a fire was needed. The actors had the familiar medieval task of performing in the round, with the principal spectators on one side and the bulk of the audience on the other.

For a long time scholars assumed that plays in dining-halls were performed in front of the screens at the bottom of the hall because this chimed with their theatrical intuitions. A backdrop of screens would have defined and isolated the fictional world of the play, allowing audiences to see the faces of the actors and so lose themselves in the dramatic fiction. At Gray's Inn in 1594, however, the principal actor in *Comedy of Errors* was unambiguously the principal spectator. A councillor contrasted the elected 'Prince' of the Grayans with a king in the theatre who ought to look calm and majestic but actually looks 'troubled' because he is trying to remember his lines: the student Prince, in other words, performed better than a professional actor. The same councillor urged the Prince to dedicate himself to variety and solace – 'after serious affairs, admitting recreation, and using pleasures as sauces for meats of better nourishment'. The culinary metaphor fits with the festive ideal of 'variety'. The proper pleasures of a monarch are listed as feasting, music, dancing, triumphs, comedies, love, ladies.[41] The performance of Shakespeare's comedy was thus one item in a royal variety show. The necromancy of Dr Pinch in Shakespeare's play inspired an elaborate set of improvisations two days later, when the breakdown of order on the 'night of errors' was attributed to a sorcerer. We see the same quality of active viewing in *A Midsummer Night's Dream*, where the plebeian actors of *Pyramus and Thisbe* try to present a formal neo-classical play, but courtiers engaged in recreation after dinner prefer to use the actors as material for their own performance of extemporal wit.

On Twelfth Night the audience at Gray's Inn was more select and better organized. A devised piece of allegorical drama was presented, incorporating an altar screened off at the side of the hall, and the event culminated in the arrival of unexpected guests in the traditional manner of a mumming. A mock-ambassador from Russia became the guest of honour, and shared in a traditional running banquet served by courtiers. This visit must have inspired the Russian embassy in *Love's Labour's Lost*, a play which would have been batted back to the circuit of aristocratic feasts a year or so later. The visit of Count Orsino on Twelfth Night, 1601, inspired the creation of Orsino in Shakespeare's *Twelfth Night*, and that Orsino was offered back to at least one of the Inns of Court in 1602, and doubtless to Elizabeth also.[42] The creative to-and-fro between text and post-prandial recreation is easily forgotten in a modern cultural environment focused on Shakespeare as text, and on Shakespeare as precursor of the modern 'professional' theatre. In medieval parlance the word 'play' was a synonym of 'game', two variant translations of the Latin *ludus*.[43] The Italian system of perspectival staging and detached viewing introduced a divide between play and game. Smell, touch and taste were excluded from the realms of art, and theatre privileged vision, whilst instrumental music developed into an autonomous form. The 'hot culture' of the medieval feast gradually gave way to a 'cold culture' that privileged literature.

John Orrell has analysed the tensions set up when Italian staging was first introduced to the English dining hall in 1605. King James was required to move from the raised and central position of principal performer to that of principal spectator, enjoying an optimal perspective close to the stage where 'the auditory could but see his cheek only'. His courtiers objected, and the traditional seating was restored.[44] These tensions became easier to reconcile once the Stuart court cut itself off from the public domain. The architectural focus of aristocratic houses in the seventeenth century ceased to be the public space of the dining-hall. Dining henceforth belonged to dining-rooms, and theatre to theatres.

In England, the year 1843 marks a crisis in the theatrical regime established at the Restoration. The Theatres Act abolished the unenforceable principle that only the two London theatres in possession of the royal patent could provide the public with drama.[45] A new distinction was created between plays, which could be given in licensed theatres anywhere, and other buildings – later to be called music halls – where people could smoke and buy drinks whilst watching entertainments other than plays. Of course, there would be much haggling over what did and did not constitute a 'play' for purposes of the act. The birth of music-hall stemmed from the pressures of industrialization. In the countryside, where the alehouse had largely taken over from the church as the focus of collective festivity, the rhythms of the agricultural calendar continued to structure a pattern of outdoor celebrations, often linked to fairs. The new urban working class, driven from the countryside by enclosures and the lure of factory wages, needed a new form of collective celebration, structured by the rhythm of the working week. At the same time, the middle classes wanted to take control of the theatre auditorium, which they achieved through abolition of the pit and the installation of expensive seats in the stalls. There was a related change in the theatre repertoire, which moved from variety programmes towards the ideal of the serious play. While theatres evolved into houses for art, the saloons of public houses expanded to become palaces for variety entertainment.[46]

The early purpose-built music halls of the 1850s and 1860s, like the celebrated Canterbury Hall in Lambeth, can be seen as an amalgam of the public house, the aristocratic supper room and the theatre.[47] They did not differ so very greatly from the medieval dining-hall. The chairman, commonly the owner, extended hospitality to the surrounding area, and invitations to sit at his table were sought after, though guests now had to pay for the hospitality of the house, and the chairman's high table was placed in front of the stage, not on it. A neo-classical doorway functioned like the cloth of state, emphasizing the importance of the solitary singer who commanded the stage. As in medieval times, the tables were often arranged so that the public sat at right-angles to the host's table, and food and drink were supplied from the bottom of the hall. Three walls were lined with galleries, for more spectators. Rushes on the floor gave way to carpet in the nineteenth century, frescoes and mirrors replaced tapestries, and bright gas-lit chandeliers replaced candles, but the structure remained essentially medieval. The main change lay in the way the minstrels (now often female) directed their numbers at the whole body of the hall. The chairman mediated the relationship, but less authoritatively than a medieval monarch. The early halls attempted to cash in on the status now vested in notions of 'art'. The library and picture gallery at the Canterbury, and the evening dress worn by the earliest singers, were all part of a battle for status, contesting the social implications of the 1843 act.

The equipoise which prevailed in the 1860s between mental and comestible sustenance did not long survive a capitalist logic that required more space for more customers. Tables gradually vanished from the large music halls in the 1870s, and chairs or benches were turned to face the stage, though nothing eroded the principle that drinking and smoking were a necessary part of the pleasure involved in watching a music-hall turn. In the old dining-hall arrangement, the performer's demand that the eyes of the spectator should turn sideways away from the bottle and conversation towards the stage contributed to the audience's pleasure. The fight for attention was a ritualized contest which could be won or lost.[48] When seats were turned to the stage, the performers were more secure, and able to develop their art to greater degrees of refinement, but managers by the same token were able to exercise more control over content and timing, restricting audience participation and squeezing two houses into an evening. The loss of tables did not in itself rule out the creation of an antiphonal balance when the solo voice of the singer presenting the verses was answered by the collective voice of the hall joining in the chorus – but a steady movement towards passive spectatorship had begun.

Parliamentary enquiries give us a very full picture of the tensions between 'theatre' defined as art, and 'music-hall' devoted to recreation. The variety presented in music-hall appealed to the five senses, and might include the taste of beer, the smell of tobacco and the touch of a prostitute's hand. Theatre, on the other hand, was expected to reach the soul, and sensory pleasures were alien to it. When the committee in 1866 interrogated Nelson Lee, an actor, author and manager speaking on behalf of theatre, they asked him why he thought the working classes should be deprived of Shakespeare. His reply was sarcastic: 'During the time I am speaking Hamlet's soliloquy, perhaps a man asks for potatoes and a kidney.' When the committee responded that, even if *Hamlet* did not aid the digestion, it would do the man no harm, he could offer only the lame response that dance routines were sufficient, having no way of rationalizing his assumption that Shakespeare transcends the material world. For Lee, the essence of the theatrical experience was the quality of attention:

Nobody could sit down in front of my stalls with drinking, eating and smoking going on and listen to a serious piece; if you go to the Adelphi and see 'Rip Van Winkle,' you can hear a pin drop; or go to the Olympic and see the refined acting of Kate Terry, if anybody sitting next to you was even to speak a word, everybody would look round, and say 'silence'.[49]

He feared nevertheless that if these plays were given in some nearby music hall, much of his audience would decamp; some would be silent at the right moments but some would not. The Victorian desire for serious drama seems to have been painfully at odds with the desire for conviviality and sensory satisfaction.

Another actor–manager in 1892 expressed himself more soulfully:

– I very often myself have to play characters in which there is a little tragedy mixed with the comedy, and I do not know how it is with me, but when I get to those little bits of pathos I always cry myself, really cry. I could not do it if a gentleman was opening a bottle of soda.
– Do you think a gentleman would ever open a bottle of soda?
– I do not know.[50]

The new focus on the interiority of the actor assumes that a passive audience will lose itself in the emotions of the fictional character. The parliamentary interrogation exposes the class-based nature of the new aesthetic code. The agonistic challenge of reducing a convivial audience to silence is not something the theatre-manager can contemplate in the gentrified environment of the theatre. The young Bertolt Brecht articulated the opposite view, claiming 'that in a Shakespearean production one man in the stalls with a cigar could bring about the downfall of Western art . . . In my view it is quite impossible for the actor to play unnatural, cramped and old-fashioned theatre to a man smoking in the stalls.'[51]

Male concerns about the performing female are at the centre of the Victorian debate. It is a woman, Ellen Terry's sister, who epitomizes perfect refinement in the theatre, but it is woman in her fallen aspect who epitomizes the music hall. The theatre spokesman of 1892 declares:

I have a sort of cast-iron voice and cast-iron constitution, I am thankful to say; but very many of our delicately organised ladies, and not only ladies but gentlemen, could not pursue their avocation if there was smoking. In Mr Gilbert's opera, which I am playing in now, our principal lady, our prima donna, Miss Ulmar, has a very delicate organ; it may be powerful but it is very delicate; the least thing upsets her . . . If the Lyric were to allow smoking in some part of the auditorium she could not sing a bit.[52]

Though Bernhardt and other theatre actresses might be seen as examples of the 'new woman', the rift between theatre and music-hall did much to reinforce dominant attitudes to English femininity. Smoking was a sign of masculinity, and the music hall was a place of male display.

An eye-witness account of one of the new music halls clarifies the new cultural divide by virtue of its sustained misreading. James Burnley, proclaiming himself a devotee of theatre and in particular Shakespeare (the unquestioned touchstone of aesthetic merit) visited Henry Pullan's 3,000-seat Theatre of Varieties in Bradford in around 1870, in order to write an article on the new phenomenon for the *Bradford Observer*.[53] He seats himself on one side of the gallery, and immediately distinguishes the tobacco smoke rising from the 'mill hands, mechanics, masons and artizans' in the pit below him from the cigar-smoke of the petite bourgeoisie ('clerks, shopmen, small tradesmen . . .') wafting through the gallery. Waiters circulate with ham sandwiches, and programmes that double as newspapers, for this is where private individuals come to discover the world. He takes note of all the prostitutes circulating in the promenade, the seatless area in front of the bar at the far end of the gallery facing the stage, then studies a German 'Don Juan'

Plate 1   Acrobat using the auditorium in a music-hall performance. From a poster in the John Johnson collection.

who sits conspicuously in the front row, and eavesdrops on gossip about him, for watching the audience is part of the pleasure of music-hall. The programme begins with a sequence of solo acts. Though regarding music-hall as an undesirable French import, Burnley approves the opening male singer whose song about an oak tree defines the Englishness of the event. He is less happy with the woman who follows, particularly when she offers a medley, variety within variety; being unfamiliar with the ingredients of this medley, since he is not a member of the new urban community created by music-hall, he cannot grasp what generates the deafening applause. Next a man performs a comic mime-and-dance routine, followed by a woman doing character turns. Locked into mimetic assumptions about art, Burnley cannot grasp why a washerwoman should be wearing blue satin. For the same reason, he cannot interest himself in the dramatic duologue given by two sisters (one in drag) because they 'play so to the audience instead of trying to be natural'. This playing to the audience is taken further in the next act, when 'Good for Nothing Sarah' picks out Burnley's male companion, and asks if he would have her. The man of letters who came to observe the amusements of the lower orders suddenly finds himself the centre of attention, identified by the crowd as a conspicuous outsider. The evening comes to its climax with an ensemble act that includes a chorus of girls. As in modern pantomime, the inclusion of local children helps to break down the amateur–professional divide, and seals the bond between Pullan's hall and the city around it. The final act is given by a male trapeze artist swinging over the auditorium (plate 12). Burnley condemns this as too dangerous, though he does not find it sexually offensive – unlike the female gymnast he would see on his next excursion.

Burnley's final verdict is couched in aesthetic not moral terms: the numbers are repetitive and conventional; music-hall needs an 'original genius' who will 'give us true pictures of life'. His phrase 'pictures of life' points towards the picture-frame stage, not the interactive environment of the music hall where it is the unique moment of the event, not the originality of the artist, that is celebrated. Burnley is soaked in the 'cold' literary aesthetic of Aristotle, not in the 'hot' aesthetic of the symposium. Historians have not reached a consensus on how far the symposium in the ancient world was the preserve of an elite, in contrast to theatre which belonged to the many. In the Victorian world this tendency was reversed: theatre was associated with the elite end of the spectrum, the sympotic environment with the popular end, though there was much common ground in the middle. Towards the end of the nineteenth century, another shift can be seen. Numerous modernists turned away from realist notions of art towards symbolism, and

Figure 25   Sketch of Manet's *Café-concert*.

other forms that emphasized the subjectivity of perception. This generation found much more to value in the conventions of music-hall.[54]

In his *Café-concert* of 1878 (fig. 25), Manet portrayed spectators at the small Brasserie Reichshoffen in Paris.[55] In the foreground a drably dressed prostitute looks vacantly at the viewer of the painting whilst an elderly gentleman beside her focuses on the singer, who is visible only in a mirror behind the spectators. Behind the couple, a barmaid quaffs a glass of Bocks beer. A vertical line passing through the beer on the table seems to divide the three working women from the male. Manet links the performance to alcohol, suggesting that the relationship between man and prostitute is mediated both by drink and by the man's response to a performance. This is a world of illusion, where the man cannot look at any of the three women who serve his desires and see them as they are. The man could be the subject of an official portrait, but the prostitute is partly cut off by the frame. Music-hall performers in much the same way derived their energy from a refusal to confine themselves to the frame of the stage. In his famous *Bar aux Folies-Bergère*, painted four years later, Manet moved to the other end of the spectrum, a huge and expensive variety theatre.[56] Here an expressionless barmaid faces the viewer, but in the mirror behind her the pose is different, and appears to signify sexual availability as she leans forward towards an affluent customer. The mirror includes a view of wealthy spectators in the gallery opposite. The bar is set on the promenade of the Folies-Bergère which, as in all large music halls, was a notorious venue for prostitution. Manet uses the mirror, with its impossible perspective, to problematize the stance of anyone who views the painting, since logically the viewer should be the man engaged in a sexually charged encounter. An acrobat swinging above the stalls is conspicuous by her eclusion from the frame, only her legs being visible, and she may be seen as an alter ego for the barmaid in sober attire behind the safety of the counter. Manet's paintings, like music-hall, implicate the spectator in the work of art, and break down the stability of Cartesian representation. The illusory world of the stage may echo the mysterious nature of human emotions, but there is no mystery about the harsh social conditions of the time. Neither in painting nor in the theatre were classical rules of representation adequate to depict what was felt to be real.

Walter Sickert was an English Bohemian, much influenced by Manet, who tried in a sequence of paintings to capture the distinctive ambience of music-hall. Sickert was more interested than Manet in the performer, perhaps because he had spent three years of his youth as a professional actor. One of his most complex paintings is *Little Dot Hetherington at the Bedford Music Hall* (1888–9), (plate 13).[57] Everything apart from the empty stalls seats at the bottom of the picture is seen reflected in a mirror, so the spectators have no more materiality than the performer. Justifying his low-life subject matter, Sickert once recalled a moment in a small hall in Islington:

A graceful girl leaning forward from the stage, to accentuate the refrain of one of the sentimental ballads so dear to the frequenters of the halls, evoked a spontaneous movement of sympathy and attention in the audience whose sombre tones threw

Plate 12   Walter Sickert: *Little Dot Hetherington*. Preparatory drawing.

into more brilliant relief the animated movement of the singer, bathed as she was in a ray of green limelight from the centre of the roof, and below in the yellow radiance of the footlights.[58]

The intensity and momentariness of the audience's gaze inspired that of the impressionist artist. The dominant line of tension in the painting links the child star, lit by electricity not limelight, to the group of working-class men in the gallery lit by a chandelier. The child points up and sings 'The boy I love is up in the gallery', a song later made famous by Marie Lloyd. Sickert developed the image of these working men in the Bedford gallery in a series of paintings which contrast the opulence of the architecture with poverty of dress, vicarious affluence contributing to vicarious emotional satisfaction.[59] The expressionless, rapt attention of these men in the gallery communicates the power of the child performer, who merges innocence and knowing sexuality, the unattainability of her young innocence emphasized by rails in front of the stage. The chairman mediates between stage and auditorium, looking over his shoulder at the performance. The affluent in the stalls do not display the same overt emotion as the men in the gallery, and the presence of a woman's hat suggests that some can afford to purchase satisfaction afterwards. The view through a mirror, doubled by a second mirror image on the left, makes the performer look younger and more angelic, but also contributes to the self-effacement of the artist, who once declared to pupils: 'banish your own person, your life and that means you and your affections and yourself from your theatre'.[60] The sense of Sickert as an absent subject is reinforced by the empty chairs at the side of the stalls, the only solid reality not seen through a mirror. Sickert's own attitude to sexualized childhood is left in decent obscurity.

Mirrors in these impressionist paintings, as in *Las Meninas*, are a philosophical device. Mirrors played an important part in music-hall architecture, being placed around the walls, and in some cases also around the stage.[61] They not only expanded the space and removed its sense of material limitation, but also encouraged self-reflexivity in the spectators, who could catch glimpses of themselves performing social identities as they sauntered in the promenade. Mirrors emphasize the uncertain nature of the actor–audience divide. The strength of a solo performance lay in the way it allowed actor and role to merge, and the spectator to feel a personal bond with the personality on stage. The new capitalist world of mass production generated a craving for individual identity, and social inclusion. The neo-classical principle that the stage should be a framed mirror of society was no longer relevant in an age when social identities were homogenized in broad bands of class. In a mass society, music-hall satisfied a widely felt need to feel that one had a unique individual, embodied and localized existence, and this need could never be answered by Cartesian viewing in a realist theatre. Going to music-hall was, as Foucault might have put it, a *techne* of the self, a mode of forming and performing identity.

Thirty years later, Sickert would lament the disappearance of 'the dear old oblong Bedford, with its sliding roof, in the "days beyond recall", before the music-halls had become two-house-a-night wells, like theatres to look at'.[62] In his old age he did three paintings of the Plaza Tiller Girls, whose regimented legs epitomized the new production-line world of 'variety'. Managers like Stoll and Moss controlled chains of theatres, and offered lavish spectacle to the passive gaze as an alternative to the cheaper spectacle of cinema. The wide stage designed for choral compositions no longer served as the frame for vulnerable solo performers who apparently sought to escape their isolation on stage in the companionship of the audience. A darkened auditorium, sealed off from the bar and promenade, created a safe environment for family units to view the performance, not forced to interact either with others. The poor were obliged to peer into a well, isolated from the affluence that lay behind the stage curtain. A sliding roof was no longer required to remove the stench of men's tobacco. A place of social encounter had become a place for spectating.

In France, the *café-concert* was liberated in 1863, when the prohibition on anything beyond songs sung in evening dress was lifted, and the repressive monopoly of 'theatre' was ended.[63] Here and elsewhere on the continent, the artistic community at the end of the century helped to steer many of these cafés towards cabaret, driven by the anti-realist aesthetic that drew Sickert to music-hall. The attraction of 'variety' in the social environment of the café was the possibility of bringing together the different art forms: poetry, painting, puppetry, jazz and other forms of music, dance and theatre. Dada is the most famous artistic movement to have emerged in the cabaret environment.[64] In Britain the class associations of the public house were too strong, and bohemians could not so easily step off the boulevard into the café. The synthesis of performance, eating and drinking flourished best in the male-dominated world of working-men's clubs, until de-industrialization in the second half of the twentieth century slowly changed the British social structure. By the 1930s the male performer had replaced the female performers of music-hall, and comic patter had replaced song as the major component in sympotic performance.[65] Controls on soliciting went hand in hand with a new tolerance of female nudity, and the strip club was another sympotic form available to satisfy the male eye,[66] whilst the stand-up comic articulated in language working-class male frustrations. The skill of the music-hall artiste lay in creating ambiguities around the level of her sexual knowledge. When she became free to reveal her body in public, the same tensions could no longer be exploited.

The birth of the Comedy Store in 1979 was an important milestone, launching a classless American-style 'alternative' comedy in London as heir apparent to a declining club culture centred in the industrial north.[67] The Banana Cabaret in London is a representative example, and will serve to illustrate the present state of the classical divide between theatre and symposium. The 'cabaret' is located in a converted circular dance hall that once opened onto the main bar of the Bedford Arms public house in Balham. The area was once a noted red-light district, and the sleazy associations of the area add to the appeal for a young upwardly mobile audience. The audience sit at tables, crowd the walls, or peer down from the gallery. Four comedians perform in an evening, the most experienced taking the longest final slot. There is no raised stage and the role of the compère is minimal, because the focus of the circular space is so intense that such aids to attention are unneeded. The performer stands on the edge of the circle, and faces the ground-floor bar with lights, microphone and a painted rear wall to focus attention on him. Food is available upstairs beside the gallery bar. People eat, drink and smoke as they watch the comedian.

The intensity and energy of the communication in this space is linked to crowding and the close proximity of bodies.[68] This intimacy is possible because the Theatres Act of 1968 (which refers to the 'playing of a role' as the criterion of a 'dramatic piece') does not apply, so there is no regulation of aisles, spacing and gangways with glowing emergency exit signs. The Cabaret has a public entertainment licence because the comedy turns are followed by a disco, and this does impose some ceiling on numbers. If there were no dancing involved, the Bedford's liquor licence (under the Licensing Act of 1964) would allow one or two performers at a time to do comedy turns without anything but the most rudimentary health and safety considerations.[69] A social ambience is created that can never be achieved in a 'theatre', and this does much to draw in the audience. The great divide established in 1843 remains, in a modified form, fundamental to the way modern performance culture is organized. The law becomes an immovable force that perpetuates time-honoured practices, the price of safety in the high-status milieu of 'theatre' being a certain sterilization.

Whilst the audience is of both sexes, the comedians at the Banana Cabaret are usually male – though the number of women is increasing. This tendency relates partly to male logocentricity, and partly, as in Covent Garden, to the projection of the grotesque body. The comedian presents a version of his own inadequacies and frustrations in order to reassure the spectators that their lives are better. The comedians wear informal, everyday wear to signify their authenticity, the fact that they are presenting self and not a theatrical role. The absence of spectacle in the form of costumes, elaborate props or scenic decoration assures the audience that they are watching truth, not the artifice of theatre. The acts all depend upon interaction, and the creation of fellowship. An important ritual consists in asking spectators where they come from, identifying and absorbing visitors and occasional foreigners within an ethnically homogeneous audience. Collective laughter both creates and depends upon a shared recognition of and empathy with emotions described. Resisting the comedian and waiting for him to win them over is part of the audience's pleasure. The actor will often insult the audience, welding them into a group set against him, the better to win them over.

Sitting at tables is crucial to the quality of this interaction, for the table allows couples and groups to acknowledge their responses to each other, and to choose whether they will give the audience their gaze, or look away in embarrassment or boredom. Smoking, no longer a marker of gender, more a defiance of the new puritanism, contributes to the relaxation of many, albeit the discomfort of some. Food can be eaten because there is no pressure on the audience to construct their bodies as beautiful in this anti-aesthetic environment. Heckling charges the atmosphere, but also endangers the performer if he fails to assert control. The danger risked by the comedian is much like the danger of the acrobat, his problems exacerbated by the fact that under stage lighting he can only see the faces of the front row, though the audience can all see each other. The founder of the Comedy Store favoured the analogy of 'Christians versus the lions'.[70] The fact that the Bedford Arms is a public house and not a theatre allows the audience to feel that they are going for relaxation and recreation, not for improvement. The rhythm of the evening, with the jokes becoming more personal and sexually explicit, is bound up with the rhythm of drinking, and the lowering of defences.

I shall describe a typical evening in 2001 in order to suggest how the event is shaped.[71] The first act was a Glaswegian, defining the audience as a community by his geographical otherness. His high-energy act took the audience on a journey through the London underground and onto an aircraft; these journeys evoked a shared area of experience, but also reminded spectators of the journeys that had brought each of them to this special space of performance. The second act was surreal, and could afford to be less intense now the audience had relaxed. The comedian's persona was highly educated, placing him as the social equal of the audience. Ineffectual jokes allowed the audience the pleasure of mockery. The third act, after the interval, was the shortest – a try-out slot for a beginner, who adopted a combative teenage persona. The fourth and major act was given by a black American from Atlanta. He was able to create stillness, following the very mobile performances by the earlier acts, and succeeded in creating concentration on every word, with an audible response following every utterance – the two-way communication found so rarely in the regimented institution of modern 'theatre'. He began by placing himself as an American, dealing with complex British emotions about being led by America into a war with Afghanistan. The cabaret was presented as a place where truth could be told and feelings of mistrust shared. He dealt next with race, and genially encouraged the audience to call him a 'nigger'. He then moved on to sexual encounters, dealing with different male and female attitudes to guilt, completing a kind of collective therapy. His last anecdote turned on whether he was a comedian or philosopher.

If the fare in music-hall was more varied, that may reflect the greater social diversity of the Victorian audience. The division of modern society into fragments, defined by sexual orientation and ethnicity as well as age, education and profession, requires each fragment to express its own recreational preferences, which perforce limits diversity within any single consumer choice. The potency of sympotic performance is undiminished, although (and perhaps because) it is not vested with cultural prestige in the form of state subsidy, and academic and journalistic attention. The Plutarchan aesthetic remains a latent cultural force, as it has been since antiquity, with little recognition of its deep historical continuities.

CHAPTER 6

The cosmic circle

The western dramatic tradition differs from the eastern in the passion it displays for the circle. The creators of the notorious Millennium Dome in London, for example, chose to set a circular performance space at the centre of a structure intended to embody in microcosm a unified and idealized Britain, and this space within a space fused the idea of the piazza with that of the circus.[1] The designers fell back on the Greek form of the circle for lack of any more compelling symbolism rooted in the present. The performance traditions of the east, on the other hand, are mostly governed by the square, its orientation marked by the four points of the compass. In the *Natya Sastra,* as we saw in chapter 2, the four directions correspond with particular castes, colours and deities, and complex rituals govern the embedding of the theatre in the earth, allowing the classical Indian theatre to represent and embody in microcosm the order of the universe. The Japanese Noh stage is bound by a similar logic. The stage faces south, which is the direction of the red phoenix, of the fire god and of summer; the west belongs to the white tiger, to the god of harvest and to the autumn. The ghostly figure represented by the *shite* is not new-born but returns from death, and thus naturally enters from the west.[2] The use of cardinal points ties the spatial order indissolubly to the temporal order. The siting of the Dome on the Greenwich meridian attempted a similar force, but the time-line, a product of the imperial past, had little contemporary resonance. My subject in this chapter will be the historical devotion of western culture to circular playing spaces, which symbolically unify and centre the world. The mystique of the circle stems from the Greek and in some small part from the Celtic tradition, but owes nothing to the Jewish inheritance. St John in the *Apocalypse,* like the prophet Ezekiel, envisages a heavenly Jerusalem that is square with four equal sides.[3]

The Swedish designer Per Edström begins a manifesto for 'arena theatre' by observing that people form a circle when engaged in an important de-bate, and gather on all sides round a fight; they define a narrow angle when listening to and watching a monologue, but the angle widens when several actors play in front of a picture.[4] Irrespective of symbolism, a certain physical logic thus governs theatrical form. Speeches generate frontality, whilst interaction and displays of physical action generate circularity. Western theatre has always had to negotiate these opposing impulses. At the time of writing, I have just returned from seeing a production of Aristophanes' *The Birds* performed by a group of circus artistes on trapezes before a frontal auditorium of the National Theatre in London.[5] The flying routines were impressive as spectacle, and the critique of American imperialism was clear as message, but the possibility of interaction was removed by the lack of an encircling audience. To recover a Greek spatial relationship combining physicality with narrative, concelebration with political statement, is an elusive El Dorado for many modern practitioners.

The early French structuralist Etienne Souriau in a lecture of 1948 found the essence of theatre in the antinomy of sphere and cube. In different periods of theatre history, he found, one or the other tends to be dominant. It is part of the human condition, he argued, to be both in the world – within the sphere – and confronting the world – seeing through the missing wall of a cube. He elaborated on the principle of the sphere:

No stage, no auditorium, no boundaries. Rather than section off a fixed fragment of the world you have decided to construct, you must find its dynamic centre, its beating heart . . . The group of actors who incarnate this heart, this *punctum saliens*, this dynamic centre of the play's universe are officiants, magicians, and when they exert their power no boundaries exist . . . They are the centre and the circumference is nowhere – forced to recede into infinity, absorbing the spectators themselves, catching them within the unbounded sphere.[6]

Souriau's tension between cube and sphere offers a simplified way of understanding the tension between *scaena* and orchestra in the classical theatre, or stage and circular auditorium in the Elizabethan theatre. The *théâtre à l'italienne*, the dominant European form from the seventeenth until the nineteenth century, draws on the principle of the cube for the perspectival or pictorial setting behind the proscenium, but retains the principle of the sphere for the auditorium. By the mid twentieth century the principle of the cube had also overwhelmed the auditorium, prompting Souriau to reassert the values of the sphere. Much modern rhetoric about the evils of 'proscenium theatre' ignores the auditorium. Peter Brook's conversion of the Bouffes du Nord illustrates the ease with which the latent sphericity of a *théâtre à l'italienne* built for music-hall can be recaptured. All he needed to do was to raise the floor of the stalls and push the stage forward.

The music-hall audience wanted its own social encounters, stimulated by the performance, to be the beating heart, the *punctum saliens*, but the late twentieth-century audience preferred Brook's work of art to take priority. In my final chapter I shall pursue the issues raised by Brook's theatre.

Souriau diverged from classical antiquity in denying his circular space a visible circumference. He envisaged a theatre where the actors were lit whilst the boundaries of the auditorium were shrouded in darkness, echoing the thinking of his age about a boundless cosmos. Souriau's lecture was chaired by André Villiers, who was a prime mover and intellectual apologist for the Théâtre en Rond in Paris in 1954. A year later Stephen Joseph launched his 'Theatre-in-the-Round' in Scarborough, both having been influenced by experiments in the democratically minded USA, where eighty-two arena theatres could be counted in 1950.[7] Whilst the French theatre-in-the-round had a circular playing space, Joseph maintained vigorously that 'theatre-in-the-round' should actually be rectangular. Post-war French intellectuals were soaked in classicism in a way that the English were not. Villiers begins his manifesto by denying that promoters of theatre-in-the-round were concerned with Platonist metaphysics, arguing that tradition rather than symbolism has led him to the circle. He reiterates the claim that a circular space allows one to rediscover 'the circle of society'. Joseph, in his more pragmatic manifesto, castigates the circle on two practical grounds. First is focus. He argues that the circle is not vectored and has but a single strong point, namely the centre, which makes it a less interesting space to play in. He makes an analogy with the interior of a lighthouse, saying that lighthouse-keepers are known to go mad because they have no point of orientation. Secondly, he remarks that the circle is unsympathetic to the spaces which plays most commonly represent: rooms, roads, fields and so forth.[8]

Villiers, and the republican French tradition that lay behind him, were interested in the social relationships which theatre engenders, while Joseph was concerned with the world that is represented. Joseph's rectangular theatre 'in the round' did much to inspire the dramaturgy of Alan Ayckbourn, in whose comedies a regular domestic setting is complicated by the refusal of a single point of view. The real/unreal tension in his plays relates to a particular performance challenge: actors inhabit a room without the artifice of facing front, yet the audience have a heightened sense of artifice because they face each other. The potential of the circular form was not realized in Britain until 1976 when a tent-like module was created inside Manchester's huge Royal Cotton Exchange. The rhetoric of the founder, Michael Elliott, was closer to Villiers than Joseph. He spoke of theatre being a

"He doesn't like theatre-in-the-round."

Plate 14 Cartoon by Ionicus (1977).

'happening', and declared that 'we want the theatre to be rooted in a community, and serve it, not open the doors to the endless anonymous mass that is London'.[9] The Royal Exchange has thriven on an epic repertory, where Joseph's strictures about rooms, roads and fields are irrelevant. Yet none of these three theatres, in Paris, Manchester and Scarborough, has generated the wave of imitations that their founders hoped. Ionicus' cartoon (plate 14) reflects a widespread traditionalist response to theatres like the Exchange. These remain curiosities with local appeal in a world that has internalized a different mode of seeing. In order to understand the modern mode of seeing, we have first to recognize the differentness of the ancient.

Plato's *Timaeus* was a kind of Bible for the Graeco-Roman world, medieval Christendom and the renaissance. Plato's account of a single benevolent creator, who privileged soul over body, provided a vision of the universe that merged seamlessly into Christianity, and his spherical cosmos remained a compelling visualization as long as the earth was held to be the centre of the universe. There were areas of disagreement in antiquity. Though the Epicureans insisted that the earth was flat, the general principle that the earth stood at the centre of a circular universe roofed by concentric spheres was universally granted in antiquity. Around Plato's spherical earth, seven translucent rotating spheres supported the sun, moon and five other planets. Outside these seven, another sphere supporting the fixed stars rotated in the opposite direction (see plate 1). The *Timaeus* maps a structural correspondence between macrocosm and microcosm. The universe is described as a kind of body, and the body is a miniature version of the universe. The numberless fixed stars are human souls before and after their life on earth. Plato's other works establish a correspondence between the threefold order of human society and the tripartite human body, which located the highest part of the soul in the 'sphere' of the head, the passions in the heart and appetite in the belly. Of most direct relevance to the theatre in *Timaeus* is Plato's description of planetary movement as a chorus, an idea which astrological commentators like Ptolemy and Macrobius would extend.[10] The new cosmology of Copernicus and Galileo tore the foundations from this integrated intellectual system. The rotating circle could no longer be a key to understanding the universe, and astrology lost its intellectual credibility. The new Cartesian mode of viewing lent itself to the principle of the cube. However, in the late nineteenth century, the collapse of scientific rationalism and the possibility of political revolution caused a new interest in the circle to emerge. When Wilhelm Dörpfeld at the end of the nineteenth century excavated the Theatre of Dionysus in Athens and discovered, behind the Romanized semicircular orchestra, an arc of stones suggesting a circular form for the original orchestra, it became possible to rewrite theatre history. The true theatre of antiquity could now be understood as a ritual space around which the community gathered, and not as a Wagnerian space of frontal display.

Plato's cosmic circle was indebted to the astral religion of the Egyptians, to the mystical mathematics of the Pythagoreans, and to the astrology of the Babylonians. Herodotus described Ecbatana, capital city of the Medes, as a microcosm where seven concentric rings of fortification, each coded with a different colour, protected the king at the centre.[11] Plato's circle also has roots in the Homeric world.[12] The earliest Greek geographers conceived of the inhabited earth as a circular land mass surrounded by ocean. Thus in Aeschylus' *Prometheus*, the hero stands chained to a rock on the northern perimeter of the earth, and the god who personifies Ocean rides round the perimeter of the acting space on a chariot pulled by some sort of aquatic horse. The circularity of the early Athenian theatre space must in the first instance derive from its use for the dithyramb, a circular dance for fifty people.[13] Dancing in a circle round an altar was a standard ritual practice. The introduction of a stage building in the *Oresteia* gave a new frontality to the performance, and introduced a new focal point before the door. Aeschylus' plays had a chorus of twelve, a cosmic number related to the hours of the day and the signs of the zodiac, which is to say the months of the year, correlating therefore with the rotational cycle of the sun. The choruses of Sophocles and Euripides numbered fifteen, forming a rectangle three deep and five wide.[14] The change of number relates to the new rectilinearity imparted by a lateral stage wall (see figure 2), and a gradual relinquishment of cosmic concerns.

The circular auditoria of the Hellenistic world were not only intended for tragedy and comedy, but were in most instances also places of political assembly, and thus embodiments of the social structure. In *Tragedy in Athens* I examined Megalopolis, capital of the Arcadian federation, a new model city built in the mid fourth century BC. Here a wooden stage building was laid across the floor of the circular orchestra, allowing the dithyrambic circle to be converted into a more frontal performance space for tragedy and comedy. Inscriptions on the seats indicate that different wedges or segments were allocated to different tribes, and it is likely that the central wedge, as in Athens, was used for serving office-holders drawn from all the different tribes. Epidaurus, built a generation or more later, is located in a shrine to the god of healing. Here there was no city to assemble, only visitors from across the Greek world. The stage building is set further back, and the dancing circle fixed by a stone border and a *thymele* (sacred stone) in the centre. The architecture is governed by Pythagorean mathematics to create a space of perfect geometric harmony. The singing of paeans to Apollo was probably a more important ritual in this space, with its emphatic focus on the orchestra, than the performance of tragedy and comedy.[15] Whilst Megalopolis embodies the order of the *polis*, Epidaurus embodies the order of the cosmos. The difference is one of emphasis: the former symbolizes the bonding of the merged Arcadian cities, the latter symbolizes the healing that stems from harmony of mind, body and environment. The political space, geared in the first instance to the speaker, is more frontal than the ritual space geared to the dancing chorus.

Wagner set the pattern for the twentieth century in idealizing the Greek auditorium, which he saw as the antithesis of the elitist, stratified and ugly theatres of his day. In a pair of essays published in the wake of the 1848 European uprisings, he located the origins of tragedy in the 'spirit of community' which had sadly 'split itself along a thousand lines of egoistic cleavage'. A new approach to theatre design was needed because 'no architect in the world will be able to raise our stratified and fenced-off auditoria – dictated by the parcelling of our public into the most diverse categories of class and civil station – to conformity with any law of beauty'. The Greek ideal of 'community' for Wagner shaded into the idea of 'communion' with Dionysus, an experience which supposedly allowed the collectivized audience 'in noblest, stillest peace to live again the life which a brief space of time before, they had lived in restless activity and accentuated individuality.'[16] In early nineteenth-century Germany the prevailing view of Greek tragedy held it to be characterized by serenity, repose and calm grandeur, just like the Parthenon frieze. Wagner's ideal of a communitarian auditorium was realized in the Bayreuth Opera House of 1876, which has been described as 'the beginnings of contemporary theater design' (fig. 26).[17] The paradox of Bayreuth is obvious, a traditional baroque stage coupled to an innovative Greek-style auditorium. Complete with its royal box, added to satisfy the monarch who funded the enterprise, Bayreuth was and is an elite environment, the preserve of a group that shares Wagner's aesthetic. Wagner's idealization of the German *Volk*, dissolving class differences in an image of national unity, has in retrospect some painful political implications. His ideal audience seems to have been disciplined into silence by the aestheticism of the elite.[18] When Greece became the ideal for Wagner and many intellectuals of his day, Roman theatre had to be cast as the negative antithesis of Hellenic perfection. 'The brutal Romans,' Wagner declared, 'wallowed in realism, not imagination.'[19] Adolphe Appia rejected Wagner's pictorialism in order to stage his operas in a manner that emphasized the human body.

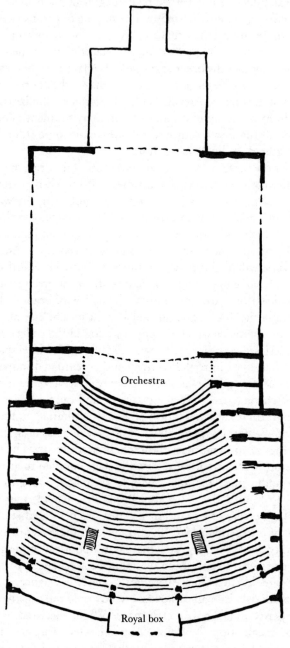

Figure 26   Bayreuth.

It was the Greeks, Appia maintained, who began with the living human body, while the Romans fashioned their theatres 'with the fundamental triviality of the Latin race'.[20]

Wagnerian principles shape the Olivier auditorium in Britain's National Theatre, where as in Bayreuth a Greek-style fan is moderated to become a frontalized and controlling space, where the actors can command the audience and never feel that someone is viewing them from behind. Peter Hall, for long the artistic director of the National Theatre, like Wagner idealizes the 'perfect simple geometry' of Greek theatre, specifically Epidaurus, and he condemns the Roman theatre (citing the theatre of Herodes Atticus in Athens) as a 'brutal confrontation' where spectators look down on 'their victims'.[21] Richard Negri, designer of the Royal Exchange, shares the same rhetoric, rejecting the 'standard proscenium arch as a Roman aberration. For him, the great ages of the theatre were in Ancient Greek and Elizabethan times, when the actors were right out in front and little or no scenery was used'.[22] Theatre history at this point dissolves into theatre myth.

Not all theatre designers echo this idealization of Hellas. Iain Mackintosh in *Architecture, Actor and Audience* declares himself deeply disillusioned by the cosmic pretensions of the Olivier Theatre, a space which suits a very limited repertoire, and he champions the intimate Georgian theatre as a model for the present. He wants attention given to the vertical dimension in the auditorium, and a pricing structure that will bring a socially diverse group into an auditorium that does not conceal social difference. He also argues for the importance of 'sacred geometry', which uses classical ratios to mark out the relationship between the two spaces of actor and audience, and thereby create a strong site of interaction.[23] Roman theatre has no place in his analysis, presumably because the Wagnerian tradition has dismissed it with such scorn, yet at every turn he is arguing for a Roman set of priorities in the auditorium: a steeper rake, mapping the social hierarchy, decoration for sensory stimulation, wrapping the stage, with absolute priority given to geometry.

The Elizabethans themselves had a very different perception of theatre history. Thomas Heywood, who brought epic treatments of Greek myth to the Jacobean stage, traced the origins of the Elizabethan theatre back to Rome. Rome is the site of the earliest theatre that he mentions, a circular theatre built of earth that reminds us of Celtic hill-forts. Here, in the time of Romulus, Sabine women came to be admired, and were assaulted by Roman males. Ovid's narrative is used to legitimize the symbiotic relationship of theatres and brothels that characterized Elizabethan and Jacobean London. A certain Dionysius, declares Heywood, built a semicircular open-air

Plate 15   Isaac Cruikshank: 'Old price' riots at Covent Garden (1809). Cartoon.

stone theatre in Athens, with a stage for good visibility. The Romans put
a roof over theatres, and Pompey expanded capacity to 80,000 (echoes
of Pliny). Caesar responded by building an 'amphitheatre' (presumably
the Colosseum) equipped with fine marble columns. Over the stage was an
astrological ceiling with mobile parts – a description that recalls a celebrated
ceiling possessed by Lord Burghley.[24] The emperor and officiating senators
have seats in the gallery, but otherwise all the 'rooms' are free of access to the
plebs. Later Romans created spaces called circuses with 'the frame globe-like
and perfectly round', which doubled as spaces for jousting and gladiatorial
combat. These circular spaces are presented as the direct ancestor of the
Elizabethan playhouse. Heywood's narrative is teleological, building up to
his own perfect cosmic form where theatre architecture presents 'the world'

> As by the roundness it appears most fit,
> Built with star galleries of high ascent
> In which Jehove doth as spectator sit . . .[25]

It is easy to dismiss Heywood's narrative as one that falls short of modern
historiographic standards – but in dismissing him we should not forget
that the modern world too shapes theatre history to fit modern requirements. The cosmic aspect of Roman theatre, which seemed so important
to Heywood, has been written out of modern narratives centred on the
issue of democracy. The architectural overlap in Rome between spaces of
combat and spaces of dramatic performance, which seems abhorrent to the
modern world, was taken by Heywood as a matter of course. The clown
Tarlton, for example, became the queen's master of fence. The lord mayor
of London in 1583 made a sweeping complaint about the theatres that would
be used by Shakespeare a decade later, lamenting 'the assembly of people
to plays, bear-baiting, fencers, and profane spectacles at the Theatre and
Curtain'.[26] Bear-baiting was seen to descend from the Roman *venatio* in
the arena, and prize-fighting from gladiators, just as drama descended from
ancient tragedy. In Heywood's world, baiting, fighting and stage-plays were
equivalent in status, ennobled by the same classically inspired architectural
form.[27]

The Roman ideal was still in play at the start of the nineteenth century when rioters at Covent Garden refused to let Kemble's new pricing
structure change the social dynamics of the playhouse (plate 15). When the
rioters presented theatre-going as an Englishman's constitutional right, the
basis for their claims lay unmistakably in Cicero. Cicero was the paradigmatic wise and ethical politician at the start of the nineteenth century,
and his friend Roscius the paradigmatic actor. The Roman constitution,

with its mixture of monarchical, aristocratic and democratic elements, was the model for the British polity.[28] Cicero maintained that the opinion of the Roman People was manifested in three environments: the meeting, the assembly and the games, but that the games were much the best indicator. Here the audience was representative, which is to say less easily gerrymandered, and any attempt to manipulate public responses through the employment of claques was transparent.[29] During his exile from Rome, Cicero was deeply concerned about the way the public responded to him and his enemies. He seems to have found broad support from theatre audiences, partly because he consorted with actors skilled in manipulating their material, partly because at festival time more conservatively minded Romans from the countryside entered the city. Whatever the true representativeness of the theatre audience, Cicero leaves us in no doubt that the theatre and gladiatorial games were pivotal in the functioning of the political system.[30] We should avoid the modern cliché which declares that Greek theatre was democratic, Roman theatre was not, for Roman auditoria played a vital role in articulating the voice of the people.

The Roman political system did not tolerate the Greek notion of seated assembly-places where the whole citizen body could listen to complex debates, and vote upon policy. This was a major reason why theatres in the republic were temporary structures, erected for the duration of a festival.[31] These temporary theatres were the only place where Roman citizens could sit and contemplate themselves and their leaders as a corporate body. Senators sat on the perimeter of the orchestra, not unlike priests and ambassadors in the Greek theatre. This position on the one hand defined their pre-eminent status, but on the other turned them into performers and exposed them to the potential hostility of the crowd towering above them. Facing the stage, senators could not control the crowd through the power of the gaze, and they had to be content to let wreathes of honour on their heads bespeak their authority. Because they sat in the orchestra, senators had to make a formal entry from the side, much like actors, and this exposed them to whistles or applause, responses that could in no way be disciplined. Cicero speaks of hands stretched out and tears when his ally arrived, curses, fists and shouts when his rival walked in.[32] It was in the collective interest of the elite to provide engrossing entertainments and a spectacular environment, and so to win the hearts of the people – but in the late republic the elite did not function as a collective.

During a Roman theatre performance, audience responses could reflect on nobles in the orchestra. Cicero describes how actors in a comedy leant towards his enemy and urged him to kill himself, causing the senator to walk out in a state of shock, made suddenly aware of the popular mood. In another performance, the actor Aesopus played Eurysaces, who laments the fact that his father Ajax has been banished from the Greek army. Cicero was identified with Ajax, by virtue of the catch phrase that named him 'father of the People'. The audience applauded the writer, the emotions displayed by the actor, and the imminent prospect of Cicero's recall from exile. Aesopus was a friend of Cicero, and manipulated the text, adding lines from elsewhere to point up topicality. He addressed the audience as if they were themselves the Greek army guilty of banishing Ajax. Cicero gives us a vivid sense of the audience's line-by-line reactions to the text, expressed through applause, encores and tearful lamentations. This was an interactive performance, where the emotions of the crowd swept up Cicero's opponents as well as his friends.[33] The performance unfolded as an encounter between the actors on stage and senatorial performers present or conspicuously absent from the orchestra. The front line of the stage bisected an imaginary circle that embraced both contemporary politicians and figures from Greek myth. The audience on the seats above savoured the relationship.

It was a basic republican principle that office-holding was temporary, and this was another reason why the theatres of the Roman republic were temporary structures, reflecting glory on the elected office-holders who built them and hosted 'games' inside them. Permanent theatres were built by men who sought life-long power, and immortalization in the public memory. Pompey had every reason to understand the importance of theatre. Cicero tells us that Pompey the Great used to be applauded vociferously, but in 59 BC was derided: the line 'By our misery are you *Great*' received a dozen encores. Years later the tide turned and the theatre audience called for peace, when Antony and Augustus (Octavius as he was then called) had driven Pompey from Rome and sat on their thrones in the orchestra.[34] It was the collapse of republican ideals that allowed Pompey to build a stone theatre. We saw in chapter 4 how the Forum Romanum was the most symbolically resonant performance space in the city. Pompey, the outsider adopted by the plebs, built not merely a theatre but an alternative to the Forum Romanum, a new urban focus outside the old city centre that would embody new values (fig. 27).[35] His architectural complex embraced a gigantic semicircular auditorium topped by a temple to Venus at the west end, and a new Senate House at the east end dominated by a statue of himself, most probably holding a globe in his hand to symbolize his conquest of the world. Between them gardens were laid out in arcades with Grecian statues, and at the sides the under-spaces were filled by shops. As we saw in

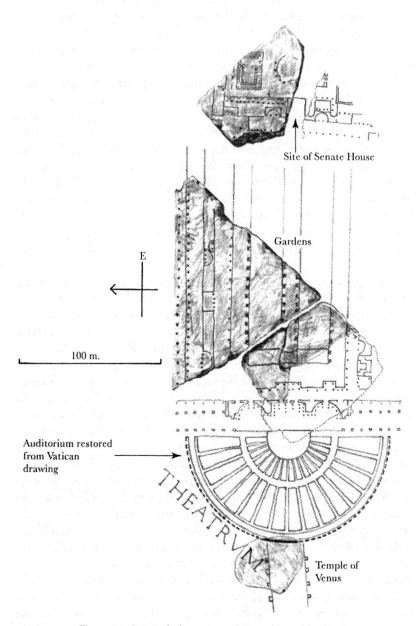

Site of Senate House

Gardens

E

100 m.

Auditorium restored
from Vatican
drawing

THEATRVM

Temple of
Venus

Figure 27   Pompey's theatre according to the marble plan.

chapter 2, the original stage wall may have been a wooden structure, creating better acoustics than the later stone façade, and capable of being removed to create a single unified microcosm of Rome. As an alternative to the bustling, gladiatorial, riot-inducing Forum Romanum, Pompey provided the people with a tranquil park, which trees, fountains and female statues made into an urban utopia. Somewhere in the complex stood statues personifying the fourteen nations (seven on each side – the magic planetary number) that Rome had conquered. Built with the loot, this was to be the symbolic and honorific centre of the Roman empire.

Augustus had other ideas. He moved the seat of the Senate back to the Forum and moved Pompey's statue to the theatrical end of the park. Pompey's theatre was now twinned with a pleasure garden, and separated from the centre of power. It was to be a space where people would come not to practise politics but to enjoy leisure in what we might term the world's first arts centre. Augustus meanwhile built his own theatre with an even larger capacity, on ground which Caesar had cleared in order to put a theatre below the Capitol.[36] Masks above the archways announced that this was to be a space for Greek-style drama, not for political triumphalism. At the great Ludi Saeclorum that ushered in Augustus' golden age, plays in Greek were given in the two stone theatres, identifying them as cultural rather than political spaces.[37] In Pompey's theatre the logic of the stage wall was to serve as backdrop to his own triumphal procession.[38] Augustus' theatre appears from the marble plan to have been much closer to a Greek theatre in its conception. The lines of the semicircular auditorium in many cases extend across the line of the stage, and in wrapping the stage the auditorium created a better focus for the actor. The stage wall is shown to be flat, making it suitable for Greek-style scene-painting as well as embedding decorative materials. The seating on the side of the stage must have been reserved for groups like the vestal virgins and praetorian guard. It has been plausibly suggested on the basis of the marble plan that the theatre was convertible, with a removable stage and stage wall allowing the space to be converted into an arena.[39] What seems clear is that Augustus rejected some of Pompey's processional monumentality in favour of a more centred space that worked better for the theatrical performer. It may also have served the performance given by a hunter of wild beasts.

Augustus' political agenda was different from that of Caesar and Pompey. Securely established as an emperor and god, he used the theatre to certify that he was also a man of the people in the best Grecian and republican tradition. He did not name his theatre after himself, but was more discreetly dynastic, dedicating it to his deceased nephew and heir apparent

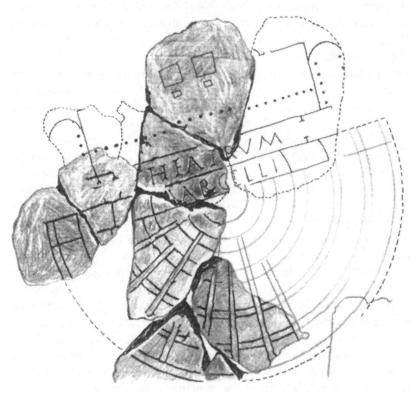

Figure 28   Theatre of Marcellus according to the marble plan.

Marcellus, whose golden image sat on a throne in the orchestra. If Augustus sat modestly on the right hand side of the statue, he would have sat on the axis line leading to Apollo's temple.[40]

The marble plan shows that the Augustan auditorium was more complex than surviving Roman theatres, and the multiple lines suggest some five concentric (or nearly concentric) rings of seating echoing the circuit of the planets (fig. 28). Augustus' primary interest lay in structuring the audience, and his architectural project was linked to a scheme to order the unruly audience, using space to instil a new morality based on the equation of his political order with the cosmic order. There had been much ill-feeling in Plautus' day when senators were placed in the orchestra, and in the late republic when the first fourteen rows were reserved for the equestrian class. Augustus attempted a comprehensive further structuring of the auditorium in defiance of the libertarianism that had always governed behaviour in the theatre. Men honoured with the civic crown sat behind the senators, displaying their prestige to those above. The orchestral area was purified of potential ex-slaves who might once have come as ambassadors. Women were separated from their husbands and consigned to the back. Only the vestal virgins remained towards the front, seated under the watchful eye of the praetor who sat above a side entrance charged with discipline. Roman boys sat in one wedge like Greek ephebes, their tutors in the adjacent wedge. Separate areas honoured those who fought as soldiers, and those who had helped reproduce the city by taking wives. The colour-coding of Roman costume made this scheme workable and eloquent. Senators had broad purple bands on their togas, knights had narrow bands. The Roman males in the central band of the theatre were required to wear their white togas, and anyone who was not entitled to a toga or could not afford one sat at the back. The semicircular auditorium was the ideal place to display a perfectly ordered society.[41] Gladiator-fights in the Forum and chariot-races in the Circus were covered by the same legislation.

How far this attempt at social engineering was transformed into reality we do not know, but we hear of some defiance. Augustus was mobbed for having a soldier killed in the Circus for presuming to sit amongst the knights. Against Augustus' championship of marriage we must set Ovid's account of amorous encounters at the theatre and the Circus. In Ovid's poems, couples are forced into body contact, and inspired by the eroticism of the dramatic performance, and the youth who wants to avoid the temptation of prostitutes is advised to sit in the front row. We can also read Horace's elitist diatribe, complaining of how the plebs in the public Augustan theatre may call for a bear, or boxers, or engage in a slanging-match with the knights. Horace evokes the terrifying boom of many thousand voices, likening it to the sea, or wind amidst trees exposed on a promontory. He himself preferred to write for a reader, but had some grudging admiration for the 'tightrope walker' or 'magician' who could transport the audience to Thebes or Athens, and then wring, enrage, melt and terrify the collective audience.[42] Taming this audience was thus no easy task. Augustus' measures would have challenged the power of the senatorial elite by making it harder for them to pack parts of the theatre with clients acting as claques. Whatever the success of Augustus' reforms, one thing is clear: the Roman imperial auditorium was a space for collective self-contemplation, and was socially patterned in complex ways. As in Greece, so in Rome a formal tribal structure may have been one element in this patterning. Our most nuanced picture of actual audience composition comes later from the Graeco-Roman theatre of Aphrodisias in Asia Minor, where membership of different associations – associated with public office, trade guilds, locality of residence or in the case of Jews ethnicity – entailed entitlement to specific seats in the theatre. In the late empire, when other aspects of the urban social structure started to break down, the 'factions' became an important empire-wide identity group. Thus in Aphrodisias, the north end of the auditorium belonged to the 'greens', clearly identifiable through their green jackets.[43]

The Roman semicircle had a double force. On the one hand, it was a symbol of unison, on the other it was a structured space where individuals could perform their social identity and assert the views of their class. The threefold banding of the *cavea* or auditorium, with the first fourteen rows reserved for the knights, the mid level for citizens in white togas, and the upper seats for slaves, freedmen, foreigners, paupers, women and the rest, corresponded with the three tiers of columns that shaped the stage wall and the external façade of the building. The conception corresponds with the tripartite social structure of Plato's *Republic*, and the tripartite soul of the *Timaeus*. The Augustan regulation of the auditorium was not so much an attempt to silence the audience as to channel its expressivity, for the theatre and other spectacles remained the principal way in which the Roman people could express their views to the emperor. Our historical sources emphasize contention, but approving applause was probably the norm. The system of acclamations was increasingly formalized, with a chorus leader amidst the audience chanting a message, and the group around him repeating. One substantial text survives from the Byzantine Circus: a dialogue between the Blue faction, the Green faction and the emperor's herald. A clear difference can be discerned between the metrical regularity of the prepared text, and the looser rhythm of impromptu replies.[44] This script, archived for its political importance, indicates more vividly than any other document the extent to which the Roman auditorium was a performance space.

Augustan theatre architecture encouraged a new mode of performance. The Theatre of Marcellus belonged to Apollo, who was patron of pantomime. The 'pantomime' transformed Greek tragedy into a dance for a solo masked performer supported by instrumentation and choral singing. 'Tragedy' meanwhile became a solo form in which the actor did not dance but sing. In either form, the challenge to dominate the theatre when performing against a monumental stage wall adorned with rich columns and statues was a call to heroism. The magnificence of the stage wall invoked both the power of the emperor, whose insignia appeared upon it, and the might of the cosmos. Gilles Sauron describes pantomime as a dialogue, performed in comic or pathetic mode, between the architecture of the Golden Age and an individual representative of fallen mankind.[45]

The verticality of the Augustan theatre contrasts with the horizontality of Hellenistic theatre, where the stage wall was only one storey high. The horizontal architectural form was linked to social interaction and interpersonal dialogue on the human plane, as exemplified by the comedies of Menander.[46] The only tragic drama to survive from imperial Rome is that of Seneca. Though his rhetorical plays were probably written for elite audiences in private houses or in small odeons (miniature roofed versions of public theatres),[47] his plays exemplify the principle of verticality, containing little interpersonal dialogue and social context, but depicting the relationship of the individual suffering hero to the cosmos and the power of fate. Just like emperors, pantomimes were individual stars, and members of the equestrian class, both male and female, aspired to pantomime stardom until this was seen to offend against the social order. Republican theatre had been a competition between the different aristocratic sponsors of the games, but Augustan theatre was funded largely by the state and became a competition of star actors. The division of the Roman audience into supporters of one pantomime or another, one type of gladiator or another, diverted them from politically more dangerous schisms.[48]

Vitruvius, formerly a missiles engineer under Julius Caesar, wrote a treatise on architecture for Augustus. This treatise included a substantial essay on the Roman theatre, relevant at a time when Augustus was planning or building his own theatre in Rome, and theatres were being built in different parts of the empire. There is no sign that any Roman theatre designers took notice of Vitruvius' schema, which had too large an orchestra, and doorways too close together. It is nevertheless interesting as an example of how Romans in the Augustan age thought about theatre. On the one hand, Vitruvius writes as a philosopher, applying the Platonist principle of the microcosm to the theatre, and thereby revalidating an institution which Plato disparaged; on the other, he writes as an engineer and mathematician who had a passion for gadgets, and developed his musical ear through tuning catapults. He also writes as a Roman, concerned to distinguish Roman theatre from its Greek forebear.

The circle is the governing principle of the Platonist microcosm. Vitruvius states that the outstretched human body fits into a circle and square, with a navel as the centre point. His treatise includes a long account of astronomy, with the planetary spheres and the path of the zodiac along the ecliptic. In his account of the theatre, he is preoccupied with acoustics, and understands acoustics as a cosmological problem. Astronomers, he says 'have a common ground for discussion with musicians in the harmony of the stars and musical concords in tetrads and triads . . .'[49] The Pythagorean principle that the ratios between musical notes correspond with ratios defined by the planets underpins his understanding of sound. Plato's assumption that the movement of the spheres creates a heavenly music too perfect for the human ear to apprehend, though rejected by Aristotle, was common currency in the Roman world. Cicero, for example, explains how, within the universe that is god's temple, the eight spheres make seven notes by means of their rapid circular movement, and seven is a crucial number in almost everything. Though we cannot hear this music, wise men imitate it with voices and stringed instruments, and this opens a way back to the divine.[50] It follows from these Platonist principles that a circular theatre is the space where the most perfect music can be created.

Vitruvius' premise is that the circumference of the extended orchestra, like the zodiac, must be divided into twelve. In the Greek theatre, he maintains, the corners of three squares define the twelve points, while the Roman theatre should be based on four equilateral triangles. These triangles, he says, should be set 'at equal distances apart and touching the boundary line of the circle, as the astrologers do in a figure of the twelve signs of the zodiac, when they are making computations from the musical harmony of the stars'. The doorways, stage, stage wall and gangways are laid out in relation to these squares or triangles, forms which relate to astrological propositions about the tetrad and trigon.[51] Vitruvius' account of the geometry of the theatre follows an elaborate account of an unusual Greek gadget, *echeia* or 'echo-vases', examples of which had been brought to Rome from the theatre of Corinth.[52] Thirty-eight vases are to be arranged at three levels, following the layout of the auditorium (fig. 29). Vitruvius explains in meticulous detail how these echo-vases are to be 'placed in niches under the seats in accordance with the musical intervals . . . in such a way that when the voice of an actor falls in unison with any of them its power is increased, and it reaches the ears of the audience with greater clearness and sweetness'.[53] The tragic actor, who is now essentially a singer, should play the auditorium as if it were a musical instrument. The mathematical logic of Vitruvius' acoustical scheme is clearest when we superimpose it on his plan for a Greek auditorium.

Vitruvius states that astronomy is fundamental to optics as well as acoustics, but does not pursue the point in relation to sightlines in the theatre – though he does state that sunlight moves in straight lines, forming equilateral triangles when it encounters the outermost sphere.[54] What Vitruvius envisages in his treatise is a perfect Platonic auditorium. The three rows of

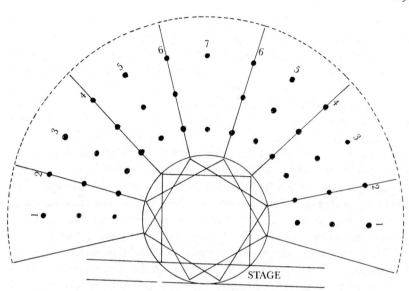

Figure 29   Vitruvian echo-vases in an idealized Greek auditorium.

vases replicate the three orders of society which occupy their separate horizontal bands and use different entrances. His architectural scheme allows
the Augustan political ideal of a balanced and ordered society to correlate with an ideal of theatrical performance in which the actor creates not
debate or narrative in the first instance but beautiful music. Pantomime
developed as a form where words were subordinated to music, and music
defined movement.

Vitruvius' precise scheme was never adopted, but the broad outline and
mode of thought are characteristic of the age. We know that Varro, who
may have served as Augustus' adviser in matters of drama, set up an aviary
in the form of a theatre to exploit the different modes of birdsong.[55] David
Small argues that most Roman theatres were in practice planned on a
relationship of circles, hence the circular embrasures often found around
doorways in the stage wall.[56] As we saw in chapter 2, it was astral religion
that made Augustus' theatre a sacred space. His orchestra did not observe
Vitruvius' twelve-point division of the circumference, but, according to
the marble plan, consistent in this point with the number of columns on
the perimeter, each 90° quarter was divided into seven wedges, the magic
planetary number. Augustus did not build a Vitruvian theatre, but his
architecture exemplifies the same philosophy.

The architectural difference between Greek and Roman theatres can be explicated in different ways: Greek sensitivity to landscape, versus a Roman determination to dominate nature, for example, or a Greek emphasis on the democratic chorus in the orchestra giving way to a Roman emphasis on the authority of the actor. Whilst the Greek theatre referred the audience outwards to the *polis* beyond and a landscape inhabited by gods, the Roman theatre, completed by an awning that shut out the sun, was a contained spatial system. Autonomous Greek communities were bonded to place, but Roman citizenship conferred membership of a global community, and place slowly gave way to a more abstract sense of space. Stoic cosmology began to envisage an infinite void surrounding the spherical universe.[57] The high stage wall of the Roman theatre communicated a sense of the invisible, which relates politically to the fact that Rome was too big for Romans ever to view themselves as a totality. The logic of astral thinking does much to explicate the semicircular Roman form. The powerful diameter line which divides actors from audience is associated with the binary relationship of day and night, summer and winter, waxing and waning moon; only half the zodiac, and half of each planetary sphere, can be in the visual field of human beings at any one time of year.

The Greek theatre is wrapped around a central point defined by the sacred *thymele*, which creates the feeling of repose that appealed to Wagner and the nineteenth-century Greek revival, and reflects the idea that the earth, the matter at the centre of the universe, is inherently stable. Roman theatre, on the other hand, sets up a tension between two balanced halves, reflecting the Stoic view that the universe is in a state of constant physical tension, with human life and the cosmos linked by the unstable principle of *pneuma* or breath. Seneca was a celebrated exponent of Stoicism, and the performance requirements of his plays can be understood in this light. One of the most interesting moments in his drama occurs when Manto, daughter of Teiresias, describes the disembowelling of a bull and heifer that symbolize Laius and Jocasta – a horrific scene that cannot be represented in any literal way on stage, but requires the physical skills of the actor to stimulate the audience's imagination. Thomas Rosenmeyer comments on how different Seneca's *Oedipus* is from Sophocles' version. 'The effect of the dramaturgy is to strip Oedipus of his lone, towering standing, and to engulf him in a cosmos, of which he is shown to be a pulsating, but feeble, constituent.'[58] Manto's description places the dying, pulsating animals amidst the breath-filled audience. In the choral hymn to Bacchus which follows the reading of the entrails, the chorus evoke the order of circling stars, ocean around the earth, cycles of Venus and moon, and one constellation that never sets. The deformed organs of sacrificial animals, which should be microcosms of universal order, threaten the stability of this cosmic system. This cosmic order is also embodied by the Roman auditorium, striving to contain the violent emotions and social tensions of the pulsating audience. The impossibility of rendering such scenes literally is precisely what gives Senecan drama its power in a Roman theatre. The virtual half-circle which incorporates the stage is completed by the actual half-circle of the audience. The Greek audience sat in judgement around the magical circle, but the Roman audience sat within it.

In accordance with his traditionalist agenda, Augustus continued to stage gladiator fights and hunts of exotic animals in the Forum, the ancient space of sacrifice, and it was not until AD 80 that the Colosseum became the major permanent site in Rome for such activities. The elliptical shape of the gladiatorial arena appears to derive from the wooden structure traditionally erected inside the rectangular Forum. The ellipse offers the advantages of a circle in denying the animals a corner to hide in, and allowing the spectators to see each other, but it has the further advantage of being, in Joseph's terms, vectored. A journey can be accomplished, each combatant can take one end as his territory; and the emperor has a position of command on the long sun-lit side.[59] In terms of symbolism, the perfect Platonic circle which shaped theatrical space was inimical to actual scenes of violence and bloodshed. Whilst the Greek tradition in the eastern empire maintained a firm distinction between circular theatre and elliptical arena, in the west distinctions were weaker, and many arenas, like the 'theatre' at St Albans (Verulamium), were designed to accommodate both types of ludic activity.[60] In the arena dedicated primarily to blood-sports, lunchtimes were regularly given over to comic entertainments, and to theatricalized executions where the victim was given a mythological role.[61]

The Colosseum inspired London's Albert Hall, a symbol of empire which it is useful to consider in this context as Britain's most Roman performance space. Whilst the artistic community in the 1860s favoured all things Greek, military men designed Prince Albert's 'Hall of Arts and Sciences', complete with a Roman-style awning hung below a glass dome to preserve the open-air feel of the original. Since the Second World War it has been the site of England's most patriotic ritual, the Last Night of the Proms. Peter Laurie offers a memorable description:

The Albert is like a big, hollow, plush egg; everything that happens there rolls to the centre. The arena is cradled in the stalls and walled by the boxes . . . Its great quality is its fireside feeling – a marvellous place for human happenings. The excitement of the Albert Hall comes from the feedback it provides. It probably has the optimum conditions for mass exchange of emotion, because from any seat you can see almost everyone else there. The stimulus to laugh, cry, boo or applaud is reinforced as strongly as it can be by the rest of the audience. Compare this self-confrontation with the stimulating view of the back of a neck provided by the conventional theatre layout.[62]

There is profundity in the remark attributed to Queen Victoria that 'It looks like the British constitution.'[63] Like the Old Price rioters at Covent Garden, she recognized that the Roman-style organization of the auditorium made a political statement. At today's Proms the social diversity provided by boxes in hereditary ownership at one extreme, and five-pound promenading tickets at the other, creates a feeling of energy that is enhanced on the Last Night by displays of participatory singing and banner-waving. Theatre, however, was prohibited by the founding constitution of the Albert Hall. When, for example, Reinhardt wanted to bring his *Oedipus* complete with mass chorus to London, he was not allowed to use the Albert Hall, and had to use the individualizing, pictorial space of Covent Garden instead. The hall was built as a space for collective activity, diverting artisans from popular theatre or early forms of music-hall, and the collectivist possibilities of theatre were politically too dangerous to contemplate. The rules were relaxed in the 1990s to allow forms like ballet, opera and circus to use the Hall, but high prices ensure that there can be no danger of glimpsing in a theatrical context any embodiment of the British polity.

The Platonist ideal of the circle passed without interruption to the middle ages. As we saw in chapter 2, Hroswitha's play *The Conversion of Thais the Prostitute* (c.960) begins with a long exposition of Platonist theory as mediated by Boethius.[64] The hermit condemns the prostitute to a closed cell where she cannot honour god through the creation of vocal music. The force of Hroswitha's polemic becomes clearer when we compare her to Hildegard who, one and a half centuries later, was enclosed in an anchorite cell at the age of seven. Though Hildegard was at least allowed to hear ecclesiastical music, and learned to play the psalms on a psaltery, in her maturity she decided to found her own convent with a more open regime where she could develop musical and dramatic performances and celebrate the body beautiful.[65] We do not know how Hroswitha's play was staged, but it is a reasonable guess that the cell, the living tomb from which the prostitute has to be resurrected, was placed close to the imperial tomb beneath the dome of the church at Gandersheim. The force of the text would thus have correlated with the force of the architecture, designed by virtue of sphericity to create heavenly music. Jean-Pierre Vernant brings out another important aspect of the classical tradition, namely that the circle was considered a female space in contrast with the masculine square.[66] The circular temple of the vestal virgins, for example, signified that Vesta–Hestia was goddess of the central hearth. Hrosvitha's account of the music of the spheres is bound up with her feminist perspective.

Though it was only in the Middle Ages that the complete 360° Platonic circle emerged as a playing space, medieval practitioners believed, like Thomas Heywood, that they were following in the classical tradition. When Chaucer evokes the 'theatre' of Athens in *The Knight's Tale*, he pictures a gladiatorial arena that recalls medieval dramatic practice.

> That such a noble theatre as it was,
> I dare well say that in this world there nas [*was not*].
> The circuit a mile was about,
> Walled of stone, and ditched all without.
> Round was the shape, in manner of a compass,
> Full of degrees, the height of sixty pas,
> That when a man was set on one degree,
> He letted not his fellow for to see.[67]

Medieval theatre was vectored by the points of the compass, in accordance with the dualist thinking of the age, and the combat here takes place on an east–west axis. Temples are built to Venus and Mars, at the eastern and western entrances, whilst the lady sits in the north. The symbolism of Chaucer's amphitheatre is explicitly bound up with the rotation of the sun and planets. Roman space reverted in the medieval world to place, the present state of the sky being part of the performance. Medieval human beings could never escape from their condition as performers in the theatre of the world, under the eyes of transcendental beings.

It is only a small step from Chaucer's astrological arena to the famous amphitheatre constructed for *The Castle of Perseverance*, probably in East Anglia in the 1420s (fig. 30). It is now seven sins rather than seven planets that act upon the human protagonist in the centre. The arena remains a space of combat, but the principal action is a siege not a duel. The privileged eastern side belongs not to the pagan goddess of love but to God in heaven. The protagonist Mankind is torn between God in the east and the attractions of this world. At the start of the play, Mankind climbs onto the stage of the World, lit by the morning sun, and at the end his soul sits on the right hand of God, lit by the evening sun. The east–west axis is complemented by a north–south axis: Hell to the north is associated with sins of the mind, the warm south with sins of the body. These two axes meet at the Castle in the centre,

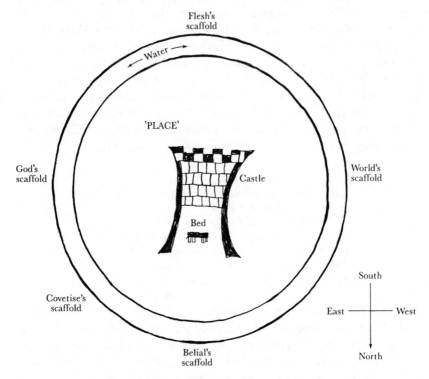

Figure 30   *The Castle of Perseverance.*

and define the sacred form of a cross. One other stage is shown in the diagram, that of Covetise whom the narrative identifies as the deadliest sin. His stage is a focus in the early part of the play, and is positioned in order that Mankind may be pulled towards Heaven by his Good Angel, towards Hell by his Bad Angel.

The Castle is another scaffold stage, with battlements on the upper level but open beneath, as is clearly shown in the diagram. The ditch has been variously explained as a barrier to keep non-paying spectators away, a moat around the castle within the playing area, and a barrier that keeps unruly spectators out of the playing area.[68] The last is the most straightforward explanation, retaining the symbolic force of the castle moat and securing sightlines. The scaffolds on the perimeter must be located amidst and above the spectators, as in Fouquet's famous miniature of *The Martyrdom of St Apollonia*, which shows such an arrangement, leaving it unclear in some

cases which are privileged spectators and which are figures in the drama.[69]
The staging diagram specifically prohibits spectators from occupying the
central scaffold 'for there shall be the best of all' – a mysterious phrase which
I take to refer to an effigy of the Virgin Mary or some similar sacred object
used to sanctify the performance space. The implication is that spectators
might well crowd onto the other scaffolds and incorporate themselves in
the action.

> Thus endeth our games
> To save you from sinning

runs the epilogue. The spectators inhabit the world of sin which surrounds
the Castle, and their impulse to cheer on the comic devils or invade the
playing space binds them to that world. The playing space represents the
cosmos, and the earthbound spectators inhabit that cosmos, playing their
parts under the eyes of God. It is also a map of the human mind, and
the space allows the audience physically to inhabit that mind. The Greek
audience sat outside and above the circle, able to contemplate its beauty.
The Roman audience could only experience half the cosmic circle. The
medieval audience sat inside the circle, with an intense sense of involvement
compensating for blocked sightlines.

When World opens the play, he calls the audience to silence, addressing
them expansively as 'worthy wights in all this world wide'. He defines the
playing space as symbolic of the inhabited earth, running through a quasi-
alphabetic list from Assyria to Rome. The Devil speaks next, narrowing the
range down to England 'from Carlisle into Kent'. Flesh narrows the focus
again to the gathered community who

> on hill
> Sitteth all still.
> And seeth with good will
> Our rich array.

Into this microcosm defined by its circular form, Mankind is born naked.
He addresses Jesus to the east 'in Heaven hall', but is lured to the stage of the
World in the west to 'dwell with Caesar, King and Knight'. Inescapably,
the action folds back on the audience. The publicity statement issued a
week before the performance evokes a tripartite social order comprising
King, 'royals of this realm' and 'good commons of this town that before us
stand', echoing the tripartite cosmic order of God, angels and 'mankind in
middle-earth'. There would have been an obvious divide in the auditorium

between the gentry who elected to sit on stands to be viewed in all their status distinctions and finery, and undifferentiated commoners who crowded beneath and around. Chaucer distinguished in this way between the nobility who process formally to the theatre 'one and other, after their degree' and take up their seats 'in degrees above', and an undifferentiated rabble: 'Unto the seats presseth all the rout.'[70] A similar theatre built in a field in Autun in 1516 contained

240 boxes in its upper part, each separated by a wooden partition wall and clad with wainscot; there sat churchmen, nobles, senators, knights, gentry. In the lower part, the degrees and seats were so disposed that the circle kept expanding as it rose. The people crowded there, sheltered by linen awnings which protected seated and standing spectators and actors from the rain.[71]

The Castle of Perseverance engages with this divide of high and low, playing upon the fact that lords and ladies have positioned themselves alongside personifications of sin, but touching also upon the perils of envy. There was no means of stepping outside the universal drama.

The Castle in the centre symbolizes on the most obvious level virtue. It is a gendered space, being inhabited by maidens who represent the seven cardinal virtues, and it evokes the sealed virginal body of Mary, humankind's protector.[72] Women in their bodies and social lives were associated with the principle of enclosure, men with openness. It is the top of the Castle which represents virtue, whilst the space below the battlements is the fallen world to which Mankind goes at the end of the siege. The vertical structure correlates with the structure of the Platonic body, with its highest faculties located in the head, and appetite down in the belly. Since the belly space below represents a bedroom, we may infer that Mankind emerges from here at the start of the play, and completes the circuit of life around the arena, before ending up in the place where he was born. When Mankind dies at the end of the play, his Soul emerges from beneath the bed, is carried to Hell and rescued by female intercession, to finish on the right hand of God in Heaven. The Castle becomes a human body, a temporary hollow container for an immortal soul. In Plato, the soul returns to the stars on the periphery of the Cosmos, but in this Christian reworking the periphery is vectored by Heaven and Hell. The cruciform pattern, defined by the two axes which intersect at the bed, suggests a further Vitruvian correlation between the circle and the outstretched limbs of a body. If Mankind's head points to heaven like St Apollonia's head in the Fouquet miniature, the cupboard at his feet marks the fact that life has drawn him in the opposite direction.

Plate 16   Frontispiece to Terence, *Comedies*, published by J. Grüninger (Strasbourg, 1496).

The cosmic circle was the normal form for medieval 'theatres' erected in an open field. We find the circular form used in the rural Cornish cycle, and probably in two long sequences of the East Anglian compilation known as the N-Town cycle.[73] It is a mistake to see medieval and classical as two competing traditions that converged in the Elizabethan playhouse, for medieval theatres in the round were rooted in classical thinking. When we look at the frontispiece to Grüninger's 1496 edition of Terence's comedies (plate 16), we see an imagined Roman theatre that could have been designed for *The Castle of Perseverance*: a tower in the centre, slender at the base, with four arches that vector the space and curve across from the tower to the edge of the auditorium. Surviving Roman amphitheatres, medieval dramatic practice and classical cosmology combined to assure Grüninger that the Roman *scaena* must have been a central castle.[74] Which of the figures are Terentian characters and which are Roman spectators remains ambiguous, for medieval theatre thrived on the intermingling of actors and audience.

Frances Yates in 1969 attempted to show that Shakespeare's Globe was a Vitruvian space, with twenty-four sides. Archaeology proved her wrong, indicating a theatre of some twenty sides, a product of standard timber lengths rather than renaissance cosmology.[75] In 1992 Joy Hancox published a set of drawings by late eighteenth-century freemasons purporting to represent Elizabethan playhouses, though excavations of the Rose had already invalidated her thesis that the documents had an archaeological basis.[76] Her drawings are nevertheless a fascinating indication of how eighteenth-century intellectuals viewed the theatre, linking theatres to Christian temples, and in a rationalist age seeking to recover the notion of a sacred space through Platonist mathematics and geometry. Iain Mackintosh has pointed to the importance of 'sacred geometry' in the planning of eighteenth-century playhouses, and applied the principle to modern theatre design.[77] It is not surprising that Yates should have been wrong, for Roman theatres themselves were never products of pure Vitruvian theory. We must not set up a false dichotomy by asking whether the Globe was essentially a medieval or a renaissance space, for Platonist thinking linked both forms. We can see the Globe as a commercial booth stage superimposed upon the medieval circle, or we can see it as a Roman-style amphitheatre with equal justification, for it was both. The major reversion from medieval to Roman thinking lay in the abandonment of the cardinal points, and the reversion from place to space, within a theatre closed off from its environment. Ernst Cassirer remarked that in renaissance philosophy space 'as a substratum' was replaced by space 'as a function' – which is to say that geometric relations became relative rather than absolute.[78] Kent Van den Berg argues that the shift of name from 'The Theatre' to 'The Globe' points to a new conception of the theatre building as a man-made model rather than an embodiment of the world.[79]

The reconstruction of Shakespeare's Globe on the south bank of the Thames gave a new and empirical direction to research into Elizabethan performance space in the late 1990s. Despite the collapse of Yates' theory, the classical placing of a square within a circle was found a helpful key to reconstruction.[80] The presence of spectators sharing space with musicians in the gallery behind the stage brought a realization that this is an audience in the round. The 'discovery space' within the stage façade which preoccupied the first half of the twentieth century, rooted in its attachment to the proscenium arch, can now be seen as a figment of the historical imagination. Two important themes emerge from Pauline Kiernan's interrogation of participants in the 1997 production of *Henry V*. In the first instance, the new Globe is a listening space, as implied by Webster's famous evocation of 'so many lines drawn from so many ears, whiles the actor is the centre'. The actor William Russell comments that continuity of sound compensates for discontinuity of focus on the speaker's face, and that actors trained in old-fashioned sonority and televisual intimacy have yet to discover a sufficient musicality in their speaking of verse. The project architect spoke of the new Globe as 'the original instrument that Shakespeare wrote for' and this conception of the theatre as a musical instrument returns us to the Vitruvian agenda, with sound rather than image as the driving concern.[81] Secondly, the new Globe is an interactive space. One actor speaks of the 'generation of energy in the circle within the building', and comments on the way both actor and spectator feel 'part of the play'; he goes on to speak of a 'spiritual dimension', a 'bridge between Shakespeare and now', a reminder that geometry is always bound up with symbolism. When Russell speaks of feeling 'double-charged' by his interaction with groundlings who move about him like the sea, sometimes silent, sometimes spontaneously noisy, sometimes irritatingly noisy in a 'manufactured and artificial' way, we catch the drift not of Vitruvius but of Cicero, thrilled by applause, dismayed by claques.[82]

The 'authenticity' of the Globe project has been the subject of heated argument. On one level, the practicalities can be debated: is the theatre too large? are the columns too intrusive? On another level, there is the question of how far spaces can generate meanings and emotional responses in a way that is not culturally determined. Shakespeare's cosmological terms of reference, for example, belong to a culture that has vanished. When Cleopatra says of Antony:

His face was as the heavens; and therein stuck
A sun and moon, which kept their course and lighted
The little O, o'th earth . . .
His legs bestrid the ocean; his reared arm
Crested the world; his voice was propertied
As all the tunèd spheres – and that to friends –
But when he meant to quail and shake the orb,
He was as rattling thunder . . .[83]

it is easy for a modern audience in the reconstructed Globe to grasp the
metaphors of scale. We can feel how the Globe stage, like the mountebank's booth, was a tool for creating dominance, and allowed the actor to
command the pit in a way that neither medieval theatre in the round nor
Roman theatre architecture permitted. When Antony bestrides the modern
Globe stage as if it were the Mediterranean, that physiological dominance
can be apprehended. However, a modern audience attuned to the psychological analysis of facial acting is likely to be mystified by the notion that a
face may contain the light of sun and moon. We have a more passive concept of viewing, tied to a different theory of optics, which cannot admit
that eyes emit rays of light. The correlation between the architectural O of
the theatre and the microcosm of the human body with its 'lights' on the
perimeter, has vanished from contemporary culture. The zodiac painted
on the heavens above the stage, so important to Heywood, has become a
quaint curiosity.

The musicality of Antony's voice may be broadly apprehended, though
its production may run against the grain of actor training. We may sense
that Cleopatra's words, spoken from the monument, lack the acoustical
support enjoyed by Antony's speeches delivered below the zodiac.[84] Yet
however alert our ears become, musicality itself has changed in a culture
of polyphonic orchestral music and artificial amplification. According to
the Platonist tradition, as understood by Hroswitha and others, voice was
the privileged instrument which established contact between the human
and the divine. When Helkiah Crooke in a treatise of 1616 stated that
'Voice is a kind of sound characteristic of what has soul in it',[85] we cannot
relate culturally to his Aristotelian and Christian terms of reference. We
are unlikely to hear Antony playing the theatre walls with his voice and
attacking them because we are not trained in collective listening, but belong
to a different 'acoustic community'.[86] We think of the play being out there
on the stage, and not amongst us, because a sense of empty space divides
us from it. We are trained to conceive space as homogeneous, infinite and
abstract, not as functions of the body and of a fixed centre.

To reconstruct the Elizabethan audience is an obvious impossibility in the twenty-first century, though much can be learned from the way the pit today generates interaction. The act of standing creates a physiologically energized spectator who both wants to be involved, and feels a greater freedom to respond – even though, alas, licensing regulations mean that the spectator can never experience standing in a packed crowd as at an outdoor concert. Tourists and schoolchildren unversed in the protocols and disciplines of modern theatre-going provide the actors with strong rather than sensitive responses. Missing from the new Globe is any meaningful social distinction between pit and gallery, or any sense that a society has gathered to contemplate its own nature. The Globe was never a model of Augustan order, and seating was governed by what people chose to pay. Within the fluid social structure of Elizabethan London, the fascination was to construct order. Dekker, in a satirical pamphlet, suggests that a young man about town should attempt to sit on the stage:

Sithence the place is so free in entertainment, allowing a stool as well to the farmer's son as to the Templar; that your stinkard hath the same liberty to be there in his tobacco-fumes which your sweet courtier hath; and that your car-man and tinker claim as strong a voice in their suffrage, and sit to give judgement on the play's life and death, as the proudest Momus among the tribe of Critic.[87]

Momus god of ridicule establishes the Roman terms of reference: like the Roman theatre, the playhouse is defined as a space of 'liberty' and 'suffrage', where the plebeian can make his voice heard. But in a Jacobean capitalistic economy, the problem was to tell who actually was a plebeian. When a wealthy farmer's son sits on stage next to an impoverished gentleman from the Inns of Court, what codes of costume or manners allow them to be distinguished? If the plebeian smokes tobacco affecting to be a gentleman, is it merely an imperceptible body odour that tells them apart? In a climate of constant anxiety about the relationship of birth and wealth, the theatre was a place where people could come and locate themselves. When Shakespeare's Antony embraced the pit along with four actors as 'friends, Romans and countrymen', we can imagine how he unified the auditorium with his gaze. His subsequent enquiry whether 'Brutus is an honourable man' raised at a deeper ethical level the question that all spectators asked as they contemplated their neighbours.[88] Just as senators in the Roman orchestra activated the collective self-awareness of the Roman people, so in Dekker's account the assertiveness of spectators on stage who wish to be seen as gentlemen triggers awareness of the social structure. The Roman senator claimed his place in the orchestra by virtue of ancestry and the broad stripe on his toga, but the Jacobean gentleman had to perform his gentility. In this uncertain environment, Dekker advises the aspiring young man exactly what to wear and how to enter. The reward is status: hobnobbing with the actors, and being recognized in the street, but the cost is humiliation when he is mocked by plebeians in the pit. Dekker pictures a scene of class warfare where the gallant will 'like a piece of ordnance be planted valiantly, because impudently, beating down the mews and hisses of the opposed rascality'. Sitting on stage was a more significant feature of the private playhouses, where the intimacy and relative exclusiveness made the activity more rewarding, but it is clear from Dekker's account that it was also a feature of many public playhouses, if not necessarily the Globe.[89] Dekker's satire allows us to sense the fluid and potentially confrontational nature of the theatrical microcosm, where rank like space had ceased to be a firm substratum with fixed points of orientation, and social relations could only be defined in relative terms.

In sixteenth-century Italy, unlike England, the Vitruvian ideal was common currency among intellectuals, and Vitruvius made particular sense in light of the theory that Greek tragedies were not spoken but sung throughout. Palladio's Teatro Olimpico at Vicenza (1585) exemplifies an insoluble problem that Vitruvianism threw up.[90] The principle of equality that united members of the elite Olympic Academy was enshrined in the perfect semicircular form of the auditorium. But the individualistic demand for perspectival viewing compelled Scamozzi, who completed the building, to install three-dimensional vistas in each of the doorways, so every spectator had a view down at least one vista. Alas, any actor entering through these doorways found his scale hopelessly distorted by the illusionist painting on the flats. This tension between circle and vista was not an insuperable problem for Serlio and others who erected temporary classical auditoria in sixteenth-century courtyards and dining halls, nor would it be a problem in baroque theatres like the huge Teatro Farnese (1618). Here the duke or noble patron sat in the centre, and was seen to enjoy the optimum view of the single-point trompe l'œil perspective, an optical privilege never enjoyed by a Roman emperor. The logic of the semicircular seating in renaissance courts was not that of Augustus, with his utopian vision of a balanced society, but of Pompey, with his celebration of personal power and organization of the theatre around its linear axis. The curve of the auditorium allowed the spectators to divide their gaze equally between the imperfect stage picture and the duke who alone could see perfectly.[91]

Tension between the virtual circle of the auditorium and the framed vista, between Souriau's principles of sphere and cube, characterizes the history of theatre architecture until the end of the nineteenth century, when the lights in the auditorium were dimmed out and seats were arranged in a fan or straight line focused exclusively on the stage. I shall return to the 'cube' in the next chapter. Here my concern will be the classical auditorium. Sir Walter Scott, in an essay of 1826, celebrated the success of John Kemble in Roman tragic roles like Cato, Brutus and Coriolanus, ideally suited to these roles thanks to his bearing and aquiline nose. This Romanity suited a theatre that Scott likened to a 'national convention'. The British theatre, Scott maintains, against the background of the French revolution a generation earlier:

unites men of all conditions in those feelings of mirth or melancholy which belong to their common humanity, and are enhanced most by being shared in a multitude. The honest, hearty laugh, which circulates from box to gallery; the lofty sentiment, which is felt alike by the lord and the labourer; the sympathetic sorrow, which affects at once the marchioness and the milliner's apprentice; – all these have a conciliating and harmonizing effect, tending to make the various ranks pleased with themselves and each other.[92]

Communication between the different parts of the theatre is seen as the essence of the Georgian theatre experience. Scott celebrates not only vertical traffic but also the horizontal whisper that is heard 'through the whole circle of the attentive audience'.[93] He goes on to deplore the new, cavernous and would-be fashionable theatres of Covent Garden and Drury Lane. When Benjamin Wyatt rebuilt Drury Lane in 1812, inspired by French neo-classical experiments to emulate the model of 'Greek and Roman amphitheatres', his new auditorium formed three-quarters of a perfect circle, on account of the circle's 'superiority over every other form, in point of beauty'. Since the success of the Old Price riots obliged Wyatt to retain a balanced tripartite division of the auditorium into pit, galleries and boxes, he used the Platonic circle to create a disciplinary space in which everybody could see everybody and misdemeanours would be harder to commit. Classical beauty was linked to control. The proscenium arch was meanwhile identified as 'a line of separation' between the 'scene' and the 'spectatory'.[94] Lying outside the magic circle defined by the front line of the boxes and gallery, the world of the play could not now be touched by unruly spectators. Wyatt sought to give the circle a new meaning, but the conceptual isolation of acting space from auditorium was a fatal flaw to his design. The preferred

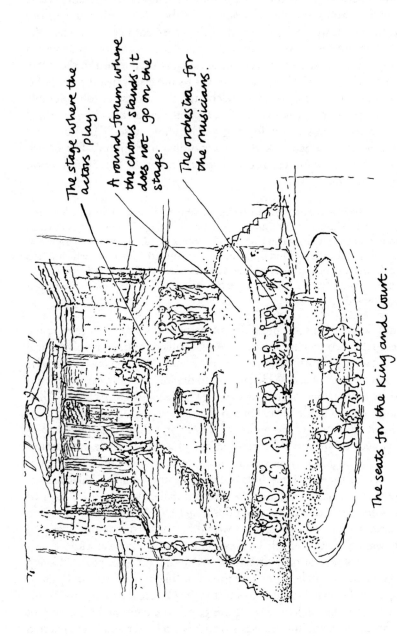

The stage where the actors play.

A round forum where the chorus stands: it does not go on the stage.

The orchestra for the musicians.

The seats for the King and Court.

Figure 31   Stage design for *Antigone* at Potsdam (after a sketch by Mendelssohn).

nineteenth-century forms of egg, ellipse and horseshoe would bond the audience to the stage in a more satisfactory manner.

It is not my purpose here to trace the complex history of European theatre architecture, but merely to indicate underlying shifts in the actor–audience dynamic. Late eighteenth- and nineteenth-century circus throws up particularly interesting issues of historiography. From one point of view early circus can be seen as an awkward hybrid, pending the emergence of its natural form, the unitary ring, in the later nineteenth century. From another point of view, we can see early circus as the perfect expression of its age, reproducing the Hellenic balance of stage and orchestra. The first thesis sets up a binary opposition between circus as a space where things are done for real and the theatre as space of illusion, and the ensuing historical narrative allows us to naturalize certain highly questionable assumptions about what theatre essentially is.[95] The second thesis helps us to see early circus as a means of resolving the aesthetic tensions evident in Wyatt's Drury Lane, in a direct line of continuity with the Teatro Farnese, where the orchestra was used for tournaments.[96] Wilhelm Schlegel at the start of the nineteenth century identified the classical ideal of performance with sculpture, the romantic ideal with painting, the former emphasizing the body, the latter the face.[97] Early circus was an oscillation between the three-dimensional action in the ring and the pictorial display on stage, balancing the two traditions. From a classical point of view, circus set up a balance between the pleasures of the gladiator in the arena and the pantomime in the theatre. In the ring, a hero exposed himself to physical danger, whilst on stage a mythic other world was created. The first attempt at a textually and archaeologically authentic Greek performance was the *Antigone* at Potsdam in 1842 (fig. 31), best known for Mendelssohn's music. A circular 'orchestra' was set in front of a deep raised stage, in an arrangement scarcely distinguishable from that of the circus, whilst the Prussian king sat in the centre of the baroque auditorium.[98] In social terms, early circus was a space of relative equilibrium, not contested so bitterly as theatre. People of fashion came, but do not seem to have felt threatened by the massed plebs as they did in the theatre, where the commercial pressure to expand could not be reconciled with good acoustics.

The diameter of the circus ring was defined, if not by the length of a lunging rein, then by the degree of centifugal force exerted upon a rider standing on a circling horse, ensuring his or her stability.[99] The basis of the form lay in the relationship of human being and horse, which exemplified, both literally and metaphorically, the power of a heroic individual to dominate nature. This great romantic theme related to empire and the conquest of savages, to capitalism and the triumph of the machine, to sexuality with its emergent, guilty distinction of ego and id, and to class, with the nobility of the horse symbolizing the nobility of the lower orders. The circle was the perfect form to exploit this theme. The focal point in the centre belonged to the ringmaster, the human being, while the periphery belonged to the horse, the embodiment of nature's power. The challenge was for the human being to conquer that periphery. Andrew Ducrow in *The Vicissitudes of a Tar* rode on the back of a horse dressed as a man o' war. Held down by centrifugal force, he mimed a long narrative, taking leave of his wife, joining ship, looking sadly at her picture, wrecked, swimming to safety and reunited. The feelings engendered by this narrative of a humble sailor triumphing against all the odds correlate with those engendered by watching a rider's miraculous triumph over gravity. Ducrow's monodramas give us some idea of what Roman pantomimes must have achieved, engaging with fate in the huge theatres of Rome. Ducrow had another specialism when he occupied the centre of the ring, the sacred space of the *thymele* in classical tradition. Standing on a pedestal and deploying his mimetic skills, he earned the praise of connoisseurs by bringing classical statues to life.[100] The Roman term 'circus', the classical iconography of the building and Ducrow's statues combined to validate circus as a respectable art form.

In Astley's first amphitheatre, known as the Royal Grove (1786–91), painted trees all around the auditorium gave spectators the sense that they shared a single pastoral environment with the performers (plate 17). By 1803 the second amphitheatre, displaying a zodiac on the roof and Britannia receiving gifts from all four corners of the earth, was proclaiming the circus ring a microcosm, placing spectators at the centre of empire.[101] The circus ring was the natural milieu of the horse, and the horse-borne human protagonists tended to be lower-class figures: tars, flower-girls, highwaymen, couriers and the like. Echoing the Greek space of the circling chorus, the ring belonged to ordinary mortals beings. Nobility was the magical construction of the perspective stage, a space where plebeians escape environmental dangers and discover they have noble blood. The logic of early circus was a binary one. The beauty of the material body was displayed by athletic horsemanship (or horsewomanship) and by living sculptures in the ring, while nobility of spirit and the ethereal beauty of exotic landscapes were displayed within the idealist world of the stage. When horses in 'hippodrama' invaded the high-status space of the stage which did not naturally belong to them as members of a lower order, tragedy might follow. The Byronic

Plate 17 Astley's 'Royal Grove'. Print in the John Johnson collection.

Mazeppa of 1831, for example, presents the death of the Tartar horse which has carried Mazeppa to safety, its wildness and beauty expressed by the painted stage mountains. Mazeppa pronounces an epitaph over the equine hero: 'Of mortal mould it cannot be but the chosen instrument of Heaven to restore to Tartary a sovereign, to a doting sire a long-lost son!'[102] The real impossibility of social transformation for the spectator, and the economic necessity of exploitation which the ideology of the time did not concede in respect of human beings, was expressed through the metaphor of the horse.

In Paris in 1843, Jaques-Ignace Hittorf designed the Cirque d'Eté as a unified space without a stage. The planning authorities who refused to allow a stage wanted to localize circus within the heterotopia of an urban park, whilst theatres were to be the focus of municipal vistas. Nature and culture were prised apart. In London the Royal Circus and Astley's Amphitheatre had enclosed boxes for royalty and aristocracy, framed by the pillars that supported the roof, but Hittorf introduced an amphitheatre of open seats, with slender columns defining a gallery, and in 1853 he succeeded in abolishing columns altogether in his Cirque d'Hiver. Whilst English circus represented an aristocratic polity, Parisian circus embodied the values of republicanism. The Ciceronian ideal of social balance gave way in France to the Greek ideal of social equality. Hittorf was inspired by the design of Greek theatres, and was impressed by the discovery that Greek buildings and sculptures were once brightly painted, which allowed him to reconcile classicism and festivity in his creations. A decorative awning, as in the Albert Hall, hung over the ironwork of the roof, inspired by the awnings that covered Roman amphitheatres.[103] The idea that circus belongs in a tent began in the USA in the early nineteenth century, but the French awning created a similar association between circus and ephemerality. European theatres and opera houses with their classical façades became monuments to the indestructibility of high culture, while circuses came to be associated with the passing moment of performance.

In 1910 Max Reinhardt presented *Oedipus* in the Circus Schumann in Berlin, and then toured other circus spaces in Europe, failing as we have seen to secure the ideal venue in London, and he followed this production with an *Oresteia*. The aim of Reinhardt's 'Theatre of the Five Thousand' was to bring theatre to a lost popular audience.[104] An eye-witness explained the success of his staging, showing how the chorus in the circus ring merged into the audience:

The drama has broken through the wall that separated it from real, everyday life; it has stepped right into the centre and radiates a magnetic power of attraction that draws everything toward it. The masses gathered around it become a frame, a sounding board. Herein lies the secret effectiveness of the Arena, it is built out of the masses of the people, the thousands around become the mute chorus, a wall against which the powerful waves of the drama throw themselves only to float back to the centre, back and forth in alternating rhythm . . . Thus the Arena is the medium which opens the soul of the people once more to the drama and makes this very soul visible.[105]

This rapturous account captures not only the political but also the spiritual aspect of Reinhardt's project, inspired by Wagner's ideal of community and Nietzsche's ideal of communion. In 1919 Reinhardt transformed the Berlin circus into a formal theatre with revolve and cyclorama, but his purpose-built Grosses Schauspielhaus lost the rawness and sense of authenticity that characterized the old circus.

In 1919 victorious Paris responded to vanquished Berlin with its own circus-based version of *Oedipus* – Sophocles' pertinent tale of a heroic individual who destroys himself to save his assembled people. Firmin Gémier, the director who also took the role of Oedipus, saw the roots of the French radical tradition in Rousseau, and Rousseau's desire to substitute popular festivals for the class-bound theatre of the ancien régime. Gémier realized Rousseau's ideal in Switzerland by orchestrating 20,000 spectators gathered in a circular arena to mark the confederation of the French-speaking canton of Vaud.[106] Now in Hittorf's Cirque d'Hiver he sought to turn the

Greek play into a festival, filling the circus ring with processional dances and athletic contests. Since the Greek theatre had been 'a sort of temple to Dionysus', Gémier would seek to create 'civic faith in a new secular religion'. This theatre was to be filled with beauty and nobility of thought, an alternative to the dumbing spectacles of music-hall. Gémier saw the circular form of the circus as a figure of beauty, which the chorus adorned like a frieze. Behind the influence of Rousseau lay Plato, and the idea that beauty of the athletic body correlates with beauty of mind. In his socially unified circus auditorium Gémier envisaged laughter and anguish passing over the audience like ripe crops, emotions propagating themselves and growing as they moved towards the back.[107] Jean Vilar, in a speech given on the centenary of Gémier's birth, identifies space as the problem that prevented Gémier developing any further his ideal of a people's theatre. The government endowed the Théâtre National Populaire with the 'sarcophagus' of the Trocadero, believing the 'people' required a utilitarian tool not a place of beauty.[108]

In Moscow, Meyerhold admired the skills of circus performers and sought to absorb them into the theatre, but had no truck with the romantic project of placing ancient tragedy in the circus ring.[109] The Platonist aesthetic was incompatible with angular constructivism, its spiritual idealism incompatible with materialist principles. In a Russian context, it was clear too that spatial reform was not sufficient to achieve a classless audience. In 1930, inspired by the thinking of the Bauhaus, Meyerhold planned to create an adaptable theatre allowing performance in different conformations. He mapped out a production in the round of a controversial new play about eugenics, which required the audience to intervene. This, declared the author, was not a play 'that ends by closing an aesthetic circle'.[110] The set was to be on split levels with transparent floors. In this disorientating and asymmetrical environment, Meyerhold planned to exploit not the spiritual unity of his audience but its divisions. The romantic vision of a popular audience, bonded by the unifying spatial principles of Greece and Rome, seemed to be over. This was the age of Stalin, however, the play failed to conform to the new realist agenda, and the theatre became a concert hall. Meyerhold's theatre-in-the-round was nevertheless resurrected by his pupil Okhlopkov in 1961 for a production of *Medea* that ran for twenty years, and dealt with the problem of dictatorship. A full symphony orchestra was used. In this theatre-cum-concert-hall, the dominance of music over oratory and characterization, and the use of ritual features like masks, made sense of the circular space and gave new life to the western dream of resurrecting the democratic Greek arena.[111]

In London back in 1886, William Godwin, father of Edward Gordon Craig, staged a Grecian *Helen* in Hengler's Circus as an experiment in archaeological authenticity, causing Oscar Wilde to lament that Wagner was a much better exponent of the Greek style.[112] Lacking a republican tradition, London did not provide the conditions in the early twentieth century for adapting ancient spatial principles to build a new popular audience. It was only in the 1960s, the era of student revolution, that the Roundhouse emerged as the 'temple of the alternative society', a space vested with comparable meanings.[113] In 1961 Arnold Wesker identified this former turning shed for railway engines as a suitable venue for a theatre funded by the trade unions in order to bring the highest form of art free of charge to the working class. The classical overtones of the space, with its twenty-four iron columns, combined with its industrial origins to make it the ideal site. Wesker's failure to raise funds to realize his vision relates to flaws in that vision. Rooted in the 'arts and crafts' aesthetic of Ruskin and William Morris, he was more interested in textures than spaces. He wanted a container of quality to put plays into, plays that could transfer to school halls and meeting rooms, and he thought of plays as a function of playwrights, not performances as a function of spatial relationships. He thought ambitiously in terms of an adaptable space that could be used in different configurations, and put too little value on the rough found qualities of the Roundhouse. The dynamics of the auditorium were not an important consideration within his humanist, individualizing conception of art. It may be true, Wesker conceded, that 'to be one of many hundreds of people watching the same play adds an intellectual illumination and emotional dimension to the experience' – but he declared his equal respect for the opposite view that 'watching a play alone, or with a dear friend or a family, makes the experience a more private and hence more profound one . . .'[114] Wesker gave up the struggle in 1970, the building in its raw state having become a venue both for rock concerts and for theatre, serving an audience that was interested in releasing personal identity (sometimes through drugs as well as art), that had little commitment to notions of high art, and that defined community in relation to values rather than class.

Peter Brook was the first theatre practitioner to discover the merits of the Roundhouse with his *Tempest* of 1968, the year when he formulated in *The Empty Space* his ideal of 'rough theatre', and he is alleged to have called it 'the most exciting playing space in Europe'.[115] Andrew Lloyd Webber lamented in 1982 the closure of 'London's only real "event" space, certainly of any substantial size'.[116] Within a capitalist system of mass production, theatre and 'event' seem to have split into separate concepts. Mnouchkine with

1789, Savary with his *Grand Magic Circus*, Barrault with *Rabelais*, Stomu Yamashta with his Red Buddha Theatre and Beck with his Living Theatre were amongst those who brought to the Roundhouse an un-English sense of theatre as event, theatre as an expression of collectivity. In 1970, Tynan's *Oh Calcutta!* was perceived as an event in the sexual revolution of the time. By the late 1970s, the political climate had changed and a more traditional repertory had taken over. In the 1980s, in an era of 'political correctness' there was an attempt to impose 'community' and turn the Roundhouse into a centre for Black Arts. This merely resulted in the fittings that had given the Roundhouse its ambience being stripped out. In summer 2002, the Royal Shakespeare Company temporarily took over the building in an attempt to attract a more youthful audience. Meanwhile the Roundhouse Trust was raising millions in order to restore lost Victorian features such as the glass roof, and create a multi-purpose youth-oriented arts centre.

The circularity of the Roundhouse is the basis of its power to create a feeling of collectivity, when spectators contemplate each other as equals, and feel that theatre has the actuality of circus, with embodied human beings risking something of themselves in what they present. Peter Brook in 1985 declared that the Roundhouse 'has a special humanity that Arnold Wesker realised when he first discovered it for the theatre. You could rebuild the building exactly and not get that living feeling.'[117] When Vitruvius wrote of placing the human form in the square and circle that articulate his model of Greek theatre, he had a clear notion of how 'humanity' related to space. But Brook's elusive conception of 'humanity' implies that geometry is not enough, and his thinking, based on his experience of seeing dynamic found spaces fixed and sanitized by institutional forces, offers a challenge to those about to restore the Roundhouse. The issues are complex. It is clear that the particular social energies of circa 1970 cannot be recreated, but they may be a memory that the space needs to conserve if it is to avoid the twin perils of heritage and aestheticism.

As Lefebvre demonstrates, space is social, and the architectural object is conjoined inseparably to the audience as subject. On the one hand, our formal representations of space have changed since the renaissance, and we do not use the same Platonist cosmological scheme to analyse the physical universe. The decision of the Victorian architect to give the Roundhouse twenty-four columns belongs to a residual cosmic mode of thinking that has faded away. Yet on the other hand, unlike the renaissance, the modern world uses the circle for round-table meetings to settle international differences and, in most western capitals apart from London, for democratic assemblies. The political symbolism of the circle, inherited from antiquity, has given it the potential to shape twentieth-century performance spaces. The continuities are subtle and shifting. The power of a performance space like the Roundhouse turns on cultural memories, and memories rely on texture as well as geometry. The spatial logic of the building is bound up with Greek democracy, medieval cosmology, circus and railway turntables. Conserving the richness of such memories is no easy task.

CHAPTER 7

The cave

Mos' people live on a lonely island
Lost in the middle of a foggy sea
Mos' people long for anudder island
One wher dey know dey would lak to be . . .

Bali Ha'I may call you,
Any night, any day.
In your heart you'll hear it call you
'Come away, come away'
(Bloody Mary in *South Pacific*)[1]

Bali Ha'I, with its two breast-like volcanoes, was represented in 1949 through the traditional use of Euclidian perspective: dead centre, framed by trees, beyond the long beach, a sense of the sea and infinite skies created by the cyclorama. Scenes played in front of the tabs represent the banality of everyday life remote from the war (fig. 32), whilst the space behind the tabs becomes the space of a dream. Bali Ha'I is specifically the dream of a young doomed lieutenant, and his carnal alter ego, Billis the engineer. A different perspective is visible from the terrace of Emile, the man of sexual experience, the island at his vanishing point having the suggestively feminine name of Marie Louise. Inhabited by Japanese, Marie Louise is known to be a space of danger, but the man of experience knows the dangers and survives to get the heroine, Nellie. The perspective stage, preferably harnessed to music, has proved to be one of the most powerful tools of western culture for manufacturing dreams.

The Chinese entrepreneur Bloody Mary gambles her daughter's virginity on Bali Ha'I in hope of an American marriage. 'The tabs open to reveal the interior of a native hut. The scene is lit beautifully, a kind of setting for a jewel.' When the tabs close again, native girls walk across the forestage with baskets of fruit and flowers to symbolize the sexual act. The dream of

Figure 32　*South Pacific*, Act 1 Scene 2 (after a photograph by A. McBean).

Bali Ha'I means many things. On an overt ethical level Bali Ha'I is a world where ethnic differences dissolve; but it is also the sexual fantasy of an Anglo-Saxon male, for whom the orient signifies desire; it is a class-based dream that cannot be shared by the good-hearted engineer waylaid by topless dancers; it is a dream conjured up by the Chinese entrepreneur, who has supplanted the colonial economy with small-scale capitalism; and Bloody Mary is herself a third-world victim, dreaming of access to the privileged first world. These ideological strands are not likely to be recognized by spectators seated in darkness on individual seats, the better to be drawn into Bloody Mary's dream and listen to their own hearts calling 'Come away.'

The basic western device to create a theatre of dreams is the curtain which reveals and conceals, effecting a gap between the embodied human being in the here-and-now and the 'heart' which has its place elsewhere. The curtain creates the spectre of a more profound truth behind it, which commonly extends from the truth of private emotion to a higher more spiritual reality. Act I having culminated in the rape, Act II starts by carnivalizing the dream of sexual fulfilment: Nellie dresses as a butch bosun, whilst Billis plays the desirable woman, parts which they act before the assembled troops at Thanksgiving. The set then revolves to show behind the temporary curtain the true emotions of the protagonists. The metaphor of Nellie's stage performance before the curtain supports an interpretation of human nature similar to that advanced by Erving Goffman in 1959 in *The Presentation of Self in Everyday Life*.[2] Goffman's proposition that we all have frontstage and backstage modes of behaving is symptomatic of a modern devaluing of public life in favour of a more authentic private domestic life.

In the last chapter we saw how Souriau's principle of the 'sphere' placed the audience inside the world of the play; in this chapter I am concerned with Souriau's 'cube' which leaves the audience outside and facing that world. In his account of the perfect circle Plato articulated a spatial principle that would shape western theatre practice, and his thinking about the 'cube' is equally fundamental. In his simile of the Cave, Plato equated our everyday experience of the world with the act of watching a shadow mime (fig. 33). In his simile, a fire replaces the sun, and the roof of a cave replaces the vault of heaven. Human beings are condemned to sit facing the rear wall of the cave, manacled with their heads locked into place so they can only see shadows cast by a fire behind them onto this wall. They cannot see their neighbours in this darkened auditorium, but think they see them in the shadows opposite. Other shadows are created by people walking up and down behind a partition, carrying effigies of animals, people and objects

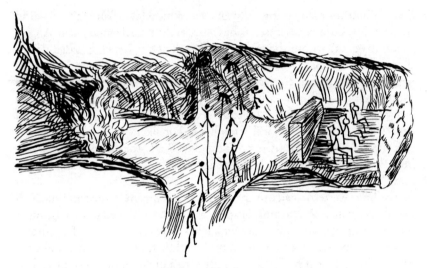

Figure 33   Plato's cave.

that protrude above the partition. Life, the simile declares, is lived as a form of theatre. Plato envisages the possibility that one of the prisoners turns, sees the shadow-mime for what it is, leaves the cave and gradually accustoms his eyes to looking at shadows, at the moonlight and finally at the sun itself, which equates with ultimate goodness and truth. The escapee, destined now to be the political ruler, is obliged to redescend into the cave, where of course he can now see almost nothing, and explain to the prisoners what true reality is.[3]

It is not clear where Plato got the inspiration for his simile. One may recall the thousands of slaves who languished in the silver mines of classical Athens, but the major inspiration probably came from the practice of initiation. Athenians processed by night to the town of Eleusis, where a cave marks the spot where Persephone disappeared into the underworld.[4] Initiates crowded into the huge covered Hall of the Mysteries, the Telesterion, where, in the nocturnal darkness, a door was suddenly opened, giving onto a subterranean chapel. We know only that a blaze of light reduced everyone to awed silence. Things were done, things were said, and things were shown. Whatever exactly was heard and seen, this was an important spiritual experience for many Athenians, relating to an anticipation of life after death. The principal myth was that of Persephone and her mother the goddess of the harvest, but the story of Orpheus who descended into the underworld in search of his dead wife was also bonded onto the Eleusis ceremonies in Plato's lifetime. The Mysteries were addressed to individuals irrespective of their gender or citizenship, so this was not a civic experience like tragedy, even though the power of collective emotion remained crucial. This was an indoor mode of performance which differed both semiologically and experientially from outdoor modes like tragedy. The climax of the Mysteries was a visual experience, and a function of artificial light. As in Plato's simile, ultimate truth was a function of seeing rather than hearing.

Plato's simile throws up a paradox.[5] If we live already a life of illusion, then theatre qua mimetic art merely compounds illusion and adds another layer of falsification to that which is already false, and on such grounds Plato banished tragedy and comedy from his utopian Republic. But we can also imagine the escapee, the ruler who has acquired enlightenment, returning in the role of theatre director in order to simulate, for the benefit of those who remain pinioned in their seats, a vision of what ultimate truth looks like, a glimpse of the sunlight at the end of the tunnel. Much subsequent debate about 'theatrical illusion' turns upon this ambivalence. On the one hand, the 'fourth wall' of an enclosed cube may open to reveal a pretence or 'mimesis', a shadow-mime of the *real* life lived by the audience, and constitute a potentially useful mirror of that life; on the other hand, the rock blocking the mouth of the cave may be rolled away, to reveal the distant prospect of a world *more real* than that of an enslaved audience. The first proposition turns upon a materialist philosophy of life, the second upon a spiritual and idealist philosophy.

Plato's idealism rests upon a distinction between soul and body, between intelligible and sensory realms of experience. The slave pinned to his subterranean seat is a metaphor for the condition of the soul shackled to a body, striving to take leave of the body, and pass to the mystical world of light. In neo-Platonist theatre, the boundary between cave and sunlight corresponds with the boundary between the auditorium (for which the Latin term is *cavea*) and the scenic world. *South Pacific* is a fine specimen of neo-Platonist theatre, with its representation of a banal, meaningless and alienated life on the forestage, and a dream of true love, true freedom realized by the proscenium, dimmers and cyclorama.

Ancient theatre architecture – if I may simplify greatly – bequeathed to posterity three broad spatial models. First came the early theatre of classical Athens, the gathering of the *polis* around the dancing circle in a Dionysiac rite. This model had little impact on posterity until the twentieth century. The second model was Hellenistic theatre, where the actors stood as if in relief on a narrow stage, and the empty space of the orchestral circle created aesthetic distance, with choral songs helping to separate the imitators of life from those imitated. The art of trompe l'œil scene-painting was developed, to enhance the proposition that the stage was a two-dimensional mirror. Greek scene painters developed the art of perspective to create depth – not the single-point perspective beloved of renaissance princes but a looser form that satisfied spectators in all parts of the auditorium.[6] The major theoretician of Hellenistic theatre was Aristotle, whose theory of *mimesis* turned upon materialist assumptions. Aristotle saw the visionary aspect (*opsis*), like music, as a mere accessory to the practical business of imitating life.[7] The values of Hellenistic theatre were no longer those of the closed political community but of a cosmopolitan Greek-speaking world, and its concerns were with individual rather than corporate morality. The third model was the theatre of Rome, where actors and audience engaged with each other as equal and opposite parties across the diameter line of the architectural circle. Roman theatre was in a double sense a space of confrontation, for here also different classes of spectator asserted their collective identities. We saw in chapter 4 how Plautus played with different social groupings, and with the status of his own performance. Whilst Aristotle spoke of *mimesis* or 'imitation', the Romans preferred the more participatory notion of *ludus* – 'game' or 'sport'.

Whilst the Greeks developed trompe l'œil representations of painted palaces, city-scapes, and landscapes, the Romans went on to mingle illusion with true opulence. A temporary theatre built in 58 BC incorporated columns of marble, glass and gilded wood, and the portable marble columns were later incorporated by Augustus in the stage wall of the Theatre of Marcellus.[8] The metatheatrical techniques of Plautus demonstrate how Roman theatre was based on an interplay of reality and illusion. Whilst Hellenistic theatre relied on aesthetic distance, Roman theatre drew its energy from physical convergence. The deep Roman stage allowed actors to move from a heroic up-stage position framed by columns and doorways to an intimate and complicit down-stage position. The curtain was an important Roman device invented in order to create and then dissolve the separation of two worlds.[9]

Our best account of the curtain in use is found in Apuleius' late second-century novel *The Golden Ass*, where the account of a dramatic performance turns out to be a Platonist parable. The hero's enslavement to the body is symbolized by his transformation into an ass. In the penultimate book of the novel he finds himself condemned to be exhibited in the course of a three-day gladiatorial festival in the theatre of Corinth, a Greek city rebuilt in the Roman style under Augustus.[10] The playing space was still a theatre in Apuleius' day, but in the next century it would be transformed into an arena. The archaeological remains confirm that a decorative curtain was wound up and down from a trench at the front of the stage. In the novel, the performance begins with choral dancing in the orchestra. Then the curtain is lowered and drapes removed to reveal the set, a model of Mount Ida complete with goats and a beautiful youth playing Paris. The youth chooses between the three women playing goddesses, and in accordance with the myth he selects the goddess of love. The actress playing Venus is naked save for a diaphanous veil, and she gives a skilled display of erotic pantomime dancing. Apuleius' description is lyrical, and emphasizes the aesthetic beauty of the performance. Once Paris has been seduced, the climax of the performance is marked by a phallic eruption on the part of Mount Ida, which ejaculates sweet-smelling saffron into the air. At this point the audience can no longer contain themselves, and call for illusion to be transformed into reality. The mountain is removed and a cage brought on, inside which the ass is supposed to copulate with a condemned murderess, a scene conceived as a parody of the mythical rape of Pasiphae by a bull. The ass is canny enough at this point to make good his escape whilst the audience are distracted by the scene change.

In the final book of the novel, the Platonist moral is drawn. The hero is transformed into human form after undergoing initiation into the Mysteries of Isis. He stands on the 'threshold of Persephone' in order to glimpse ultimate truth. His body is admired as though it were a beautiful statue, for it is no longer driven by its appetites. Total transformation is completed by the arrival of spring, and a journey from Greece to the idealized city of Rome. In his novel Apuleius sets up as antitheses a vision of the goddess in the Mysteries, where the highest faculties of the soul are engaged, and a vision of carnal beauty, where base appetites are engaged. After engaging his reader in the seductions of theatre, Apuleius demonstrates that this was a mere pornographic display. Visions of beauty yield to ugliness as the body imposes its sexual demands. It is hard to tell how fair Apuleius was in his critique of theatre. He seems to have taken nude dancing as found in the Floralia, the feast of the courtesans, together with practices of the gladiatorial arena, such as the display of mechanical mountains and the theatricalizing of executions, and he has merged such practices with pantomime dancing, the highest art-form of the Roman theatre. Different modes of viewing have been conflated in order to support the Platonist argument that popular theatre is essentially voyeuristic. For the philosopher Apuleius, what the curtain unveils is the antithesis of the Ideal. Reading against the grain of Apuleius' text, we can imagine how a clothed, male dancer impersonating Venus might well have been admired for his grace and athleticism, and construed indeed as the embodiment of human perfection.

Christianity rejected materialism, and thus the principle of replicating material reality in art. At the same time, it conceived of a fallen world in which the Ideal could not be made visible. It laid its emphasis upon the Word, and thus could not admit the principle of Greek Mystery religions that truth is something we see with our eyes. It was only in the high gothic era, as we saw in chapter 2, that denial of vision through the screening of the choir became a road to spiritual experience, and the light of Easter candles became an expression of a ultimate truth. Medieval art consistently avoids interior spaces. Gabriel annunciates, Magi visit the Christ-child, and hermits meditate before façades in outdoor locations, and the viewer's eye is never led into an interior. The sepulchre of Christ, far from marking an entrance to the underworld as in the Greek Mysteries, is represented in liturgical drama by a perforated structure that the audience sees to be empty. In a French convent, we hear of an audience coming into the sepulchre after the *Quem Queritis* performance in order to handle relics appropriate to the context: a cross, a lantern and a lock of Mary Magdalene's hair. In the Barking Easter ceremonies, there was no question of purgatory being a mysterious interior viewed from without. Nuns and priests crowded into a chapel which represented purgatory, and a priest impersonating Christ hammered on the door from outside.[11] In both these cases, the interior space representing the world of death was not a mystery to be viewed from without, but a space that the body could enter. Detached viewing belonged only to God.

The principle of the frame is very important in medieval art to enhance the sanctity of a statue or icon, and in medieval dramaturgy to give focus to an actor standing on a scaffold or a wagon, but the frame by no means implies interiority.[12] The representation of an interior is associated with the birth of perspectival theatre in Italy, and my major concern in this chapter will be the *théâtre à l'italienne*, which came to be regarded as the natural architectural form of theatre within western culture. We can define the 'Italian' form as a conjunction of two things: an encircling auditorium alluding to the *cavea* of Roman antiquity, and a perspectival stage laid along a central axis. The latter found its validation not in Roman archaeology but in Roman writings, notably Vitruvius' account of perspectival scene-painting and Servius' reference in his commentary on Virgil to a *scaena versilis* (revolving façade) and *scaena ductilis* (sliding façade).[13] The strength of this arrangement lies in the way the circle makes the audience function as a single organism, whilst perspective allows this audience to see the same face and the same action at the same moment.

I shall examine the *théâtre à l'italienne* in regard to four major modalities, which I set out schematically below. To each, I have attached a system of lighting, a philosophy, and a configuration of the pit. I shall touch more briefly on a second route from the renaissance to the romantics via baroque Italian opera. I have concentrated on France because here intellectual and political ferment generated a wealth of theoretical material.

	set	philosophy	technology	pit
renaissance court theatre	deep perspectival flats + forestage	neo-Platonism	wax candles and hidden oil lamps	seated nobility
French neo-classical	spectators on stage framing *palais à volonté*	Descartes + enlightenment	tallow candles	standing and socially mixed
romantic	painted scenes + shrinking forestage	Kant + idealists	argan lamps, then gas and limelight	mixed, with chairs and benches
early modernist	box set, permeable rear wall	psychoanalysis + materialism	gas, then electricity	on chairs and affluent

In 1435 Alberti established the principle of separation between viewer and viewed with his famous remark that 'I draw a rectangle of whatever size I want, which I regard as an open window through which the subject to be painted is seen.' In an acid Marxist riposte to Alberti, John Berger maintained that the renaissance painting should be seen not as a window in the wall but as a safe in the wall, locking up something the patron owns.[14] One of the dangers in writing about the *théâtre à l'italienne* is to take the world inside and outside the window (or safe) as autonomous entities with independent histories. The difficulty in transferring the principles of painting to the stage, which caused more than a century's delay in the introduction of single-point perspective, was the collective nature of theatrical viewing. The patron, as we saw in the last chapter, could be given an ideal view of the stage world that highly paid artists and carpenters had created, but others had to be content with an inferior angle of vision, and with seeing the image vicariously through the patron's eyes. The tensions in this arrangement were eased when Italians agreed that Greek tragedies must originally have been sung in their entirety, and opera emerged as the dominant Italian form. When musicians occupied the orchestra, formerly the space of the chorus, singing actors had an excuse to step forward and separate themselves from the picture plane. The visibility of the set might be inequitable, but the mingled sound of voices and instruments carried equally to all parts of the *cavea*.

The Italian renaissance prioritized vision. Because we can see the beauty of the world with our eyes, wrote Leonardo da Vinci, 'the soul is content to stay imprisoned in the human body, for through the eyes the various things of nature are represented to the soul. Who loses his eyes leaves his soul in a dark prison without hope of again seeing the sun, the light of all the world.'[15] The dichotomy of soul and imprisoning body implies, as in Plato's simile, a system of representation which invites the viewer to penetrate an interior. Plato and the idealist tradition in antiquity held that vision was an active process, with the eyes emitting rays or spirit,[16] and this theory of optics supported the notion that the eye was a privileged instrument, allowing the soul to probe where the body could not follow. When we read Serlio's influential treatise on architecture published in 1545, we find that magic not realism was his aim.[17] He sought 'to yield admiration, pleasure to sight, and to content the fantasies of men', and the key to achieving this was light. Coloured lights shining through windows are likened to different jewels. He writes of sun and moon rising and setting, and gods descending amidst shooting stars. Silk vegetation and costumes of cloth of gold create comparable shimmering effects in pastoral plays. Serlio's much reproduced engravings of comic, tragic and pastoral scenes, because they replace the play of light and painted shadow with analytic line, create a misleading impression of the viewer's experience. Nevertheless the church door at the vanishing point of the comic scene (plate 18), and the triumphal arch and memorial obelisk at the vanishing point of the tragic scene, demonstrate how perspectival art was bound up with idealism, creating a visible locus of unattainable perfection. Mystery is enhanced by the fact that the actor, because of his scale, cannot pass through the door at the vanishing point. An empty space between forestage and orchestra enhanced aesthetic distance.

Serlio's auditorium echoes that of Rome, but ladies now occupy the rows behind the senatorial thrones, where Roman knights once sat. Sabbattini, in his handbook of 1638, went on to suggest that the most beautiful ladies should be placed in the centre, to encourage the actors to perform with more zest and *joie de vivre*.[18] The *théâtre à l'italienne* was a feminized environment,

Plate 18   Sebastiano Serlio: Comic scene. Engraving from *Tutte l'opere d'architettura* (1545).

both aesthetically and sexually a space of seduction. The church door and brothel in Serlio's comic scene confirm that love stories were the staple of his theatre. When opera first removed the anomaly of people using ordinary speech in a space of perspectival magic, the Orpheus myth emerged as a paradigmatic narrative, subject of the first surviving score. Rooted in the ancient Mysteries, the myth catches all the major themes of neo-Platonist theatre, with the Ideal represented by the beautiful woman. In Monteverdi's celebrated 1607 version, which would become the first opera exported to France, the hero, whose music gives him power to charm the guardians of the underworld, leaves the public milieu of Thrace, crosses the symbolic barrier of the Styx, and enters the cavern. At the vanishing point of the cavern he finds the woman who represents the 'soul of my soul', his 'heart upon an altar'. The unruly passions of his body prevent him from bringing her back to the fields of Thrace, and sliding flats conceal the underworld from view. The receding horizontal axis which points to an ideal of femininity is replaced, as Apollo appears in the heavens, by a vertical axis that signifies male power.

In England, the court masque pushed to an extreme the ambivalence in Plato's theory of viewing. *Albion's Triumph* in 1632 was designed as a vehicle for King Charles to impersonate an idealized Roman emperor.[19] A triumphal arch, perhaps inspired by Serlio's title page, formed a proscenium arch, and within it another triumphal arch at the vanishing point of the Forum framed a miniature cut-out triumphal procession passing behind, a trick described by Serlio. The triumphal procession has just passed through a Roman public theatre, and this theatre auditorium becomes the setting for a debate between a Platonist philosopher who despises the theatre, and a common working man who has enjoyed the spectacle. The debate between the pair echoes a tension between two figures on the proscenium arch who represent theory and practice. The philosopher argues that he does not need to see the spectacle, for the eyes of understanding in his mind allow him to penetrate the inner perfection of the monarch. Nevertheless, he is inveigled into watching a display of popular entertainment with combat, mimicry and grotesques. This material and earth-bound spectacle yields to an ethereal one when the painted shutters slide back to reveal the emperor on the Capitol. Charles as emperor advances through the triumphal proscenium arch, drawn by rays emanating from the eyes of the principal spectator, Queen Henrietta-Maria, seated on the perspectival axis, and the two worlds of stage and *cavea* merge in a dance. At this point, the logic of the space is turned about. The Ideal has hitherto been located at the vanishing point of the stage, but now it seems that the stage is merely a cavern, a place of popular entertainment, and the true light of goodness is constituted by the radiant eyes of the queen. The stage changes to reveal a picture of Whitehall Palace, a mirror of the place where the masque is being presented. The world of the Ideal, conjured up by the Italian stagecraft of Inigo Jones, has now been turned around and located in the here-and-now of the courtly audience, whilst the stage now represents a lower, mimetic level of reality. The entry into Plato's cavern has become the exit.

The fall of the English monarchy in the 1640s was related to the gap between theory and practice which Jones portrays. There was a divide between two modes of seeing and representing the world in pre-revolutionary England: the elitist, neo-Platonist mode associated with the *théâtre à l'italienne*, and the word-based, collectivist mode associated with the public playhouse, both forms laying equal claim to the authority of Roman tradition. The culture of the Protestant word, at least in the short term, triumphed over the cult of the royal image. In France, neo-classical tragedy developed in part as a response to Italian cultural hegemony, and here a theatre of the spoken word had very different political implications.

Louis XIV supported an Italian-style theatre of machines and visual illusions of a kind that only a royal court could afford, but unlike Charles I of England he distanced his person from the theatre. The power of gods to bestow amorous favours on mortals, and to change the scene from a palace to a gloomy grotto, echoed the absolute power of the French monarch to control his kingdom. The techniques of this theatre were now familiar, and the audience celebrated its mechanics as much as its magic.[20] The disciplined genre of neo-classical tragedy emerged meanwhile in the public playhouse, and defined itself by its difference from the machine play. Lucien Goldmann famously related the world of Racine, in which no divine intervention or unveiling of neo-Platonist truth, is allowed, to the 'hidden god' of Pascal and Jansenism.[21] Equally relevant to Racine is Descartes's distinction between intelligible truth and sensible truth.[22] For Descartes, the eyes can only reveal sensible truth, and when we look at the human body we see in fact a mere machine, but words direct us to intelligible truth, and are a better means of apprehending the invisible soul which animates the body. Descartes examined the retina scientifically, and allowed the eye no metaphysical privileges, regarding it as a mere conduit to the brain. The unique focus in neo-classical drama was the actor's body. The actor's words, voice and movement were the only means of access to an invisible reality within. Racine's final play, *Athalie*, written in 1691 after his religious conversion and retreat from the professional stage, broke the iron Cartesian discipline. The doors open in the final act to reveal a vision of the temple of Jerusalem, and inside it the boy ruler who preserves the male line of David. Perspectival magic reveals a divine will at work, and the music of a chorus furthers the idea that human senses are not confined by material things. Hitherto in Racine's work no such feasting of the eye and ear had been allowed.

In a book entitled *Racine: a theatrical reading* (1991), David Maskell opens with a lament: 'It is hard to imagine any venue less suited to the enjoyment of drama than the public theatres in seventeenth century Paris.' He cites the rowdiness of the audience, the discomfort of the pit, poor acoustics in the *amphithéâtre* behind the pit, and poor sightlines in the boxes such that 'Most of the spectators would have had great difficulty in

seeing the stage at all.' Spectators on stage, moreover, 'might break the theatrical illusion for the spectators in the auditorium'. These considerations
oblige him to postulate a 'hypothetical spectator' able to watch a kind of
virtual performance.[23] On this basis he performs a semiotic analysis of stage
action, and offers a 'reading' of what he implies is the real Racinian play.
Maskell's book illustrates the methodological difficulty of a semiotic approach. He – or should one say his detached Cartesian ego – views Racine
as if from the dark and comfortable seat of a modern cinema auditorium,
and not from the physically demanding and constrictive environment of a
baroque playhouse. It is a basic principle of the *théâtre à l'italienne* that the
spectators are also performers – a principle which also obtains in medieval
and Roman theatre. Maskell's starting point is the text, which exists out
there in the world, available to be 'read'. My contention in this book is
that performance is first and foremost a relationship in space, and Racinian
drama should therefore be understood as a function of space, and not as
an autonomous thing slotted into a more or less unsatisfactory container.
We need to establish why the qualities of the seventeenth-century French
playhouse, which so dismayed a late twentieth-century English critic, are
bound up with the particular words that were once declaimed and now survive in a printed and canonized form. In a mediatized age, it is important
for us to understand how different historical forms of theatre generated a
particular physical sense of inhabiting the present.

I shall base my analysis of the French playhouse around an engraving
which depicts a scene from the final act of Corneille's *Cinna: or the mercy of
Augustus* (plate 19). The engraving is one element in an allegorical portrait
of 'Poetry', and the scene is thus to be regarded as the quintessence of tragic
poetry. The engraving claims to reproduce a painting by Julien Alexandre,
who died in 1679. Whilst the painting probably evoked in some measure
the original performance of 1640–2, probably at the Marais theatre, the en-
graver's choice of costume points to the revival at the Guénégaud theatre in
1679–80.[24] The artist adjusts the normal frontal perspective in order to
represent tragic poetry as an interaction between actors and spectators.
The angle of vision reflects the experience of a spectator in a box.

To begin with the two actors: on the right, Augustus extends the hand of
mercy, while on the left Cinna, the courtier who has betrayed his emperor
for love, grovels and dissimulates, using his posture to express a gamut
of emotions. Both actors wear Roman dress from the waist down, but
sport fashionable French wigs and hats. The antique statues viewing the
action alongside courtiers on stage reinforce the sense of interface between
past and present. Voltaire in the mid eighteenth century would mock this

Plate 19   Corneille, *Cinna*, Act V. Detail from 'Allegory of Poetry' in Charles Perrault, *Le Cabinet des beaux-arts* (1690).

anomalous visual rendition of Corneille's Augustus,[25] for his own dramaturgy aimed to isolate the stage in order to create an illusion of a historical world. Corneille, however, was creating a reenactment of history for present political purposes, and in the interface lay the point.[26] His noble emperor signified the brutal Richelieu, and in subsequent revivals Louis XIV. Roman theatre provided the spatial model for baroque theatre, and the major literary authority was Horace, court poet of Augustus, so the affairs of the first Roman emperor were an obvious source for dramatic narrative.

At the rear of the stage, beyond the right-hand edge of our engraved image, lay a perspectival representation of a *palais à volonté*, a generalized palace. This standard motif can be understood as a visual metaphor signifying that inside each protagonist is an inaccessible interiority. To the left of the engraving beyond the spectators, again unseen, is a proscenium door. It is likely that this door gave onto the apartment of Emilie, Cinna's beloved, whilst the door on the right gave onto Augustus' apartment, in accordance with the gendered logic that would later place the queen's box on the left, the king's on the right.[27] The single fictional place which Corneille created on stage is articulated by two axes: left is female and emotional, while right is male and rational; up-stage stands for an impenetrable interiority which we can interpret psychologically as the mind, politically as the court, while down-stage in the direction of the public is the public world, the world of the body, the political world that has to be ruled. Barthes in his semiotic account of neo-classical theatre rightly emphasizes the importance of the antechamber as the place where public and private worlds converge.[28]

The auditorium at the Marais was rectangular in 1640, but the Italian horseshoe form may well have been adopted at the Guénégaud by 1680. Both theatres were built in converted tennis courts, where the confrontation of two players across the net was replaced by the confrontation of two groups on either side of the footlights. Heightened declamatory speech allowed the words of the actors to drive through like tennis balls to reach the spectators banked up in the *amphithéâtre* on the rear wall. It is worth recalling that the rectangular 'shoebox' was until recently the favoured form for concert halls because of the lateral reflections off the side.[29] The convention of sitting on stage was never adopted in Italy, where the circling auditorium gave every box a good view of almost every other box, but in narrow French theatres weak sightlines from the side galleries, and the desire of some men to be more visible, encouraged the custom, said to have been introduced after the huge success of *Le Cid*.

Seating on stage was permitted because men of fashion were thought to enhance the ambience. A far-fetched story tells how an enemy of Molière booked all the stage places and gave them to hunchbacks, whose presence beside the proscenium arch caused proceedings to be ridiculed.[30] The presence of aristocracy would normally have had a reverse impact. Our engraving somewhat aggrandizes the stage, which would have been crowded with more spectators than the five shown. These five – four gentlemen and a young cleric – have distinct and expressive postures, and their faces are better lit than the face of Augustus. For spectators on the opposite side who cannot make out the emperor's features, these five become a mirror, reflecting to others what they see and feel. On-stage spectators generally enter the historical record when they cause annoyance, and their positive contribution to the performance is too easily obscured. Jan Clarke provides a misleading caption to this engraving in the Cambridge Documentary History when she writes: 'the fashionable young spectators on stage seem to be competing with the actors for the attention of the rest of the audience by adopting remarkably similar attitudes'.[31] This is no negative representation of competition, but an image which depicts a high point of tragic poetry. The attention of four figures is rapt, while the fifth checks his companion's reactions. Yet Clarke is not entirely wrong to discern a self-consciousness in the body-language of these spectators. Descartes, in a letter of 1645, offers the experience of watching a tragedy as evidence that soul and body have their separate pleasures. The sadder we become, he remarks, the more pleased we become. The pleasure which the soul receives 'from crying when watching some sad or tragic play in a theatre derives principally from the fact that the soul seems to perform a virtuous action by having compassion for the afflicted. Generally the soul is pleased when it feels passion arise in itself, no matter what passions they are, on condition that it remains in control of them.'[32] Descartes captures the paradox that a deeply felt reaction may at the same time be a performed reaction. The baroque theatre was a space which allowed people to perform their feelings. The architecture of the baroque theatre only makes sense when we recognize that the performances which mattered most were those of the principal spectators. The actors were a catalyst, not the be-all and end-all of an aesthetic experience.

Whilst men sit on stage, women command the interior space of the box. Georges Banu writes eloquently in his study of the *théâtre à l'italienne*:

The box is a stage. The stage of woman. Leaning on the balustrade, that border to a void which is the frame round a theatre box, she gives herself over to that most difficult thing to perform, namely presence. There may be no lack of speech inside the box, yet, facing outward, she performs with no support save gesture and costume. You can only dominate a box – this the task of woman – by alternating seduction, usually associated with the interior, and display, which is aimed outwards at the whole auditorium. The actress of the box gives her all to creating variety, so her performance will delight the eye and awaken desire.[33]

Cloaks draped over the balustrade serve to personalize each box and call attention to it. There is, however, no sign yet of those crucial eighteenth-century accoutrements of viewing, the fan and the opera glass. The opera glass allowed the female user to demonstrate whether or not she was attending to the stage. Its protocols allowed the male to scan the auditorium, and place a second frame around the one constituted by the edge of the box. The woman then used her fan as a theatrical curtain in order to conceal or reveal her beauty, the world of the Ideal.

A fictional eighteenth-century account, attributed to a Jew visiting the Parisian opera, gives a fuller picture of the dynamics of the gaze. Upon seeing a group of men in the pit scanning the boxes, the Jew remarks: 'As soon as the glasses were fixed on someone, she gracefully averted her eyes, smiled in an agreeable manner, and simpered flirtatiously with the help of her muff or fan. This behaviour continued until the viewers started to examine her neighbour, who at once played the same part.' These voyeurs construct narratives around the performers in the boxes, praising one for her new lover, condemning another for her dull eyes and graceless smile, evidently a sign of failure in love. It was a convention that wives and husbands did not sit together, for this would have undermined the performance of sexual roles. The Jew is then diverted by the opera on stage, and is surprised to learn that the actresses are not princesses but excommunicated whores.[34] The low nature of the official performers becomes a touchstone against which the performers in the boxes can be measured. Returning from the eighteenth century to our seventeenth-century engraving, however, we find that the women here are unambiguously watching the play. The artist contrasts a female sensibility visible in the boxes with a public male sensibility presented by male spectators on the stage. In the drama, Cinna shows himself torn between emotion – the pull of the off-stage Emilie to his right – and rationality – the pull of the male emperor to his left. In the studied casualness of the male spectators, who sit back, and the posture of the female spectator who peeps round, pulling forward, we see the same tensions at play. The suggestion in this image may be that the women are more fixed on Cinna's love, the men on Augustus' magnanimity. Substituting for the ancient chorus that had vanished from neo-classical tragedy, the spectators behind the proscenium complicated and enriched the theatrical experience.

We pass finally to the rows of heads that represent the pit. Diderot in 1758 lamented the way the spontaneity of the pit was being quelled by the presence of armed guards, and he addressed it sorrowfully:

You stirred and shifted and heaved, your soul transported. And I know of no mood to suit the playwright better. The play had trouble in starting, with many interruptions, but reach a fine passage and the fracas was unbelievable, encores repeated endlessly, and such infatuation with the actor and actress! The crazed feeling passed from pit to *amphithéâtre*, and from *amphithéâtre* to the boxes. You came heated, you left intoxicated. Some went off to whores, others into society. It was like a storm passing on, its distant rumble heard long after the sky had cleared. This was pleasure.[35]

Such feelings prompted Diderot, as editor of that bible of the Enlightenment, the *Encyclopédie*, to commission an analysis of the pit from the playwright Jean-François Marmontel. The standing pit was now threatened not just with soldiers but with seats.

Marmontel describes the theatre as a form of republic, and argues that if seats were introduced, 'the democracy of the pit would degenerate into aristocracy'. In the collectivity of the pit lies its 'freedom'. Aristocratic viewing is conceived as an individualistic affair, with each person forming their own view, and this isolation of the spectator's soul is deleterious to the performance, because there is no consensus about the merits and failings of the play, and thus no scope for collective applause. Marmontel ponders how one might calculate the extent to which emotion is enhanced by membership of a constricted crowd, and finds his metaphors in physics:

Imagine five hundred mirrors, each beaming its reflected light to the next, or the same sound echoed five hundred times . . . First you are made to laugh by the impact of the comic object, or respond directly to the object of pity; but then, you laugh to see others laugh, or weep to see others weep. The result of these multiplied emotions may often be that you are convulsed with laughter, or choked with grief. Now it is particularly in the pit, and in the standing pit, that this kind of electricity comes suddenly, quickly and powerfully. The physical cause lies in the more painful, less indolent, position of the spectator, who is kept active by a state of constant discomfort and perpetual flux.[36]

Marmontel supports his argument about the unified pit by noting how each pit in each different theatre has a unique character because of its local identity, while the aristocracy moves indifferently from one theatre to the next. He shares the view of Diderot that the response of the pit is decisive for a play's success. The pit's distinctive qualities are 'by contagion transmitted to the boxes, and create as it were the spirit of place, the sense of the moment'.[37] Gender adds a further dimension to his analysis. The box is a female-dominated space, and its responses are sensitive but capricious, but the male pit embodies solid common sense, and cannot be seduced. In an appendix to his article published after the Comédie Française had installed seats, Marmontel declared that he had been proved right. The audience was harder to arouse. The imaginative and responsive younger generation could no longer afford to attend.[38]

Marmontel perhaps had the Italian seated pit in mind when he comments that in less constrained cultures seats might well be appropriate. Limojon de St-Didier in 1680 portrayed Venetian theatre-going as an extension of carnival, marked by the spectators' custom of wearing masks. As a Frenchman he was shocked at the libidinous behaviour of Italians, dismayed to see the pit ruling the actors, and the nobility bombarding the pit with missiles.[39] The different dynamics of French theatre were also a function of its intimate scale. Marmontel comments on the greater size of Italian theatres, which encouraged the art of stage design, and sees the move to expand French theatres as a threat to the speech-based traditions of his country,[40] but here he was swimming against the tide of change. Theatres would soon become urban monuments, their grandiose proportions inhibiting spontaneity and interaction. Squalor and overcrowding were necessary conditions for the theatre of Racine and Corneille, a theatre in which the constraints of the body were transcended by language that expressed the soul.

Diderot's aesthetic values turned upon a moral critique of the *Ancien Régime*, the ideology of which was bound up with Parisian theatre practice. The falsity of this theatre, he wrote to an Italian actress in 1758, dismayed him so much that he had attended but ten times in fifteen years. The actress in question had read Diderot's experimental bourgeois comedy *Le Père de famille*, and had offered him the wisdom of an experienced practitioner: his set should be symmetrical in order to hold attention; actors in order to be seen and heard should stand no more than three feet from the footlights and declaim in the direction of the pit. 'It is not through ignorance that actors play as they do,' she declared. 'It is because the space [*salle*] in which they perform demands this style of playing.' Diderot responded that actors should not be mere furnishings for spaces, but theatres should be made for actors. He argued that actors should be able to turn their backs, retreat upstage, and deliver lines into the wings, and he urged the actress to rehearse her plays before an audience on all sides in order to create a more natural style. The ideal of being 'natural' places Diderot and his contemporaries at a far philosophical remove from the mechanized world of Descartes, where nature was an evil to be controlled.

It was Diderot's principal contention that the stage image should resemble a good painting, and paintings in his day avoided symmetry, caught figures from the side, and stimulated the imagination through selective use of light and shade. He fails to develop any new conception of theatre architecture, beyond the obvious correlative that an adequate stage picture requires the removal of spectators from the stage, and he declares lamely that his play had received many a successful performance in the privacy of his study.[41] The tension between rationality and feeling animates every corner of Diderot's thought, most famously his account of the acting process, where he tipped the balance towards rational self-awareness. His Dionysiac account of the pit is at odds with a remark to the actress that he often finds himself out of sympathy with it, wanting simple expressions of emotion when the pit goes wild over bloated rhetoric.

Diderot's rational side led him to the genre which he attempted himself, sentimental bourgeois comedy. His ideal here was to create a real room on stage. When he describes to the actress his method of composition, taking the bookshelves in his study for upstage, and the window side for the direction of the pit, he anticipates the notion of the fourth wall, and the tradition of playwriting that led via Beaumarchais to the late nineteenth-century convention of the box set. But his pictorial conception of the stage pointed also to romanticism, and to drama that privileges feeling over moral judgement.

1758 was the year when Rousseau threw down the gauntlet to Parisian radicals, using the arguments of Plato to support his thesis that theatre had no place in the model republic of Geneva; only festivals in the open air were admissible.[42] We do not know whether it was Rousseau, or the lack of any acceptable theatre, that discouraged Diderot from writing any more plays. Diderot engaged with Plato, and revealed his deep ambivalence about the romantic turn in the arts, when he reviewed a painting exhibited by Fragonard in 1765.[43] This extravagant proto-romantic painting depicts a young priest of Dionysus killing himself rather than sacrifice the girl whom he loves. Diderot claims not to have seen the painting, but to have dreamed it as a prisoner in Plato's cave. He dreams the painting as a stage tableau at the climax of a five-act drama, evidently recalling how the myth had been treated in an opera by Destouches. He admires Fragonard's magic, intelligence and technique, also the side-lighting, half-tones, and hinted figures in the background, and he notes how successfully the painting induces emotions of fear. But he likens his feelings to those experienced in a riot, in a crowd driven on by emotion before the facts are known. He ponders what critics mean when they accuse the painting of being 'theatrical'. In his dream he finds himself condemned by his peers when he turns round to watch the showmen operate their shadow-puppets. He claims that he can commune with the painting in darkness, but in daylight is unable to believe in it. Diderot uses the vehicle of Plato's parable to explore his own unease before a theatre of visual and emotional assault.

Beethoven's post-revolutionary opera *Fidelio* (1814) offers a convenient illustration of the two competing traditions at the turn of the century, classical and romantic. The first act, set in a well-lit courtyard, is shaped by the genre of bourgeois comedy. A group of prisoners emerge from their cells into the spring sunlight, evoking the liberation of the Bastille. The liberation portrayed in Act I is socio-political, and the audience's mode of viewing is detached and ironic. The second act, however, is effectively a reworking of the Orpheus myth. The heroine dressed as a man charms her way into the underworld of the dungeon. Dimly seen through a grill at the point of perspective, the heroine realizes the hero's dream of a rescuing angel. Another light signifies in the nick of time that salvation has arrived from outside the prison. The final sequence restores the daylight, before the sign of a royal statue, and completes the characteristic cycle of neo-Platonist and romantic drama: a descent into the world of darkness, dreams and glimpsed perfection, followed by a return to normality and order. The liberation that takes place in Act II is not political but personal, a union of two hearts. The spectator is no longer allowed a stance of detachment, but is drawn into the space of the dream. Dim lighting ensures that the audience will be in no position to judge the quality of scene-painting, and costuming, but allows a complete merging of the starving hero with the environment he inhabits. Here in his dungeon, the isolated hero stands for the isolated ego of the romantic subject. The space of the stage no longer seems to the spectator material and other, but accords with the conception of Kant that space is an extension of the consciousness of the viewer. The final version of *Fidelio* opened in Vienna in the year of Napoleon's defeat; and the opera was frequently chosen to reinaugurate German opera houses after the Second World War.[44] It portrays, however, the only kind of liberation that the *théâtre à l'italienne* admits: the liberation of the individual soul. This is the inescapable logic of Plato's cave.

The nineteenth-century auditorium was subject to competing pressures. Schlegel, for example, lamented in 1808 the 'unavoidable defects' of perspectival staging, a system devised for and best adapted to opera. But despite his admiration of Shakespeare, and dismay at the fashion of introducing new painted settings for every scene, he cannot envisage any return to the principles of the Elizabethan stage.[45] Though there seemed no alternative to the universal *théâtre à l'italienne*, gradual changes took place within the constraints of the form. The pressures of capitalism and urban growth meant larger auditoria, which were more compatible with romantic pictorial staging than with French classicism. Increased scale encouraged the spectator's sense of viewing as an individual ego rather than part of a closed community. Theatres became urban monuments, sited at the head of public squares or boulevards. Their frontages, modelled on Greek temples, presented theatres as temples of art, substituting for mediaeval churches and palaces in a secular and more republican society.[46] The action moved rear of the proscenium, framing the play as an object of aesthetic contemplation. Affluent seventeenth- and eighteenth-century spectators had dressed up in wigs and make-up in order to play out social roles in the auditorium, but the would-be natural human being of the romantic era had no such accoutrements to hide the soul behind, and so required the greater privacy offered by comfortable, upholstered seats. The theatre gradually became a space in which one escaped one's public role, free to indulge in private emotions. Grand foyers, saloons and staircases compensated for greater personal privacy at the point of viewing, and insisted that theatre-going was still a social event.[47] Despite the drift to privacy and silent, passive spectatorship, the spatial principles of the *théâtre à l'italienne* did not lose all their ability to generate excitement in the manner that Marmontel describes. The key to this energy was still the pit with its distinctive local identity. Though the poorest members of the urban crowd were banished to the galleries, and the rest pushed further from the stage by rows of stalls seating, the pit continued to be a conduit of emotion. Henry Irving tried in 1885 to decollectivize the pit at the Lyceum by making places reservable, but his experiment failed. He found that 'from an artistic point of view the pit did not applaud, and the applause of the pit is most inspiring, for, as I have said before, the pit is the backbone of theatre'.[48] Though Irving failed, the Bancrofts at the Haymarket did succeed in abolishing the pit, after enduring the inevitable riot.[49] The abolition of the pit at the Haymarket went hand in hand with the final triumph of the picture frame. Theatre became the preserve of polite society, and the *théâtre à l'italienne* lost its *raison d'être*.

The logic of romantic viewing was understood and followed through by Wagner, whose dark auditorium and single fan of seating at Bayreuth focused all eyes on the stage (figure 26). His theatre was not a grand urban monument, but a building oriented upon its interior where individuals could lose their imprisoning individuality in the work of art. It was no longer the collective act of viewing that mattered, but the aesthetic object. Leo Tolstoy condemned Bayreuth as 'counterfeit art', a space of illusion, and wondered what an honest peasant would say watching the cream of the upper classes engaged in voluntary hypnosis.[50] But Tolstoy was swimming against the tide with his classical and ethical conception of art. Bayreuth was a place where the romantic ideal of art as a waking dream could be realized, in a conscious surrender to the imagination that transcended Diderot's dichotomy of rationality and feeling.[51] Wagner carried the logic of Plato's cave to its conclusion, releasing the theatre finally from the public, interactive Roman mode of viewing, casting the spectators into darkness, and tying them with invisible bonds that prevented them from looking to left or right.

Figure 34 Antoine's set for *The Wild Duck*.

André Antoine, the celebrated director of naturalistic drama, was an enthusiastic advocate of Wagner's theatre space. He launched his plan for a Parisian replica with a fierce diatribe against the *théâtre à l'italienne:*

The circular form in general usage condemns two thirds of the audience on the upper levels to sit, literally and without any exaggeration, facing *each other*. Although ultimately everyone seated in the front row of a gallery can enjoy the performance at the cost of endurable torture, the occupants of the two or three rows behind are obliged to stand, contort themselves and lean into the void in order to see a tiny part of the stage . . . It would not be wrong to claim that out of twelve hundred people, there are *six hundred*, three hundred on each side, who *do not see* the integral performance . . . One third of the audience *cannot hear* . . . The *circular* form of auditorium is thus illogical and contrary to any rational mode of performing.[52]

He went on to argue for perfect sightlines, and the comfort that the public now expected. Actors in the *théâtre à l'italienne*, he lamented, perform like statues, as if wearing evening dress, and his plea for a theatre of natural movement and speech echoes Diderot.

On the face of it, Antoine argued for a theatre that would create on stage a replica of material existence, but when we look more closely at high naturalism, we find that Platonist viewing has by no means disappeared. Amongst Antoine's most celebrated productions were two plays of Ibsen, *Ghosts* (1890, written 1881) and *The Wild Duck* (1891, written 1884). Despite the solid box set, and electric light capable of revealing the physical authenticity of the props, the theme of both plays relates to the inner world of the cavern that opens up at the back of the stage, the space where ghosts return and the wild duck is shot. In both plays the main box set represents at once the false façade of bourgeois society, and the front which an individual puts before the world, whilst perspectival depth reveals inner truth. Antoine's set for *The Wild Duck* reveals, despite solid timber structures and studied asymmetry, a triangular form that leads the eye back to the mysterious half-lit inner room.

The Wild Duck is a meditation on Platonist notions of truth. The plot is driven by the attempts of Gregers, son of an industrialist, to assert the 'claim of the ideal', a messianic call to absolute truth that seems to be driven by some kind of Oedipal impulse. The set represents a photographic studio, a space for the manufacture of illusions (fig. 34). A doctor, healer of the body, speaks up for what Plato termed the 'noble lie' as a foundation for happiness. The mystic garret behind Ibsen's box set, constantly changing according to the light, is a home-made fantasy world, an attempt to recreate the Scandinavian forests where human beings were once happy before being alienated from their natural selves by industrialization. On another level, the garret represents the soul of the innocent heroine, housing the wounded wild duck that symbolizes her inner self. Though a space of nature and innocence, the garret is also associated with the violence of the hunter. Ibsen's technique in *Ghosts* was similar: the perspectival vista with its stormy fjord and burning orphanage evokes the sexual guilt inherited by the protagonist, a guilt that is cleared on death to reveal a sunlit snowscape. The work of Ibsen the naturalist was shaped by a romantic quest for self, and for a spiritual truth that lies in the interior of the individual. The traditional techniques of the *théâtre à l'italienne* remained his only recourse.

Freud was evidently inspired to formulate his theory of the Oedipus instinct after watching Mounet-Sully's renowned rendering of Oedipus at the Comédie Française. Mounet-Sully's performance was designed for the *théâtre à l'italienne*, and its success turned upon its exploitation of guilt.[53] Freud's best-known spatial representation of the mind recreates the features of a *théâtre à l'italienne*.[54] I have turned his diagram upside-down in accordance with the normal representation of theatres (fig. 35).

The small horseshoe of the perceptual-conscious equates with the Italian auditorium, where the audience watch the play moment by moment. The box set equates with the preconscious, and presents the family circumstances and other environmental influences that have shaped the protagonists' behaviour. Behind the box set lies the space of the unconscious, energized by the id. Freud's broken lines represent the permeable rear of the box set, which opens at climactic moments to reveal the mysteries of the soul. Freud's superego enters down-stage left, the traditional side used by the Victorian villain who blocks desire, while up-stage right, typically used by the heroine, is the doorway to the repressed. We see these conventions operating in *The Wild Duck*, where stage left is used for the entry of Gregers, the malign voice of conscience, while stage right leads to the kitchen area, controlled by the photographer's wife who knows all and says nothing. Freud's conception of the human Ego cannot be dissociated from his conception of the theatre. European theatre in the late nineteenth century was still a privileged medium for shaping human experience.

The vocabulary of naturalism remains potent in the twenty-first century, for it continues to accord with conceptions of the human being as container for an inner life. In February 2002, I watched a sell-out naturalist play at the Royal Court Theatre in London. The Royal Court has thrived over five decades as a space for new writing because it combines the energies generated by the *théâtre à l'italienne* with the intimate scale of neo-classical

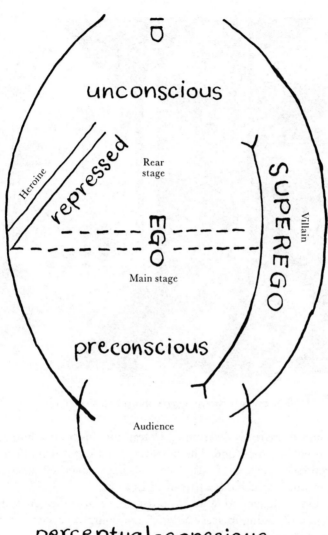

id

unconscious

Heroine

repressed

Rear
stage

SUPEREGO

Villain

EGO

Main stage

preconscious

Audience

perceptual-conscious

Figure 35   Freud's theatre of the mind.

French auditoria, and an audience committed to intense listening. In the final tableau of the play the hero stands in front of a Victorian hearth, placed centrally and framed by two doorways, and imagines himself crucified. Stage left is commanded by his mother's dresser (his superego), stage right is used for the entry and exit of his homosexual lover. The woman society

Plate 20   *Look Back in Anger.* Cartoon by Ionicus (1961).

requires him to marry is determined to tear out this hearth, and replace
it with an ugly modern one. The hearth with its warm flames and long
history represents his soul, heart, deepest feelings, inner self, or whatever
term we favour for the hidden part of an Ego.

The room, as Raymond Williams observed, defined the genre of stage
naturalism, articulating in space a critique of bourgeois society. Williams
identifies in Ibsen and Chekhov

A repeated search for some means of defining the humanity that cannot be lived, in
these well-ordered rooms – the forces outside, the white horses or the seagull, the
tower or the cherry orchard, which have meaning because there are forces inside
these people in these rooms, which cannot be realized in any available life.[55]

In naturalist theatre at the end of the nineteenth century there was a creative
tension between the private space of the room and the public space of the

theatre where people gathered to escape the entrapment of domesticity. A Punch cartoon of 1961 (plate 20) shows tension turned to anomaly. John Osborne's celebrated kitchen-sink drama *Look Back in Anger* (1956) is being played not in the Royal Court but in the grander Lyric Theatre, Hammersmith. The affluent first-night audience, gathered for an ostentatious rite of display, is set to gain vicarious satisfaction from the idea of slumming in a garret. However, the cartoonist has eliminated all sense of picture frame, creating a shallow open stage on which actors confront their class enemy, reflecting Osborne's antagonistic view of the British public. The *théâtre à l'italienne* is seen to reflect and support an antiquated set of social values. Originally designed to create mystery through concealment and revelation, the *théâtre à l'italienne* does not easily lend itself to the authentic representation of squalor.

In the first decades of the twentieth century, modernism involved a radical challenge to received notions of self, space, society and representation.[56] The cubists abandoned the fundamentals of perspectival viewing, preferring the intersection of planes upon a surface. Einstein like the cubists complicated the relationship between time and space, and denied that there was an objective position from which to view material reality. Theatre encountered also the challenge of cinema, which allowed angles of viewing to be shifted at will by the camera, and time sequences to be intercut. The function of theatre as a representational medium became uncertain, alongside its social function. The two major ways forward for theatre as an autonomous art can be associated with the names of Craig and Appia, the first heir to the romantic tradition, the second to the classical.

Romantic theatre tried to emulate painting, but always had a technical difficulty in merging human heroes with painted renderings of the natural world. Craig solved this problem partly through the use of light, partly through down-grading the status of the actor, whom he famously termed a super-marionette. The resources of electricity allowed him to create suggestions of open and infinite space – as for example in Ibsen's *Rosmersholm*, where he abandoned the box set the better to open up the 'inner life' of the play.[57] It is characteristic of Craig's designs that architectural structures tower over diminutive human silhouettes with all the grandeur of Roman stage façades. The new Roman emperor in Craig's conception was the stage director, who subordinated text and actors to his unifying aesthetic vision. It was not the actor–audience relationship that interested Craig, so much as the aesthetic object. When the stage director emerged in the early twentieth century as the major creative artist, closely allied to the designer or 'scenographer' (to use the more assertive French expression), the spectators were expected to share the artist's point of view. The space of the audience was low on Craig's agenda, because the spectators were to be overwhelmed by the force of the stage image. 'Art is revelation', as Craig remarked in a programme note to *Rosmersholm*,[58] and whatever his aspirations to modernity some form of proscenium staging suited that goal in most instances.

Adolphe Appia was concerned with the sculptural form of the human body, and not with the inner life. He provided eurhythmic dancers with solid platforms, steps and subtle lighting. Where Craig anticipates the tradition of 'directors' theatre', Appia can be associated with the more democratic ideal of 'actors' theatre'. He was much more interested than Craig in actor–audience relationships, and in an essay of 1922 he pondered how best to create a 'people's theatre'. Despite his passion for Greek antiquity, he did not follow Reinhardt and Gémier and resurrect the Greek circle. Cubist art was his major inspiration, and frontal presentation made it easier to use light as an expressive medium. Frontality, however, posed the problem of the frame needed to unify the image. Appia observed that the gilded picture frame had been made redundant by modern art, and was now just a device that allowed paintings to hang as objects on a museum wall. He was hostile to the proscenium arch, and sought to bring the performance ever closer to an active audience. At Hellerau, where eurhythmic theatre was developed in 1911–14, the rectilinear steps of the auditorium echoed the rostra used by the dancers. There was no formal division between spectators and performers, not even one of light. Appia had no sympathy with the prevailing configuration of theatre spaces:

The position given the actors directly influences the spectator, and we must begin by changing this position. Its most characteristic quality is the remoteness of the actor from the audience, emphasized inside the auditorium by the footlights, outside by separate entrances, and throughout by a mode of behaviour that is far removed from that of the spectator. The audience, for its part, idly perpetuates the custom of paying for and selecting its seat, then expecting the actor to do all the rest. But such conditions are anachronistic, and both the actor and the audience can no longer agree to these humiliating relations.[59]

Yet the possibilities of Hellerau were limited. Neither Appia nor anyone else in the twentieth century had an easy answer to the question of how to make the actor–audience relationship closer, once the proscenium arch had gone. What sort of activity was now expected of the spectator? How should the seats be arranged? What degree of merging between actor and spectator was possible? How was interaction to be reconciled with aesthetic distance?

For Tadeusz Kantor as an east European, modernism was tied to the Russian revolution, which brought in its wake the 'destruction of the "Winter Palace" of Illusion'. Seeking to obliterate the gulf between art and life, Russian constructivists opened up the aristocratic *théâtre à l'italienne* in order to expose the proletariat working the mechanisms behind the trickery:

> In the jargon of theatre historians, this process of changes was called *the disappearance of the demarcation line between the stage and the auditorium* . . . The work ceased to be a *reflection* of life, which connoted a safe perception and a comfortable condition for the spectator . . . The acting space was detached from the imaginary horizon and pushed forward towards the audience.[60]

For Kantor, this desire to bring actors and audience closer resulted in contradiction. Some experimenters in environmental theatre invited the audience to enter the performance space, and become co-creators of illusion; others transferred the performance from a theatre to an appropriate 'authentic' found space, generating yet another level of pretence. Attempts to destroy illusion only recreated it. Kantor was driven to the conclusion that the whole debate rested on a false premiss, because it begged the question: what is reality?

Kantor's radical step forward – or backward – at the end of his life was to raise the postmodern question of self. Casting aside once fashionable Marxist modes of analysis, he sought to find truth in the so-called 'individual human life'. In 1990 he decided to place himself on stage in a painter's studio that embodied the reality of his imagination:

> The space of Reality must be expanded for it to embrace
> such nonphysical territories as
> MEMORYS.
> One needs to place an equals sign between Memory and Reality.

He goes on to explain that

> Such a site is presented in
> my current production,
> *Today is my Birthday.*
> On stage *(sic!)*,
> I am putting together (CONSTRUCTING) my home,
> my POOR Room of Imagination.

His controlling device in the production was a huge picture frame that allowed figures to appear both inside and outside it. Actors moved between the empty, framed, theatrical space of the imagination and the immediate face-to-face world of the audience. The audience could feel itself to be real, more real than the play, because it was in a position to gaze at the stage picture; but its identity was at the same time destabilized, because it was the object of the author's gaze, and the gaze of the actors. Kantor argued that the picture-frame is a principle that we can neither accept nor abandon:

> I accept illusion
> because by accepting its existence,
> I can keep destroying it interminably.[61]

The *théâtre à l'italienne* was a space that turned upon competing and contradictory premisses: the idealist proposition, harking back to Plato, that one can look into the human soul; the materialist proposition, harking back to Aristotle, that reality exists out there to be observed and imitated on a stage; and the collectivist proposition, harking back to the practices of Roman theatre, that we are social beings before we are individuals, and so naturally gather in a circular auditorium to assert our social identity. Through denying the stability of the ego, and identifying self as a locus of intersecting images, Kantor offers a new legitimacy to picture frame theatre. After a lifetime of refusal, Kantor's decision to place a dramatic action 'On stage (*sic!*)' marked a sign of the times – the end of the modernist impulse to jettison the past.

By the end of the twentieth century, a new respect for the *théâtre à l'italienne* was apparent amongst theatre practitioners.[62] Faith in eternal progress had been discredited, and the desire to discard the past was replaced by a desire to play upon the memories embedded in architectural forms. The *théâtre à l'italienne* was seen to have stood the test of time. Brecht, for example, had developed his dramaturgy in a *théâtre à l'italienne* in socialist East Berlin without any hint of anxiety. Bourgeois architecture allowed him the better to challenge bourgeois values. The Czech scenographer Josef Svoboda stated in the early 1990s: 'I've always been an advocate of the proscenium stage because it is the most theatrical space available; moreover, the routine transformation of theatre into mere spectacle isn't readily possible in it.'[63] Reaffirmations of the *théâtre à l'italienne* stem from this recognition. Framing the scenic image problematizes the relationships of viewers and viewed in endlessly interesting ways. By the end of the twentieth century it was widely recognized that 'proscenium theatre' had been a false bogey. Rhetoric about the evils of the 'proscenium arch' stemmed from the failure of twentieth-century architects to understand and learn from the past. Though architects were not the only culprits. When Antoine and other modernists called for a theatre of comfortable seats and good sightlines, rather than an environment that stimulated the senses and encouraged social interaction, they led theatre architecture into a cul-de-sac.

CHAPTER 8

The empty space

The Committee for Revolutionary Action (C.A.R.), together with the militants of the revolutionary student movement, has occupied the ex-theatre of France and transformed it into a permanent meeting place for all. During the night of May 16, it transferred the responsibility . . . to a Committee of Occupation made up of actors, students, and workers whose political position is in line with their own. The goals of the occupation remain the same:

   – The sabotage of all that is 'cultural': theatre, art, literature, etc. (right-wing, left-wing, governmental or 'avant-garde') and the maintenance of the political struggle in highest priority.

   – The systematic sabotage of the cultural industry, especially the industry of show business, in order to make room for true collective creation.

   . . . Never again must a ticket be sold in the ex-theatre of France; its free status must be maintained . . . The only theatre is guerrilla theatre . . . .

      Comité d'Action Révolutionaire de l'ex-Théâtre de France 17 May, 1968

The occupation of the Odéon in Paris in 1968 marks a turning point. It was the boldest attempt, by a section of society which saw itself as 'alternative', to discard all that belonged to tradition. The Paris radicals took it for granted that aesthetic, economic and political structures were entirely caught up with each other, and art could not be separated from the institutions that defined and contained it. The revolutionaries of 1968 believed that art could somehow be 'freed' from the past, and a new form of theatre be created, based on open public spaces, and on interactive relationships not passive audiences of consumers. *The Drama Review* in 1968 published a manifesto by an activist in the occupation and stager of Happenings, Jean-Jacques Lebel. Lebel wrote of the irrelevance of history, finding an emotive chord only in the pre-logical art of primitive peoples. He argued that if artistic activity was to renew and intensify human perception, then it needed to escape from supposedly sacred places like theatres and galleries.[1]

The Marxist aesthetician, Theodor Adorno, writing in the same period, saw modern art as a response to industrialization, and identified much the same tension between art and capitalism:

Modern art is equally determined socially by the conflict with the conditions of production and inner-aesthetically by the exclusion of exhausted and obsolete procedures. Modernity tends rather to oppose the ruling Zeitgeist, and today it must do so . . . The murderous historical force of the modern is equated with the disintegration of all that to which the proprietors of culture so desperately cling . . . Only works that expose themselves to every risk have the chance of living on, not those that out of fear of the ephemeral cast their lot with the past.[2]

It is a necessary condition of successful modern art, in other words, to oppose dominant socio-economic structures, and to reject the past insofar as that past belongs to 'the proprietors of culture'. Adorno preserves a space for art as a category, unwilling to reduce it to a function of institutional structures.[3] He offers a more nuanced picture than Lebel of the way modernity is duty-bound to reject the past, arguing that art has always proceeded dialectically through a critique of past practice. It is fundamental to his analysis that art of the twentieth century differs from previous centuries in the 'murderous' extremity of its rejection of the past, and in its consistent sense of oppositionality. The split between mainstream capitalist culture and a dissident avant-garde is a defining feature of the modern period, and has obvious consequences for any account of theatre space.

My concern in this chapter will be the twentieth century, and its attempt to start afresh, finding no roots in the historical past. My focus will be the notion of the 'empty space' as an ideal locus for performance, a space emptied of any attributes that associate it with a particular place and time. Peter Brook's famous quartet of lectures, *The Empty Space*, was published in 1968, the year when the occupiers of the Odéon planned to change the world, and his book will serve as an anchor for my analysis. Brook is a pivotal figure because of his searching experimentation with theatre space. In 1968 he was a figure who belonged neither to mainstream culture nor to alternative culture, but straddled the two.

From the perspective of the twenty-first century, we can see the historical particularity of the 1960s. Affluence was new, and middle-class youth were content to put ideals before career. Women and minorities felt newly empowered. Contraception allowed the sexual morality of the past to seem irrelevant – in contrast to the millennium when AIDS would foster a new puritanism. The 'alternative' or 'counter' culture rested on a sense of us and them, and the prime symbol of 'them' was the Vietnam War, which in its turn was a symbol of technocracy, an industrial–military machine running out of control. The desire to live intensely in the present was encouraged by an awareness that thermo-nuclear immolation could occur at any moment. By the millennium, the ending of the Cold War and the passing of time had reduced such fears. The alternative culture was characterized also by its spiritual searching. By the millennium drugs had become associated either with social deprivation or with communal pleasure-seeking, but in the sixties LSD offered an avenue to inner realities and truths born of contemplation. In mainstream culture the power of technology produced an infatuation with the new and a faith in progress. There was not yet any collective awareness of global warming and the degradation of the planet. The prime symbol of the new was modernist architecture, which swept away city centres, old forms of housing and many old theatres.

This is the socio-political context in which we have to read *The Empty Space*. The first lecture is a diatribe against 'deadly theatre', and Brook's symbol of deadliness is early twentieth-century proscenium theatre:

I can take any empty space and call it a bare stage. A man walks across this empty space whilst someone else is watching him, and this is all that is needed for an act of theatre to be engaged. Yet when we talk about theatre this is not quite what we mean. Red curtains, spotlights, blank verse, laughter, darkness, these are all confusedly superimposed in a messy image covered by one all-purpose word. We talk of cinema killing the theatre, and in that phrase we refer to the theatre as it was when cinema was born, a theatre of box office, foyer, tip-up seats, footlights, scene changes, intervals, music, as though the theatre was by definition these and little more.[4]

In 1968, this proved an inspirational text, offering an ideal that was, if not guerrilla theatre, then a more contemplative indoor equivalent. Brook goes on to explain how Edward Gordon Craig was infatuated by Victorian illusionist theatre in his early youth, but as time went by the stage curtain ceased to uncover surprises. Reflecting the progressivist bias of his age, Brook equates that historical transition with a collective loss of childhood.[5] In place of the Victorian theatre, he offered his readers not the functional buildings of the modern movement, but an empty space of fresh beginnings. His views were born of a professional crisis. In 1970 he was still trying to reconcile the irreconcilable with his production of *A Midsummer Night's Dream*, a play that encloses theatre inside theatre. He created a white box as a stage set, the epitome of an empty space, and placed this box on the stage of the Royal Shakespeare Theatre at Stratford-upon-Avon. By means of bright colours in a white box, he attempted to bring the action closer to an audience seated too far away. He condemned the RST as a large, cold and uninteresting space, and spoke of a terrible temptation to burn the building down and use the insurance money to pay eighteen months' wages to actors.[6] He did not attempt this compromise again, recognizing that his creative project had to embrace the entirety of the theatre space.

In the context of 1968 Brook's ruthless discarding of old institutional structures generated enormous creative energy. However productive it may have been of good work, Brook's ideal of 'empty space' was always philosophically untenable. In order to *take* an empty space and *call it* a bare stage, he (the unseen director) needs to frame that space, and separate it from the clutter round about. The shape and contour of the frame confers an identity on that which is framed. And human figures within the frame have to be seen against a background. Brook toured Africa using a Persian carpet to define the boundaries of an 'empty' playing space designed to liberate the imagination and transcend cultural divisions. It was only when he tried to use the same carpet in his set for *The Tempest* that he recognised how the woven pattern suited one narrative and negated another.[7] The idea that this carpet could actually demarcate an empty space was seen to be an illusion.

Brook's second lecture articulates his spiritual ideal of 'holy theatre' where the invisible is made visible. The theatrical past merited little more than contempt in 1968:

In the theatre, the tendency for centuries has been to put the actor at a remote distance, on a platform, framed, decorated, lit, painted, in high shoes – so as to help persuade the ignorant that he is holy, that his art is sacred. Did this express reverence? Or was there behind it a fear that something would be exposed if the light were too bright, the meeting too near? Today we have exposed the sham.[8]

The newly discovered work of Grotowski epitomized Brook's ideal of the holy. Here, ascetic actors were creating a theatre of monastic poverty, offering to tiny audiences an intense spiritual experience. This theatre, he wrote, 'responds to a need the churches can no longer fill'.[9] Grotowski's *Towards a Poor Theatre* was published in 1968, with a preface by Brook, in which Brook distanced his own 'Shakespearean' tradition from Catholic Poland, and argued that in his own culture the rough had necessarily to be blended in with the holy. Sketches in *Towards a Poor Theatre* indicate the importance of spatial relationships in Grotowski's work, but the text of the book concerns itself exclusively with the techniques of the holy actor. As we saw in chapter 2, the locus of Grotowskian holiness was the disciplined body of the actor, not the space of performance, nor (back in the mid 1960s) the mind of the committed spectator. Actors might substitute for monks, but theatres could not replace churches. Grotowski's interest lay in proxemics. It was the relative relationship of embodied actor and embodied spectator that shaped the dramatic event, whilst the shell that surrounded that relationship and cut it off from the corrupt, materialist world outside was of no account. In the introspective 1960s, spiritual human beings could be separated from their material environment in a way that would seem more difficult come the millennium.

Brook's notion of the empty space has a spiritual basis. He wrote of his personal searching that one 'must start from zero, clear an empty space in oneself . . .' As a long-term devotee of Gurdjieff, he stands at the spiritual rather than the political end of the radical 1960s value system.[10] When he staged a protest play about Vietnam in the bourgeois Aldwych Theatre in 1964, he challenged the performance traditions of the Royal Shakespeare Company, but ended up by aestheticizing protest.[11] Finding himself in Paris in May 1968, he pursued his original programme of research and refused to take to the streets.[12] His celebration of 'rough theatre' is based more on metaphysics than politics, and recalls the dualism of medieval artists who depicted grotesques as the complement of angels.

One of Brook's most powerful exemplars of rough theatre is a post-war performance of *Crime and Punishment* in a crowded Hamburg garret, where he discovered 'the essence of an art that stems from the story-teller'. The lack of stage machinery helped the performance match the complexity of Dostoievski's novel, and the flexibility of cinema.[13] The RSC designer Sean Kenny had heard Brook tell of this legendary performance, and in 1964 drew an appropriate Brookian moral: 'Theatre equals proscenium arch, and that really is all it means today. It doesn't mean a place where you can make anything happen . . . We haven't designed a place where theatre can begin from a white canvas, from a negative expression.'[14] Kenny failed to consider how the power of this performance related to the packed crowd of some two hundred spectators, and more precisely to the lack of any *empty* space, given that the actors were confined to an area 6 foot by 12. The audience became the set. There was nothing here to equate with white canvas. Brook's formalist account of the event underplays the dimensions of place and social space. The historical centre of Hamburg had been destroyed by allied bombing, so a Victorian house standing in the environs held a particular meaning. Dostoievski's novel is an empathetic study of guilt following a murder, and the performance was intense because these actors and watchers were coming to terms with Nazism. The political context is erased in Brook's account, which seeks to extrapolate a universal moral. Nevertheless despair of an unmotivated English audience is a consistent strand running through *The Empty Space*. In his sequel published in 1993, he gave increasing emphasis to the principle that: 'Another aspect of the empty space is that the emptiness is shared: it's the same space for everyone who is present.'[15] Brook's excursions around the globe furnished ever more examples of the fact that a performance depends on the mentality of its audience.

Brook was again unwilling to refer the quality of a performance back to the mentality of its audience when he attended the Berliner Ensemble's Marxist *Coriolanus*, and he pronounces authoritatively upon Brecht's rewriting that: 'we carry a less insistent memory with us'. Pursuing his celebration of Shakespeare as the ideal dramatist, he goes on: 'The Elizabethan stage was like the attic I was describing in Hamburg: it was a neutral open platform.' He follows William Poel in stressing the priority of language over scenery, but goes further, noting the view of historians that 'the permanent structure of the Elizabethan playhouse . . . was a diagram of the universe as seen by the sixteenth-century audience . . . a perfect philosopher's machine'. From this conception of a philosopher's machine, he adduces that Shakespeare's language takes us not only across continents but also into an inner psychic world, for it is Shakespeare's ultimate greatness to deal with 'the whole condition of man'.[16] Brook glides over the historical specificity of the Elizabethan playhouse in order to offer the 'empty space' as the foundation for an aesthetic capable of engaging with the human condition. Running through Brook's work is a tension between on the one hand a concern for universal spiritual truths, and on the other an awareness that each performance event is a unique moment of communication. Emptiness finally becomes a metaphysical, Zen conception, where material existence can be escaped. A materialist analysis of Brook's thinking about empty space may discern echoes of the 1960s property developer, seeking cleared slums or a green-field site in order to create an ideal lifestyle; echoes too of the demise of empire, which left Europeans hungry for new empty spaces to colonize.[17]

The title of Brook's final lecture 'Immediate theatre' alludes to the 1960s phenomenon of the Happening, but the lecture turns out to be a lesson in how to perform Shakespeare in mainstream theatre. We can read the chapter in retrospect as a desperate attempt by Brook to reconcile his vision of theatre with a personal future inside the Royal Shakespeare Company. The sixties Happening was another manifestation of the utopian impulse that drove Brook to escape from alienating traditions, to find authenticity in the experience of the moment, to seek truth in the world of the invisible.[18] Brook had not yet abandoned mainstream British institutions, or made his pilgrimage to the empty spaces of the Persian mountains and Sahara desert. *The Empty Space* ends with an affirmation of what theatre ought to be, but no sense of how, in the European context of 1967, that end could be achieved. The enduring importance of the book as a work of performance theory lies in its insistence that theatre can only be understood phenomenologically. The vogue for semiotics has waxed and waned since 1968, and Brook's questions about the quality of live experience seem to have returned to the head of the intellectual agenda, new forms of virtual reality having supplanted cinema as the necessary point of reference.

The 1960s was a utopian era when new beginnings seemed possible. In an influential conference paper delivered in 1961, the Parisian theatre historian Denis Bablet pronounced the *théâtre à l'italienne* to be a dead thing. His key text was an unpublished statement by Edward Gordon Craig:

Theatre must be an empty space with only a roof, a floor, and wall. Inside this space one must set up for each new type of play a new sort of stage and temporary auditorium. We shall thus discover new theatres, for every type of drama demands a particular type of scenic space.[19]

Bablet could equally well have quoted Appia in a text written for the same international exhibition of 1921/2:

We do wrong to make the same buildings serve both for the standard repertory and for modern experimentation. The implications of that fixed form palpably hold us back from attaining our quest for freedom. So let us relinquish those theatres to an expiring past, and build rudimentary structures designed simply as a covering for the space we work in. No more stage, no circle of seats. Just a bare and empty room [*salle*], in anticipation.[20]

Bablet used Craig's text as a rallying cry for an adaptable theatre where the seating could be reconfigured to suit any historical or experimental lay-out. The Marxist bent of his generation encouraged him to think in terms of specific socio-economic formations. He saw his own 'society' as one in a state of transformation. When a new society, and corresponding way of writing plays, finally emerged, then would be the time for a definitive architectural form.

Bablet invoked many other twentieth-century practitioners to support his thesis. Jacques Copeau's call for the *tréteau nu*, the bare boards of the commedia dell'arte, identifies him as another pioneer of 'empty space'. At the Vieux-Colombier in Paris, Copeau removed all decoration, blanked off the balcony at the side of the auditorium, and stripped out as much of the proscenium arch as he could, seeking to reduce theatre to its essential: contact with the words and body of the actor.[21] Like most great practitioners of the twentieth century, Copeau sought for the quality that can variously be defined as 'reality', 'presence' or 'authenticity' – a quest that relates both to the challenge of cinema, and to the feeling that no touchstone of ultimate reality can be found in God or science. On stage he found the quality he wanted in the stage carpenter, and in the cleaning lady as she swept and scrubbed the steps, whilst actors were compulsively false.[22] The bare stage allowed truth to be revealed. What Copeau soon discovered was that architectural space could not be dissociated from social space. The problem of theatrical communication lay in the audience as much as in the actors:

There is a professional audience just as there are, in the worst sense of the word, professional actors and playwrights. They have lost their truthfulness. The theatre needs truthfulness, and authenticity, on stage. These things are no less necessary in the auditorium.[23]

The falsity of Parisians drove him to seek a more truthful audience in rural Burgundy. A semi-industrial space once used for making wine-casks yielded a more authentic environment.[24]

Bablet cites Copeau as an exemplary pioneer seeking new architectural forms. Max Reinhardt is presented as the foremost experimenter in theatrical 'place', having used a circus for *Oedipus* and the urban landscape of Salzburg for *Everyman*. Bablet cites Reinhardt as saying: 'Let good actors perform in a barn or a theatre today, tomorrow in an inn, inside a church, or even, Heaven help us, on an expressionist stage – if the place corresponds with the play, the result will be superb.'[25] Such experiments, Bablet argues, constitute a 'laboratory' allowing us to uncover the true architectural needs of our society. Whilst Reinhardt was able to realize most of his experiments, all too many pioneers – Meyerhold, Artaud, Bel Geddes – were not. Most important of these, perhaps, is Walter Gropius, for Gropius was a member of the Bauhaus, the grouping of artists that did so much to shape modernist architecture. Though fascism prevented any development of the project, Gropius designed for Piscator a 'total theatre' that could be reconfigured for three fundamental historical forms: the deep proscenium stage, the open or thrust stage of classical antiquity with its semicircular auditorium, and the full arena with audience on all sides. Gropius wanted to create a space that would serve for assemblies, concerts and sporting events as well as plays. He envisaged 'a great keyboard for light and space, so objective and adaptable in character that it would respond to any imaginable vision of a stage director'. The new versatility of lighting was the key to flexibility, and the vagaries of acoustics were largely forgotten. The versatility of space, made possible by modern technology, was for Gropius a source of inspiration: 'a flexible building capable of transforming and refreshing the mind by its spatial impact alone'.[26] Here was the vision that would lie behind many a post-war arts centre or *maison de culture*.

This is the ideal to which Bablet's manifesto pointed at the start of the utopian 1960s: a laboratory that can be adapted to any experiment, an arts centre that will serve for any vaguely theatrical purpose. We hear the lyrical tones of Gropius in a poem written by an English architect when commissioned in 1970 to build a cut-price regional arts centre:

> Why a finite stage
> that can impose
> limited order
> to the vision of man?
> Arena, apron, proscenium
> are terminals
> that reduce the spatial world
> to numbered formulae.
> So man
> in free space
> moving only in time,
> can create
> his own order at will,
> as actor within
> spatial infinity,
> where boundaries are drawn
> by light and visual angle
> to define.[27]

The reality of such arts centres did not correspond with the dream. The dream was of free and infinite space controlled by the dimmer switch, involving intellectual and moral liberation from the spatial constraints of the past. The reality was a space in which every configuration proved a compromise. Bablet in 1961 failed to pinpoint a deep incompatibility between Copeau's ascetic bare boards and the technological revolution. The former rooted theatre in the authenticity of the body, the latter denied the body.

The most articulate exponent of multi-purpose theatre design has been George C. Izenour, who commenced his architectural practice in 1955, and went on to build numerous theatres in American municipalities and universities. In 1977 he published the first edition of a monumental history of theatre design, which offered a progressivist view of the past. Izenour identifies as the first modern visionary the engineer John Scott Russell who declared in 1838:

A perfectly good seat is one in which, without uneasy elevation of the head or eye, without straining or stretching, we can calmly and quietly take any easy position or variety of positions, which we may be disposed to assume, and yet may in all of them see and hear the speaker with equal clearness and repose, so as to give him patient and undisturbed attention. The person who occupies such a seat feels as if the speaker were speaking principally to and for him; he finds that no-one else stands in his way, and that he hears well, and sees as well, as if there were no one else in the room but himself and the speaker. A room so constructed that every man in it should feel in this manner, that he had got one of the best places and that no one else was in his way – such a room would be perfect.[28]

Izenour nails his colours to this scientific visionary, with his chilling ideal of an emotionless, individualized spectator released from the horrors of the standard Victorian auditorium. Nineteenth-century theatre design, Izenour maintains, rested on pre-democratic rules of hierarchy combined with 'architectural caprice'. Innovators like Wagner, the acoustician Walter Clement Sabine, and the engineer Dankmar Adler who designed a dual purpose theatre–concert hall in Chicago in 1889, are identified as key figures in a Copernican revolution that at last provided a 'rational solution to the problems of sight lines and auditorium seating geometry'.[29] Izenour's own major contribution lay in the design of acoustical shells that could be placed over a stage to transform a theatre designed for speech into a hall for symphonic music. Large multiple-use theatres seemed to him an inescapable product of economic logic.

Not surprisingly, Izenour had no patience with a 'strident counterculture' concerned with obliterating the performer–audience relationship. The youth counter-culture would never succeed in redefining that relationship, he argued; in spite of youth's "back-to-the-trees" impulse, the need for buildings would always reassert itself.[30] Yet most people now who look back on the 1960s see the counter-culture as the main locus of creativity. The historian Arthur Marwick, in his compendious account of the decade, describes experimental theatre as a 'mighty atom' effecting political and artistic change in a manner quite disproportionate to the number of persons involved.[31] We see in the sixties an extreme form of the split between avant-garde and mainstream which characterizes the century. The implications for late twentieth-century theatre are profound. On the one hand, there is mainstream theatre which inhabits either inherited Victorian spaces or else a functionalist modern *machine à jouer*, a machine for performing in.[32] And on the other hand there is a fringe theatre which inhabits spaces that receive almost no mention in histories of stage architecture.

Izenour echoes the common view that Tyrone Guthrie was the major post-war innovator in mainstream theatre design. In an appendix he cites without comment a text by Guthrie that flatly contradicts his own position. Guthrie explains how he rejected a flexible design for his new theatre at Minneapolis (1963) 'on the ground that an all-purpose hall is a no-purpose hall – that insofar as a purpose is flexible it is not wholehearted'.[33] Guthrie's understanding of the actor–audience relationship was entirely at odds with that of John Scott Russell:

It is axiomatic in my philosophy of the theatre that the audience has got to be packed into the place . . . Anybody who has got any sense knows that when human beings get together in large numbers a great performer will fuse their identity; each single person ceases to be himself and becomes a tiny bit of a single collective personality, that of the audience.[34]

In calling the attention of architects to the dynamics of the audience, Guthrie's contribution was enormously positive. The open, thrust stages that he created, with their allusions to a Greek and Elizabethan inheritance, did much to liberate the classics from the constraints of naturalism. His bare stage freed the actor to use language in order to stimulate the imagination. Such theatres were perfect spaces for a classic repertory, and for an institutional structure whereby directors made their name for directing the classics. But their historical allusiveness made them far less congenial for contemporary dramatic writing and experimentation.

By and large, if I may generalize rather broadly, the twentieth-century plays that are deemed to have endured, and to be worth reperforming, were designed for intimate spaces. If we exclude the domains of musical theatre and classic revivals, we can see the 450-seat Royal Court as representing a maximum size for intense verbal communication in the second half of the century. Intimacy has proved a necessary condition for the expression of an avant-garde or alternative culture. Samuel Beckett, for example, noted how much better *Endgame* worked in the 140-seat Studio des Champs-Elysées than in the Royal Court; in the studio theatre, he found, 'the hooks went right in'.[35] The atmosphere of claustrophobia and entrapment, and the idea of a world stripped down to the bare essentials, made sense when the audience too inhabited a closed minimalist environment. The Royal Court, with its ambiguous identity midway between alternative and mainstream sectors, was an ideal place for socialist-minded British writers to negotiate their relationship with the past, and speak out front to an audience that was at once a general public and an intimate subculture. Though the formal proscenium frame had gone, the Court's nineteenth-century configuration could not serve the needs of a more metaphysical theatre rooted in the physical presence of the actor.

The great quest of the twentieth century, as I suggested in regard to Copeau, has been for authenticity and presence. The existentialism of Jean-Paul Sartre and the phenomenology of Merleau-Ponty are two of the most important post-war attempts to define our sense of the real. Before the war the Marxist aesthetician Walter Benjamin attempted to dismiss 'aura' and 'authenticity' in favour of the reproductive technology that made art available to the masses.[36] Benjamin's views may command more sympathy today, in the wake of Derrida's challenge to the Artaudian myth of presence, but in the post-war period practitioners wanted to find positive qualities in live theatre that differentiated it from cinema. In the wake of fascism with its manipulated mass rallies, the quest for a mass people's theatre lost its momentum. Intimacy became the necessary condition for a sense of body-to-body contact capable of transcending Cartesian ocularity. The sixties cult of stage nudity was a corollary, symbolizing the removal of all social barriers.[37]

Grotowski stated in 1964 that:

There is only one element of which film and television cannot rob the theatre: the closeness of the living organism . . . Let the most drastic scenes happen face to face with the spectator so that he is within arm's reach of the actor, can feel his breathing and smell the perspiration. This implies the necessity of a chamber theatre.[38]

By the end of 1967, he had revised his opinions: 'If the contact between the spectator and the actor is very close and direct, a strong psychic curtain falls between them. It's the opposite of what one might expect.'[39] Alternative theatre slowly waned as an ideal in the last part of the century as practitioners came to terms with this paradox. Grotowski himself could only take his quest for authenticity forwards by developing a new conception of performance space in which all symbolism was eliminated: 'The space does not represent any other space. If something happens in a room, then it happens in a room.'[40]

Several key terms characterize alternative performance spaces of the twentieth century, spaces that were once marginal but in retrospect seem culturally central. These include 'fringe' theatre, the 'intimate theatre', the 'studio', the 'workshop', the 'laboratory', and the 'black box'. 'Fringe' for example, emerged in the late 1950s to describe companies that were not part of the official programme of the Edinburgh festival. It was a proudly worn term in the 1960s, but fell into disuse outside its Edinburgh context when marginality came to be resented. I shall examine these categories, which are united by one essential feature, smallness of scale.

Strindberg is one of the most important pioneers of intimacy. In his chamber plays written for his 160-seat 'Intimate Theatre' in Stockholm in

1907–10, he engaged in ruthless psychic self-exposure. He declared in a poem:

> When the performance starts
> And the curtain rises
> Under more than 100 lights we shall be stripped
> While you are hidden in darkness
> And your feelings like your faces are protected.[41]

Writing in the age of Freud and recovering from his own mental breakdown, Strindberg used actors to play out the workings of his own psyche. *Ghost Sonata* is the most famous of these chamber plays, its central motif being the removal of a domestic façade. Strindberg illustrates a spatial dynamic that would recur throughout the twentieth century: the use of theatre space as a psychoanalyst's consulting room, a privileged and secret environment where the innermost workings of the self can be revealed.

The conception of the theatre as an artist's 'studio' originates with Meyerhold. In 1905 relations between Stanislavski and Nemirovich-Danchenko, his co-director of the Moscow Art Theatre, had broken down, Chekhov was dead and the realist style seemed to have become sterile. Stanislavski encouraged Meyerhold to begin experimental work based on principles of improvisation to release theatre from the tyranny of the text, on breaking the illusion of the fourth wall to transcend materialism, and on using symbolism to explore the inner life of the human being. Developmental work carried out in a barn by a close-knit community of young actors so excited Stanislavski that he renovated at huge personal expense a large Moscow theatre. Unfortunately work that had meaning and integrity in a barn failed in the environment of a conventional theatre. The actors seemed merely Meyerhold's puppets.[42] Stanislavski had yet to grasp how far theatrical meaning was a function of theatrical space.

In 1912 Stanislavski went on to rent a flat above a cinema, where he established the first of four successive Moscow Art Theatre 'Studios', whose remit now included possibilities for a 'new theatrical architecture'. The first studio simply comprised an acting area at floor level, a cloth curtain, lights but not footlights, some chairs, and a table around which to analyse the script.[43] A curved auditorium was then built to seat 150 people. In the first instance, the studio was a developmental space where Stanislavski could train young, open-minded actors in his intense, self-exploratory method, but the training proved inseparable from a new performance ethic. Stanislavski's teachings are paradoxical, on the one hand demanding observation of external reality, on the other packed with spiritual terms like truth, faith, communion and soul. In a protective environment uncontaminated by the trappings of material civilization, Stanislavski felt that the actor could come into contact with the highest part of his or her inner being. The Studio actors lived as a community in the Crimea, and built their own stage objects, which added to the intensity of their public performances. Stanislavski discovered that the intimate performance space, which made the spectators feel they were in the same room as the characters, was bound up with the quality that he demanded of his actors, acting from the heart without affectation.[44] Crossing back to the main theatre became an impossibility, and a series of Studios went on to develop autonomous identities. The conception of the 'studio' soon spread to the west. In the USA, Stanislavski's early ideas spawned the 'Actors Studio' where naturalism was pursued without the ingredient of Orthodox spirituality, and intimacy served to prepare actors for the demands of playing before the camera. In the 1970s the 'studio' became a regular appendage of mainstream English subsidized theatres with a rather uncertain brief: in theory a place where new experimental work could be developed, but in practice increasingly a place where new work could be marginalized.[45] The philosophical and ethical drive that turned Stanislavski's studios into spaces of truth gradually lost its momentum.

The French term *atelier* subsumes the two English concepts of 'studio' and 'workshop', places where privileged visitors can see artistic work in the process of being made. The second term provides a rougher Anglo-Saxon edge. The first 'Theatre Workshop' was created by George Pierce Baker at Harvard in 1913, as a place where students of playwriting could learn that the craft of writing involved not just plot and dialogue but the manipulation of movement, scenery, props and lighting. Baker's workshop was not an empty space but a long hall packed with flats, furniture and objects that could be set up on a portion of floor that matched the unsatisfactory stage of the university theatre.[46] In England in 1945 the term was taken up by Ewan MacColl and Joan Littlewood who found in it a double resonance. On the one hand 'workshop' evoked an experimental stagecraft which sought to create 'a flexible theatre art, as swift-moving and plastic as the cinema'; on the other it recalled from the 1930s the traditions of workers' theatre. The new stagecraft relied on light, recorded sound and black drapes in order to maximize possibilities of representation with minimum budget.[47] To reconcile this avant-garde aesthetic with rough working-class traditions was a hopeless contradiction, resolved by the move to an old-fashioned music-hall theatre in East London suited to a more colourful mode of staging.

Whilst the term 'workshop' suggests raw incompleteness, the connotations of 'laboratory' are more clinical. Both Stanislavski and Baker conceived of their experimental spaces as laboratories.[48] The term gained currency in France in 1911 when the Laboratoire Art et Action introduced the experimental principles of Meyerhold, Reinhardt and Appia to a non-paying Parisian audience. Unfortunately the company's work was restricted to a *théâtre à l'italienne*, and bold plans for a *Théâtre de l'Espace* never materialized, like so many projects of the 1930s.[49] The term came to prominence again with Grotowski, who adopted the term 'Laboratory Theatre' to replace his 'Theatre of 13 Rows' in 1962. On the face of it, the term sits oddly with the spirituality of Grotowski's enterprise, but Grotowski liked to invoke the research institute set up by the physicist Niels Bohr on the grounds that great acting is a product of method, not inspiration.[50] The term 'laboratory' accords with the assumption that the theatre building is an inert shell surrounding live human organisms. Grotowski resembles Stanislavski in his desire to yoke science and spirituality, but his laboratory differs from Stanislavski's studio in its disposition of space. Stanislavski assumed that actor–audience 'communion' should be indirect, and avoid the perils of music-hall, so stage and curtain separated the audience from the closed circles of concentration in which the actors enfolded themselves. For Grotowski, in an age when audiences had learned to be restrained, the abolition of the actor–audience boundary was the spatial principle that defined a laboratory situation.[51] When the Arts Lab was set up in London in 1968 as a focus for the counter-culture, the term 'laboratory' passed into common currency.

In a temporary studio in around 1907, Stanislavski held a brainstorming session to address the problem that stage scenery seemed irrevocably coarse and ugly. He felt he had discovered America when he hit upon the idea of black velvet. Black drapes would allow him to dematerialize the setting for Maeterlinck's *Blue Bird*, and represent reality in symbolic terms. The result, alas, was 'gloomy, sarcophagal, awful and airless', quite unsuited to the light mood of Maeterlinck's play.[52] By the end of the 1960s, however, though Littlewood's Theatre Workshop had moved elsewhere, the dominant spatial form adopted by the alternative fringe/laboratory/workshop theatre was an uncompromising 'black box' studio. The black box became the quintessential 'empty space', the form that responded best to the complex of aesthetic demands made by Brook in 1967/8. It purported to be a neutral environment, allowing any desired configuration of seating. Its walls being invisible, lighting could make the space seem as tiny or expansive as the director might desire. Such was the theory, but with the passage of time it became clear, as Stanislavski discovered, that there is nothing neutral about blackness. The black box makes a historically specific architectural statement just as forcefully as Shakespeare's Globe. Like the proscenium theatres of London's West End, black boxes have become a piece of historical baggage that contemporary practice must struggle to accommodate. I search through my own memories in an effort to recall the sense of liberation that those spaces once generated in me and my generation. Today the illusion of flexibility has gone. The insistent rectilinearity of walls and of seating units positioned according to the dictates of the safety officer, the fixed position of the control box and the glowing green exit signs impose their iron discipline.

Because of its anonymity and notional invisibility, the history of the black box has gone almost unrecorded. The most influential flexible space of this broad type is generally taken to be Royce Hall 170, set up at University of California Los Angeles in 1942 in order to accommodate some half a dozen different configurations.[53] Black curtains played an important part in most designs. The original architectural identity of the hall was defined by an honorific apse, and this feature had to be concealed in order to turn the room into a spatial emblem of democratic society where anyone is free to do anything. For the pure form of black box theatre, a representative example might be *Kaspariana*, the opening production by Odin Teatret in their new laboratory-style theatre at Holsteboro, staged in 1967. The ceiling, floor and walls of the rectangualar room were all painted black. The 80 audience seats were divided into small blocks forming an arena which the actors could walk behind; this generated a multiplicity of individual points of view, and broke any sense of stage–auditorium division. The play told of Kaspar Hauser, a young man taken like the space to be a tabula rasa, a mental empty space, and given an identity through various forms of forced cultural, sexual and religious initiation.[54] In the enclosed black space with its vaguely subterranean ambience, in the remote Danish town where this international company had found refuge, it was easy for the audience to feel that they were escaping from the cultural, sexual and religious mores of mainstream society. Though society denied Kaspar his individuality, they at least in their individualized seats could celebrate their personal autonomy.

The British playwright Howard Barker is noted for his expansive, neo-Jacobean style of writing. In 1988 he suggested that an expansive space was the necessary concomitant: 'If the new writer is taught economy the theatre will itself shrink to the size of an attic. It is probably time to shut the studio theatres in the interests of the theatre.'[55] Perhaps it was the sight of David Hare filling the Olivier Theatre with a journalistic state-of-the-nation trilogy in 1990 that caused him to shift his emphasis, and write an eloquent apologia for black-box theatre, arguing for theatre as an art, not theatre as message:

Let me suggest that the theatre is literally a box, physically and morally a box. What occurs in the box is infinite because the audience wishes it to be infinite . . . It is a black box when the lights are off because as we all know darkness permits the criminal and the promiscuous act . . . When Brecht commanded that the box be filled with light he was driven by the passion for enlightenment, and he knew instructions require light just as the imagination hates light and flees from it. Imagination also flees its neighbours. In light you are only half-conscious of the stage and half-conscious of your neighbour. In all collective culture your neighbour controls you by his gaze. In darkness he is eliminated and you are alone with the actor . . . In the black box you are trusted to be free, to be solely responsible. To enter it is to be engulfed by the possibility of freedom through the powers of the actor and the dramatist, the onus is placed on the audience not as a collectivity but as individuals. No disciplines, no recall to conscience . . . What else can explain the residual excitement we still experience in dark theatres?

Barker's black box is thus a privileged space where society is kept at bay:

Against the walls of the theatre there washes continuously the sea of morality and debate. Inside the black box, the imagination is wild and tragic and its criminality unfettered.[56]

His messianic tones and celebration of tragedy echo Nietzsche, while his individualism harks back nostalgically to the values of the sixties.

Barker's manifesto helps us see how the black box functioned as a 'perfect philosopher's machine' in the same historically specific way as the Elizabethan playhouse. The most obvious defining quality is *blackness*. Semiotically, blackness in western culture signifies tragedy, magic and evil, its connotations broadly romantic and gothic. Physiologically, it lowers the audience's arousal level, and dampens any tendency to laughter.[57] Organizationally, it places the control of space in the lighting box, and thus not with an ensemble but an individual, not with actors but (despite the anti-technocratic rhetoric of alternative culture) with technology. A generation earlier, Le Corbusier had idealized white as a sign of the liberated spirit, released from the clutter of bourgeois decoration. He associated white with a medieval world that had just escaped the dark ages. Untroubled by any thought about the way Protestants whitewashed colourful Catholic churches, he states that theatre took place in cathedrals, and these 'cathedrals were white, thought was clear, spirit was alive, the spectacle clean'.[58] When Theodor Adorno in the late 1960s wanted to define the parameters of a modernist aesthetic, he took the opposite view: 'Radical art today is synonymous with dark art; its primary color is black. Much contemporary production is irrelevant because it takes no note of this and childishly delights in color.' The holocaust, Stalin and Hiroshima more than Vietnam inform Adorno's historical moment. 'The injustice committed by all cheerful art, especially by entertainment, is probably an injustice to the dead; to accumulated speechless pain. Still, black art bears features that would, if they were definitive, set their seal on historical despair; to the extent that change is always still possible they too may be ephemeral.' Blackness is not altogether lacking in the capacity to create pleasure, for 'ever since Baudelaire the dark has also offered sensuous enticement as the antithesis of the fraudulent sensuality of culture's facade'.[59] The morbidity of radical 1960s was always tinged with eroticism. Thus Adorno sums up the Zeitgeist that generated black box theatres, so different from the optimism of modernists in the pre-war period.

Portraying the modern movement as a form of puritanism, Charles Jencks offers a succinct definition of modernist architecture as 'the overpowering faith in industrial progressivism and its translation into the pure, white International style (or at least the Machine Aesthetic) with the goal of transforming society both in its sensibility and social make-up'. Though he finds modernism in the other arts to be less progressivist and optimistic, he believes that 'the various Modernisms agree in two key areas, and that is over the value of abstraction and the overriding importance of aesthetics'.[60] Though the black box studio expresses the pessimistic and broadly antiprogressive strand in twentieth-century modernism, it remains a form that encourages abstraction, and creates a closed environment in which aestheticism can flourish. The black box is also bound up with the modernist goal of transforming society, which may seem paradoxical in view of the way it cuts itself off from any contact with an implicitly corrupt and false social world outside, and attempts to obliterate all social signals from its interior. The flexibility of the auditorium is expressive of a libertarian and democratic ideology, for there is a theoretical freedom of choice here to adopt any mode of organizing the theatrical microcosm. The governing philosophy is 'democratic' rather than 'socialist' for spectators in this space, whatever the communitarian rhetoric, are constructed as individuals. As Barker notes, spectators are allowed by the darkness to retain their personal privacy. The black box is a depoliticizing space in the sense that no body politic can be placed on view, whatever the overt political content of works performed. The black box also rules out Ibsenesque naturalism, for any stage set framed by a black wall is revealed to be mere stage artifice. It fosters Grotowski's notion of the 'secular *sacrum*', sacredness devoid of any link to place or to social institutions, and rooted in the human body. This body is made tantalizingly available through proximity and three-dimensionality, but abstract and mysterious through dim lighting. The dead acoustic created by drapes and prefabricated plywood units (though not by brick-lined Polish cellars) yields a voice that comes from nowhere but the actor's body. There is no sense of acoustical life in the environment. The singular spectator is placed in a linear relationship to the singular sound-source, not enveloped in a shared sound. Words in a dead acoustic ask to be stripped to their bare semantic function, and to their rhythmic function of punctuating silence. This is Barker's unsolved problem with the black box: the failure of his language to resonate.

The black box places theatrical performance firmly in the domain of the aesthetic, isolating it from other social practices. Peter Brook in *The Empty Space* lamented the failure of theatre to find a lively audience comparable to that which flocked to the Museum of Modern Art in New York, but rather than consider the fundamental issue of space he blamed economics.[61] MoMA (1939) is in fact the first and most celebrated example of the 'white cube' conception, the characteristic form taken by the modernist art gallery. Brian O'Doherty in 1976 published an influential critique of that form, and his thesis can in large measure be applied to the black box. He argued that, whilst modern art-works are a function of innumerable differentiated '-isms', a white ideal space can be seen as the single archetypal image behind twentieth-century art. The white cube gallery is 'constructed along laws as rigorous as those for building a medieval church'. The walls are white, the light source hidden, floors clinically wooden or soundlessly carpeted, and in this environment any object is perceived as an aesthetic, almost sacred artefact:

The ideal gallery subtracts from the artwork all cues that interfere with the fact that it is 'art' . . . Some of the sanctity of the church, the formality of the courtroom, the mystique of the experimental laboratory joins with chic design to produce a unique chamber of esthetics. So powerful are the perceptual fields of force within this chamber that once outside it, art can lapse into secular status. Conversely, things become art in a space where powerful ideas about art focus on them.[62]

Analysts of theatre have been slower than analysts of modern art to perceive how far meaning is a function of space, and how performance in the second half of the twentieth century has been the product of a particular aestheticizing environment. The myth of the black box as an inert container has been too strong. O'Doherty explores the symbiotic relationship which bound up abstract art and the white cube. The same processes were at work in theatre, but are harder to discern in a medium that relies on living bodies.

Perspectival painting is traditionally tied to a *Beaux arts* picture frame just as perspectival theatre is tied to a golden proscenium frame. In early nineteenth-century galleries, the viewer used the frame in order to isolate one canvas amidst a crowded wall, in much the same way as the theatre spectator used the frame and opera glasses to isolate images within a bustling, fully illuminated environment. In the modernist gallery, the white wall effectively replaced the frame. Without challenging the two-dimensionality of the picture plane, and the marketability of an easel painting, abstract painting engaged creatively with the white surface. Expressionist and absurdist theatre in much the same way challenged naturalism in the theatre without redefining the actor–audience relationship. The black box proved a convenient medium for conserving a time-honoured institution called theatre.

O'Doherty identifies as a decisive moment the emergence of collage in 1911, when Cubism 'poked out' the picture plane. Behind the three-dimensional collage 'is simply a wall or a void; in front is an open space in which the viewer's sense of his own presence becomes an increasingly palpable shadow'. Perspectival art fixed the position of the viewer, impressionism made point of view problematic, but collage turned the gallery into that new twentieth-century category – *space*. Within sculpture and painting,

a trinity of changes brought forth a new god. The pedestal melted away, leaving the spectator waist-deep in wall-to-wall space. As the frame dropped off, space slid across the wall, creating turbulence in the corners. Collage flopped out of the picture and settled on the floor as easily as a bag lady. The new god, extensive, homogeneous space, flowed easily into every part of the gallery.[63]

Modernist space, O'Doherty goes on, 'redefines the observer's status, tinkers with his self-image'.[64] He wittily describes how he visits a gallery space in a threefold persona, as if accompanied by his snobbish cousin the Eye who sees reality in terms of the picture plane, and his faceless, confused and well-meaning alter ego the Spectator, who is bombarded with sensations and forced into different physical positions by new uses of the gallery. Environmental stagings, through productions like *Kaspariana*, turned the theatre into a *space* in much the same way, leaving spectators with a similar sense of personal fragmentation. Theatre space is not so much a given, but rather a concept produced by a specific spatial practice. The black box is a locational, textured and dimensional *place* that purports to be mere homogeneous *space*. All that differentiates the theatrical black box from the white cube of the gallery, and indeed the dance studio, is in the last analysis blackness. The excitement of black box theatre for young fringe audiences would not yet have been in Brook's mind when he stood outside MoMA in around 1960. Nor did he perceive the challenge that the white cube was about to face.

The art critic Michael Fried in 1967 published a manifesto in which he wrote of a 'war going on between theatre and modernist painting', his thesis being that 'art degenerates as it approaches the condition of theatre'. He discerned theatricality entering the art gallery when the 'presence' or 'objecthood' of art-works was emphasized, and a new aesthetic started to incorporate the beholder, vesting meaning not in the art-work itself but in the relationship of object and beholder within the structuring space of the room.[65] At least in the short term, Fried's defence of conventional genres and artistic values was a lost cause. Conceptual and performance art proved irresistible, and it was from colleges of art that the major radical alternative to the black box conception of theatre emerged. Allan Kaprow staged the first so-denominated 'happening' in a New York gallery in 1959. Other artists like Yves Klein in France in the late 1950s and then Joseph Beuys in Germany broke down the boundary between art and performance through attacking received perceptions of the gallery.[66] The logical next step was to escape altogether the confines of the institution. Kaprow proclaimed in *The Drama Review* in 1968:

Our space now-a-days is no space. It used to be that space was those places that you couldn't get to, that were too far away. Now we can get anywhere. In the past we had a closed, relatively focused space. Today we feel a lot freer and we can celebrate extended space. I think this new feeling needs to be recognised by the traditional theatre . . .[67]

This confused utopian vision of an extended 'no space' was the other side of the coin of the black box, an alternative means of idealizing empty space in the name of freedom. It was the impulse that drove Brook to the Sahara desert, and Odin Teatret to the streets of Southern Italy and altiplano of Peru.

The French performance artist Daniel Buren in the early 1970s developed a more rigorous position. Starting from the premiss that the aseptic white cube is a 'value-giving repository' allowing art-works to function as transportable commodities, and that every place imbues a work or creation with its meaning, he argued for a dialectical relationship between work and architectural frame. 'It is a question of a conflict relationship, where both parties are on trial concerning a difference.' He saw transient site-specific creations as the only way to expose the false neutrality of the gallery, and the false impression that art-works have an *a priori* existence. The old system of production whereby the artist created in the studio work that could be placed in any of the world's ubiquitous white cubes had to be discarded.[68] Buren's conception of a dialogue between the work and the architecture has become a commonplace in postmodern museum design. As O'Doherty puts it, the gallery 'joins the picture plane as a unit of discourse'.[69] Whilst the Guggenheim in Bilbao is a flamboyant expression of architecture as art, the Musée d'Orsay and Tate Modern rely upon found industrial spaces to create a positive and assertive context for the display of modern art-works.

My own most recent visit to a gallery of modern art took me to Les Abattoirs in Toulouse, opened in 2000 in a converted slaughterhouse. The nineteenth-century industrial architecture of the slaughterhouse in its turn paid tribute to the sacred architecture of St Servin, the city's great abbatial church, turning the modern gallery into a palimpsest of contradictory memories. The gallery is divided into three sectors. The crypt built to suggest a theatre houses a huge and fragile stage curtain by Picasso. This is the holy of holies, a giant white box built to house a modernist masterpiece. Above the side aisles are a series of flexible white and coloured boxes, though fashion rules against the obvious logic of the space, which is to construct the visitor's circuit as a linear journey through time in the manner of MoMA. The nave opens onto a vista of the city, marking a refusal to separate contemporary art from life. The nave housed at the time of my visit a set of installations by a Montenegrin artist in memory of a French friend who killed himself in 1961.[70] The side spaces became chapels with reliquaries on the walls containing found objects from the Bosnian war, and paintings by the dead artist. The central space housed installations, like the torso of a car covered in bones. The use of found objects in this found space made it clear that the aesthetic can no longer be a closed category: the exhibition dealt with a real suicide and a real war. The building, associated with the death of animals and at a further remove with the symbolism of Christian sacrifice, was an inseparable part of the artistic concept. The bonding of the work to its space fostered an enhanced awareness of time. An empty space is a timeless space, but a space packed with memories creates a sense of presence in the here-and-now.

The same impulse to occupy abandoned industrial spaces has been apparent in theatre in the last thirty years. Major British examples include the Royal Exchange in Manchester, the Tramway in Glasgow and the

Roundhouse in London. In France Ariane Mnouchkine converted an old gunpowder factory into the Cartoucherie de Vincennes. Such spaces create a sense of authenticity in a post-industrial age, and pander perhaps to a certain nostalgia for the raw physicality of manual labour. They contest the idea that theatre is a closed aesthetic category. And they are invested with memories, creating a sense of the present moment. This trend has lead to the creation of many small theatres in former warehouses, boilerhouses, breweries, corn exchanges, fire stations and the like. In most cases, however, the aesthetic principles of found space apply strikingly to the exterior, partially to the bar and foyer, but minimally if at all to the performance area, where the black box aesthetic is likely to prevail. Just as the white cube continues to serve the need of a market in paintings, so the black box continues to serve the needs of a project-funded touring circuit, where shows can be slotted in and out, free from any need to create a dialectic with the architectural frame.

Having effectively coined the term 'empty space', Peter Brook has done more than anyone to develop an aesthetic of the characterful found space. In his continuing practice he has demonstrated the need to turn space into place if communication with a flesh-and-blood audience is to be achieved. His decision to install himself in the Bouffes du Nord in Paris in 1974, after a period of wandering the world, epitomizes the transition from what we may think of as 'sixties' values to a new and emphatic rejection of modernism. Rightly or wrongly, the oil crisis of 1973 is often seen as the catalyst of transition, when the radical utopianism of the sixties yielded before a desire to conserve a culture at risk. Brook's decision to settle in a nineteenth-century theatre chimed with that historical moment. The fact that Brook has based his research centre for nearly thirty years in a single theatre with distinctive architectural qualities and a fixed disposition of seats marks a rejection of the sixties principles of infinite adaptability and the multiplicity of individual points of view. His move was a reaffirmation of faith in theatre as an institution, and an acceptance that art's relationship to the past should be one of creative continuity rather than rupture.

Brook wrote in 1976 that a theatre should not be anecdotal. It should have a good acoustic, and it should be a 'neutral' space in the sense of escaping definitions, so as to avoid placing performances within an ideology.[71] The Bouffes du Nord, built a century earlier, retains the acoustic of a music hall, where the fold-back of the audience's response helps shape the performance. The unusual shallow ellipse creates both intimacy and a sense of epic breadth. It is a 'post-modern' space insofar as it is a historical composite, subsuming historical references with a view to transcending history and ideology.[72] It retains the outline of a Victorian social space, which once invited an audience in the balconies to interest itself in the floor of the auditorium. By removing the elevated stage, levelling the stalls and pushing the acting area out towards the centre, Brook changed the overt historical references. His circle of benches provides a flavour of democratic Greece, with shoulder-to-shoulder contact removing the sense of individuation. The interiority and intimacy recall Restoration theatre, whilst the verticality and circularity are reminiscent of Elizabethan theatre. When the foundations of the Rose were excavated, Brook felt that his theatrical intuitions had been confirmed because the ground-plans matched so well.[73] Yet what he lacked at the Bouffes du Nord was any means of replicating the social diversity of the Elizabethan or indeed Victorian playhouse; he could and frequently did take work out to prisons and deprived audiences, but he could not bring those audiences to his theatre. Brook's passion for Shakespeare is made clear in *The Empty Space*, and in his choice of productions. His dramaturgical taste is linked to his architectural taste, and that architectural taste sits squarely within an anglo-centric performance tradition.

Brook's strategy was to preserve the found qualities of the Bouffes du Nord, with the signs of its previous life and decay. He was initially attracted to the Bouffes because 'the "cultural" skin of architectural decoration had been cauterised away', revealing it as a very particular space, no longer specifically Victorian:

The Bouffes was unimaginable for us; it told us what to do. It had two characteristics which struck us immediately: the very unusual playing configuration presented by the voiding of the stalls seats. And the fact that it was materially wounded, with wrinkles, pock-marks and signs of having passed through life.[74]

Over recent years these signs of a theatrical past followed by years of decay have had superimposed upon them signs of previous Brook productions. David Williams comments that 'this numinous, charged space possesses a quality of weathered, textured humanity, the environment bearing silent witness to the passage of time, revealing the traces of its pasts like stigmata'.[75] The old sixties distinction between organic human beings and an inert container no longer obtains when we are encouraged to think of spaces having a life of their own, a life constituted by multiple traces of other human lives. As Mike Pearson's manifesto suggests, one of the most important shifts in the Zeitgeist since the 1960s has been the awareness that human beings and their environment are interdependent.

Brook's aesthetic of 'foundness' resolved his Manichaean dichotomy of rough and holy, material and spiritual. On the one hand the Bouffes is a rough theatre that resists any attempt to decorate, prettify and sanitize – Brook regrets the way so many of the raw found spaces which he created on world tours have had their life removed when sponsored by local authorities, smartly fitted out and packed with technology.[76] On the other hand, as Williams' reference to 'stigmata' implies, the Bouffes is felt to be a 'holy' space, invested with a presence that transcends everyday living in the here-and-now. If Brook's phenomenology of the sacred is not to our taste, we could substitute a drier post-structuralist vocabulary and speak of scarred walls that double-code past and present and preserve Derridean traces of former utterances. But the difficult issue of the sacred keeps returning whenever we frame the question of what we value in theatre and why.

Brook describes the Bouffes, stripped bare and yet full of stimuli, as a 'chameleon space' which 'allows the imagination to wander freely'.[77] But on a theoretical level, he has never satisfactorily resolved the relationship of space as emptiness and space as *plenum*. He stated rather unhelpfully in 1991: ' "Theatre" is one thing, whereas "the theatres" is something quite different. "The theatres" are boxes; a box is not its content any more than an envelope is a letter.'[78] This separation of form and content does not accord comfortably with his own practice since 1974, working in a building that is far more than a box or envelope for his work. This theoretical vacuum makes it hard for others to draw conclusions about how best to work.

Vitez and Lefebvre, as we saw in chapter 1, felt that modern practitioners had to choose between a theatre that is a mere covering and theatre as a monument.[79] Michael Elliott, who conceived the Royal Exchange Theatre, despaired of the modernist monumentality in 1973 when he argued that one should no longer build for posterity.[80] The lack of any agreed architectural vocabulary for monumental architecture has encouraged the recycling of Victorian buildings that did benefit from an aesthetic consensus. Monumental buildings like the Royal Exchange are all the more acceptable today because they were associated with working people rather than organs of government. The Bouffes has similar qualities of monumentality, but its continuing vitality stems also from the way that it exists in a state of flux, subject to constant reworking. Brick and plaster are easier to modify and remodify than reinforced concrete. When Denys Lasdun designed in concrete the Olivier Theatre, he 'searched for an open relationship that looked back to the Greeks and Elizabethans and, at the same time, looked forward to a contemporary view of society'. A sixties design by an architect whose taste was shaped by Le Corbusier perforce no longer offered a 'contemporary' view of society by the time the theatre opened in 1976.[81] Though his attention to the past, to modernism as much as to Greece, allowed him to create an acceptable monumentality, he did not create a space that later generations could easily modify and revitalize.

There is an obvious correlation between monumental buildings and classic plays. In all the arts, there is a pressing issue of how to present period works to a contemporary audience. Modern concert halls have to accommodate a repertoire that includes both baroque music written for intimate aristocratic music rooms and the symphonic music of the romantics which demands a much higher reverberation time.[82] In the late 1960s Stockhausen's experiments briefly reminded the world that music is necessarily a function of performance space.[83] In the visual arts, an assertive found space like Les Abattoirs tends to be designed for modern art. Across the river in Toulouse, a recently established collection of period art puts modernity (impressionists and post-impressionists) on one floor defined as an aesthetic space by empty walls, yellowed rather than stark white to create a sense of historicity, while earlier works from Cranach to Canaletto are located in furnished period apartments to signal that art before modernity had a social function.[84] In theatre, the creative role of the director makes the relationship between past and present works more fluid, but there is always a tension between duty to an inherited masterpiece, and the duty to create a performance for the present. The layering of present upon past allows the Bouffes to create a dialectic more subtle than anything achievable in the Olivier.

The crisis of space is particularly evident in the Royal Shakespeare Company at the time of writing. The possibilities of modifying Elizabeth Scott's modernist Stratford auditorium of 1932 have been exhausted, but Scott's building has become a listed monument, making it impossible to start again from scratch. In London, the company has abandoned the Barbican, a sixties design within a concrete urban environment, reflecting a bygone taste for cinema-style productions that need a broad epic stage. The success of Shakespeare's Globe prompted a temporary move to the Roundhouse in the summer of 2002 to develop a more interactive mode of performance, and attract a younger audience. Underlying such local difficulties is a bigger issue: the passing of modernism, and the retreat from what Lefebvre terms 'abstract space'. Lefebvre explained how modernist architects 'offered – as an *ideology in action* – an empty space, a space that is primordial, a container ready to receive fragmentary contents, a *neutral* medium into which disjointed things, people and habitats might be introduced'.[85] The Bouffes du Nord offers a very different 'ideology in action' that we may consider to be radically new, or deeply conservative in the way it draws on the past. It is bound up with a desire to bond self to a social and physical environment, a desire to escape personal fragmentation by becoming an embodied participant, a desire to create theatre in places rather than containers. To achieve these contemporary goals must involve looking at the past afresh.

Notes

The following abbreviations appear in the notes and select bibiliography:

CNDP   Centre National de Documentation Pédagogique
CNRS   Centre National de la Recherche Scientifique
GITA   Le Groupe Interdisciplinaire du Théâtre Antique
IFTR   International Federation for Theatre Research
PAJ   Performing Arts Journal
PUF   Presses Universitaires de France
RKP   Routledge & Kegan Paul

I INTRODUCTION

1. Reported by A. C. H. Smith in *Orghast at Persepolis* (London: Methuen, 1972), 225.
2. Exercise devised by Emma Govan.
3. *History of the Theatre* (4th edn, Boston, Mass.: Allyn & Bacon, 1982), 1. Brockett's italics.
4. Mike Pearson, 'My balls/your chin', *Performance Research* 3.2 (1998), 35–41.
5. Pierre Bourdieu, *Outline of a Theory of Practice*, tr. R. Nice (Cambridge University Press, 1977), 2.
6. *Environmental Theater* (New York: Applause, 1994), xxiii–xxiv.
7. *The Empty Space* (London: MacGibbon & Kee, 1968), 9; *There Are No Secrets: thoughts on acting and theatre* (London: Methuen, 1993), 4.
8. See Daniel C. Dennett, *Consciousness Explained* (Harmondsworth: Penguin, 1993), 107–8.
9. See for example Joseph R. Roach, *The Player's Passion: studies in the science of acting* (Ann Arbor: University of Michigan Press, 1993).
10. 'Questions on geography' in *Power/Knowledge: selected interviews and other writings 1972–1977*, ed. C. Gordon (Brighton: Harvester Press, 1980), 70.
11. 'Of other spaces', tr. J. Miskowiec in *Diacritics* 16 (1986), 22–7.
12. 'The eye of power' in *Power/Knowledge*, 149.
13. Cf. *The Order of Things* (London: Tavistock Publications, 1970), xviii.
14. *The Order of Things*, 3–16.
15. A. M. Moreno, *Las Meninas*, tr. N. Williams (Madrid: Aldeasa, 2000).

16. *The Production of Space*, tr. D. Nicholson-Smith (Oxford: Blackwell, 1991), 406–7.
17. *Ibid.*, 26.
18. *Ibid.*, 93–4.
19. *Ibid.*, 33.
20. *Ibid.*, 162.
21. See for example Anne Ubersfeld, *Lire le théâtre* (Paris: Editions sociales, 1982); *L'Ecole du spectateur* (Paris: Editions sociales, 1981); Patrice Pavis, *Dictionnaire du théâtre* (Paris: Editions sociales, 1980); 'L'espace des *Fausses confidences* et les fausses confidences de l'espace' in *Voix et images de la scène: vers une sémiologie de la réception* (Presses Universitaires de Lille, 1985); G. Banu and A. Ubersfeld, *L'Espace théâtral* (Paris: CNDP, 1992); A. Helbo, J. D. Johansen, P. Pavis and A. Ubersfeld (eds.), *Approaching Theatre* (Bloomington: Indiana University Press, 1991).
22. For a recent and eloquent critique along phenomenological lines, see Marie-Madeleine Mervant-Roux, *L'Assise du théâtre: pour une étude du spectateur* (Paris: CNRS, 1998), 48–50.
23. *The Production of Space*, 236–40.
24. *Ibid.*, 301–6.
25. *Ibid.*, 286.
26. See Martin Jay, 'In the empire of the gaze: Foucault and the denigration of vision in 20th-century French thought' in *Foucault: a critical reader*, ed. D. C. Hoy (Oxford: Blackwell, 1986).
27. Michael Barron, *Auditorium Acoustics and Architectural Design* (London: Spon, 1993), 265, 281.
28. Mervant-Roux, *L'Assise du théâtre*, 149–55.
29. *The Production of Space*, 220.
30. *Ibid.*, 222–5.
31. *Ibid.*, 175 and note, 223, 383–5.
32. Cited in Gay McAuley, *Space in Performance: making meaning in the theatre* (Ann Arbor: University of Michigan Press, 1999), 38.
33. *Ibid.*, 383–5.
34. *A Journey through Other Spaces: essays and manifestos, 1944–1990*, ed. and tr. M. Kobialka (Berkeley: University of California Press, 1993), 217.
35. *Ibid.*, 75; cf. 33–4.
36. *Ibid.*, 123.
37. *Ibid.*, 37.
38. 'Carnet de notes' in *Voies de la création théâtrale* 18 (1993), 115ff.
39. *The Oxford Illustrated History of Theatre* (Oxford University Press, 1995), 1–10.
40. Manifesto relating to the Lancelot Quail project.
41. 'The new theatre' in *Happenings and Other Acts*, ed. Mariellen R. Sandford (London: Routledge, 1995), 29–50, p.29.
42. *Postmodern Culture*, ed. Hal Foster (London: Pluto Press, 1985), 31–42.
43. Citations from Louis Riccoboni, *Reflexions historiques et critiques sur les differens théatres de l'Europe* (Amsterdam, 1740), sig. s3v, 1, 37, 67. First published in Paris in 1738, with an English translation published in 1741. For a historical

survey of theatre historiography, see R. W. Vince, 'Theatre History as an academic discipline' in *Interpreting the Theatrical Past: essays in the historiography of performance*, ed. Thomas Postlethwait and Bruce A. McConachie (University of Iowa Press, 1989), 1–18.

44. *Ibid.*, 67.
45. *Ibid.*, 71.
46. Hans Kellner, 'Language and historical representation' in *The Postmodern History Reader*, ed. Keith Jenkins (London: Routledge, 1997), 127–38, p.127.
47. *Ibid.*, 136–7.
48. Richard Southern, *The Seven Ages of the Theatre* (London: Faber, 1964), 26.
49. *Space in Performance*, 14, 281.
50. Cf. David George, 'On origins: behind the rituals', *Performance Research* 3.3 (1998), viii–14.
51. *Happenings: an illustrated anthology* (London: Sidgwick & Jackson, 1965), 14ff.
52. *Liveness: performance in a mediatized culture* (London: Routledge, 1999).
53. I borrow the phrase *machine à jouer* ('a machine for performing in') from the introduction to Jean Chollet and Marcel Freydefont, *Les Lieux scéniques en France 1980–1995* (Paris: Scéno+, 1996), 25.

2 SACRED SPACE

1. *The Production of Space*, tr. D. Nicholson-Smith (Oxford: Blackwell, 1991), 234.
2. *Ibid.*, 235.
3. *Ibid.*, 44.
4. *The Sacred and the Profane: the nature of religion*, tr. W. R. Trask (New York: Harcourt, Brace & World, 1959), 11–14.
5. *Ibid.*, 28.
6. *Ibid.*, 44–5.
7. *Passing Strange and Wonderful: aesthetics, nature and culture* (Washington, D.C.: Island Press, 1993), 172.
8. *Ibid.*, 182–3.
9. 'Sacred space: explorations of an idea' in *Dimensions of Human Geography: essays on some familiar and neglected themes*, ed. K. W. Butzer (Dept of Geography, University of Chicago, 1978), 84–99.
10. 'Of divine places', tr. M. Holland in *The Inoperative Community* (Minneapolis: University of Minnesota Press, 1991), 110–50, p.148.
11. *A Midsummer Night's Dream* I.ii.102, *Merry Wives of Windsor* IV.iv.25ff. Cf. Ronald Hutton, *The Pagan Religions of the Ancient British Isles* (Oxford: Blackwell, 1991), 293–7.
12. As J. Ronayne notes in *Shakespeare's Globe Rebuilt*, ed. J. R. Mulryne and M. Shewring (Cambridge University Press, 1997), 121–2. In 2003 a rethink was in progress.
13. *Production of Space*, 235.
14. Robert Parker, *Athenian Religion: a history* (Oxford University Press, 1996), 168–9.
15. Exodus XXXVIII.15, XL.20–4.

16. For Christian symbolism see George Lesser, *Gothic Cathedrals and Sacred Geometry* (London: Alec Tiranti, 1957).

17. Bharatamuni, *The Natya Sastra*, tr. A Board of Scholars (Delhi: Sri Satguru Publications, 1996), chapters 2–3.

18. I owe this account to Dick McCaw.

19. *Greek Religion*, tr. J. Raffan (Oxford: Blackwell, 1985), 92.

20. *Poetics* 1.iv.1449a.

21. *Pindar II*, ed. and tr. W. H. Race (Cambridge, Mass.: Loeb Classical Library, 1997), 311; A. Pickard-Cambridge, *Dithyramb, Tragedy and Comedy*, rev. T. B. L. Webster (Oxford University Press, 1962), 21, 38.

22. Dionysius of Halicarnassus, *On Literary Composition*, 22.

23. Joseph Fontenrose, *Python* (Berkeley: University of California Press, 1959), 453–6.

24. Pickard-Cambridge, *Dithyramb, Tragedy and Comedy*, 72–4.

25. A. Pickard-Cambridge, *Dramatic Festivals of Athens*, rev. J. Gould and D. M. Lewis (Oxford University Press, 1968), 48. For archaeological sources, see David Wiles, *Tragedy in Athens: performance space and theatrical meaning* (Cambridge University Press, 1997), 27–9.

26. For the issues see Simon Goldhill, 'The Great Dionysia and civic ideology' in *Nothing to Do with Dionysos? Athenian drama in its social context*, ed. John J. Winkler and Froma Zeitlin (Princeton University Press, 1990), 97–129; P. E. Easterling, 'A show for Dionysus' in *The Cambridge Companion to Greek Tragedy*, ed. P. E. Easterling (Cambridge University Press, 1997), 36–53.

27. Pickard-Cambridge, *Dithyramb, Tragedy and Comedy*, 32–3.

28. *Erechtheus* fragment 370K, 67–74. For full text and translation see Euripides, *Selected Fragmentary Plays I*, ed. C. Collard, M. J. Cropp and K. H. Lee (Warminster: Aris & Philips, 1995). On the rock, see R. E. Wycherley, *The Stones of Athens* (Princeton University Press), 188.

29. See for example W. R. Connor, 'Sacred and secular: *hiera kai hosia* and the classical Athenian concept of the state', *Ancient Society* 19 (1988), 161–88; Michael H. Jameson, 'The spectacular and the obscure in Athenian religion' in *Performance Culture and Athenian Democracy*, ed. Simon Goldhill and Robin Osborne (Cambridge University Press, 1999), 321–40. On tragedy and hero cults, see Richard Seaford, *Reciprocity and Ritual: Homer and tragedy in the developing city-state* (Oxford University Press, 1994).

30. My account follows R. Turcan, *The Cults of the Roman Empire*, tr. A. Nevill (Oxford: Blackwell, 1996). See also M. J. Vermaeren, *Cybele and Attis* (Thames & Hudson, 1977), W. Burkert, *Ancient Mystery Cults* (Cambridge, Mass.: Harvard University Press, 1987), 77–8.

31. J. A. Hanson, *Roman Theater–Temples* (Princeton University Press, 1959), 13–16; Sander M. Goldberg, 'Plautus on the Palatine', *Journal of Roman Studies* 88 (1988), 1–20.

32. *De Haruspicum Responsis*, 11.

33. Tertullian, *De Spectaculis* 10.5. On the theatre, I draw particularly upon Pierre Gros, 'La fonction symbolique des édifice théâtraux dans le paysage urbain de la Rome Augustéenne' in *L'Urbs: espace urbain et histoire* (Rome: Ecole

Française de Rome, 1987), 319–46; Gilles Sauron, *Quis Deum? L'expression plastique des idéologies politiques et religieuses à Rome* (Paris: Ecole Française de Rome, 1994); Filippo Coarelli, *Il Campo Marzio – dalle origini alla fine della repubblica* (Rome: Quasar, 1997), 539–80.

34. I follow the persuasive argument of Kathryn L. Gleason in 'Porticus Pompeiana: a new perspective on the first public park of ancient Rome', *Journal of Garden History* 14 (1994), 13–26. Cf. Richard C. Beacham, *Spectacle Entertainments of Early Imperial Rome* (New Haven, Conn.: Yale University Press, 1999), 263 n.18.

35. Hanson, *Roman Theater–Temples*, 46.

36. For the evidence of the Severan marble plan, see chapter 6 below, p.176.

37. Diodorus Siculus XVI.92–4.

38. Socrates of Rhodes cited in Athenaeus IV.148; for Antony as Dionysus, see E. G. Huzar, *Mark Antony* (Minneapolis: University of Minnesota Press, 1978), 156.

39. See Bruno Poulle, 'Le théâtre de Marcellus et la sphère', *Mélanges de L' Ecole Française de Rome* III (1999), 257–72; Paolo Fidenzoni, *Il teatro di Marcello* (Rome: Liber, 1970). On Apollo's temple see the entry on Apollo Palatinum in *Lexicon Topographicum Urbis Romae, Vol. I*, ed. E. M. Steinby (Rome: Quasar, 1993); also Karl Galinsky, *Augustan Culture: an interpretive introduction* (Princeton University Press, 1996), 346.

40. See M. R. Wright, *Cosmology in Antiquity* (London: Routledge, 1995), 156–62.

41. Vitruvius I.vii.1. For Caesar's project see Coarelli, *Campo Marzio*, 580–90.

42. See Gros, 'La fonction symbolique des édifices théâtraux', 319–46, p.342.

43. See the decree cited in Hanson, *Roman Theater–Temples*, 92.

44. Jonas Barish, *The Antitheatrical Prejudice* (Berkeley: California University Press, 1981), 61–2.

45. Gospel of St John IV.21–3.

46. Matthew XVII.1–9.

47. L. Michael White, *The Social Origins of Christian Architecture* (Valley Forge, Penn.: Trinity Press International, 1990).

48. Cf. Joan E. Taylor, *Christians and Holy Places: the myth of Jewish–Christian origins* (Oxford University Press, 1993), 308.

49. See Robert L.Wilken, *The Land Called Holy: Palestine in Christian history and thought* (New Haven, Conn.: Yale University Press, 1992), esp. 89–94; Taylor, *Christians and Holy Places*, 113–42, 308ff.; also Charles Coüasnon, *Church of the Holy Sepulchre in Jerusalem*, tr. J. P. B. and C. Ross (Oxford University Press, 1974).

50. J. Wilkinson, *Egeria's Travels* (3rd edn, Warminster: Aris & Phillips, 1999).

51. E. D. Hunt, *Holy Land Pilgrimage in the Later Roman Empire A.D. 312–460* (Oxford University Press, 1982), 152.

52. See Jacques Le Goff, 'Body and ideology in the medieval world' in *The Medieval Imagination*, tr. A. Goldhammer (University of Chicago Press, 1988), 83–5.

53. A. J. Gurevich, *Medieval Popular Culture: problems of belief and perception*, tr. J. M. Bak and P. A. Hollingsworth (Cambridge University Press, 1988), 65–8.

54. On Greek parameters see Wiles, *Tragedy in Athens*; also *The Masks of Menander: sign and meaning in Greek and Roman performance* (Cambridge University Press, 1991), 44–7, 65–6.

55. See A. J. Gurevich, *Categories of Medieval Culture*, tr. G. L. Campbell (London: RKP, 1985), 72.

56. Procopius, *Buildings* I.i.61.

57. Acts VII.47–9.

58. See Thomas F. Mathews, *The Early Churches of Constantinople: architecture and liturgy* (University Park: Pennsylvania State University Press, 1971), 120.

59. C. C. Schnusenberg, *The Relationship between the Church and the Theatre* (Lanham: University Press of America, 1988), esp. 315–17; O. B. Hardison, *Christian Rite and Christian Drama in the Middle Ages* (Baltimore: Johns Hopkins University Press, 1965), esp. 61.

60. Karl Young, *The Drama of the Medieval Church* (Oxford University Press, 1933), I.83. My translation.

61. For the architectural implications, see Otto Von Simson, *The Gothic Cathedral* (New York: Pantheon Books, 1956), 22–43.

62. Cited from the translation by M. M. Butler in *Medieval and Tudor Drama*, ed. J. Gassner (New York: Bantam, 1971), 23. Note that this translation omits much of the crucial opening scene. The most performable translation remains Christopher St John [alias Christabel Marshall] *The Plays of Roswitha* (London: Chatto and Windus, 1923).

63. See David Wiles, 'Hrosvitha of Gandersheim: the performance of her plays in the tenth century', *Theatre History Studies* 19 (1999), 133–50.

64. Von Simson, *Gothic Cathedral*, 8–11, 37–8.

65. I follow the suggestion in Peter Dronke, *Women Writers of the Middle Ages* (Cambridge University Press, 1984), 63, as against the alternative theory that the text accompanied a sequence of paintings; the text is translated in E. H. Zeydel, 'On two minor poems in the Hrosvitha codex', *Modern Language Notes* 60 (1945), 373–6.

66. Rudolph Wittkower, *Architectural Principles in the Age of Humanism* (University of London Press, 1949).

67. Gurevich, *Categories of Medieval Culture*, 56.

68. Elie Konigson, *L'Espace théâtral médiéval* (Paris: CNRS, 1975), 13–37.

69. *The Production of Space*, 259–60.

70. See Jacques Le Goff, *Medieval Civilization 400–1500*, tr. J. Barrow (Oxford: Blackwell, 1988), 158.

71. Francis Bond, *Screens and Galleries in English Churches* (London: Henry Frowde, 1908); Eamon Duffy, *The Stripping of the Altars* (New Haven, Conn.: Yale University Press, 1992), 96.

72. Herrad of Landsberg cited in Young, *Drama of the Medieval Church*, II.412–13.

73. *Victoria County History: Essex*, vol. II (London: Constable, 1907), 117.

74. Text in J. B. L. Tolhurst (ed.), *Ordinale and Customary of the Benedictine Nuns of Barking Abbey* (Bradshaw Society, 1927); part translated in *The Medieval European Stage 500–1550*, ed. W. Tydeman (Cambridge University Press, 2001),

83–7. A generation of Darwinian theatre historians have argued that western theatre was reborn in the tenth century from the textual seed of the *Quem Queritis* trope: Hardison, *Christian Rite and Christian Drama*, explores the roots of this theory in E. K. Chambers, *The Mediaeval Stage* (Oxford University Press, 1903) and Karl Young, *The Drama of the Medieval Church* (Oxford University Press, 1933).

75. See Roberta Gilchrist, *Gender and Material Culture: the archaeology of religious women* (London: Routledge, 1994), 138. On Barking see A. W. Clapham, 'The Benedictine abbey of Barking', *Transactions of the Essex Archaeological Society* 12 (1913), 69–87; *Royal Commission on Historical Monuments: Essex*, vol. 11 (London: HMSO, 1921).

76. Normally a male priest would administer confession: see Dunbar H. Ogden, 'Women play women in the liturgical drama of the middle ages', *On-Stage Studies* 19 (1996).

77. Though I have not followed her in every detail, my analysis of the space owes much to Kate Matthews, 'The Bride of Christ: an exploration of convent drama c.1100–1500', (PhD thesis, Royal Holloway University of London, 2002).

78. For the ceremonies of Easter week, see Hardison, *Christian Rite*, 80–177; Blandine-Domininique Berger, *Le Drame liturgique de Pâques: liturgie et théâtre* (Paris: Beauchesne, 1976); John Harper, *The Forms and Orders of Western Liturgy from the Tenth to the Eighteenth Century* (Oxford University Press, 1991); Duffy, *Stripping of the Altars*, 22–37; Ronald Hutton, *The Stations of the Sun: a history of the ritual year in Britain* (Oxford University Press, 1996), 182–97.

79. Simson, *Gothic Cathedral*, 51–5; Tuan, *Passing Strange and Wonderful*, 138–42.

80. *Architecture, Actor and Audience* (London: Routledge, 1993), 106.

81. See Millar Maclure, *The Paul's Cross Sermons* (University of Toronto Press, 1958), 3–19. Cf. Larissa Taylor, *Soldiers of Christ: preaching in late medieval and reformation France* (Oxford University Press, 1992), 29.

82. *Sermons* 2.3.114 – cited in Bryan Crockett, *The Play of Paradox: stage and sermon in renaissance England* (Philadelphia: University of Pennsylvania Press, 1995), 173.

83. Cf. John Bossy, *Christianity in the West 1400–1700* (Oxford University Press, 1985), 100.

84. 'The idolatrous eye: iconoclasm, anti-theatricalism and the image of the Elizabethan theater', *ELH* 52 (1985), 279–310, pp.296–7. Cf. S. Greenblatt, *Renaissance Self-Fashioning* (University of Chicago Press, 1980).

85. 'Of other spaces', tr. J. Miskowiec, *Diacritics* 16 (1986), 22–7, p.22.

86. *Le Rouge et or* (Paris: Flammarion, 1989), p.67.

87. *Ibid.*, 31.

88. Wagner cited in R. Hartford (ed.), *Bayreuth: the early years* (London: Gollancz, 1980), 29.

89. G. Skelton, *Wagner at Bayreuth* (London: White Lion, 1976), chapter 1; Barry Millington and Stewart Spencer (eds.), *Wagner in Performance* (New Haven, Conn.: Yale University Press, 1992), 148–51.

90. Peter Bürger, *Theory of the Avant-garde*, tr. M. Shaw (Manchester University Press, 1984), 28.

91. 'Monumentality' in *Texts on Theatre*, ed. Richard C. Beacham (Routledge, 1993), 137.

92. Paul Claudel (1913) cited in Denis and Marie-Louise Bablet, *Adolphe Appia 1862–1928: actor – space – light* (London: John Calder, 1982), 85; cf. 'The work of living art' in Appia, *Texts on Theatre*, 167ff.

93. Denis Bablet, *The Theatre of Edward Gordon Craig*, tr. D. Woodward (London: Eyre Methuen, 1981), 168–71.

94. *The Theatre and its Double*, tr. V. Corti (London: Calder & Boyars, 1970), 74–5, 29.

95. *Towards a Poor Theatre* (London: Methuen, 1969), 49.

96. *Ibid.*, 43, 89.

97. *Ibid.*, 32.

98. *Ibid.*, 213–14.

99. *Ibid.*, 42.

100. *The Grotowski Sourcebook*, ed. Lisa Wolford and Richard Schechner (London: Routledge, 1997), 156.

101. Rudolf Steiner, *The Story of my Life* (London: Anthroposophical Publishing Co., 1928), 236, 338.

102. *The Four Mystery Plays*, tr. A. Bittleston (London: Rudolf Steiner Press, 1982); *Speech and Drama*, tr. M. Adams (London: Rudolf Steiner Press, 1960).

103. See Hegen Bresantz and Arne Klingbord, *The Goetheanum: Rudolf Steiner's architectural impulse*, tr. J. Schmid (London: Rudolf Steiner Press, 1979); for the context see also Johannes Hemleben, *Rudolf Steiner: a documentary biography*, tr. L. Twyman (East Grinstead: Henry Goulden, 1975).

104. Rudolf Steiner, *The Architectural Conception of the Goetheanum*, cited in Rex Raab, Arne Klingborg and Ake Fant, *Eloquent Concrete* (London: Rudolf Steiner Press, 1979), 32.

105. Colin Wilson, *Rudolf Steiner: the man and his vision* (Wellingborough: Aquarian Press, 1985), 154–5.

106. Rudolf Steiner, *Ways to a New Style in Architecture*, tr. H. Colliston (London: Anthroposophical Publishing Co., 1927), 23; see also *And the Temple becomes Man*, tr. D. S. Osmond (London: Rudolf Steiner Press, 1979).

107. See Raab, Klingborg and Fant, *Eloquent Concrete*.

108. See Oswald Spengler, *The Decline of the West: form and actuality*, tr. C. F. Atkinson (London: George Allen & Unwin, 1926).

109. *Collected Plays* (London: Faber, 1962), 53–4. For the performance context see E. Martin Browne, *The Making of T. S. Eliot's Plays* (Cambridge University Press, 1969).

110. See for example Raymond Williams, *Drama from Ibsen to Brecht* (Harmondsworth: Penguin, 1968).

111. *On Poetry and Poets* (London: Faber, 1957), 79. For Eliot's populism see Peter Ackroyd, *T. S. Eliot* (London: Abacus, 1985), 296.

112. Lyndall Gordon, *Eliot's New Life* (Oxford University Press, 1989), 36.

113. Humphrey Carpenter, *Benjamin Britten: a biography* (London: Faber, 1992), 409. On the architecture see Louise Campbell, *Coventry Cathedral: art and architecture in post-war Britain* (Oxford University Press, 1996).

114. *Architecture, Actor and Audience*, 84.

115. *Theatrical Space: a guide for directors and designers* (Lanham: Scarecrow Press, 1995), 160.

116. 'Dr Strangelove: or how I learned to trust in the Globe and set fire to my dreams', *The European English Messenger* 4.1 (1995), 14–16.

117. *The Globe: the newsletter of the International Shakespeare Globe Centre* (summer, 1995), 5.

118. The documents are published by Joy Hancox in *The Byrom Collection* (London: Jonathan Cape, 1992).

119. *The Sacred and the Profane*, 23–4.

120. Tony Coult and Baz Kershaw (eds.), *Engineers of the Imagination: the Welfare State handbook* (London: Methuen, 1990), 219.

121. John Fox, *Eyes on Stalks* (London: Methuen, 2002), 164.

122. John Fox, 'Exploring to fulfil a genuine need' in *Live 4 Freedom Machine* (London: Nick Hern, 1996), 33–9. I am grateful to Alec Bell, the manager of Lanternhouse, for explaining to me some of the thinking behind the building.

3 PROCESSIONAL SPACE

1. *Independent Review of Parades and Marches*, chaired by Peter North (London: Stationery Office, 1997), 41–2 – citing Desmond Bell, *Acts of Union: youth culture and sectarianism in Northern Ireland* (London: Macmillan, 1990).

2. Victor Turner and Edith Turner, *Image and Pilgrimage in Christian Culture* (Oxford: Blackwell, 1978).

3. My account follows Edward Muir, *Civic Ritual in Renaissance Venice* (Princeton University Press, 1981), 119–34.

4. David Wiles, *Tragedy in Athens* (Cambridge University Press, 1997), 30–4. The Sacred Way which leads from the Temple of Nemesis to the Theatre of Rhamnous provides another example. See Vasileios Petrakos, *Rhamnous* (Athens: Ministry of Culture, 1991).

5. On the route of the procession, see Christiane Sourvinou-Inwood, 'Something to do with Athens: tragedy and ritual' in *Ritual, Finance, Politics*, ed. Robin Osborne and Simon Hornblower (Oxford University Press, 1994), 269–90.

6. Wiles, *Tragedy in Athens*, 63ff.

7. See Froma Zeitlin, 'The Argive festival of Hera and Euripides' *Electra*', *TAPA* 101 (1970), 645–69, and more generally F. de Polignac, *Cults, Territory and the Origin of the Greek City-State* (Chicago University Press, 1995); Athena Kavoulaki, 'Processional performance and the democratic polis' in *Performance Culture and Athenian Democracy*, ed. Simon Goldhill and Robin Osborne (Cambridge University Press, 1990), 293–320.

8. Dated to the reign of Hadrian. See Stephen Mitchell, 'Festivals, games and civic life in Roman Asia Minor', *Journal of Roman Studies* 80 (1990), 183–93.

Cf. the processional route at Ephesus: Guy M. Rogers, *The Sacred Identity of Ephesos: foundation myths of a Roman city* (London: Routledge, 1991).

9. I am grateful to Richard Beacham and the *Theatron* project at the University of Warwick for allowing me to test this proposition on a computer-generated model.

10. Figure 6, based on Richard Beacham's computer-generated model, depicts a solid building over the side approach, while the reconstruction of the marble plan marks an open avenue of columns and suggests a more processional dynamic. See chapter 6 below, n.35.

11. See Richard C. Beacham, *Spectacle Entertainments of Early Imperial Rome* (New Haven, Conn.: Yale University Press, 1999), 65, 70.

12. Diane Favro, *The Urban Image of Augustan Rome* (Cambridge University Press, 1999), 242–3 and fig. 4; Josephus, *Jewish War* vii.131. The term 'theatres' would have included the great stadium for chariot-racing, the Circus Maximus.

13. Cf. W. R. Connor, 'Tribes, festivals and processions: civic ceremonial and political manipulation in archaic Greece', *Journal of Hellenic Studies* 107 (1987), 40–50.

14. Kallixeinos of Rhodes, *On Alexandria*, extracted in Athenaeus v.196–203. Background information is taken from E. E. Rice, *The Grand Procession of Ptolemy Philadelphus* (Oxford University Press, 1983); Victoria Foertmeyer, 'The dating of the Pompe of Ptolemy II Philadelphus', *Historia* 37 (1988), 90–104; André Bernand, *Alexandrie des Ptolémées* (Paris: CNRS, 1995); K. M. Coleman, 'Ptolemy Philadelphus and the Roman amphitheater' in *Roman Theater and Society*, ed. W. J. Slater (Ann Arbor: University of Michigan Press, 1996), 49–68.

15. See H. S. Versnel, *Triumphus: an inquiry into the origin, development and meaning of the Roman triumph* (Leiden: Brill, 1970); H. H. Scullard, *Festivals and Ceremonies of the Roman Republic* (London: Thames & Hudson, 1980), 213–18; Ernst Kunzl, *Der römische Triumph* (Munich: C. H. Beck, 1988); Diane Favro, 'The street triumph: the urban impact of Roman triumphal parades' in *Streets: critical perspectives on public space*, ed. Z. Çelik, D. Favro and R. Ingersoll (Berkeley: University of California Press, 1994), 177–88; Diane Favro, *The Urban Image of Augustan Rome* (Cambridge University Press, 1999), esp. 235–6.

16. See Harriet I. Flower, *Ancestor Masks and Aristocratic Power in Roman Culture* (Oxford University Press, 1996).

17. *De Spectaculis* vii–x.

18. Karl Young, *The Drama of the Medieval Church* (Oxford University Press, 1933), II.461–3, 691–3; Elie Konigson, *L'Espace théâtral médiéval* (Paris: CNRS, 1975), 27–30.

19. Young, *Drama of the Medieval Church*, II.225–45; Konigson, *L'Espace théâtral médiéval*, 39–45; Peter Meredith and John E. Tailby (eds.), *The Staging of Religious Drama in Europe in the Later Middle Ages: texts and documents in English translation* (Kalamazoo: Medieval Institute Publications, 1983), 207–25.

20. Jacques Le Goff, *Medieval Civilization 400–1500*, tr. J. Barrow (Oxford: Blackwell, 1988), 158.

21. *Records of Early English Drama: York*, ed. A. Johnstone and M. Rogerson (University of Toronto Press, 1979), 1.137–51. Interpretations in L. Attreed 'The politics of welcome: ceremonies and constitutional development in later medieval English towns' in *City and Spectacle in Medieval Europe*, ed. B. A. Hanawalt and K. L. Reyerson (Minneapolis: University of Minnesota Press, 1994), 208–31; Sydney Anglo, *Spectacle, Pageantry and Early Tudor Policy* (Oxford University Press, 1997), 21–8; Gordon Kipling, *Enter the King: theatre, liturgy and ritual in the medieval civic triumph* (Oxford University Press, 1998), 134–9.

22. *Records of Early English Drama: York*, 1.154–5.

23. See Charles Phythian-Adams, 'Ceremony and the citizen: the ceremonial year in Coventry 1450–1550' in *Crisis and Order in English Towns 1500–1700* (London: Routledge, 1972), 57–85; François Laroque, *Shakespeare's Festive World: Elizabethan seasonal entertainment and the professional stage*, tr. J. Lloyd (Cambridge University Press, 1991), 81ff.

24. Useful broad-based studies include Mervyn James 'Ritual, drama and the social body in the late medieval English town', *Past and Present* 98 (1983), 3–29; Miri Rubin, *Corpus Christi: the Eucharist in medieval culture* (Cambridge University Press, 1991); Sarah Beckwith, 'Making the world and the York cycle' in *Framing Medieval Bodies*, ed. S. Kay and M. Rubin (Manchester University Press, 1994), 254–76; Anne Higgins, 'Streets and markets' in *A New History of Early English Drama*, ed. J. D. Cox and D. S. Kastan (New York: Columbia University Press, 1997), 77–92. For a specialist bibliography on the York cycle, see Richard Beadle (ed.), *The Cambridge Companion to Medieval English Theatre* (Cambridge University Press, 1994), 350–1.

25. M. M. Bakhtin, 'Forms of time and of the chronotope in the novel: towards a historical poetics' in *The Dialogic Imagination*, tr. C. Emerson and M. Holquist (Austin: University of Texas Press, 1981), 84–258.

26. *Categories of Medieval Culture*, tr. G. L. Campbell (London: RKP, 1985), 74.

27. *Ibid.*, 302–3.

28. *Ibid.*, 109–13.

29. Reproduced in Bryan Holme, *Princely Feasts and Festivals: five centuries of pageantry and spectacle* (London: Thames & Hudson, 1988), 46–9. My analysis follows that of Meg Twycross in 'Some approaches to dramatic festivity, especially processions' in *Festive Drama*, ed. Meg Twycross (Woodbridge: D. S. Brewer, 1996), 1–33. See also Meg Twycross, 'The Flemish *ommegang* and its pageant cars', *Medieval Theatre* 2 (1980), 15–41, 80–98.

30. Primary documents are assembled in *Records of Early English Drama: Somerset*, ed. James Stokes (University of Toronto Press, 1996), 261–367, with commentary on 464–73, 709–28, 932–57. Contextual information in David Underdown, *Revel, Riot and Rebellion: popular politics and culture in England 1603–1660* (Oxford University Press, 1985); M. Langley and E. Small, *Wells: an historical guide* (Bradford-on-Avon: Ex Libris Press, 1990); D. G. Shaw, *The Creation of a Community: the city of Wells in the middle ages* (Oxford University

Press, 1993); Ronald Hutton, *The Stations of the Sun: a history of the ritual year in Britain* (Oxford University Press, 1996), 244–61.

31. For London processions, see Glynne Wickham, *Early English Stages 1300–1660, Vol. I* (London: RKP, 1959), 51–63; Lawrence Manley, *Literature and Culture in Early Modern London* (Cambridge University Press, 1995), 212–93.

32. See E. P. Thompson, 'Rough music' in his *Customs in Common* (London: Merlin Press, 1991), 467–538; Martin Ingram, 'Ridings, rough music, and the "reform of popular culture" ', *Past and Present* 105 (1984), 79–113; Henri Rey-Flaud, *Le Charivari: les rituels fondamentaux de la sexualité* (Paris: Payot, 1985).

33. See R. Green, *Wells Charter Fairs and Markets* (Wells: St Andrew's Press, 1996).

34. *Records of Early English Drama: Somerset*, 371–7.

35. See A. E. Green, 'Popular drama and the mummers' play' in *Performance and Politics in Popular Drama*, ed. David Bradby, Louis James and Bernard Sharratt (Cambridge University Press, 1980), 139–66.

36. Peter Burke, *Popular Culture in Early Modern Europe* (London: Temple Smith, 1978), 216.

37. N. D. Shergold, *A History of the Spanish Stage: from medieval times until the end of the seventeenth century* (Oxford University Press, 1967), 424.

38. *The Gentle Craft* (London: 1597): in *The Novels of Thomas Deloney*, ed. M. E. Lawlis (Bloomington: Indiana University Press, 1961), 115–39. The book is not mentioned in James Stokes, 'The Wells cordwainers' show: new evidence concerning guild entertainments in Somerset', *Comparative Drama* 19 (1985/6), 332–46.

39. *The Fall of Public Man* (Cambridge University Press, 1977), 54. Cf. Peter Borsay, ' "All the town's a stage": urban ritual and ceremony 1660–1800' in *The Transformation of English Towns 1600–1800*, ed. Peter Clark (London: Hutchinson, 1984), 228–58, p.249. For a broad survey of material, see Robert Withington, *English Pageantry: an historical outline* (Cambridge, Mass.: Harvard University Press, 1918–20).

40. See for example Lewis Mumford, *The City in History: its origins, its transformations and its prospects* (London: Secker & Warburg, 1961), 368–70; David Garrioch, *Neighbourhood and Community in Paris 1740–1890* (Cambridge University Press, 1986), 199.

41. See Richard Ingersoll, 'Piazza di Ponte: the military origins of panopticism' in *Streets*, 177–88.

42. Mona Ozouf, '*Festivals and the French Revolution*, tr. A. Sheridan (Cambridge, Mass.: Harvard University Press, 1988), esp. 147–52.

43. *Flesh and Stone: the body and the city in western civilization* (London: Faber, 1994), 296.

44. *Ibid.*, 375–6.

45. 'The *Flâneur*' in *Charles Baudelaire*, tr. H. Zohn (London: Verso, 1976), 35–66.

46. 'Practices of space' in *On Signs: a semiotics reader*, ed. M. Blonsky (Oxford: Blackwell, 1985), 122–45. This edition of the essay contains important complementary photographs.

47. For a limited experiment, see John McKinnell, 'Producing the York *Mary* plays', *Medieval English Theatre* 12 (1990), 101–23. More sustained academic

revivals have taken place in Toronto: see for example David Parry 'The York Mystery Cycle at Toronto, 1977', *Medieval English Theatre* 1 (1979), 19–31; Megan S. Lloyd, 'Reflections of a York survivor: the York Cycle and its audience', *Research Opportunities in Renaissance Drama* 39 (2000), 223–35. For an overview of recent work, see John Marshall, 'Modern productions of medieval English plays' in *The Cambridge Companion to Medieval English Theatre*, ed. R. Beadle (Cambridge University Press, 1994), 290–311.

48. Stefan Brecht, *The Bread and Puppet Theatre* (London: Methuen, 1988), 584–5, 286–7; Peter Schumann, 'The Bread and Puppet Theatre in Nicaragua, 1985', *New Theatre Quarterly* 39 (1989), 3–22.

49. For background information see David Cressy, 'The fifth of November remembered' in *Myths of the English*, ed. Roy Porter (Cambridge: Polity Press, 1992), 68–90; Jim Etherington, *Lewes Bonfire Night* (Seaford: S. B. Publications, 1993); David Wiles, 'The Lewes Bonfire Festival', *New Theatre Quarterly* 46 (1996), 177–91. The modern festival is described in Andy Thomas, *Streets of Fire* (Seaford: S. B. Publications, 1999).

50. See J. E. Etherington, 'The Lewes bonfire riots of 1847', *Sussex History* 6.6 (1978), 2–16.

4 PUBLIC SPACE

1. 'On national–popular drama and the play *Martha the Seneschal's Wife*' in *Russian Dramatic Theory from Pushkin to the Symbolists*, ed. and tr. L. Senelick (Austin: University of Texas Press, 1981), 8–15.

2. Mikhail Bakhtin, *Rabelais and his World*, tr. H. Iswolsky (Bloomington: Indiana University Press, 1984), 153–4.

3. 'The fairground booth' (1912) in *Meyerhold on Theatre*, ed. E. Braun (London: Methuen, 1998), 122–3.

4. *Rabelais and his World*, 158; Rabelais, 'La Sciomachie' in *Œuvres complètes*, vol. ii, ed. P. Jourda (Paris: Garnier frères, 1962), 579–99.

5. 'The fairground booth', 155.

6. See for example the aquatint of 1721 analysed by Sybil Rosenfeld in *The Theatre of the London Fairs* (Cambridge University Press, 1960), 25–6. For early farce stages, see Michel Rousse, 'L'espace scénique des farces' in *Le Théâtre au moyen age*, ed. G. R. Muller (Quebec: Univers, 1981), 137–46. For early fairs, see Katrin Kröll, 'Theatrum Mundi versus Mundus Theatri: a study of the history of fairground arts in early modern times', *Nordic Theatre Studies* 2/3 (1989), 55–90.

7. W. M. H. Hummeln, 'The boundaries of the rhetoricians' stage', *Comparative Drama* 28 (1994), 235–51.

8. Henry Morley, *Memoirs of Bartholomew Fair* (London: Chapman & Hall, 1859), 146.

9. My analysis is based on the version in the Fitzwilliam Museum; there are others in Brussels, Amsterdam and Vienna. It is likely that all derive from a lost original by P. Brueghel the Elder.

10. Translation in *Dutch Crossing* 24 (1984), 32–81.

11. Photius on 'ikria' and 'orchestra'; Suda on 'Pratinas': Eric Csapo and William J. Slater, *The Context of Ancient Drama* (Ann Arbor: University of Michigan Press, 1995), 133, 101.

12. Noel Robertson, *Festivals and Legends: the formation of Greek cities in the light of public ritual* (University of Toronto Press, 1992), 42–8 and fig. 3.

13. See David Wiles, *Tragedy in Athens: performance space and theatrical meaning* (Cambridge University Press, 1997), 36–8.

14. *The Laws* 701 – tr. T. J. Saunders (Harmondsworth: Penguin, 1970), p.154.

15. *Ibid.*, 817 – p.310 (slightly adapted).

16. There is no reason to associate the trestle stages pictured on so-called 'phlyax' vases with the agora rather than the orchestra of a theatre. For an analysis of the form see Oliver Taplin, *Comic Angels – and other approaches to Greek drama through vase-paintings* (Oxford University Press, 1993), esp. p.93.

17. F. H. Sandbach, 'How Terence's *Hecyra* failed', *Classical Quarterly* 32 (1982), 134–5; E. J. Jory, 'Gladiators in the theatre', *Classical Quarterly* 36 (1986), 537–9.

18. *The Ten Books of Architecture* v.i.1–2 – tr. M. H. Morgan (Cambridge, Mass.: Harvard University Press, 1914), 131–2.

19. J.-C. Golvin, *L'Amphithéâtre romain* (Paris: Boccard, 1988).

20. My account of the Forum draws mainly on the following: Marcello Gaggiotti, 'Plauto, Livio, la più antica "basilica" del foro romano e la politica edilizia degli Aemilii' in *Roma: archeologia nel centro I* (Rome: De Luca, 1985), 56–65; L. Richardson Jr, *A New Topographical Dictionary of Ancient Rome* (Baltimore: Johns Hopkins University Press, 1992); Florence Dupont, *Daily Life in Ancient Rome*, tr. C. Woodall (Oxford: Blackwell, 1992), 136ff.; John R. Patterson, 'The city of Rome: from republic to empire', *Journal of Roman Studies* 82 (1992), 186–215; N. Purcell, *s.v.* 'Forum Romanum' in *Lexicon Topographicum Urbis Romae*, ed. E. M. Steinby (Rome: Quasar, 1995), II.325–42.

21. For the sources, see Stefan Weinstock, *Divus Julius* (Oxford University Press, 1971), 249–355, 400.

22. Plutarch, *Life of C. Gracchus* 33.5–6.

23. *Curculio* 465–86. I have inverted lines 483 and 484. The standard critical edition is by C. Monaco (Palermo: Palumbo, 1969).

24. Plautus confronts this problem in the prologue to his *Captives*.

25. *Rabelais and his World*, 7.

26. Cf. *The Little Carthaginian*, 17–18. Plautus' prologue refers to prostitutes trying to gain a seat on the stage, implying the presence of stage spectators.

27. *Problems of Dostoevsky's Poetics*, tr. Caryl Emerson (Minneapolis: University of Minnesota Press, 1984), 122–3. Original Russian publication in 1963.

28. Dupont, *Daily Life in Ancient Rome*, offers a fine analysis of this unique sense of place.

29. See N. Gauthier, 'La topographie chrétienne entre idéologie et pragmatisme' in *The Idea and Ideal of the Town between Late Antiquity and the Middle Ages*, ed. G. P. Bragoglio and B. Ward-Perkyns (Leiden: Brill, 1999), 195–209.

30. See Paul Zucker, *Town and Square: from the agora to the village green* (New York: Columbia University Press, 1959), 63–98.

31. Cf. Robert Tittler, *Architecture and Power: the town hall and the English urban community c.1500–1640* (Oxford University Press, 1991), 134–5.
32. *Records of Early English Drama: Somerset*, ed. James Stokes (University of Toronto Press, 1996), 358.
33. Experiments in performing the N-Town plays on different sites around Lincoln Cathedral confirm the difficulty of using the parvis: see a forthcoming study by K. Normington.
34. For medieval markets see Zucker, *Town and Square*, 63–98; A. E. J. Morris, *History of Urban Form* (London: George Goodwin, 1979), 75–7.
35. 'La Place du Weinmarkt à Lucerne: remarques sur l'organisation d'un espace dramatisé', *Les Voies de la création théâtrale* 8 (1980), 43–90. Further documentation in M. Blakemore Evans, *The Passion Play of Lucerne* (New York: Modern Language Association of America, 1943).
36. Cliff Moughtin, *Urban Design: street and square* (Oxford: Architectural Press, 1999), 100. On the renaissance square see also Zucker, *Town and Square*, 99–142, Morris, *History of Urban Form*, 127–8, 153–4.
37. Cited in Leonardo Benevolo, *The Architecture of the Renaissance*, tr. J. Landry (London and Henley: RKP, 1978), 458.
38. *Habiti d'huomeni et donne venetiane con la processione della serenissima Signoria et altri particolari cioe trionfi feste et cerimonie publiche della nobilissima città di Venetia* (Venice, 1610). Commentary in Ludovico Zorzi, *L'attore, la Commedia, il drammaturgo* (Turin: Einaudi, 1990), 172–82.
39. The paintings are reproduced and analysed in in Bianca Tamassia Mazzarotto, *Le feste veneziane: i giochi popolari, le ceremonie religiose e di governo* (Florence: Sansoni, 1961); Giorgio Busetto (ed.), *Cronica veneziana: feste e vita nella Venezia del Settecento* (Venice: Fondazione Querini Stampalia, 1991).
40. Thomas Hirthe, *Il 'foro all'antica' di Venezia: la trasformazione di piazza San Marco ne Cinquecento* (Venice: Centro Tedesco di Studi Veneziani, 1986); Edward Muir, *Civic Ritual in Renaissance Venice* (Princeton University Press, 1981), 163.
41. Thomas Coryate, *Coryat's Crudities* (London, 1611), 170.
42. Fernand Braudel, *Civilization and Capitalism Vol. III: The Perspective of the World*, tr. S. Reynolds (London: Collins, 1984), 118–38.
43. Muir, *Civic Ritual*, 223–30.
44. See Elizabeth Crouzet-Pavan, 'Espaces urbains: pouvoir et société à Vénise à la fin du moyen âge' (PhD thesis, University of Lille, 1989), 583–622, 658–68; on the festival cf. Muir, *Civic Ritual*, 135–56.
45. Muir, *Civic Ritual*, 167–74.
46. See Mazzarotto, *Feste veneziane*, 141–3.
47. Limojon de St-Didier, *La Ville et la république de Vénise* (Paris, 1680), 368; cf. Zorzi, *L'attore*, 180.
48. Muir, *Civic Ritual*, 160–4; St-Didier, *La Ville et la république de Vénise*, 385–9.
49. Painting in the Louvre: reproduced by Mazzarotto as plate II.
50. Sandro Piantanida 'Ciarlatani' in *La piazza: spettacoli popolari italiani*, ed. R. Leydi (Milan: Gallo Grande, 1959), 215–74, p.227; cf. *Coryat's Crudities*, 274.

51. Fynes Morrison in *Shakespeare's Europe*, ed. C. Hughes (London: Sherratt & Hughes, 1903), 465 – account originally written in 1596/7.

52. See Thomas Henke, 'The Italian mountebank and the *commedia dell'arte*', *Theatre Survey* 38 (1997), 1–29; M. A. Katritsky, 'Was *Commedia dell'arte* performed by mountebanks? *Album amicorum* illustrations and Thomas Platter's description of 1598', *Theatre Research International* 23 (1998), 104–25.

53. Carlo Goldoni, *Memoirs of Carlo Goldoni*, tr. J. Black (New York: Knopf, 1926), 126–8.

54. Cf. Platter's view of Bragetta's two female performers in Katritsky, 'Was Commedia dell'arte performed by mountebanks?', 145.

55. Christian Norberg-Schulz, *Genius Loci: towards a phenomenology of architecture* (London: Academy Editions, 1980).

56. *Coryat's Crudities*, 272–3.

57. *Cultural Geography: a critical introduction* (Oxford: Blackwell, 2000), 136–7.

58. H. Lefebvre and C. Régulier, 'Rhythmanalysis of Mediterranean cities' in Henri Lefebvre, *Writings on Cities*, tr. E. Kofman and E. Lebas (Oxford: Blackwell, 1996), 228–40. Cf. De Certeau's account of walking in the city: chapter 2 above.

59. I follow the account of Dante Cappelletti in *Teatro in Piazza: ipotesi sul Teatro Popolare e la scena sperimentale in Italia* (Rome: Bulzoni, 1980); also Richard Andrews, *A Theatre of Community Memory: Tuscan sharecropping and the Teatro Povero di Monticchiello* (Society for Italian Studies, University of Exeter, 1998). An account by Mary-Kay Gamel is forthcoming.

60. Ann Jellicoe, *Community Plays: how to put them on* (London: Methuen, 1987).

61. Victor Fournel, *Les Spectacles populaires et les artistes des rues* (Paris: F. Dentu, 1863), 99–115. Gringoire's *Prince des Sots* is examined by Philip Crispin, 'Scandalizing the monarchy: the Kingdom of the Bazoche and the Kingdom of France, 1460–1550' (PhD thesis, Royal Holloway University of London, 2003).

62. See R. Héron de Villefosse, *Nouvelle histoire de Paris: solennités, fêtes et réjouissances parisiennes* (Paris: Hachette, 1980); Leonardo Benevolo, *The Architecture of the Renaissance*, tr. J. Laudry (London: RKP, 1978), 696–9.

63. *Les Œuvres de Tabarin*, ed. Georges d'Harmonville (Paris: Garnier, n.d.), 212–13. On Tabarin, see Fournel, *Spectacles des rues*, 250ff., W. L. Wiley, *The Early Public Theatre in France* (Cambridge, Mass.: Harvard University Press, 1960), 71–9; Jonathan Marks, 'The charlatans of the Pont-Neuf', *Theatre Research International* 23 (1998), 133–41.

64. Cf. David Garrioch, *Neighbourhood and Community in Paris 1740–1790* (Cambridge University Press, 1986), 198–9. On the logic of baroque space, see Zucker, *Town and Square*, 232–6; Lewis Mumford, *The City in History: its origins, its transformations, its prospects* (London: Secker & Warburg, 1961), 363–77; Siegfried Giedion, *Space, Time and Architecture* (Cambridge, Mass.: Harvard University Press, 1967), 75–106; Morris, *History of Urban Form*, 124ff.; Richard Ingersoll, 'Piazza di Ponte and the military origins of panopticism' in *Streets: critical perspectives on public space*, ed. Z. Çelik, D. Favro and R. Ingersoll

(Berkeley: University of California Press, 1994), 177–88; Charles Burroughs, 'Absolutism and the rhetoric of topography: streets in the reign of Sixtus V' in *ibid.*, 189–202. Also Pierre Couperie, *Paris Through the Ages*, tr. M. Low (London: Barrie & Jenkins, 1970).

65. Wiley, *Early Public Theatre*, 130.
66. Richard Sennett, *Flesh and Stone: the body and the city in western Civilization* (London: Faber, 1994), 308.
67. *Ibid.*, 304; cf. Zucker, *Town and Square*, 185.
68. See Evan John, *King Charles I* (London: Arthur Baker, 1933), 299–302. Cf. Andrew Marvell's 'Horatian Ode'.
69. Sennett, *Flesh and Stone*, 329–32 offers a succinct account.
70. [Théâtre du Soleil], *1789: the French Revolution – Year One*, tr. A. Trocchi in *Gambit* 20 (1970), 5–74, p.60.
71. See Konstantin Rudnitsky, *Russian and Soviet theatre: tradition and avant-garde*, tr. R. Permar (London: Thames & Hudson, 1988), 44; also Robert Leach's account in *A History of Russian Theatre*, ed. R. Leach and V. Borovsky (Cambridge University Press, 1999), 304–5.
72. Mumford, *City in History*, 348.
73. The events are traced in Chuck Anderson (with Ray Green), *Save the Jubilee Hall!* (London: Random Thoughts Ltd, 1992). The market reopened in 1980. The Jubilee Hall in Covent Garden was still threatened until 1984.
74. Audrey Woodiwiss, *The History of Covent Garden* (London: Robert Conway, 1980).
75. *Ibid.*, 20–1.
76. The issues are well analysed in Jon Goss, 'Disquiet on the waterfront: reflections on nostalgia and utopia in urban archetypes of festival marketplaces', *Urban Geography* 17 (1996), 221–47.

5 SYMPOTIC SPACE

1. Original in Catalan.
2. 'Playing to the senses: food as a performance medium', *Performance Research* 4.1 (1999), 1–30, p.25.
3. See *The Noble Mirror of Art* extracted in *The Renaissance Stage*, ed. Barnard Hewitt (Coral Gables: University of Miami Press, 1958), 246–51.
4. See Sylvain Pinard, 'A taste of India: on the role of gustation in the Hindu sensorium' in *The Varieties of Sensory Experience*, ed. David Howes (University of Toronto Press, 1991), 221–30; Bharat Gupt, *Dramatic Concepts Greek and Indian: a study of the Poetics and the Natyasastra* (Delhi: D. K. Printworld, 1994), 260–73.
5. *Gorgias* 465a. Augustine, *Confessions* x.31. I have translated *opsopoikê* as 'dainties' rather than 'cookery' because of the emphasis on the visual. On the aesthetic tradition, see Michel Jeanneret, *A Feast of Words: banquets and table talk in the renaissance*, tr. J. Whiteley and E. Hughes (Cambridge: Polity Press, 1991).

6. 1 Corinthians XI.17–34.
7. 'The modern theatre is the epic theatre' (1930) in *Brecht on Theatre: the development of an aesthetic*, ed. and tr. John Willett (London: Methuen, 1964), 33–42. See also Lisa Appignanesi, *The Cabaret* (London: Studio Vista, 1975), 130–1.
8. 18 January 2001.
9. I have used the text in Xénophon, *Banquet*, ed. Jean-Claude Carrière (Paris: Les Belles Lettres, 1996). Carrière argues for a date of composition in the 360s. Xenophon joined the Socratic circle in approx. 408 BC and knew the participants. See further David Wiles, 'Théâtre dionysiaque dans le *Banquet* de Xénophon', *Cahiers du GITA* 13 (2000), 107–18.
10. On Athenian domestic architecture, see Fabrizio Pesando, *Oikos e ktesis: la casa greca in età classica* (Perugia: Quasar, 1987); on the organization of space in the classical symposium, see Birgitta Bergquist, 'Sympotic space' in *Sympotica*, ed. Oswyn Murray (Oxford University Press, 1990), 37–65, and Katherine Dunbabin, 'Ut Graeco more biberetur: Greeks and Romans on the dining couch' in *Meals in a Social Context: aspects of the communal meal in the Hellenistic and Roman world*, ed. I. Nielsen and H. S. Nielsen (Aarhus University Press, 1998), 81–101; on entertainment, Christopher P. Jones, 'Dinner theatre' in *Dining in a Classical Context*, ed. W. J. Slater (Ann Arbor: University of Michigan Press, 1991), 185–98; Eric Csapo, 'Les mosaïques de Ménandre à Mytilène: leur contexte sociale et leur tradition iconographique', *Pallas* 47 (1997), 165–82.
11. Plato, *Symposium* 176e; *Protagoras* 347c–d.
12. Diodorus xvi.92–3.
13. Manolis Andronicos, *Vergina: the royal tombs and ancient city*, tr. L. Turner (Athens: Endotike Athenon, 1994), pp. 42–4 and figs. 18–20; R. A. Tomlinson, 'Ancient Macedonian symposia' in *Ancient Macedonia: papers read at the first international symposium–Thessaloniki 1968* (Thessaloniki: Institute for Balkan Studies, 1970), 308–15.
14. Plutarch, *Life of Crassus*, 33.
15. *Table Talk* VII.8.
16. *Ibid.* IV.I; ii.preface.
17. *Ibid.* I.4.
18. *The Use of Pleasure: the history of sexuality Vol. II*, tr. R. Hurley (Harmondsworth: Penguin, 1992).
19. *L'Invention de la littérature: de l'ivresse grecque au livre latin* (Paris: Editions de la Découverte, 1994).
20. Homer, *Odyssey* VIII.55ff.; XIII.1ff.
21. *Cena Trimalchionis*, ed. Martin S. Smith (Oxford University Press, 1975) – seating plan on p.66. Translation by P. G. Walsh in *The Satyricon* (Oxford University Press, 1996). My reading draws on Niall W. Slater, *Reading Petronius* (Baltimore: Johns Hopkins University Press, 1990).
22. C. E. Baehrens, *The Origins of the Masque* (Groningen: Drukherij Dijkhuisen and Van Zauten, 1929), 79–85, cites examples from Rome and Burgundy.

23. See Inge Nielsen, 'Royal banquets: the development of royal banquets and banqueting halls from Alexander to the tetrarchs' in *Meals in a Social Context*, 102–33; Katherine Dunbabin, 'Convivial spaces: dining and entertainment in the Roman villa', *Journal of Roman Archaeology* 9 (1996), 66–80; also her essay 'Ut Graeco more biberetur' cited above. Paul Veyne and Yvon Thébert provide an overview of imperial banqueting in *A History of Private Life Vol. I*, ed. P. Veyne and tr. A. Goldhammer (Cambridge, Mass.: Harvard University Press, 1987). For later arrangements see also Katherine Dunbabin, 'Triclinium and stibadium' in *Dining in a Classical Context*, ed. Slater, 121–48; J. Rossiter, 'Convivium and villa in late antiquity' in *ibid.*, 199–214, esp. p.203 on entertainments.

24. *Table Talk* 1.3.

25. See Susan P. Ellis, 'Power, architecture and décor: how the late Roman aristocrat appeared to his guests' in *Roman Art in the Private Sphere*, ed. E. K. Gazda (Ann Arbor: University of Michigan Press, 1991), 117–34.

26. Felicity Heal, *Hospitality in Early Modern England* (Oxford University Press, 1990), 29. On dining-hall staging, see Glynne Wickham, *Early English Stages 1300–1660 Vol. I* (London: RKP, 1959), 179–253. For the architectural overview, see Stephen Gardiner, *Evolution of the House* (London: Constable, 1975).

27. Variant texts in *Nouveau recueil complet des fabliaux Vol. V*, ed. W. Noomen and N. van den Boogaard (Assen: Van Gorcum, 1990), 285–311; modern French translation in *Fabliaux*, ed. Gilbert Rouger (Paris: Gallimard, 1978), 111–14.

28. *Littérature et société arrageoises au XIIIe siècle: les chansons et dits artésiens* (Arras: Commission départementale des monuments historiques, 1981); 'Le Jeu de la feuillée: quelques notes' in *Arras au moyen âge: histoire et littérature*, ed. J.-P. Martin (Arras: Artois Presses Université, 1994), 221–7. The text is translated in Richard Axton and John Stevens, *Medieval French Plays* (Oxford: Blackwell, 1971), 209–55.

29. Axton and Stevens exemplify the old view. Berger's thesis is accepted without question in, for example, Pierre Bougard *Histoire d'Arras* (Arras: Editions des Beffrois, 1988), 75, and Adam de la Halle, *Œuvres complètes*, ed. Pierre-Yves Badel (Paris: Livre de Poche, 1995), 8. On the hall and curfew, see Berger, *Littérature et société*, 115.

30. *Saint Nicholas* and *Courtois d'Arras*, both translated by Axton and Stevens.

31. See Bakhtin's classic analysis of the grotesque medieval body in *Rabelais and his World* – cf. chapter 4 above.

32. On the fork see Norbert Elias, *The Civilizing Process*, tr. E. Jephcott (Oxford: Blackwell, 2000), 59–60, 107–9.

33. *The Great Chronicle of London*, ed. A. H. Thomas and I. D. Thornley (London: G. W. Jones, 1938), 251–2. Sydney Anglo cites another brief record which mentions a castle built in the hall: *Review of English Studies* 10 (1959), 348.

34. Michael Kirby (ed.), *Happenings: an illustrated anthology* (London: Sidgwick & Jackson, 1965). Since a matrix of narrative remains, Peter Brook's term 'immediate theatre' may be more appropriate: *The Empty Space* (London: MacGibbon & Kee, 1968).

35. *Fulgens and Lucres*, performed at around this time, probably at a Christmas feast for the Archbishop of Canterbury, demonstrates how much apparent spontaneity can be injected into a script: *The Plays of Henry Medwall*, ed. Alan H. Nelson (Woodbridge: D. S. Brewer, 1980).

36. *The First Night of Twelfth Night* (London: Mercury Books, 1961).

37. I have discussed the issues in my *Shakespeare's Almanac: A Midsummer Night's Dream, marriage and the Elizabethan calendar* (Woodbridge: D. S. Brewer, 1993), 8–12, and suggest Dekker's *Phaethon* as the most likely contender.

38. Hotson, *First Night of Twelfth Night*, 180, 202.

39. *Gesta Grayorum, or, the history of the high and mighty prince Henry Prince of Purpoole, anno domini 1594*, ed. Desmond Bland (Liverpool University Press, 1968).

40. Margaret Knapp and Michal Kobialka, 'Shakespeare and the Prince of Purpoole: the 1594 production of *The Comedy of Errors* at Gray's Inn hall', *Theatre History Studies* 4 (1984), 70–81. Their research is extended in Robert E. Burkhart 'The surviving Shakespearean playhouses: the halls of the Inns of Court and the excavation of The Rose', *Theatre History Studies* 12 (1992), 173–96. For the galleries running on all four sides, cf. Alan H. Nelson's account of staging in Queens' College hall: *Early Cambridge Theatres: college, university and town 1464–1720* (Cambridge University Press, 1994).

41. *Gesta Grayorum*, 55–6.

42. See Wiles, *Shakespeare's Almanac*, 11, 13, 31–2, 41–2.

43. See Glynne Wickham, *Early English Stages 1300–1660 Vol. II, Part 1* (London: RKP, 1963), 166.

44. John Orrell, *The Human Stage* (Cambridge University Press, 1988) 126. The performance was at Christ Church, Oxford.

45. See Watson Nicholson, *The Struggle for a Free Stage in London* (London: Constable, 1906).

46. Good contextual studies include Brian Harrison, *Drink and the Victorians: the temperance question in England 1815–1872* (London: Faber, 1971); Hugh Cunningham, *Leisure in the Industrial Revolution c.1780–c.1880* (London: Croom Helm, 1980).

47. See especially John Earl, 'Building the Halls' in *Music Hall: the business of pleasure*, ed. Peter Bailey (Oxford University Press, 1986), 1–32; Peter Bailey 'Custom, capital and culture in the Victorian music hall' in *Popular Culture and Custom in Nineteenth-Century England*, ed. Robert D. Storch (London: Croom Helm, 1982), 180–208.

48. See Jerome K. Jerome's classic account in 'Variety patter', *The Idler* 1 (March 1892), 121–35.

49. *Parliamentary Papers*, 1866, vol. XVI, items 5002–4, 4996.

50. *Ibid.*, 1892, vol. XVIII, items 3535–6.

51. *Brecht on Theatre*, 8–9.

52. *Parliamentary Papers*, 1892, item 3534.

53. *Phases of Bradford Life: a series of pen and ink sketches* (London: Simpkin, Marshall & Co. and Bradford: W. M. Byles, 1871), 54–61. See also Dagmar

Kift, *The Victorian Music Hall: culture, class and conflict* tr. R. Kift (Cambridge University Press, 1996), 28–31.

54. Bohemian attitudes are analysed in Barry J. Faulk, *Aesthetics and Necessity: London professionals and the fortunes of music hall* (Cambridge University Press, 2001).

55. Walker Art Gallery, Baltimore; analysis in F. Cachin and C. S. Mottett (eds.), *Manet 1832–1883* (Paris: Réunion des Musées Nationaux, 1983), 414–16.

56. Courtauld Institute, London. See the celebrated analysis by T. J. Clark in *The Painting of Modern Life: Paris in the art of Manet and his followers* (rev. edn, London: Thames & Hudson, 1999), 205–58. Peter Bailey qualifies Clark's interpretation of the barmaid in *Popular Culture and Performance in the Victorian City* (Cambridge University Press, 1988), 168–71.

57. Reproduced with commentary in *Sickert: Paintings*, ed. Wendy Baron and Russell Shone (London: Royal Academy of Arts, 1992), 74–5. Further discussion in Anna Gruetzner Robins, 'Sickert: painter-in-ordinary to the music-hall' in *ibid.*, 13–24.

58. Walter Sickert, *Complete Writings on Art*, ed. Anna Gruetzner Robins (Oxford University Press, 2000), 41–2.

59. Baron and Shone, *Sickert: Paintings*, 96–101.

60. *Ibid.*, 4.

61. See for example J. S. Bratton, *Wilton's Music Hall* (Cambridge: Chadwyck-Healey, 1980), 13. John Stokes analyses mirrors in 'Prudes on the prowl: the view from the Empire promenade' in *In the Nineties* (Hemel Hempstead: Harvester Wheatsheaf, 1989), 53–93. On the trope see Anna Gruetzner Robins, *Walter Sickert: drawings* (London: Scolar Press, 1996), 18.

62. Baron and Shone, *Sickert: Paintings*, 100.

63. André Sallée and Philippe Chauveau, *Music-hall et café-concert* (Paris: Bordas, 1985), 13.

64. See Appignanesi, *Cabaret*; Harold B. Segel, *Turn-of-the-century Cabaret* (New York: Columbia University Press, 1987); Laurence Senelick, *Cabaret Performance Vol. I: Europe 1890–1920)* (New York: PAJ Publications, 1989).

65. See Oliver Double, *Stand up! on being a comedian* (London: Methuen, 1997); also John McGrath, *A Good Night Out – Popular theatre: audience, class and form* (London: Nick Hern, 1996), 22–35.

66. Limited documentation is provided in Lucinda Jarrett, *Stripping in Time: a history of erotic dancing* (London: Pandora, 1997).

67. See Roger Wilmut and Peter Rosengard, *Didn't You Kill My Mother-in-law? The story of alternative comedy in Britain from The Comedy Store to Saturday Live* (London: Methuen, 1989).

68. On the impact of density, see Iain Mackintosh, *Architecture, Actor and Audience* (London: Routledge, 1993), 22–5.

69. I am grateful to Sheila Brass, Area Manager of Licensing at Wandsworth Borough Council, for an explanation of the law.

70. Wilmut and Rosengard, *Didn't You Kill My Mother-in-law?*, 10.

71. The performers on 26 October 2001 were Geoff Boyz, Dan Antopolski, Alex Zane and Reg D. Hunter.

6 THE COSMIC CIRCLE

1. See Adam Nicholson, *Regeneration: the story of the Dome* (London: Harper-Collins, 1999), 176–9, 176–9.
2. See Kunio Komparu, *The Noh Theater: principles and perspectives* (New York and Tokyo: Weatherhill, 1983), 117–21.
3. See Yi-Fu Tuan, *Topophilia: a study of environmental perception, attitudes, and values* (Englewood Cliffs: Prentice Hall, 1974), 161.
4. *Why not theaters made for people?* (Värmdö, Sweden: Arena Theatre Institute, 1990), 12–23.
5. *The Birds* directed by Kathryn Hunter opened on 26 July 2002 in a transformed Lyttelton Theatre. Plans to create an arena had not proved feasible.
6. 'Le cube et la sphère' in *Architecture et dramaturgie*, ed. André Villiers (Paris: Flammarion, 1950), 63–83, pp.66–7.
7. James H. Butler in *The American Theatre: a sum of its parts* (New York: Samuel French, 1971), 360. For the circular Penthouse Theatre in Washington (1940), see for example Richard and Helen Leacroft, *Theatre and Playhouse: an illustrated survey of theatre building from ancient Greece to the present day* (London: Methuen, 1984), 186–7.
8. *Le Théâtre en rond* (Paris: Librairie Théâtrale, 1958), 9, 73; *Theatre in the Round* (London: Barrie & Rockliff, 1967), 115.
9. *Architectural Review* 1976, cited in D. Fraser (ed.), *The Royal Exchange Theatre Company: an illustrated record* (Manchester: Royal Exchange, 1988), 19.
10. *Timaeus* 40C. See my discussion in *Tragedy in Athens: performance space and theatrical meaning* (Cambridge University Press, 1997), 93–4; William Mullen, *Choreia: Pindar and the Dance* (Princeton University Press, 1982), 221–9.
11. *Herodotus* 1.98.
12. The best account of Greek thinking about the circle is Jean-Pierre Vernant, *Myth and Thought among the Greeks* (London: Routledge, 1983).
13. *Tragedy in Athens*, 49. I have assumed an early date for the introduction of the circular orchestra in figure 3, on the basis that the space was created for the dithyramb, but some argue that early theatrical orchestras were rectilinear. On this hypothesis it is hard to explain how the theatrical circle originated. See most recently Rush Rehm, *The Play of Space: spatial transformation in Greek tragedy* (Princeton University Press, 2002), 40–1.
14. *Tragedy in Athens*, 94–6.
15. *Ibid.*, 36–43.
16. 'Art and Revolution' and 'Art-Work of the future' in *Richard Wagner's Prose Works Vol. I*, tr. W. A. Ellis (London: Kegan Paul, 1892), 47, 185n., 34.
17. George C. Izenour, *Theater Design*, 2nd edn (New Haven, Conn.: Yale University Press, 1996), 282.

18. Thus Richard Sennett, *The Fall of Public Man* (Cambridge University Press, 1977), 208.
19. *Prose Works*, 36.
20. 'Monumentality' (1922) in *Texts on Theatre*, ed. Richard C. Beacham (London: Routledge, 1993), 137.
21. *Peter Hall's Diaries*, ed. J. Goodwin (London: Oberon, 1983), 173.
22. Cited by Braham Murray in *The Times* 11 November 1988.
23. *Architecture, Actor and Audience* (London: Routledge, 1993).
24. A. Jessop *et al.*, *William Cecil, Lord Burghley* (London: Jack, 1904), 64.
25. *An Apology for Actors* (London: 1612).
26. Glynne Wickham, *English Professional Theatre, 1530–1660* (Cambridge University Press, 2000), 86.
27. See David Wiles, *Shakespeare's Clown: actor and text in the Elizabethan Playhouse* (Cambridge University Press, 1981), 12, 21, 167–72.
28. See Frank M. Turner, 'Why the Greeks and not the Romans in Victorian Britain?' in *Rediscovering Hellenism: the Hellenic inheritance and the English imagination*, ed. G. W. Clarke (Cambridge University Press, 1989), 61–82.
29. *For Sestius*, 106–27.
30. See for example Paul J. J. Vanderbroeck, *Popular leadership and Collective Behaviour in the Late Roman Republic (Ca.80–50 B.C.)* (Amsterdam: J. C. Gieben, 1987), 77–81; Shadi Bartsch, *Actors in the Audience: theatricality and doublespeak from Nero to Hadrian* (Cambridge, Mass.: Harvard University Press, 1994), 71–5; Holt N. Parker, 'The observed of all observers: spectacle, applause and cultural poetics in the Roman theater audience' in *The Art of Ancient Spectacle*, ed. B. Bergmann and C. Kondoleon (Washington: National Gallery of Art, 1999), 163–79.
31. E. Frézouls, 'La construction du theatrum lapideum et son contexte politique' in *Théâtre et Spectacles dans l'antiquité* (Leiden: Brill, 1984), 193–214.
32. *For Sestius*, 118.
33. *Ibid.*, 120–3.
34. *To Atticus* 2.19.3; Dio, *Roman History* 48.31.
35. For sources on Pompey's theatre, see chapter 2 notes 34–4 above. For a broad survey, see Richard C. Beacham, *The Roman Theatre and its Audience* (London: Routledge, 1991), 154–69. My sketch is based on fragments of the marble plan carved in around AD 210. See *La pianta marmorea di Roma antica: Forma Urbis Romae*, ed. G. Carettoni, A. M. Colini, L. Cozza and G. Gatti (Rome: Comune di Roma, 1960), 91–3, 104–6 and plates 14, 29, 32. Restorations of the auditorium and sides of the stage rely on a renaissance sketch of a lost fragment preserved in the Vatican.
36. On the theatre see especially Pierre Gros, 'La fonction symbolique des édifices théâtraux dans le paysage urbain de la Rome Augustéenne' in *L'Urbs: espace urbain et histoire* (Rome: Ecole Française de Rome, 1987), 319–46. This forms the basis of his article in *Lexicon Topographicum Urbis Romae Vol. IV*, ed. E. M. Steinby (Rome: Quasar, 1999), 35–8. For the context of Augustan policy, see

Paul Zanker, *The Power of Images in the Age of Augustus*, tr. A. Schapiro (Ann Arbor: University of Michigan Press, 1988); Diane Favro, *The Urban Image of Augustan Rome* (Cambridge University Press, 1996).

37. The reference to 'thymelic' and 'astic' games is found in *Corpus Inscriptionarum Latinorum* VI.i no. 32323 lines 156–8.

38. See chapter 3 above, p.67.

39. See Richard C. Beacham, *Spectacle Entertainments of Early Imperial Rome* (New Haven, Conn.: Yale University Press, 1999), 122. Beacham follows L. Richardson Jr, *A New Topographical Dictionary of Ancient Rome* (Baltimore: Johns Hopkins University Press, 1992), 383. Richardson also provides an un-satisfactory Vitruvian reconstruction of the theatre. The principle of convert-ibility from theatre to amphitheatre had been established by Curio's theatre described in Pliny *Natural History* 36.24.

40. See chapter 2 above, p.37.

41. See Elizabeth Rawson, 'Discrimina ordinum: the Lex Julia Theatralis' in *Roman Culture and Society: Collected Papers* (Oxford University Press, 1991), 508–45.

42. Z. Yavetz, *Plebs and Princeps* (Oxford University Press, 1969), 21–2; Ovid, *Art of Loving* 1.89ff., 1.497–503, III.394; Horace, *Epistles* II.i.

43. Charlotte Roueché, *Performers and Partisans at Aphrodisias in the Roman and Late Roman periods* (London: Society for the Promotion of Roman Studies, 1993); cf. Alan Cameron, *Circus Factions: blues and greens at Rome and Byzan-tium* (Oxford University Press, 1978); David B. Small, 'Social correlations to the Greek *cavea* in the Roman period' in *Roman Architecture in the Greek World*, ed. Sarah B. Macready and F. H. Thompson (London: Society of Antiquaries, 1987), 85–93.

44. Cameron, *Circus Factions*, 318–32.

45. *Quis Deum? L'expression plastique des idéologies politiques et religieuses à Rome* (Paris: Ecole Française de Rome, 1994), 558.

46. See David Wiles, *The Masks of Menander: sign and meaning in Greek and Roman performance* (Cambridge University Press, 1991), esp. 65–6.

47. On Odeons, see G. C. Izenour, *Roofed Theaters of Classical Antiquity* (New Haven, Conn.: Yale University Press, 1992). For Seneca in the Odeon, I follow George W. M. Harrison ' "Semper ego auditor tantum?" ' Performance and physical setting of Seneca's plays' in *Seneca in Performance*, ed. G. W. M. Harrison (London: Duckworth, 2000), 137–50.

48. See E. J. Jory, 'The literary evidence for the beginnings of imperial pan-tomime', *Bulletin of the Institute of Classical Studies* 28 (1981), 147–61; W. J. Slater, 'Pantomime riots' *Classical Antiquity* 13 (1994), 120–44.

49. Vitruvius III.i.3, IX.i–vi, I.i.16. Cf. Pierre Gros, 'Le schéma vitruvien du théâtre latin et sa signification dans le système normatif du *De Architectura*', *Revue archéologique* (1994), 57–80.

50. *Scipio's Dream* v.iii.

51. Vitruvius v.vi.1. Cf. B. A. Kellum's analysis of the trigon in Augustus' Temple of Concord: 'Display in the aedes concordiae Augustae' in *Between Republic*

and Empire: interpretations of Augustus and his principate, ed. Kurt A. Raaflaub and Mark Tober (University of California Press, 1990), 276–307.

52. My analysis follows Bruno Poulle, 'Les vases acoustiques du théâtre de Mummius Achaicus', *Revue archéologique* (2000), 37–50.

53. Vitruvius I.i.9.

54. *Ibid.* I.i.16, IX.i.11–13.

55. *Res Rusticae*, III.5 – see Sauron, *Quis Deum?*, 137–67.

56. 'Studies in Roman theater design', *American Journal of Archaeology* 87 (1973), 55–68. Kathryn L. Gleason in 'Porticus pompeiana: a new perspective on the first public park of ancient Rome', *Journal of Garden History* 14 (1994), 13–26, argues that Pompey planned his complex on the basis of two circles, but there are some difficulties with her geometry.

57. See Edward S. Casey, *The Fate of Place: a philosophical enquiry* (Berkeley and London: University of California Press, 1997), 86–8.

58. *Senecan Drama and Stoic Cosmology* (Berkeley: University of California Press, 1989), 98. Rosenmeyer does not consider the Manto scene stageable. John Fitch, 'Playing Seneca' in *Seneca in Performance*, 1–12 sums up the critical debate on this scene, agreeing that it is unplayable. I have, however, seen how powerful the scene can be, with a performer trained in physical theatre taking the role of Manto, in a production of Ted Hughes' translation (*Seneca's Oedipus* (Faber, 1969)) at the University of Manchester, directed by Wylie Longmore in 1979 with Helen Scott as Manto.

59. See Jean-Claude Golvin, *L'Amphithéâtre romain: essai sur la théorisation de sa forme et de ses fonctions* (Paris: Boccard, 1988), I.298–310. On seating, see J. C. Edmondson, 'Dynamic arenas: gladiatorial presentations in the city of Rome and the construction of Roman society during the early empire' in *Roman Theater and Society*, ed. W. J. Slater (Ann Arbor: University of Michigan Press, 1996), 69–112.

60. See C. Landes (ed.), *Le Gout du théâtre à Rome et en Gaule romaine* (Lattes: Musée archéologique de Lattes, 1989), 23–90.

61. Georges Ville, *La Gladiature en occident des origines à la mort de Domitien* (Rome: Ecole Française de Rome, 1981), 393–5; K. M. Coleman, 'Fatal charades: Roman executions staged as mythological enactments', *Journal of Roman Studies* 80 (1990), 44–73.

62. 'London's jumbo village hall', *Sunday Times* 11 September 1966. For historical documentation see *Survey of London*, vol. XXXVIII (London: Athlone Press, 1975), 177–95.

63. *Times* 27 July 1990.

64. *The Plays of Roswitha*, tr. C. St John (London: Chatto & Windus, 1923), 96–100. Cf. my 'Hrosvitha of Gandersheim: the performance of her plays in the tenth century', *Theatre History Studies* 19 (1999), 133–50, and chapter 2 above, pp.42–3. For medieval thinking about the microcosm, see A. J. Gurevich, *Categories of Medieval Culture*, tr. G. L. Campbell (London: RKP, 1985). For Christian attitudes to classical theories of music, see Kathi Meyer-Baer, *Music of the Spheres and the Dance of Death* (Princeton University Press, 1970), 33–9.

65. See Sabina Flanagan, *Hildegard of Bingen 1098–1179: a visionary life* (London: Routledge, 1998), 29ff.; Fiona Maddocks, *Hildegard of Bingen: the woman of her age* (London: Headline, 2001).

66. 'Hestia-Hermes: the religious expression of space and movement in ancient Greece' in *Myth and Thought among the Greeks*, 127–75.

67. *Knight's Tale* 1027–34. See my analysis in *Shakespeare's Almanac: A Midsummer Night's Dream, marriage and the Elizabethan calendar* (Woodbridge: D. S. Brewer, 1993), 75–8. On tournament staging, see Glynne Wickham, *Early English Stages 1300–1600 Vol. I* (London: RKP, 1959), 13–41 and frontispiece.

68. Natalie Crohn Schmitt counters one extreme view with another in 'Was there a medieval theatre in the round? A re-examination of the evidence' in *Medieval English Drama: essays critical and contextual* ed. Jerome Taylor and Alan H. Nelson (University of Chicago Press, 1972), 292–315. For a photograph of the 1979 Toronto production see Richard Proudfoot, 'The virtue of perseverance' in *Aspects of Early English Drama*, ed. Paula Neuss (Woodbridge: D. S. Brewer, 1983), 92–109. See also Clifford Davidson, *Visualizing the Moral Life: medieval iconography and the Macro morality plays* (New York: AMS Press, 1989), 47–82. I have used the edition in David Bevington, *Medieval Drama* (Boston: Houghton Mifflin, 1975).

69. I have reproduced and analysed the miniature in *The Oxford Illustrated History of Theatre*, ed. John Russell Brown (Oxford University Press, 1995), 79–81.

70. *Knight's Tale*, 1712–22.

71. Elie Konigson, *L'Espace théâtral médiéval* (Paris: CNRS, 1975), 108.

72. Crohn Schmitt, 'Was there a medieval theatre in the round?', 297–301.

73. For a staging reconstruction, see Bevington, *Medieval Drama*, 480. Neville Denny ignores the significance of orientation in 'Arena staging and dramatic quality in the Cornish Passion Play' in *Medieval Drama*, ed. N. Denny (London: Arnold, 1973), 124–53.

74. See Henri Rey-Flaud, *Le Cercle magique* (Paris: Gallimard, 1973), 87–106; also T. E. Lawrenson and Helen Purkis, 'Les éditions illustrées de Térence dans l'histoire du théâtre' in *Le Lieu théâtral à la renaissance*, ed. J. Jaquot (Paris: CNRS, 1968). For the central *scaena* cf. Francesco di Giorgio's sketch of a Roman amphitheatre complete with Vitruvian *echeia* reproduced by Robert Klein and Henri Zerner, 'Vitruve et le théâtre de la renaissance italienne', in *ibid.*, 49–71, fig. 4; also the *Térence des Ducs* miniature of the late fourteenth or early fifteenth century, reproduced in *Oxford Illustrated History of Theatre*, 67.

75. *The Theatre of the World* (London: RKP, 1969). Cf. *Shakespeare's Globe Rebuilt*, ed. J. R. Mulryne and Margaret Shewring (Cambridge University Press, 1997).

76. *The Byrom Collection: Renaissance thought, the Royal Society and the building of the Globe Theatre* (London: Jonathan Cape, 1992).

77. *Architecture, Actor and Audience*, 144, 161–6.

78. *The Individual and the Cosmos in Renaissance Philosophy*, tr. M. Domandi (Oxford: Blackwell, 1963), 174.

79. *Playhouse and Cosmos: Shakespearean theater as metaphor* (Newark, N.J.: Associated University Presses, 1985), 33–4.
80. *Shakespeare's Globe Rebuilt*, ed. Mulryne and Shewring, 197.
81. Pauline Kiernan, *Staging Shakespeare at the New Globe* (Basingstoke: Macmillan, 1999), 9, 133–4; Jon Greenfield in '*Henry V* at the Globe', Euphoria Films for Channel 4, broadcast in 1997.
82. Kiernan, *Staging Shakespeare at the New Globe*, 138–9 (Rory Edwards), 133.
83. *Antony and Cleopatra*, v.ii.79–86 – ed. Michael Neill (Oxford University Press, 1994).
84. On the acoustics of the Globe, and its generation of a broad epic voice, see Bruce R. Smith, *The Acoustic World of Early Modern England: attending to the O-factor* (University of Chicago Press, 1999), 211–14; cf. 236–7 on Cleopatra.
85. *Ibid.*, 98, citing *Microcosmographia: a description of the body of man*.
86. *Ibid.*, 46.
87. *The Gull's Hornbook* (1609) extracted and identified with Bankside in G. E. Bentley, *The Seventeenth-Century Stage: a collection of critical essays* (University of Chicago Press, 1968), 3–9.
88. *Julius Caesar*, iii.ii.73–107.
89. For sources see E. K. Chambers, *The Elizabethan Stage* (Oxford University Press, 1923), ii.534–8. Andrew Gurr, intellectual mainstay of the new Shakespeare's Globe, denies on grounds of sightlines and of Webster's induction to *The Malcontent* that spectators sat on the public stage: *Playgoing in Shakespeare's London* (Cambridge University Press, 1987), 30. Dekker, however, is explicit in his references to Bankside, penny entrance, the yard and a 'public or private playhouse'. Cf. Davies' sonnet of 1593 which speaks of sitting on stage at 'the Theater', cited in Gurr, *Playgoing*, 204, and Hall's reference to 'scaffolders' in *The Collected Poems of Joseph Hall*, ed. A. Davenport (Liverpool University Press, 1949), 14.
90. For the Teatro Olimpico and its successors, I have benefited from Karina Mitens, 'The Roman Theatre and its "Reappearance" in the Renaissance' (PhD thesis, University of London, 1998). For a broad survey see Michael Anderson, 'Plays and playhouses in the Italian renaissance' in J. R. Mulryne and Margaret Shewring, *Theatres of the English and Italian Renaissance* (Basingstoke: Macmillan, 1991), 3–20.
91. There have been many accounts of this dynamic. See for example Jean Duvignaud's classic, *Sociologie du théâtre* (Paris: PUF, 1965). For early experiments, see Fabrizio Cruciani, *Lo spazio del teatro* (Rome/Bari: Laterza, 1992), 18–22.
92. Anonymously published review of James Boaden's *Life of John Philip Kemble* in *Quarterly Review* 34 (1826), 196–243, p.200.
93. *Ibid.*, 236.
94. Benjamin Wyatt, *Observations on the design for the Theatre Royal, Drury Lane* (London: J. Taylor, 1813), 33–4, 5; cf. Anastasia Nikolopoulou, 'Panopticism and the politics of the proscenium frame theatre: Benjamin Wyatt's Drury Lane, 1812', *Essays in Theatre* 12 (1994), 141–56; also *Survey of*

London, vol. XXXVIII (London: Athlone Press, 1970). For French antecedents, see also Leacroft and Leacroft, *Theatre and Playhouse*, 88–92; and Izenour, *Theater Design*, 52–9.

95. The modern dichotomy, as formulated by Hippisley Coxe, is supported in George Speaight, *A History of the Circus* (London: Tantivy Press, 1980), 38, and interrogated in Helen Stoddart, *Rings of Desire: circus history and representation* (Manchester University Press, 2000), 79–80. My account of the early English circus draws particularly on Marius Kwint, 'Astley's Amphitheatre and the Early Circus in England 1768–1830' (PhD thesis, University of Oxford, 1994), with some further material in Jaqueline S. Bratton and Jane Traies, *Astley's Amphitheatre* (Cambridge: Chadwyck-Healey, 1980).

96. Donald C. Mullin, *The Development of the Playhouse: a survey of theatre architecture from the renaissance to the present* (Berkeley: University of California Press, 1970), 23.

97. *A Course of Lectures on Dramatic Art and Literature*, tr. J. Black (London: Bohn, 1846), 343.

98. The original is reproduced in Hellmut Flashar, *Felix Mendelssohn-Bartholdy und die griechische Tragödie: Bühnenmusik im Kontext von Politik, Kultur und Bildung* (Stuttgart and Leipzig: Sächsischen Akademie der Wissenschaften zu Leipzig, 2001), 16. The siting of the musicians is an important difference.

99. Speaight, *History of the Circus*, 44; Christian Dupavillon, *Architectures du cirque des origines à nos jours* (Paris: Editions du Moniteur, 1982), 32–3.

100. A. H. Saxon, *The Life and Art of Andrew Ducrow, and the Romantic Age of the English Circus* (Hamden: Archon, 1978), 212–14, 150–1.

101. Kwint, 'Astley's Amphitheatre', 204–8.

102. A. H. Saxon, *Enter Foot and Horse: a history of hippodrama in England and France* (New Haven, Conn.: Yale University Press, 1968), 185. The text is printed in James L. Smith, *Victorian Melodramas: seven English, French and American melodramas* (London: Dent, 1976), 1–38.

103. Dupavillon, *Architectures du cirque*, 67–79; cf. Kwint, 'Astley's Amphitheatre', 193–6.

104. Erika Fischer-Lichte, 'Between text and cultural performance: staging Greek tragedies in Germany', *Theatre Survey* 40 (1999), 1–30.

105. Robert Breuer in *Max Reinhardt and his Theatre*, ed. Oliver M. Sayler (New York: Brentano, 1924), 151–2.

106. F. Gémier, *Le Théâtre*, ed. Paul Gsell (Paris: Bernard Grasset, 1925), 266–74; Jacqueline Jumaron, *La Mise-en-scène contemporaine. II. 1914–1940* (Paris: La Renaissance du Livre, 1981), 82–7.

107. Gémier, *Théâtre*, 15, 53, 217.

108. 'Firmin Gémier' in *Le Théâtre: service public* (Paris: Gallimard, 1975), 393–400.

109. Béatrice Picon-Vallin, 'L'atelier de Foregger et le courant comique dans le théâtre soviétique' in *Du Cirque au théâtre*, ed. Claudine Amiard-Chevrel (Lausanne: L'Age d'Homme, 1983), 133–56.

110. The project for Tretyakov's *I Want a Child* is examined in Edward Braun, *Meyerhold: a revolution in theatre* (London: Methuen, 1995), 239–42, and Lars Kleberg, *Theatre as Action: Soviet Russian avant-garde aesthetics*, tr. C. Rougle (Basingstoke: Macmillan, 1993), 109–11.

111. Nick Worrall, *Modernism to Realism on the Soviet Stage: Tairov–Vakhtangov–Okhlopkov* (Cambridge University Press, 1989), 192–5; Dmitri Troubotchkine, 'Agamemnon in Russia' in *Agamemnon in Performance*, ed. Edith Hall, Fiona Macintosh and Pantelis Michelakis (Oxford University Press, forthcoming 2004).

112. See John Stokes, *Resistible Theatres: enterprise and experiment in the late nineteenth century* (London: Elek, 1972), 52–6.

113. *Financial Times*, 28 November 1998.

114. *Fears of Fragmentation* (London: Jonathan Cape, 1970), 90.

115. Publicity puffs echoed in numerous newspaper articles, e.g. *Observer*, 23 March 1997.

116. *Times*, 16 August 1982.

117. *Guardian*, 12 December 1995.

7 THE CAVE

1. Richard Rodgers and Oscar Hammerstein, *South Pacific* (London: Williamson Music, 1956), 22.

2. (New York: Doubleday Anchor Books, 1959).

3. *Republic*, VI.513–21.

4. The standard source is G. E. Mylonas, *Eleusis and the Eleusinian Mysteries* (Princeton University Press, 1981). I am grateful to Richard Seaford for suggesting the link between cave and Mysteries.

5. Cf. Georges Banu, *Le Rouge et or: une poétique du théâtre à l'italienne* (Paris: Flammarion, 1989), 49–50.

6. Erwin Panofsky, *Perspective as Symbolic Form* (New York: Zone Books, 1991), 37–45.

7. *Poetics*, VI.4–9.

8. Sources are gathered in William Beare, *The Roman Stage: a short history of Latin drama in the time of the Republic* (London: Methuen, 1955), 285–92. For the Theatre of Marcellus, see Richard C. Beacham, *Spectacle Entertainments of Early Imperial Rome* (New Haven, Conn.: Yale University Press, 1999), 120.

9. Sources on the curtain: Beare, *Roman Stage*, 257–64.

10. See Richard Stillwell, *Corinth Vol. II: the Theatre* (Princeton: School of Classical Studies of Athens, 1952), esp. 77–82 on the curtain. On curtain mechanics, cf. A. Ducaroy and A. Audin, 'Le rideau de scène du théâtre de Lyon', *Gallia* 18 (1960), 57–82. For the performance in Apuleius, the best commentary is Ellen Finkelpearl, 'The judgement of Lucius: *Metamorphoses* 10.29–34', *Classical Antiquity* 10 (1991), 221–36.

11. Origny Ste Benoite: Edith Wright, 'The Dissemination of the Liturgical Drama in France' (Dissertation, Bryn Mawr College, 1936), 186; Barking:

William Tydeman, *The Medieval European Stage, 500–1550* (Cambridge University Press, 2001), 84. See Tydeman, 88–9, for representations of sepulchres.

12. Framing principles are examined in George R. Kernodle, *From Art to Theatre: form and convention in the renaissance* (University of Chicago Press, 1944).

13. Beare, *Roman Stage*, 288–90, reprints the sources.

14. L. B. Alberti, *On Painting and On Sculpture*, ed. and tr. C. Grayson (London: Phaidon Press, 1972), 55; John Berger, *Selected Essays and Articles: The Look of Things* (New York: Viking Press, 1974), 216.

15. Cited in James S. Ackerman, 'Leonardo's eye' in *Distance Points: essays in theory and renaissance art and architecture* (Cambridge, Mass.: MIT Press, 1991), 97–150, p.97.

16. *Ibid.*, 103; cf. Alberti, *On Painting*, 41.

17. The 1611 English translation is printed in Tydeman, *Medieval European Stage*, 472–80.

18. Barnard Hewitt (ed.), *The Renaissance Stage: documents of Serlio, Sabattini and Furttenbach* (Coral Gables: University of Miami Press, 1958), 96.

19. Aurelian Townshend, *Albion's Triumph* in *Inigo Jones: the theatre of the Stuart court*, ed. Stephen Orgel and Roy Strong (London: Sotheby Parke Bernet, 1973), II.452–79.

20. See Perry Gethner, 'Staging and spectacle in the machine tragedies' in *The Age of Theatre in France*, ed. D. Trott and N. Boursier (Edmonton: Academic Printing and Publishing, 1988), 231–46; Jean Duvignaud, *Sociologie du théâtre: essai sur les ombres collectives* (Paris: PUF, 1965), 266ff.

21. *The Hidden God*, tr. P. Thody (London: RKP, 1964).

22. Cf. Pierre Frantz, *L'Esthétique du tableau dans le théâtre du XVIIIᵉ siècle* (Paris: PUF, 1998), 3ff. I have also benefited from a paper given by Ronnie Mirkin to the IFTR conference in Tel Aviv in 1996: 'Cabinets of the mind: parallel developments in relation to space in stage and interior design in seventeenth-century France'.

23. *Racine: a theatrical reading* (Oxford University Press, 1991), 9–12.

24. Background information in Jacques Heuzey, 'Du costume et de la décoration baroque au XVIIᵉ siècle', *Revue d'histoire de théâtre* 12 (1960), 20–33; Jan Clarke, *The Guénégaud Theatre in Paris 1673–1680* (Lewiston: Edwin Mellen, 1995), 20.

25. Cited by Wilhelm Schlegel in *Course of Lectures on Dramatic Art and Literature*, tr. J. Black (London: Bohn, 1846), 336.

26. Cf. Jean Marie Apostolidès, *Le Prince sacrifié: théâtre et politique au temps de Louis XIV* (Paris: Editions de Minuit, 1985), 46.

27. James H. Johnson, *Listening in Paris* (Berkeley: University of California Press, 1995), 13. For the significance of left and right in the theatre, see David Wiles, *Tragedy in Athens: performance space and theatrical meaning* (Cambridge University Press, 1997), 135ff.

28. Information about the playhouse is gathered in T. E. Lawrenson, *The French Stage and Playhouse in the XVIIth Century: a study in the advent of the Italian order* (New York: AMS Press, 1986). Corneille describes the illusion of spatial unity in *Cinna: Writings on the Theatre*, ed. H. T. Barnwell (Oxford: Blackwell,

1965), 77–8. See finally Roland Barthes, *Sur Racine* (Paris: Editions du Seuil, 1963), 11, with further discussion in Peter Holland, 'Space: the final frontier' in *The Play out of Context: transferring plays from culture to culture*, ed. Hanna Scolnicov and Peter Holland (Cambridge University Press, 1989), 45–62.

29. L. Gerald Marshall and David L. Klepper, 'Acoustical design: places for listening' in *Architectural Acoustics: principles and practice*, ed. William J. Cavanaugh and Joseph A. Wilkes (New York: John Wiley, 1999), 151–81, p.161.

30. Barbara G. Mittman, *Spectators on the Paris Stage in the Seventeenth and Eighteenth Centuries* (Ann Arbor: UMI Research Press, 1984), 33; cf. her citation of Chapuzeau on p.10.

31. *French Theatre in the Neo-classical Era, 1550–1789*, ed. William D. Howarth (Cambridge University Press, 1997), 370. Mittman adopts the same broadly negative stance.

32. Letter to Princess Elizabeth in *Meditations and Other Philosophical Writings*, ed. D. M. Clarke (Harmondsworth: Penguin, 1998), 157.

33. *Le Rouge et or*, 130. Banu's subtle study of the *théâtre à l'italienne* owes much to the documentation in Henri Lagrave, *Le Théâtre et le public à Paris de 1715 à 1750* (Paris: Klincksiek, 1972).

34. Jean-Baptiste de Boyer, *Lettres juives* (The Hague: Pierre Paupie, 1738), 1.17–21.

35. 'Réponse à la lettre de Mme Riccoboni' in *Diderot's Writings on the Theatre*, ed. F. C. Green (Cambridge University Press, 1936), 216.

36. Marmontel, *Eléments de littérature* (Paris: Firmin–Didot, 1879), III.83.

37. *Ibid.*, 85.

38. *Ibid.*, 87.

39. A. M. Nagler, *A Source Book in Theatrical History* (New York: Dover, 1959), 265–7.

40. *Eléments de littérature* III.30, III.396–7.

41. 'Réponse à la lettre de Mme Riccoboni' in *Diderot's Writings on the Theatre*, 211–22.

42. *Lettre à M. D'Alembert*: see Marvin Carlson, *Theories of the Theatre: a historical and critical survey from the Greeks to the present* (Ithaca, N.Y.: Cornell University Press, 1984), 150–2.

43. D. Diderot, *Salon de 1765*, ed. E. M. Bukdahl and A. Lorenceau (Paris: Hermann, 1984), 253–64, reviewing Fragonard's *Le grand-prêtre Corésos s'immole pour Callirhoé*.

44. *Fidelio: English National Opera Guide* (London: Calder, 1980).

45. *Course of Lectures on Dramatic Art and Literature*, tr. J. Black (London: Bohn, 1846), 452–4.

46. On monumental façades see Marvin Carlson, *Places of Performance: the semiotics of theatre architecture* (Ithaca, N.Y.: Cornell University Press, 1989), esp. 109–19.

47. The work of Richard Sennett is fundamental: *The Fall of Public Man* (Cambridge University Press, 1977), esp. 205–8; and see also *Flesh and Stone: the body and the city in western civilization* (London: Faber, 1994).

48. Cited by George Taylor in *Henry Irving at the Lyceum* (Cambridge: Chadwyck-Healey, 1980), 16.

49. George Rowell, *Theatre in the Age of Irving* (Oxford: Blackwell, 1981), 61–2.

50. *What is Art?*, tr. A. Maude (Oxford University Press, 1930), 213. Russian original first published in 1898.

51. See Frederick Burwick, 'Illusion and romantic drama' in *Romantic Drama*, ed. Gerald Gillespie (Amsterdam: Jan Benjamins, 1994), 59–80.

52. *Antoine, l'invention de la mise en scène*, ed. Jean-Pierre Sarrazeau and Philippe Marcerau (Arles: Actes Sud, 1999), 62–3. Antoine's emphases.

53. See Ernest Jones' *Sigmund Freud: Life and Work*, vol. 1 (London: Hogarth Press, 1953), 194.

54. *The Essentials of Psychoanalysis*, ed. Anna Freud, tr. J. Strachey (London: Hogarth Press, 1986), 503.

55. *Drama from Ibsen to Brecht* (Harmondsworth: Penguin, 1973), 389–90.

56. See Stephen Kern, *The Culture of Time and Space 1880–1918* (Cambridge, Mass.: Harvard University Press, 1983).

57. Phrase cited by Frederick and Lise-Lone Marker in *The Cambridge Companion to Ibsen*, ed. James McFarlane (Cambridge University Press, 1994), 187; cf. Denis Bablet, *The Theatre of Edward Gordon Craig*, tr. D. Woodward (London: Eyre Methuen, 1981), 86.

58. Cited in Denis Bablet, *Esthétique générale du décor de théâtre de 1870 à 1914* (Paris: CNRS, 1965), 292. Cf. Jean-François Dusigne, *Le Théâtre d'art: aventure européenne du XXᵉ siècle* (Paris: Editions Théâtrales, 1997), 77–8.

59. Adolphe Appia, 'Monumentality' in *Texts on Theatre*, ed. Richard C. Beacham (London: Routledge, 1993), 138–9.

60. 'New theatrical space. Where fiction appears' in *A Journey Through Other Spaces: essays and manifestos, 1944–1990*, ed. and tr. M. Kobialka (Berkeley: University of California Press, 1993).

61. 'A Painting' in *Journey Through Other Spaces*, 192–5. Kantor died while the production was being rehearsed.

62. See for example C. Dupavillon's introduction to a special issue of *L'Architecture d'aujourd'hui* on theatre space (October 1978); and the introduction to Jean Chollet and Marcel Freydefont, *Les Lieux scéniques en France 1980–1995: 15 ans d'architecture et de scénographie* (Paris: Scéno+, 1996). We see the same tendency in Iain Mackintosh, *Architecture, Actor and Audience* (London: Routledge, 1993). The publication of Banu's *Le Rouge et or* (1989) is another symptom of changing values.

63. *The Secret of Theatrical Space*, ed. and tr. J. M. Burian (New York: Applause, 1993), 19.

8 THE EMPTY SPACE

1. 'On the necessity of violation', *Drama Review* 13.1 (1968), 89–105.

2. *Aesthetic Theory*, tr. R. Hullot-Kentor (London: Athlone Press, 1997), 34.

3. For this he is challenged by Peter Bürger in *Theory of the Avant-garde*, tr. M. Shaw (Manchester University Press, 1984).

4. *The Empty Space* (London: MacGibbon & Kee, 1968), 9.

5. *Ibid.*, 44–5.

6. Cited by Luc Boucris in *L'Espace en scène* (Paris: Librairie théâtrale, 1993), 145–6, n.56.

7. *There Are No Secrets: thoughts on acting and theatre* (London: Methuen, 1993), 117, cf. 28.

8. *Empty Space*, 64.

9. *Ibid.*, 60

10. *Threads of Time: a memoir* (London: Methuen, 1998), 80.

11. See for example Charles Marowitz's critique of *US* in *Tulane Drama Review* 11.2 (1966), 173–5.

12. *Threads of Time*, 146.

13. *Empty Space*, 80.

14. 'The shape of the theatre' in *Actor and Architect*, ed. Stephen Joseph (Manchester University Press, 1964), 57–65, p.60.

15. *There Are No Secrets*, 6. The point is nevertheless made in *The Empty Space* in respect of *King Lear* (pp.21–3) and Genet's *The Blacks* (p.74).

16. *Empty Space*, 86–95.

17. I owe these ideas to Boucris, *L'Espace en scène*, 143, and to Stephen Kern, *The Culture of Time and Space 1880–1918* (Cambridge, Mass.: Harvard University Press, 1983), 164.

18. For a historical perspective, see Darko Suvin, 'Reflections on Happenings' in *Happenings and other Acts*, ed. Mariellen R. Sandford (London: Routledge, 1995), 287–309.

19. My translation.

20. 'Art vivant ou nature morte?' in *Œuvres complètes*, vol. IV (Lausanne: L'Age d'Homme, 1992), 67.

21. See Paul-Louis Mignon, *Jacques Copeau, ou le mythe du Vieux-Colombier* (Paris: Julliard, 1993).

22. Text of 1920 in *Registres 1: Appels*, ed. Marie-Hélène Dasté (Paris: Gallimard, 1974), 222.

23. Text of 1927 in *ibid.*, 158.

24. Donald Roy, *Copeau and the Cartel des Quatre* (Cambridge: Chadwyck-Healey, 1993), 35.

25. 'La remise en question', 22.

26. *Theater of the Bauhaus*, ed. Walter Gropius and Arthur S. Wensinger (Baltimore: Johns Hopkins University Press, 1996) 12.

27. John L. Paterson, 'A definition of theatre' in *The Place for the Arts*, ed. Alexander Schouvaloff (Liverpool: Seel Press, 1970), 87.

28. 'Elementary considerations of some principles in the construction of buildings designed to accommodate spectators and actors' cited in George C. Izenour, *Theater Design* (New Haven, Conn.: Yale University Press, 1996), 598. The book was first published by McGraw-Hill in 1977.

29. *Theater Design*, 577.

30. *Ibid.*, 579.

31. *The Sixties: cultural revolution in Britain, France, Italy and the United States, c.1958–c.1974* (Oxford University Press, 1998), 340, 733.

32. Cf. chapter 1 above, p.22.

33. Izenour, *Theater Design*, 603, citing 'A director views the stage', *Walker Art Gallery, Design Quarterly* 58 (1963).

34. 'Theatre at Minneapolis' in *Actor and Architect*, ed. Stephen Joseph (Manchester University Press, 1964), 30–47, pp.31, 45.

35. Ruby Cohn, *From Desire to Godot: the pocket theatre of post-war Paris* (London: Calder, 1999), 14–15.

36. 'The work of art in the age of mechanical reproduction' in *Illuminations*, tr. H. Zohn (New York: Harcourt, Brace & World, 1968), 219–53.

37. See Richard Schechner's chapter on nakedness in *Environmental Theater* (New York: Applause, 1994), 87–124.

38. *Towards a Poor Theatre* (London: Methuen, 1969), 41–2.

39. 'An interview with Grotowski', *Drama Review* 13.1 (1968) 29–45, p.43.

40. 'Action is literal' (1978) in Jennifer Kumiega, *The Theatre of Grotowski* (London: Methuen, 1985), 225.

41. Jean-Pierre Sarrazac, *Théâtres Intimes* (Arles: Actes Sud, 1989), 68.

42. *The Moscow Art Theatre Letters*, ed. Jean Benedetti (London: Methuen, 1991), 234; Constantin Stanislavski, *My Life in Art*, tr. J. J. Robbins (London: Methuen, 1980), 425–38. See also Jean Benedetti's account in *A History of Russian Theatre*, ed. Robert Leach & Victor Borovsky (Cambridge University Press, 1999), 266–8.

43. *Moscow Art Theatre Letters*, 296–8; Nick Worrall, *Modernism to Realism on the Soviet Stage: Tairov – Vakhtangov – Okhlopkov* (Cambridge University Press, 1989), 84.

44. *My Life in Art*, 525–41.

45. Cf. Robin Thornber, ' "First tragedy . . . then farce": the regional reps' in *Dreams and Deconstructions: alternative theatre in Britain*, ed. Sandy Craig (Ambergate: Amber Lane, 1980), 165–75, p.174.

46. W. P. Kinne, *George Pierce Baker and the American Theatre* (Cambridge, Mass.: Harvard University Press, 1954), esp. 166–7, 215–17.

47. Howard Goorney, *The Theatre Workshop Story* (London: Eyre Methuen, 1981), 41–2, 93.

48. Stanislavski, *My Life in Art*, 430, Kinne, *George Pierce Baker*, 184; cf. Copeau cited in Jean-François Dusigne, *Le Théâtre d'Art: aventure européenne du XXᵉ siècle* (Paris: Editions Théâtrales, 1997), 194–5.

49. Michel Corvin, *Le Théâtre de recherche entre les deux guerres: le Laboratoire Art et Action* (Lausanne: L'Age d'Homme, 1976).

50. *Towards a Poor Theatre*, 95–6; *The Grotowski Sourcebook*, ed. L. Wolford and R. Schechner (London: Routledge, 1997), 22–3.

51. *Towards a Poor Theatre*, 20.

52. *My Life in Art*, 488–92.

53. Theatre designed by Ralph Freud. See Walden P. Boyle, *Central and Flexible Staging: a new theater in the making* (Berkeley: University of California Press, 1956). Earlier Californian experiments can be traced back to 1924.

54. I follow the account in Marc Fumaroli, 'Eugenio Barba's *Kaspariana*', *The Drama Review* 13.1 (1968), 48–56. Plans and further information in Ian Watson, *Towards a Third theatre: Eugenio Barba and the Odin Teatret* (London: Routledge, 1993), 121–5.

55. 'Honouring the audience' in *Arguments for a Theatre* (2nd edition, Manchester University Press, 1993), 47.

56. 'Theatre without a conscience' in *Arguments for a Theatre*, 72–8. Originally given as a lecture at U.C.W. Aberystwyth.

57. Iain Mackintosh, *Architecture, Actor and Audience* (London: Routledge, 1993), 81–2.

58. *When the Cathedrals were White*, tr. F. E. Hyslop (London: Routledge, 1947), 6 – originally published in French in 1936.

59. *Aesthetic Theory*, tr. R. Hullot-Kentor (London: Athlone Press, 1997), 39–40 – originally published in German in 1970.

60. *What is Post-modernism?* (4th edition, Chichester: Academy Editions, 1996), 23.

61. *Empty Space*, 20.

62. *Inside the White Cube: the ideology of the gallery space* (Berkeley: University of California Press, 1999), 14–15.

63. *Ibid.*, 87.

64. *Ibid.*, 38.

65. 'Art and objecthood' in *Minimal Art: a critical anthology*, ed. Gregory Battcock (Berkeley and London: University of California Press, 1995), 116–47.

66. See RoseLee Goldberg, *Performance Art: from futurism to the present* (London: Thames & Hudson, 3rd edition, 2001), 128ff.; also Kaprow's 'A Statement' in *Happenings: an illustrated anthology*, ed. Michael Kirby (London: Sidgwick & Jackson, 1965); James Meyer, 'The functional site; or, the transformation of site specificity' in *Space, Site, Intervention: situating installation art*, ed. Erika Suderburg (Minneapolis: University of Minnesota Press, 2000), 23–37.

67. 'Extensions in time and space' in *The Drama Review* 39 (spring 1968), 153–9, p.159.

68. 'Function of architecture: notes on work in connection with the places where it is installed taken between 1967 and 1975, some of which are specially summarized here', tr. H. Meakins in *Thinking About Exhibitions*, ed. Reesa Greenberg, Bruce W. Ferguson and Sandy Nairne (London: Routledge, 1996), 313–19.

69. *Inside the White Cube*, 19.

70. 'La guerre des nerfs': exhibition by Dado (Miodrag Djuric) incorporating works by Bernard Réquichot, at Les Abattoirs, February–May 2002.

71. Cited by Jean Chollet in 'Architecture et création scénique (1960–1995)' in *Etudes théâtrales* 11–12 (1997), 66–73, p.67.

72. Robert Venturi, *Complexity and Contradiction in Architecture* (New York: Museum of Modern Art, 1966) was an influential statement of the new aesthetic.

73. *Threads of Time*, 194; Andrew Todd and Jean-Guy Lecat, *The Open Circle: Peter Brook's theatre environments* (London: Methuen, 2002).

74. Cited in a lecture given to a symposium on performance space at Royal Holloway, University of London, September 1999.

75. '"Towards an art of memory": Peter Brook, a foreigner in Paris' in *The Paris Jigsaw: internationalism and the city's stages*, ed. David Bradby and Maria M. Delgado (Manchester University Press, 2002), 37–52, p.49.

76. See *The Open Circle*; also Neil Wallace, 'Peter Brook, theatre space and the Tramway' in *Making Space for Theatre: British architecture and theatre since 1958*, ed. Ronnie Mulryne and Margaret Shewring (Stratford-upon-Avon: Mulryne & Shewring, 1995), 61–3.

77. *Threads of Time*, 193–4.

78. *There Are No Secrets*, 92.

79. See chapter 1 above, pp.12–13. Vitez (1978) discussed in Gay McAuley, *Space in Performance: making meaning in the theatre* (Ann Arbor: Michigan University Press, 1999), 38, Dusigne *Le Théâtre d'Art*, 284.

80. 'On not building for posterity' in *Making Space for Theatre*, 16–20.

81. *Making Space for Theatre*, 120. On Lasdun see William Curtis, 'Perspective' in *The National Theatre: the Architectural Review guide*, ed. Colin Amery (London: Architectural Press, 1977), 52–8.

82. See Leo Beranek, *Concert and Opera Halls: how they sound* (Woodbury: Acoustical Society of America, 1996), 4ff.

83. Michael Forsyth, *Buildings for Music: the architect, the musician and the listener from the seventeenth century to the present day* (Cambridge University Press, 1985), 320–5.

84. Fondation Bemberg located in the Hôtel d'Assézat and opened in 1995.

85. Henri Lefebvre, *The Production of Space*, tr. D. Nicholson-Smith (Oxford: Blackwell, 1991), 308. Lefebvre's italics.

Select bibliography

Adorno, Theodor. *Aesthetic Theory*, tr. R. Hullot-Kentor (London: Athlone Press, 1997)

Amiard-Chevrel, Claudine (ed.). *Du Cirque au théâtre* (Lausanne: L'Age d'Homme, 1983)

Appia, Adolphe. *Essays, Scenarios, and Designs*, tr. W. R. Volbach, ed. R. C. Beacham (Ann Arbor: UMI Research Press, 1989)

 Texts on Theatre, ed. Richard C. Beacham (Routledge, 1993)

Architecture d'aujourd'hui, L', special issue entitled *Les Lieux du spectacle* (October 1970)

Arnott, James and others (eds.). *Theatre Space: an examination of the interaction between space, technology, performance and society* (Munich: IFTR, 1977)

Aronson, Arnold. *American Avant-garde: a history* (London: Routledge, 2000)

 The History and Theory of Environmental Scenography (Ann Arbor: UMI Research Press, 1981)

Bablet, Denis. *Esthétique générale du décor de théâtre de 1870 à 1914* (Paris: CNRS, 1965)

Bablet, Denis and Jacquot, Jean. *Le Lieu théâtral dans la société moderne* (Paris: CNRS, 1969)

Bachelard, Gaston. *The Poetics of Space*, tr. M. Jolas (Boston: Beacon Press, 1969)

Baer, Marc. *Theatre and Disorder in Late Georgian England* (Oxford University Press, 1992)

Banu, Georges. *Le Rouge et or: une poétique du théâtre à l'italienne* (Paris: Flammarion, 1989)

Banu, Georges and Ubersfeld, Anne. *L'Espace théâtral* (*Actualité des arts plastiques. No. 45*) (Paris: CNDP, 1992)

Barker, Clive. *Theatre Games* (London: Methuen, 1977), chapter 11

Barker, Howard. *Arguments for a Theatre* (2nd edition, Manchester University Press, 1993)

Barron, Michael. *Auditorium Acoustics and Architectural Design* (London: Spon, 1993)

Beacham, Richard C. *Spectacle Entertainments of Early Imperial Rome* (New Haven, Conn.: Yale University Press, 1999)

Beranek, Leo. *Concert and Opera Halls: how they sound* (Woodbury: Acoustical Society of America, 1996)

Berger, John. *Ways of Seeing* (Harmondsworth: Penguin, 1972)

Bieber, Margarete. *The History of the Greek and Roman Theater* (Princeton University Press, 1961)

Boucris, Luc. *L'Espace en scène* (Paris: Librairie théâtrale, 1993)

Boyle, Walden P. *Central and Flexible Staging: a new theater in the making* (Berkeley: University of California Press, 1956)

Brook, Peter. *The Empty Space* (London: MacGibbon & Kee, 1968)

There are no Secrets: thoughts on acting and theatre (London: Methuen, 1993)

Brown, John Russell (ed.). *The Oxford Illustrated History of Theatre* (Oxford University Press, 1995)

Carlson, Marvin. *Places of Performance: the semiotics of theatre architecture* (Ithaca, N.Y.: Cornell University Press, 1989)

Casey, Edward S. *The Fate of Place: a philosophical enquiry* (Berkeley and London: University of California Press, 1997)

Çelik, Z., Favro, D., and Ingersoll, R. (eds.). *Streets: critical perspectives on public space* (Berkeley: University of California Press, 1994)

Chaney, David. *Fictions of Collective Life: public drama in late modern culture* (London: Routledge, 1993)

Chollet, Jean and Freydefont, Marcel. *Les Lieux scéniques en France 1980–1995: 15 ans d'architecture et de scénographie* (Paris: Scéno+, 1996)

Condee, William Faricy. *Theatrical Space: a guide for directors and designers* (Lanham: Scarecrow Press, 1995)

Courtney, Richard. *The Drama Studio: architecture and equipment for dramatic education* (London: Pitman, 1967)

Cox, John D. and Kastan, David Scott (eds.). *A New History of Early English Drama* (New York: Columbia University Press, 1997)

Cremer, Lothar. 'Different distributions of the audience' in *Auditorium Acoustics*, ed. R. Mackenzie (London: Applied Science Publishers, 1975), 145–59

Crimp, Douglas. *On the Museum's Ruins* (MIT Press, 1993)

Cruciani, Fabrizio. *Lo spazio del teatro* (Rome and Bari: Laterza, 1992)

De Certeau, Michel. 'Practices of space' in *On Signs*, ed. M. Blonsky (Oxford: Blackwell, 1985)

Diderot, Denis. *Diderot's Writings on the Theatre*, ed. F. C. Green (Cambridge University Press, 1936)

Duncan, Carol. *Civilizing Rituals: inside public art museums* (London: Routledge, 1995)

Dupavillon, Christian. *Architectures du cirque des origines à nos jours* (Paris: Editions du Moniteur, 1982)

Duvignaud, Jean. *Sociologie du théâtre: essai sur les ombres collectives* (Paris: PUF, 1965)

Earl, John and Sell, Michael. *The Theatres Trust Guide to British Theatres 1750–1950: a gazetteer* (London: A. & C. Black, 2000)

Edström, Per. *Why Not Theatres Made For People?* (Värmdö: Arena Theatre Institute, 1990)

Eliade, Mircea. *The Sacred and the Profane: the nature of religion*, tr. W. R. Trask (New York: Harcourt, Brace & World, 1959)

Eversmann, Peter. *De Ruimte van het Theater* (University of Amsterdam, 1996)

Forsyth, Michael. *Buildings for Music: the architect, the musician and the listener from the seventeenth century to the present day* (Cambridge University Press, 1985)

Foster, Hal (ed.). *Vision and Visuality* (Seattle: Bay Press, 1988)

Foucault, Michel. 'Of other spaces', tr. J. Miskowiec; *Diacritics* 16 (1986), 22–7
'The eye of power' and 'Questions on geography' in *Power/Knowledge*, ed. C. Gordon (Brighton: Harvester Press, 1980)

Frantz, Pierre. *L'Esthétique du tableau dans le théâtre du XVIIIe siècle* (Paris: PUF, 1998)

Freydefont, Marcel (ed.). *Le Lieu, la scène, la salle, la ville: dramaturgie, scénographie et architecture à la fin du XX ^{ème} siècle en Europe* (Louvain, 1997) = *Etudes Théâtrales* vol. 11/12

Fried, Michael. 'Art and objecthood' in *Minimal Art: a critical anthology*, ed. Gregory Battcock (Berkeley and London: University of California Press, 1995), 116–47

Golvin, Jean-Claude. *L'Amphithéâtre romain: essai sur la théorisation de sa forme et de ses fonctions* (Paris: Boccard, Publications du Centre Pierre Paris, 1988)

Gombrich, E. H. *Art and Illusion: a study in the psychology of pictorial representation* (Phaidon Press, 1968)

Greenberg, Reesa, Ferguson, Bruce W. and Nairne, Sandy. *Thinking About Exhibitions* (London: Routledge, 1996)

Gregory, Derek. *Geographical Imaginations* (Oxford: Blackwell, 1994)

Gropius, Walter and Wensinger, Arthur S. (eds.). *Theater of the Bauhaus* (Baltimore: Johns Hopkins University Press, 1996)

Gros, Pierre. 'Le schéma vitruvien du théâtre latin et sa signification dans le système normatif du *De Architectura*', *Revue archéologique* (1994), 57–80

Grotowski, Jerzy. *The Grotowski Sourcebook*, ed. L. Wolford and R. Schechner (London: Routledge, 1997)

Grunnenburg, Cristoph. 'The Modern Art Museum' in *Contemporary Cultures of Display*, ed. Emma Barker (New Haven, Conn.: Yale University Press, 1999), 26–49

Gurevich, A. J. *Categories of Medieval Culture*, tr. G. L. Campbell (London: RKP, 1985)

Guthrie, Tyrone. *A Life in the Theatre* (London: Hamish Hamilton, 1960)

Hanson, J. A. *Roman Theater-Temples* (Princeton University Press, 1959)

Hewitt, Barnard (ed.). *The Renaissance Stage: documents of Serlio, Sabattini and Furttenbach* (Coral Gables: University of Miami Press, 1958)

Holland, Peter. 'Space: the final frontier' in *The Play out of context: transferring plays from culture to culture*, ed. Hanna Scolnicov and Peter Holland (Cambridge University Press, 1989)

ICA *Seven Ages of Theatre Series* 'The place of performance' including lectures by Jean-Guy Lecat, A. Burrough, Iain Mackintosh and Stephen Daldry (Audiotape transcript, May 1994)

Izenour, George C. *Theater Design* (New Haven, Conn.: Yale University Press, 1996)

Jameson, Frederic. *Postmodernism, or, the cultural logic of late capitalism* (London: Verso, 1991)

Jacquot, Jean (ed.). *Le Lieu théâtral à la renaissance* (Paris: CNRS, 1968)

Jay, Martin. 'In the empire of the gaze: Foucault and the denigration of vision in 20th-century French thought' in *Foucault: a critical reader*, ed. D. C. Hoy (Oxford: Blackwell, 1986)

Johnson, James H. *Listening in Paris* (Berkeley: University of California Press, 1995)

Joseph, Stephen (ed.). *Actor and Architect* (Manchester University Press, 1964)

Joseph, Stephen. *Theatre in the Round* (London: Barrie & Rockliff, 1967)

Kantor, Tadeusz. *A Journey through Other Spaces: essays and manifestos, 1944–1990*, ed. and tr. M. Kobialka (Berkeley: University of California Press, 1993)

Kern, Stephen. *The Culture of Time and Space 1880–1918* (Cambridge, Mass.: Harvard University Press, 1983)

Kernodle, George R. *From Art to Theatre: form and convention in the renaissance* (University of Chicago Press, 1944)

Kirby, Michael (ed.). *Happenings: an illustrated anthology* (London: Sidgwick & Jackson, 1965)

Kleberg, Lars. *Theatre as Action: Soviet Russian avant-garde aesthetics*, tr. C. Rougle (Basingstoke: Macmillan, 1993)

Komparu, Kunio. *The Noh Theater: principles and perspectives* (New York and Tokyo: Weatherhill, 1983)

Konigson, Elie. *L'Espace théâtral médiéval* (Paris: CNRS, 1975)

Lagrave, Henri. *Le théâtre et le public à Paris de 1715 à 1750* (Paris: Klincksiek, 1972)

Lawrenson, T. E. *The French Stage and Playhouse in the XVIIth Century: a study in the advent of the Italian order* (New York: AMS Press, 1986)

Leacroft, Richard and Leacroft, Helen. *Theatre and Playhouse: an illustrated survey of theatre building from ancient Greece to the present day* (London: Methuen, 1984)

Lefebvre, Henri. *The Production of Space* tr. D. Nicholson-Smith (Oxford: Blackwell, 1991)

Mackintosh, Iain. *Architecture, Actor and Audience* (London: Routledge, 1993)

Marmontel, Jean-François. *Eléments de littérature* (Paris: Firmin-Didot, 1879)

Marshall, L. Gerald and Klepper, David L. 'Acoustical design: places for listening' in *Architectural Acoustics: principles and practice*, ed. William J. Cavanaugh and Joseph A. Wilkes (New York: John Wiley, 1999), 151–81

McAuley, Gay. *Space in Performance: making meaning in the theatre* (Ann Arbor: University of Michigan Press, 1999)

Meisel, Martin. *Realizations: narrative, pictorial and theatrical arts in nineteenth-century England* (Princeton University Press, 1983)

Mercouris, Spyros and Kapon Editions. *A Stage for Dionysos: theatrical space and ancient drama* (Athens: Kapon, 1998)

Mervant-Roux, Marie-Madeleine. *L'Assise du théâtre: pour une étude du spectateur* (Paris: CNRS, 1998)

Morris, A. E. J. *History of Urban Form* (London: George Goodwin, 1979)

Moughtin, Cliff. *Urban Design: street and square* (Oxford: Architectural Press, 1999)

Mullin, Donald C. *The Development of the Playhouse: a survey of theatre architecture from the renaissance to the present* (Berkeley: University of California Press, 1970)

Mulryne, J. R. and Shewring, Margaret. *Theatres of the English and Italian Renaissance* (Basingstoke: Macmillan, 1991)

Mulryne, Ronnie and Shewring, Margaret (eds.). *Making Space for Theatre: British architecture and theatre since 1958* (Stratford-upon-Avon: Mulryne & Shewring, 1995)

Mumford, Lewis. *The City in History: its origins, its transformations and its prospects* (London: Secker & Warburg, 1961)

Nancy, Jean-Luc. 'Of divine places', tr. M. Holland in *The Inoperative Community* (Minneapolis: University of Minnesota Press, 1991), 110–50

Nicoll, J. R. A. *The Development of the Theatre: a study of theatrical art from the beginnings to the present day* (London: Harrap, 1966)

Nikolopoulou, Anastasia. 'Panopticism and the politics of the proscenium frame theatre: Benjamin Wyatt's Drury Lane, 1812', *Essays in Theatre* 12 (1994), 141–56

Norberg-Schulz, Christian. *Genius Loci: towards a phenomenology of architecture* (London: Academy Editions, 1980)

O'Doherty, Brian. *Inside the White Cube: the ideology of the gallery space* (Berkeley: University of California Press, 1999)

Orrell, John. *The Human Stage* (Cambridge University Press, 1988)

Panofsky, Erwin. *Perspective as Symbolic Form* (New York: Zone Books, 1991)

Pavis, Patrice. *Dictionnaire du théâtre* (Paris: Editions sociales, 1980)

Pearson, Mike. 'My balls/your chin', *Performance Research* 3.2 (1998), 35–41

Penzel, Frederick. *Theatre Lighting Before Electricity* (Middletown, Conn.: Wesleyan University Press, 1978)

Redmond, James (ed.). *The Theatrical Space: Themes in Drama Vol. IX* (Cambridge University Press, 1987)

Rehm, Rush. *The Play of Space: spatial transformation in Greek tragedy* (Princeton University Press, 2002)

Rey-Flaud, Henri. *Le Cercle magique* (Paris: Gallimard, 1973)

Rosselli, John. 'Opera as a social occasion' in *The Oxford Illustrated History of Opera*, ed. Roger Parker (Oxford University Press, 1994), 450–82

Ruzza, Luca and Tancredi, Maurizio. *Storie degli spazi teatrali* (Editrice Universitaria di Roma, 1987/9)

Sandford, Mariellen R. (ed.). *Happenings and Other Acts* (London: Routledge, 1995)

Schechner, Richard. *Environmental Theater* (New York: Applause, 1994)

Sennett, Richard. *Flesh and Stone: the body and the city in western civilization* (London: Faber, 1994)

The Fall of Public Man (Cambridge University Press, 1977)

Slater, W. J. (ed.). *Dining in a Classical Context* (Ann Arbor: University of Michigan Press, 1991)

Smith, Bruce R. *The Acoustic World of Early Modern England: attending to the O-factor* (University of Chicago Press, 1999)

Southern, Richard. *The Seven Ages of the Theatre* (London: Faber, 1964)

Spengler, Oswald. *The Decline of the West: form and actuality*, tr. C. F. Atkinson (London: George Allen & Unwin, 1926)

Suderburg, Erika (ed.). *Space, Site, Intervention: situating installation art* (Minneapolis: University of Minnesota Press, 2000)

Svoboda, Josef. *The Secret of Theatrical Space*, ed. and tr. J. M. Burian (New York: Applause, 1993)

Taylor, L. *Visualizing Theory* (New York: Routledge, 1994)

Todd, Andrew and Lecat, Jean-Guy. *The Open Circle: Peter Brook's theatre environments* (London: Methuen, 2002)

Tuan, Yi-Fu. 'Sacred space: explorations of an idea' in *Dimensions of Human Geography: essays on some familiar and neglected themes*, ed. K. W. Butzer (Dept of Geography, University of Chicago, 1978), 84–99

Passing Strange and Wonderful: aesthetics, nature and culture (Washington, D.C.: Island Press, 1993)

'Space and context' in *By Means of Performance*, ed. Richard Schechner and Willa Appel (Cambridge University Press, 1990), 236–44

Topophilia: a study of environmental perception, attitudes, and values (Englewood Cliffs: Prentice Hall, 1974)

Turner, Victor and Turner, Edith. *Image and Pilgrimage in Christian Culture* (Oxford: Blackwell, 1978)

Twycross, Meg. 'Some approaches to dramatic festivity, especially processions' in *Festive Drama*, ed. Meg Twycross (Woodbridge: D. S. Brewer, 1996), 1–33

Van den Berg, Kent T. *Playhouse and Cosmos: Shakespearean theater as metaphor* (Newark N.J.: Associated University Presses, 1985)

Vernant, Jean-Pierre. *Myth and Thought among the Greeks* (London: Routledge, 1983)

Villiers, André (ed.). *Architecture et dramaturgie* (Paris: Flammarion, 1950)

Villiers, André. *Le Théâtre en rond* (Paris: Librairie Théâtrale, 1958)

Vitruvius Pollio, Marcus. *The Ten Books of Architecture* v.i.1–2, tr. M. H. Morgan (Cambridge, Mass.: Harvard University Press, 1914)

Wickham, Glynne. *Early English Stages 1300–1660, Vol. I* (London: RKP, 1959)

Wiles, David. *Tragedy in Athens: performance space and theatrical meaning* (Cambridge University Press, 1997)

Zucker, Paul. *Town and Square: from the agora to the village green* (New York: Columbia University Press, 1959)

Index

Index